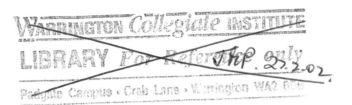

Place Promotion

otion
CITY AND
ELL TOWNS AND

ingapore

Published by John Wiley & Sons Ltd,
Baffins Lane, Chichester,
West Sussex PO19 1UD, England
National Chichester (0243) 779777
International +44 243 779777

Other Wiley Editorial Offices

John Wiley & Sons, Inc., 605 Third Avenue,
New York, NY 10158-0012, USA

Jacaranda Wiley Ltd, 33 Park Road, Milton,
Queensland 4064, Australia

John Wiley & Sons (Canada) Ltd, 22 Worcester Road,
Rexdale, Ontario M9W 1L1, Canada

John Wiley & Sons (SEA) Pte Ltd, 37 Jalan Pemimpin #05-04,
Block B, Union Industrial Building, Singapore 2057

Library of Congress Cataloging-in-Publication Data

A catalog record for this book is available from the Library of Congress

British Library Cataloguing in Publication Data

A catalogue record for this book is available from the British Library

ISBN 0-471-94834-9

Typeset in 10/12pt Times from authors' disk by Vision Typesetting, Manchester
Printed and bound in Great Britain by Bookcraft (Bath) Ltd.

Contents

List of contributors   vii

Preface   ix

1   Introduction   1
Stephen V. Ward and John R. Gold

2   Locating the message: place promotion as image communication   19
John R. Gold

3   Marketing and place promotion   39
Gregory J. Ashworth and Henk Voogd

4   Time and place: key themes in place promotion in the USA, Canada and Britain since 1870   53
Stephen V. Ward

5   'Home at Last!': building societies, home ownership and the imagery of English suburban promotion in the interwar years   75
John R. Gold and Margaret M. Gold

6   Selling the industrial town: identity, image and illusion   93
Michael Barke and Ken Harrop

7   City make-overs: marketing the post-industrial city   115
Briavel Holcomb

8   Selling the inner city: regeneration and place marketing in London's Docklands   133
Sue Brownill

9   Art-full places: public art to sell public spaces?   153
Brian Goodey

10   Transitory topographies: places, events, promotions and propaganda   181
Bob Jarvis

11   Newspapers as promotional strategists for regional definition   195
     Holly J. Myers-Jones and Susan R. Brooker-Gross

12   Marketing landscapes of the Four Corners States   213
     Ervin H. Zube and Janet Galante

13   Promoting the Forest of Dean: art, ecology and the industrial
     landscape   233
     George Revill

14   Selling the countryside: representations of rural Britain   247
     Pyrs Gruffudd

Index   265

List of contributors

Gregory J. Ashworth is Professor of Urban and Regional Planning at the University of Groningen in the Netherlands.

Michael Barke is Reader in Geography at the University of Northumbria at Newcastle.

Susan R. Brooker-Gross is Associate Professor of Geography at the Virginia Polytechnic Institute and State University at Blacksburg, Virginia.

Sue Brownill is Senior Lecturer in the School of Planning at Oxford Brookes University.

Janet Galante is a graduate student at the University of Arizona at Tucson. She is currently completing a Masters in Landscape Architecture and a Doctorate in Renewable Natural Resources.

John R. Gold is Professor of Urban Geography in the School of Social Sciences at Oxford Brookes University.

Margaret M. Gold is Principal Lecturer in the School of European and International Studies at Thames Valley University.

Brian Goodey is Professor of European Landscape Planning at Oxford Brookes University.

Pyrs Gruffudd is Lecturer in Geography at University College, Swansea.

Ken Harrop teaches in local government studies at the University of Northumbria at Newcastle.

Briavel Holcomb is Associate Professor and Chair of the Department of Urban Studies and Community Health at Rutgers University, New Jersey.

Bob Jarvis is a Senior Lecturer in the Planning Division at South Bank University, where he teaches urban design.

Holly J. Myers-Jones teaches in the Department of Geography and Environmental Planning at Towson State University, Maryland.

George Revill is Lecturer in Geography in the School of Social Sciences at Oxford Brookes University.

Henk Voogd teaches at the University of Groningen in the Netherlands.

Stephen V. Ward is Principal Lecturer in Planning History at Oxford Brookes University.

Ervin H. Zube is Professor of Renewable Natural Resources and Adjunct Professor of Geography and Regional Development at the University of Arizona at Tucson.

Preface

Most editors of collections of essays have a long story to tell about when, how and why the resulting volume came about. Our own story, however, can be told relatively quickly. This book stems not from conference or seminar proceedings – that recipe for diffuseness dressed up as seamless robe – but from the editors' interest in place promotion and from the enthusiasm of a group of colleagues to contribute to a shared project. With the assistance and wise counsel of Iain Stevenson, we were then able to refine our original ideas into the collection that you see before you.

Inevitably, as with all books, debts are incurred. The Schools of Social Sciences and Planning of Oxford Brookes University have provided finance and other assistance to facilitate our work. Colleagues and students have provided ideas and encouragement. As always the editors acknowledge the special patience of their families in putting up with them during the preparation of this volume. Scholarship is a particularly harrowing addiction that families simply have to bear, as ours always cheerfully do, even in particularly distressing cases such as the Gold household, where both its adult members are afflicted. ('It's the children you feel sorry for'.)

More specific credits arise from individual authors. John Gold would like to thank the Department of Geography, Queen Mary and Westfield College for generously affording him facilities as Visiting Professor in 1992. Much of the research for Chapters 2 and 5 was carried out during this period. Stephen Ward would like to thank the Canadian High Commission for the award of a Canadian Studies Research Award in 1990, allowing him to research bonusing municipal industrial policies in Ontario. Ervin Zube and Janet Galante would like to acknowledge their grateful appreciation for the assistance provided by: Archives Staff, Grand Canyon National Park; Joe Bowman, Editor, *New Mexico* magazine; Becky Brown, President, Grand Circle Association; Patricia Etter, Assistant Archivist for Information Services, Department of Archives and Manuscripts, Arizona State University; Patrick Fraker, Research Library, Colorado Historical Society; Hugh Harrelson, Publisher, *Arizona Highways*; Ramona Hutchinson, Librarian, Mesa Verde National Park; Orlando Romero, Librarian, Museum of New Mexico; Cathy Swarts and Robert Elliott, Arizona Raft Adventures; Bill Sykes, President, Regional Publishing Association; Ron Warren, General Manager, Grand Canyon Airlines; Val Wilson, Research Library, Utah State Historical Society; and Karen Zoltenko, Staff Archivist, State of Colorado Division of Archives and Public Records.

Contributors, authors and publishers also acknowledge the following organisations for allowing them to reproduce illustrations: Alabama Economic Development Partnership, Alloa District Council, Arizona Raft Adventures Inc., Bodleian Library,

Calderdale District Council, Central Manchester Development Corporation, Doncaster District Council, *Expansion Management* magazine, Grand Circle Association Arizona, Hartlepool Borough Council, Irvine Development Corporation, Laganside Development Corporation, London Docklands Development Corporation, National Railway Museum, Oshawa and District Historical Society, Stoke-on-Trent City Council, Telford Development Agency, Virginia State Library, Wrekin District Council. Grateful acknowledgement is made to the Abbey National and Woolwich Building Societies for permission to reproduce poster advertisements in Chapter five and on the cover of this book. All other illustrations are from the personal collections of the editors or contributors.

West Ealing and Oxford
August 1993

1 Introduction

STEPHEN V. WARD AND JOHN R. GOLD

In October 1992, the President of the Board of Trade, Michael Heseltine, announced a plan for the closure of almost half of Britain's remaining collieries. Almost immediately there was a huge, and unexpected, national outpouring of sympathy for the areas directly hit, which quickly grew into a large anti-closures campaign. Yet the realistic possibilities of a last ditch defence of such traditional sources of employment were always limited. When representatives of local authorities in the East Midlands, one of the most severely affected regions, met to draw up joint plans for an appropriate response a few days after the announcement, their decisions showed a distinct awareness of this uncomfortable truth. The main element of their chosen strategy rested not so much on contesting the closures, but on launching an extensive promotional campaign to draw new industry to their region.

It was in many respects an inevitable reaction. Indeed, in light of prevailing economic and political circumstances, which include a marked reduction in regional development incentives, it was perhaps the only available reaction. Their campaign, however, is doomed to compete in a crowded market, with the buyer very much in the dominant position. Industrial place promotion, already a commonplace activity in developed nations, becomes increasingly frenetic in times of economic recession. Mounting unemployment coupled with a dwindling supply of mobile industry leads towns, cities and regions to compete in promoting themselves to encourage investment and stimulate business.

For major prizes, such as a Japanese car-plant or a large manufacturing plant at the leading edge of microelectronic technology, the competition is particularly fierce. Areas 'with a past', often rather the worse for wear, present their freshest face to potential investors, seeking tactical advantage over their opponents. Invariably, there are hints of undisclosed deals and bribes offered behind the scenes to procure success. The stakes are high: the victors not only earn success in one specific contest but also enhance their promotional curricula vitae compared to their rivals. To have successfully gained the favours of companies such as Toyota or Mitsubishi enhances their prospects of attracting further significant inward investment in the future.

Major cities that grew as the command centres of traditional industrialisation also look to promotional activity in facing up to their post-industrial futures. As such, they often attempt to reinvent themselves. Their redundant docks, warehouses and factory districts are turned into post-modern living and working experiences, sometimes also recycling dereliction into heritage in an attempt to tap the tourist market. Such exercises in development signal their authenticity by appropriating the images and physical relics of the past into a sanitised and hyper-real present. The brightly painted dockside crane provides a perfect foil to the atrium and mirror glass of the high-tech office. The factory clock that once defined the rhythm of industrial society provides the focal point for the new leisure and niche-retailing quarter. Such juxtapositions supply the glossy images which allow still largely dowdy and grimy cities to become eminently promotable in the new post-industrial era. This is then supposed to create the impetus to transform those unregenerated parts of the cities that are not shown in the promotional pictures.

On a wider stage, the more ambitious of these cities compete for world status. As global economic and political systems experience important changes, individual cities move to stake their claim in the emergent new order. They find new ways to highlight their accumulated artistic heritage to compete for the title of 'cultural capital' within the new Europe (e.g. Deben *et al.*, 1992; Sparks, 1992). They compete to stage major international exhibitions and other events, most notably the Olympic Games. The very act of bidding becomes a promotional act in itself, asserting the credentials of a place to a wide and influential audience (Figure 1.1). Success creates the momentum for major investments in the social and physical infrastructure and gives the one-off stimulus of the event itself. Moreover, as in other spheres of promotion, success becomes a potent promotional message in itself.

Classics and clichés of place promotion

Place promotion, defined as the conscious use of publicity and marketing to communicate selective images of specific geographical localities or areas to a target audience, has a long history. During the age of colonial expansion, west European and east coast American newspapers were full of advertisements that aimed to entice migrants to venture into the unknown (Merrens, 1969; Cameron, 1974; Lewis, 1988; Zube and Kennedy, 1990). Part of the aim was to create an attractive image and, in doing so, the results were remarkably consistent. The land was always of unsurpassed fertility and ready for the plough, the climate wonderfully healthy, droughts unknown and the rivers teeming with salmon. Untold riches were available for those with the foresight to grasp this unparalleled opportunity. At the same time, promoters of colonial schemes also had to counter unfavourable images already in vogue. As Jones (1946:133) noted, one of the principal tasks for promotional literature was to combat the 'flood of slander and gossip' from which most colonial schemes suffered. This strategy is well typified by the report of a correspondent for *The Times* newspaper, who penned a report entitled 'Immense Arrival of Treasure from Australia' (quoted in the *Sheffield Daily Telegraph*, 28 May 1856). Seemingly stung by the suggestion that the new colony was anything other than a land of unlimited abundance, he announced: 'Our problem is not to find where gold is, but to find a place where it certainly is not.'

Other forms of place promotion are nearly as old and as cliché-ridden (*see* Chapter 4). Seaside resorts in search of tourists have long plied their wares through press advertisements, posters and brochures, invariably claiming to have golden sands, invigorating climates, beaches washed by sparkling waters, welcoming hotels and homely guest houses (Buck, 1977; Ward, 1988; Yates, 1988). Historic towns have well-established promotional rivalries in terms of the respective lengths of their

Figure 1.1 Success in one competitive arena is soon reflected in other aspects of place promotion. Thus, when Manchester won the right to present Britain's Olympic bid, the Central Manchester Development Corporation was quick to use this in its advertising.

antiquity and the cultural cachet associated with it. Promoters of residential developments, especially late-19th and early 20th-century suburbia, made use of messages replete with references to nature, domesticity and security (*see* Chapter 5). In each case, much of the language and imagery proved remarkably enduring, albeit updated to reflect changing social mores.

More recent forms of place promotion may have introduced new themes, but these too become quickly familiar as they are worked and reworked. Out-of-town retail centres, for instance, are promoted as supplying extraordinary retailing experiences in the hope of drawing sufficient numbers of both major retailers and affluent mobile shoppers away from the traditional centres. The same tendency is shown in the new large leisure complexes, pioneered by Disneyland and copied by a growing number of smaller variants (Lyon, 1987; Winsberg, 1992), in which the all-round 'family experience' is fervently celebrated.

We could easily add to these examples. Over the years, the practice of place promotion has been led by a handful of brilliant, and often rather simple, advertisements and slogans that have achieved lasting fame. Figure 1.2 shows one such advertisement. First issued in 1908 as part of a campaign run by the Great Northern Railway, John Hassall's image of a jolly fisherman with its 'Skegness is So Bracing' slogan evokes the heyday of the British seaside holiday before it fell victim to mass pursuit of the sun (Shackleton, 1976:44–6). More recently, New York State's 1977 'I ♥ New York' campaign has used the resources of modern advertising to create a positive feeling about a place in a truly original way (Holcomb, 1990:31). Its success, claimed to have helped the City of New York move back from the brink of fiscal collapse, has spawned countless imitations.

The process of imitation, however, demonstrates a general paucity of creative ideas and effectively ensures that the vast majority of place promotional campaigns rarely manage to cross the threshold of ephemeral indifference. Occasionally the multi-layered cleverness of 'Make It In Livingston' or 'Glasgow's Miles Better' capture wider attention (Cosgrove and Campbell, 1988; Boyle and Hughes, 1992; Paddison, 1993). Yet many campaigns of the 'B_____ Means Business', 'L_____'s Looking Up' or '_____: Capital/Heart of/Gateway to the_____' variety, simply fail to register, except as objects of ridicule. We can recall here the late Peter Sellers' gentle satire of the genre in his 'Balham: Gateway To The South' sketch, in which he parodied the narrative style of the cinema travel films of the 1950s. Evenly stressing each syllable of the place name (in contrast to the usual emphasis only on the first), an American-accented narrator extols the mock virtues of what is in reality an unremarkable south London suburb. In the process, Sellers effectively underlined the ever-present risks of banality in the promotional representation of places, although not sufficiently to deter subsequent emulation; exactly the same slogan, albeit with more justification, greeted the international air traveller arriving at Atlanta in the early 1990s.

Cliché and repetition are understandable, even forgivable, up to a point. Place promotional budgets rarely approach those for major commercial products and suffer cruelly by comparison. Inevitably, therefore, many campaigns have something of the entertaining clumsiness of low budget commercial campaigns. Moreover, despite increasing use of advertising and marketing agents, many promotional endeavours are effectively poor examples of professional practice.

Figure 1.2 A classic place promotion image by the famous advertising artist, John Hassall. First issued by the Great Northern Railway in 1908, it was widely used in the interwar years and continues to feature in Skegness' promotion even in the 1990s. The variant shown dates from the 1930s.

The example of press advertising clearly demonstrates this point. Advertising copy is often overcrowded and poorly laid out, with few limits to the amount of copy that some advertisers feel able to put into even the smallest space. It is not unusual, for example, to find over 200 words of copy, thrown together with a small photograph or illustration, and panels with slogans and addresses in a space measuring 10 square inches or less. The fact that the text appears in a spidery, semi-legible font, perhaps half the size of that used for the surrounding newsprint, appears secondary to the goal of cramming in as much material as possible. The impression of a visual swamp is common, as is the tendency to miss the presence of some advertisements completely at first, or even second glance.

These are not just minor technical defects since they point to several major deficiencies. First, there is confusion between different styles of advertising. Through their sheer wordiness, place promotional advertisements most closely resemble direct sales advertising, in which advertisers attempt to sell goods or services outside the normal retailing system. All the evidence, however, suggests that place promotion advertising is not used for this purpose but rather to create and sustain awareness. As such, the advertisement is usually seen as a first step, to be followed by dissemination of brochures and public relations activity. Other forms of advertisement, with greater visual impact or forceful exposition of a single key idea, would better serve this objective.

Secondly, they reveal a marked failure to establish a distinct selling proposition to the audience. Advertising researchers stress the significance of making a clear proposition to the audience that says: 'buy this and you will receive this benefit' (Reeves, 1961:47). While this approach may be dismissed as too simplistic for place promotion, given the multifaceted nature of the product being marketed (see below), the frequent failure to make any selling proposition calls into question the point of the exercise.

Finally, such advertisements reveal confused aims. All place promotional campaigns are founded on fragmentary assemblies of place elements, which those responsible for the creative process gather together into advertising copy (see Chapter 2). Frequently, they seem either unable or unwilling to discriminate between the importance of these different elements. In part, this expresses an inability to establish a distinct selling proposition (see above), but is also symptomatic of failing to specify the target audience accurately. As Burgess (1982) points out, there is a spectrum between weakly-targeted public media advertising and closely-targeted public relations exercises. Standing at the ill-defined end of the spectrum, press advertising is frequently designed to express local pride as well as attracting industrial migrants and, equally often, is constructed as much to appease competing local interests as to convey persuasive images to an outside audience.

These arguments about the deficiencies of press advertising can be extended to other forms of promotional materials. The net effect of those deficiencies militates against the simple and the understated. It also works against the deliberate use of humour, causing an overwhelming air of earnest worthiness to pervade most campaigns. The ample indulgence in self-mockery that typifies the best commercial advertising rarely features in place promotion. Unfortunately, it is seen as much too serious for that.

Our aim here is not to reverse this process by subjecting place promotion to sustained mockery, regardless of the fact that many elements of current practice might warrant it. Nor, by the same token, do we merely seek to highlight the falsity of the place images that promotion creates, whatever economies with the truth are exhibited by most contemporary campaigns. Rather, our concern is to offer critical analyses, explanations and some understanding of the practices and imageries of place promotion and, implicitly at least, to suggest how they might be improved. In doing so, we will touch on the three major areas on which researchers have focused to date. The first, the complex question of the place promotion as *image communication*, is a major topic that merits and receives detailed discussion in its own right (Chapter 2), but some notes on the remaining two areas, place promotion as *public policy* and as *marketing*, are useful at this stage.

Place promotion as public policy

The place promotional paradox

The first point to make is that there is a real contradiction at the heart of place promotion. On the one hand, place promotion in western Europe is traditionally an aspect of public or quasi-public policy. This means that it is expected to embody notions of the public good and social benefit. It should be effective in promoting the justifiable advantages of a place, but not at the expense of neighbouring regions and communities. On the other hand, place promotion is now strongly influenced by the spread of the market principle. This means that places must compete with each other as profit-making commercial entities, something which is commonplace in North America (e.g. see van den Berg *et al.*, 1990), but strange territory for officials in many European local or regional public authorities. As a result, it is noticeable that many of the new cadre of European professional place promoters were recruited from the world of business rather than public service. It is also noticeable that much European literature remains relatively unsophisticated, still concentrating upon inculcating awareness of such marketing issues as the policy ramifications of local economic promotion and development initiatives (e.g. Camina, 1974; Mawson and Miller, 1986; Totterdill, 1989; Collinge, 1992; Neill, 1992; see also contributions to the journal *Local Economy*).

This reorientation needs to be placed in its full perspective. The public policy dimensions of place promotion arose as part of a wider fragmentation of the traditional conception of spatial planning (Brindley *et al.*, 1988). In the three decades following World War II, it was normal for patterns of urban and regional growth and decline in western Europe to be shaped substantially by the planning process. Within the context of these mixed economy, welfare-conscious social democracies, market processes were not so much replaced as orchestrated by planners to offer a measure of certainty to the investor and social benefits to the community at large. This was significant because it discouraged active place promotion, except in a few specific instances such as tourist areas, depressed regions and new towns – all of which were subsumed within an overall spatial planning framework. In effect, the promotional impulse was compressed into the wider policy objectives of spatial planning. The broad trends were similar even in the USA, despite differences in the practice of place promotion and less tradition of a planned approach to development than in western Europe.

The pattern has changed dramatically everywhere since the 1970s. Economic instability, restructuring and an acceleration of the international mobility of capital have caused many regions to lose the traditional sources of employment that gave them their primary identity. At the same time, individual national governments have retreated from their former interventionist strategies. Taken together, these forces have fragmented the traditional planning approach as the main agency shaping and managing the processes of spatial change and have left a vacant policy niche within which local promotional activity has flowered.

An impression of the extent that policy has shifted is found in the official literature given to foreign industrialists seeking investment locations in Britain. In the late 1960s, they would have received a folder called 'Room To Expand' from the Board of Trade (the arm of government responsible for trade and related policy). This contained information about regions where central government, under its regional policies, wished to encourage development. Growth elsewhere was firmly discouraged. Such scope as there was for the promotion of individual places was firmly limited by the framework of these larger policies. By contrast, in the early 1990s foreign industrialists receive an 'Invest in Britain' booklet listing all the area-based promotional initiatives. The strong regional policy steer of the 1960s has been greatly diluted; the inward investor is pitched straight into the more locally-competitive bidding of place promotion.

Place promotion and local economic policies

Alongside these developments came new styles of small area-based policy initiative that are inherently more promotional in character. Of these, the most striking is leverage. This approach originated in the USA, having been practised with particular success in Baltimore and Boston. Under leverage, place promoters make available financial and other material incentives, such as subsidised land, to encourage private development of all kinds on the basis of maximising the gearing ratio of public to private investment. Much reliance is placed on bargaining to secure social benefits, though their attainment is far easier in an economically buoyant place rather than one which is desperate for new investment. Hence, as its British practitioners have found, the example of Boston is easier to emulate in London's Docklands than, for example, in Merseyside (Madsen, 1992). Moreover, even in the most favoured areas, social benefits must always take second place to profit and therefore tend to rely on the rather imperfect distributional mechanisms of 'trickle down'. These benefits also tend to evaporate completely during recessions – exactly the time when the need for them is strongest.

Unease at being placed in the position of supplicants to private investors encouraged some left-wing local councils in Britain to attempt a different approach during the 1980s. Many of their areas were suffering particularly badly from the effects of economic change and their initiatives attracted a great deal of interest in the policy literature. There were, for example, experiments in supporting co-operatives and taking more direct control of local businesses. Achievements were very limited, however, not least because opposition from Conservative central government ensured they remained on a very small scale. Moreover, their purpose was ideologically confused and indistinct from more conventional place promotion and development policies. A policy which seeks to support economic activity in one specific place, by whatever means, necessarily places it in competition with other places. Certainly by the end of the 1980s the pursuit of the chimera of a specifically socialist approach to local promotion and development was virtually ended. The centrally-sanctioned approach of promotion and leverage was dominant.

Place promotion as marketing

If the place-competitive promotional style sits uneasily within the public interest traditions of local policies, the same can also be said of its relationship with marketing. There is a considerable literature on this dimension, much of it American in origin. In general the concern is severely practical: namely, how to do it. Not for nothing was McDonald's (1938) early volume on the subject entitled *How To Promote Community And Industrial Development*. That mantle is now carried by journals such as *Economic Development Commentary* and studies like Ryans and Shanklin (1986) and Kotler *et al* (1993).

Belatedly, a European place-marketing literature is also now appearing, including particularly works by Bartels and Timmer (1987), Ashworth and Voogd (1990) and Gren (1992). Some of these studies, particularly that by Ashworth and Voogd, move beyond the practical dimension and acknowledge some of the underlying conceptual difficulties raised by applying marketing approaches to place. These issues are also addressed in the same authors' contribution to this volume, so we will not deal with them at any length here other than to rehearse some basic propositions.

The conceptual problem derives from the fact that marketing is a business practice devised to promote a tangible and clearly defined product that is literally sold to clearly defined consumers. The maximisation of sales provides a very specific objective of conventional marketing. It is not possible to market places in these ways for several reasons. One immediate problem is that it is not readily apparent what the product actually is, nor how the consumption of place occurs. Though marketing practices make places into commodities, they are in reality complex packages of goods, services and experiences that are consumed in many different ways. In turn this means that the clear marketing objective of sales maximisation is easily lost sight of, except in the still very uncommon circumstances of a place designed specifically as marketable commodity – a Disneyland for example. More typically only a small amount of the returns on marketing effort – the 'sales' – accrue directly to the promotional agency.

Nevertheless, as Ashworth and Voogd show, the rise of social and attitudinal marketing over the last two decades or so has provided a firmer conceptual basis for a marketing practice that can more easily be applied to places. One important consequence is that it has completely freed place marketeers from the obligation to define with any clarity the places they are promoting and how they expect them to be consumed. Increasingly the emphasis has shifted to an association of feelings with places – 'I ♥ NY' was a brilliant example of this kind of campaign.

Although earlier place promoters had occasionally stumbled intuitively on this truth, there had always been a strong tendency to temper even the most powerful image associating place and feelings with extensive factual descriptions (Figure 1.3). We tend to recall the simple and often superb railway posters promoting holiday resorts in most western countries before 1939 (e.g. Shackleton, 1976; Camard and Zagrodski, 1989;

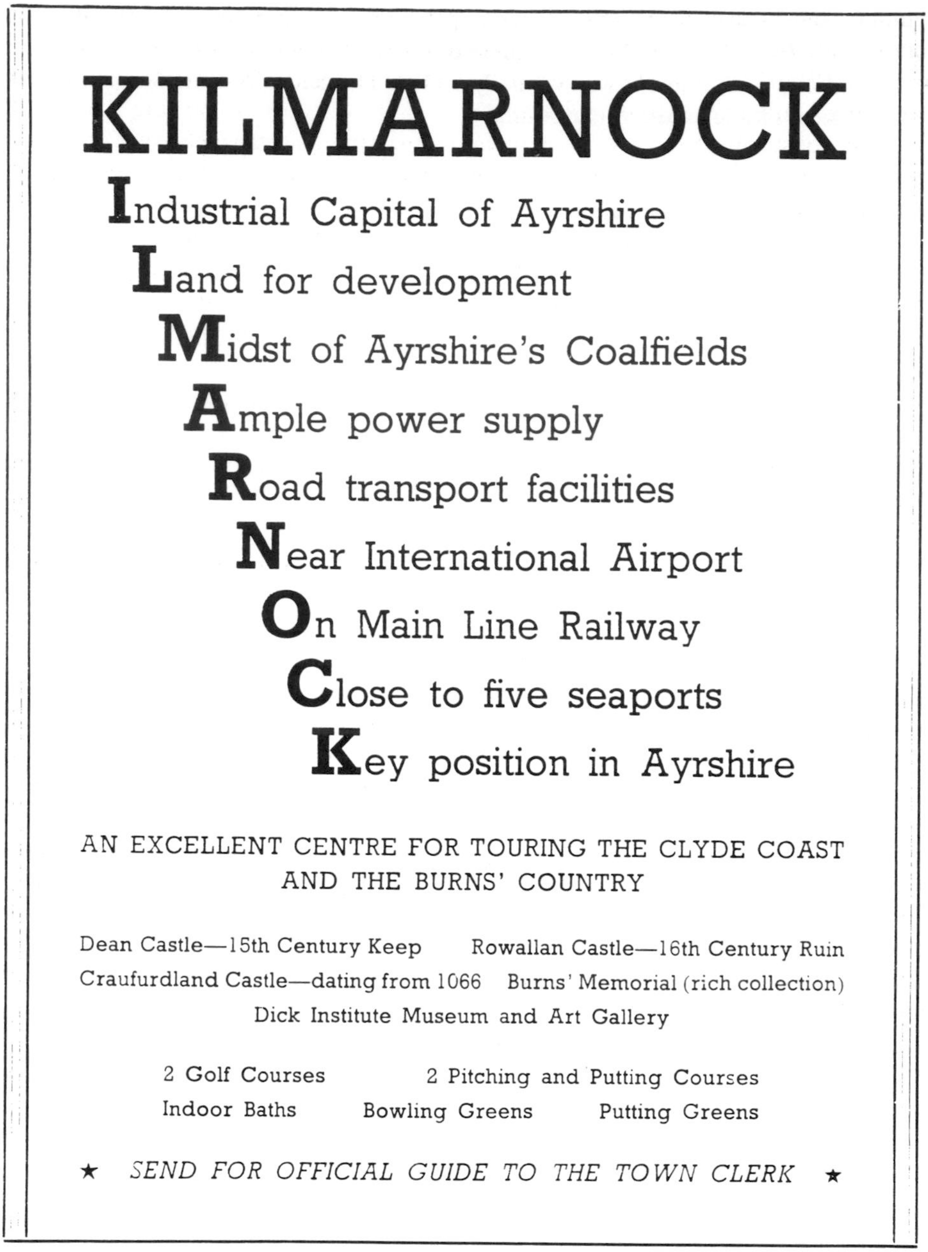

KILMARNOCK

Industrial Capital of Ayrshire

Land for development

Midst of Ayrshire's Coalfields

Ample power supply

Road transport facilities

Near International Airport

On Main Line Railway

Close to five seaports

Key position in Ayrshire

AN EXCELLENT CENTRE FOR TOURING THE CLYDE COAST
AND THE BURNS' COUNTRY

Dean Castle—15th Century Keep   Rowallan Castle—16th Century Ruin
Craufurdland Castle—dating from 1066   Burns' Memorial (rich collection)
Dick Institute Museum and Art Gallery

2 Golf Courses   2 Pitching and Putting Courses
Indoor Baths   Bowling Greens   Putting Greens

★ *SEND FOR OFFICIAL GUIDE TO THE TOWN CLERK* ★

Figure 1.3 An extreme example of a traditional approach to place promotion, from the early 1960s. Matching benefits up to the letters of the place name may have seemed conceptually attractive but it means that the resulting word picture of the place is very confused.

Reinders and Oosterwijk, 1989; Hillion, 1990, 1991; Cole and Durack, 1992; also Figure 1.2), but the most pervasive promotional artefact of these years was the brochure (Ward, 1988). This typically gave chapter and verse to about just about everything – municipal parks, cultural facilities, floral gardens, bathing pools, crazy golf, hours of sunshine, schools, local rates and the timings of market days. There was a clear reluctance to market a place solely on image association; the place itself had to be carefully and tediously delineated.

The need for that specification of place, at least from the place marketeers' point of view, has now gone. Chicago can be marketed across the Great Lakes region of the USA and Canada by television advertisements that merely show a fragment of ballet or electric blues music and associate them with the city's name. Numerous southern American towns and cities can trade on 'Y'all come down' folksiness. London Docklands can be sold simply by associating the area with particular 'smart' social attitudes, as Brownill shows in Chapter 8.

Moreover the increasing reliance on the fragmentary image allows place to be suggested in different ways to different place consumers. This can have advantages in appeasing local political pressures, for example, not to write off hopes of enhancing a traditional manufacturing base by concentrating solely on tourist development. As we have already noted (and will see further in Chapter 6), this kind of compromise, especially on a low budget, can produce very confused place marketing messages. It provides a very specific instance of the uneasy co-existence between the public policy and the marketing approaches to place promotion.

Despite these qualifications, the marketing approach offers the nearest thing to a practical expertise for those undertaking place promotion. There is, as we have already hinted, little in the traditional approach of the main public service professions that readily lends itself to this style, although this is certainly changing as local government is obliged to become more entreprencurial. It is, however, to the marketing approach that such officials will be looking. Regardless of how much critics (including the present authors) may bewail commodification and its potential for undermining the traditional multi-dimensional meanings of place, the fact is that this is precisely what almost all municipal and regional authorities everywhere are rushing to do. The marketing approach offers some tools for the job that give promotional bodies a methodology that enables them to define and target place images. It is also an approach that is capable of being refined and given a stronger public interest ethos without necessarily fully resolving the inherent contradictions referred to above. Yet individual towns, cities and regions can only go so far along this route. Its fuller achievement is at least partly dependent on changes that allow some greater mediation of spatial change at national and international levels.

Organisation and structure

Setting the context

The various chapters fall naturally into two groups. Chapters 2 to 4 are contextual in character and follow the methodological and conceptual cues which have been set down in this chapter, covering in turn the notions of place promotion as image communication, marketing and public policy. The subsequent chapters are more in the nature of case studies, using different mixes of approach to understand particular manifestations of place promotional activity.

In Chapter 2 John Gold provides extended examination of the various approaches that researchers have adopted in the study of media messages. After recognising place promotion as part of a culturally-defined system of communication, he identifies four main foci available to researchers when studying media content: content analysis, art historical approaches to pictorial representations, cognitive-behaviouralism, and cultural studies. He outlines and evaluates the progress and deficiencies of each school of research, culminating in a detailed analysis of the ideological and rhetorical meanings of promotional messages. He concludes by noting that realisation of the promise offered by cultural approaches depends on overcoming the problems associated with conceptual plurality and fragmentation.

In Chapter 3, Ashworth and Voogd, much the most thoughtful of the current crop of place marketeers, give many insights about how place promotion can be effectively tackled. Their chapter is important since it articulates a conceptual basis for those who wish to understand how places are commodified through the practices of place marketing. It also provides some conceptual and practical guidelines for those who actually wish to undertake place marketing themselves. Of particular importance is the need continually to monitor projected and received place images, changing promotional practice accordingly. More fundamentally, Ashworth and Voogd stress the limitations of place marketing and readily concede that there are problems connected with places that cannot be solved by this approach.

The final contextual chapter, by Stephen Ward, derives from the public policy tradition. In it, he explores the historical development of place promotion within the three different geographical settings of Canada, southern USA and Britain, showing how differing economic, institutional and political circumstances shaped promotional policies in rather different ways. The concern is less with imagery or the practicalities of place marketing than with policy analysis. Local economic policies, a frequent accompaniment to place promotion, are given particular emphasis. An important policy distinction is drawn between boosterism and regeneration, with particular implications for managing the politics of place promotion. In doing this, Ward reminds us that there is more to historical study than simply encouragement to current practice. Rather, careful historical study of other promotional episodes enlarges the experience of today's practitioners and facilitates greater conceptual depth.

Case study chapters

This point is reinforced in several of the case study chapters. The most explicitly historical of the later chapters is John and Margaret Gold's study of the promotion of suburban London between World Wars I and II. This builds on the earlier work of Jackson (1973) and others to explore the creation and meaning of the place images used in the promotion of suburbia. Their work considers the promotional role of the building societies. The societies played a key part in articulating the new environmental ideal of suburbia, matching their crucial financial role in facilitating the whole process.

In Chapter 5, the Golds use poster advertising to examine the messages conveyed by building societies in promoting the all important notion of home ownership. They show how the societies articulated and endlessly augmented a rhetoric that drew upon a carefully selected repertoire of environmental and social depictions to communicate, simultaneously, the idea of home ownership and the desirability of the new suburbs to their audience.

Mike Barke and Ken Harrop also include some historical references in what is primarily a contemporary study of selling industrial (or what used to be industrial) towns in Britain. Their basic approach is one largely shaped by place marketing approaches, though with a strong accompanying focus on the creation of new place images. The chapter effectively updates the studies by Gold (1974) and Burgess (1982) on typical 'run of the mill' promotional material. In many ways they show that local place promoters have learned some of the lessons from the work of their predecessors. It is clear, for example, that boosting the confidence of local inhabitants in their own town or city is now seen as a key element in the promotional process, as Burgess recommended. As regards promoting inward investment, they also show that places are amply practising what Ashworth and Voogd are preaching, tailoring their message to specific inquiries. This leads the authors to the pessimistic conclusion that any traditional conception of place itself is disappearing within promotional practice.

Their themes and arguments are set in comparative context in Chapter 7 by Briavel Holcomb. She supplies a vivid and succinct overview of current US practice, combining an approach based on image analysis and public policy. After comparing urban place promotion with the application of cosmetics, she supplies further light on the historical basis of boosterist initiatives in American urban policies. Most of her concern though is with the contemporary scene. She examines the close integration of promotion and the physical remodelling of key parts of cities that become highly visible in place marketing exercises.

Such an approach sits uneasily in the British tradition of urban policy; there are clearly many more continuities with American experiences. In Chapter 8, Sue Brownill provides a British case-study that supports this point. She focuses on the London Docklands, a project that has been highly visible in place marketing exercises during the last 15 years. The regeneration of London's Docklands was almost a model of Thatcherite urban planning policies. It was fundamentally promotional in style, dependent on encouraging new private investment and new residents in the former dereliction of redundant wharves and quays. Writing from a public policy perspective and building on the work of her influential book (1990), Brownill explores how promotion was used to market a new idea of London's Docklands that was integral to the area's regeneration. In common with much public policy literature on place promotion, the conclusion is highly critical. Place marketing is seen as part of a fundamentally flawed approach to planning and urban policy, though she admits some form of promotional policies may be necessary within a more planned and welfare oriented approach.

A point to which Brownill refers repeatedly in her chapter, particularly in relation to the Canary Wharf development, is the use of architecture and urban design as part of the promotion of place. The next two chapters continue this theme. Brian Goodey, a pioneer of interest in place promotional imagery in Britain during the 1970s, provides an important and authoritative review of the use of public art as a promotional device. His long-standing experience of the realities of making both places and promotional images of places permeates his chapter. While he underlines the major significance of dramatic pieces of art and design in making promotable places in the contemporary world, his conclusion is significant. The modern media have a very low boredom threshold and soon tire of even the most dramatic and eyecatching pieces of public art: promotable public art is therefore becoming ever more transient.

This recognition provides the point of departure for the contribution by Bob Jarvis. His chapter, rooted very much in culturalist approaches to understanding images and events, represents a plea for a celebration of the transient. As he reminds us, there is potential within the temporary event for a popular reclaiming of place. Fairs and festivals can be more than just part of the accelerating process of capital accumulation requiring the creation of new place images with ever greater rapidity. They can provide a setting for a genuine rediscovery of place and community. In his broad historical review of this phenomenon, Jarvis offers some pointers to the future that repay further study.

Most of the chapters so far have been specifically concerned with the promotional concern of specific towns and cities. While perfectly understandable, place promotion has many other dimensions, as the next four chapters remind us. The next Chapter, 11, by Holly Myers-Jones and Susan Brooker-Gross, emphasises the wider regional role of urban boosterism. Their study uses content analytic methodology to show how boosterist messages found in newspaper content are shaped and filtered within the context of the wider city region of Roanoke, Virginia. In particular, the authors show how a newspaper that embraces pro-growth sentiments shapes its editorials and reportage to fit the socio-spatial pattern of opinion in the region.

Promotion of rural regions, especially for tourism, is another important dimension of the wider practice of place promotion. This theme is introduced here by Ervin Zube and Janet Galante. They are concerned with the selling of the American west, first to settlers and then as a tourist and retirement destination. In an approach that brings together marketing and image-making concerns, the authors give an incisive historical account that focuses on the Four Corners Region – the states of Arizona, Colorado, New Mexico and Utah. They show how the area's spectacular natural landscapes and other features were and are marketed to outsiders, encouraging development that has fundamentally changed the region. They show how promotion has often been the refuge of scoundrels and charlatans. Yet their conclusion is noticeably more optimistic in tone than many of the others in this collection. Promotion, it seems, can be good for places, at least if it generates the impetus and resources to maintain the scenic and other qualities that are being promoted.

The two final chapters retain the emphasis on promotion of rural areas, with both drawing heavily on culturalist and iconographic approaches. George Revill's study of the Forest of Dean examines the promotional role of the Forest Sculpture Trail, studying the ways in which the sculptures represent changing conceptions of the industrial landscape and the wider role of art in promoting that landscape. It also considers how art can mediate the relationship between nature and industrialisation, showing how the phenomena of de-industrialisation and ecological crisis are brought together in an industrial 'heritage' landscape.

This emphasis on landscape as a socially constructed means of imposing order on the world is continued by Pyrs Gruffudd. He emphasises that interest in place promotion transcends the self-conscious activity of public or quasi-public agencies, since places are also promoted by other, less conscious means. In his study of the interpretation and presentation of rural landscapes to the public, particularly in interwar Britain, he demonstrates the subtlety with which a range of cultural products – travel books, landscape art, popular treatises on rural life, academic studies – contributed to the creation of a ruralist cultural discourse that stressed the integrity of rural life and landscapes. He argues that the promotion of the rural has as much to do with the transmission of 'enduring values' as with narrow environmental concerns; values which remain heavily promoted in the tourist and industrial place marketing of the late 20th century.

Conclusion

As these various contributions reveal, our understanding of place promotion is, like the activity itself, partial and fragmentary. Taken together our contributors point to important differences in approach that are being, but are not yet, usefully reconciled. In particular the distinctions between the critics and the practitioners remain too wide to be fully productive. The former numerically dominate the contributions here, as they do the more general body of material. The practitioners on the whole allow their work to speak for them and are to some extent reluctant to reveal the full details of their practice. In addition, despite the growth of a rational marketing approach, there remains a strong intuitive element in promotional image-making that defies precise definition. Yet if place promotion is to become an established and useful practice, it requires some real intellectual engagement between critic and practitioner.

What can be said with certainty is that place promotion is here to stay. As some of the contributors here show, it has the potential to be practised better and harnessed to rather more meaningful ends than is common at present. Certainly it deserves to be better understood. The contributions which follow are motivated towards that end.

References

Ashworth, G.A. and Voogd, H. (1990) *Selling the City*, London: Belhaven Press.

Bartels, C. and Timmer, M. (1987) *City Marketing: instruments and effects*, Athens: European Regional Science Association.

Boyle, M. and Hughes, G. (1992) 'The politics of the representation of the "real": discourses from the Left on Glasgow's role as European City of Culture', *Area*, 23, 217–28.

Brindley, T., Rydin, Y. and Stoker, G. (1988) *Remaking Planning: the politics of urban change in the Thatcher Years*, London: Unwin Hyman.

Brownill, S. (1990) *Developing London's Docklands: another great planning disaster*, London: Paul Chapman.

Buck, R.C. (1977) 'The ubiquitous tourist brochure', *Annals of Tourism Research*, 4, 195-207.

Burgess, J.A. (1982) 'Selling places: environmental images for the executive', *Regional Studies*, 16, 1–17.

Camard, F. and Zagrodski, C. (1989) *Le Train à l'Affiche: les plus belles affiches ferrovaires françaises*, Paris: La Vie du Rail.

Cameron, J.M.R. (1974) 'Information distortion in colonial promotion: the case of the Swan River colony', *Australian Geographical Studies*, 12, 57–76.

Camina, M.M. (1974) 'Local authorities and the attraction of industry', *Progress in Planning*, 3(2), whole issue.

Cole, B. and Durack, R. (1992) *Railway Posters 1923–1947*, London: Laurence King.

Collinge, C. (1992) 'The dynamics of local intervention: economic development and the theory of local government', *Urban Studies*, 29, 57–75.

Cosgrove, S. and Campbell, D. (1988) 'Behind the wee smiles', *New Statesman and Society*, 1(28), 10–12.

Deben, L., Musterd, S. and van Weesep, J., eds. (1992) 'Culture and urban regeneration: some European examples', *Built Environment*, 18, whole issue.

Gold, J.R. (1974) *Communicating Images of the Environment*, Occasional Paper 29, Centre for Urban and Regional Studies, University of Birmingham.

Gren, J. (1992) *Place-Marketing in Europe: a manual*, Grenoble: Institut d'Etudes Politiques.

Hillion, D. (1990) *La Mer S'Affiche*, Rennes: Editions S'Affiche, Editions Ouest-France.

Hillion, D. (1991) *La Montaigne S'Affiche*, Rennes: Editions Ouest-France.

Holcomb, B. (1990) *Purveying Places: past and present*, Working Paper 17, Piscataway, NJ: Centre for Urban Policy Studies, Rutgers University.

Jackson, A.A. (1973, 1991) *Semi-detached London: suburban development, life and transport, 1900–39*, London: George Allen and Unwin/Didcot: Wild Swan Publications.

Jones, H.M. (1946) 'The colonial impulse: an analysis of the promotion literature of colonisation', *Proceedings of the American Philosophical Society*, 90, 131–61.

Kotler, P., Haider, D.H. and Rein, I. (1993) *Marketing Places: attracting investment, industry and tourism to cities, states and nations*, New York: Macmillan.

Lewis, G.M. (1988) 'Rhetoric of the western interior: modes of environmental description in American promotional literature in the nineteenth century', in D.E. Cosgrove and S. Daniels, eds., *The Iconography of Landscape: essays on the symbolic representation, design and past use of past environments*, Cambridge: Cambridge University Press, 179-93.

Lyon, R. (1987) 'Theme parks in the USA: growth markets and future prospects', *Travel and Tourist Analyst*, 9, 31–43.

Madsen, H. (1992) 'Place marketing in Liverpool: a review', *International Journal of Urban and Regional Research*, 16, 633–40.

Mawson, J. and Miller, D. (1986) 'Interventionist approaches in local employment and economic development: the experience of Labour local authorities' in V. A. Hausner, ed., *Critical Issues in Urban Economic development*, Vol. 1, Oxford: Clarendon Press, 145–99.

McDonald, F.H. (1938) *How to promote Community and Industrial Development*, New York: Harper and Row.

Merrens, H.R. (1969) 'The physical environment of early America: images and image makers in colonial South Carolina', *Geographical Review*, 59, 530–56.

Neill, W. (1992) 'Re-imaging Belfast', *The Planner*, 78(18), 8–10.

Paddison, R. (1993) 'City marketing, image reconstruction and urban regeneration', *Urban Studies*, 30, 339–49.

Reeves, R. (1961) *Reality in Advertising*, New York: Knopf.

Reinders, P. and Oosterwijk, W. (1993) *Neem de Trein: Spoorwegaffiches in Nederland*, Utrecht: Veen Reflex.

Ryans, J. K. Jnr. and Shanklin, W. (1986) *Guide to Marketing for Economic Development: competing in America's second civil war*, Columbus, Ohio: Publishing Horizons.

Shackleton, J. T. (1976) *The Golden Age of the Railway Poster*, London: New English Library.

Sparks, L. (1992) 'Birmingham: a European city', *The Planner*, 78(11), 4–10.

Totterdill, P. (1989) 'Local economic strategies as industrial policy: a critical review of British developments in the 1980s', *Economy and Society*, 18, 478–526.

van den Berg, L., Klaassen, L.H. and van der Meer, J. (1990) *Marketing Metropolitan Regions*, Rotterdam: European Institute for Comparative Urban Research.

Ward, S.V. (1988) 'Promoting holiday resorts: a review of early history to 1921', *Planning History*, 10(2), 7–11.

Winsberg, M.D. (1992) 'Walt Disney World, Florida: the creation of a fantasy landscape', in D.G. Janelle, ed., *Geographical Snapshots of North America*, New York: Guilford Press, 350–53.

Yates, N. (1988) 'Selling the seaside', *History Today*, 38, 20–27.

Zube, E.H. and Kennedy, C. (1990) 'Changing images of the Arizona territory', in L. Zonn, ed., *Place Images in the Media: portrayal, meaning and experience*, Savage, MD, Rowman and Littlefield, 183–203.

2 Locating the message: place promotion as image communication

JOHN R. GOLD

An important theme in many chapters of this book is a focus on the messages created and communicated by place promotional activities, particularly through use of the media. It is a focus, however, that takes many different forms. Such diversity is typical of media research generally. Once described as a 'teeming wilderness of facts and notions, instances and generalisations, proofs and surmises' (Smith, 1968:8), media research has acquired, if anything, an ever greater assortment of approaches and perspectives with the passage of time (e.g. see Davis and Walton, 1983; McQuail, 1983, 1987; Gamson et al., 1992; Heath and Bryant, 1992; McQuail and Windahl, 1993). More specifically in the case of place promotion, the assortment of approaches also reflects the lack of explicit theorising by those interested in the subject. Empiricism has long reigned, with researchers tending to adopt whatever theoretical framework seems most appropriate at the time. The result has been a fragmentary field of study that draws its strength more from the intrinsic interest of the subject matter than from incisive and theoretically grounded analysis of promotional messages.

Progress towards a more rigorous understanding of promotional messages is possible, however, by identifying place promotion as part of a culturally defined system of communication in which 'meanings are encoded and decoded by specialist groups of producers and decoded in many different ways by the groups who constitute the audiences for those products' (Burgess, 1990:139–40). Seen in this way, three different emphases can be identified in the study of promotional messages. The first sees them as part of the production system, viewing the activity of image communication as a manifestation of the specific needs of the communicators and as a product of the broader socio-political system. The second concentrates primarily on the message of the media, searching for manifest or latent meanings in the material that is selected, encoded and communicated. The third highlights audience consumption of media messages recognising that, in contrast to traditional approaches to the media (e.g. see Gold, 1974:10–13), there is no necessary equivalence between the encodings and decodings of messages.

This chapter examines the second of these themes, aiming to supply context for subsequent chapters by examining the principal foci in research, actual or potential, concerning the messages conveyed by the media when used for place promotional purposes. There are four main sections. The first examines content analytic approaches, which supply insight into the manifest content of communicated materials. The second examines pictorial representations, commenting on the relatively meagre insights available from art historical approaches. An exploratory classification of some common advertising formats is offered as an example of directions for future analysis. The third section considers cognitive-behavioural approaches, in particular examining the use of promotional work to combat stereotypes. The fourth section turns to recent work in cultural studies. It is recognised that very little research in this area has yet dealt with place promotion, but emphasises the promise that exists. This is exemplified by detailed discussion of the ideological and rhetorical nature of place promotional messages.

Content analysis

Whether or not they choose to use the term, most researchers carry out some form of 'content analysis' when studying media messages, if only as a first step. Content analysis, as originally conceived, was rooted in social–scientific approaches to mass communication research (Weber, 1990). Conventionally defined as techniques for 'the objective, systematic and quantitative description of the manifest content of communication' (Berelson, 1952:18), content analysis remains a basic building block of media studies. It is most commonly associated with quantitative approaches to communicated materials, such as frequency counts of the mention of items, summations of column inches devoted to particular topics, or key word analysis. These are then used to make valid inferences from text about the sender(s) of messages, their audiences, or about the messages themselves.

While the preoccupation with quantitative methods and manifest content has persisted, recent developments have introduced openly qualitative and thematic approaches. As a result, the emphasis has shifted with the rise of techniques that focus more on underlying or 'latent' content. Equally the social–scientific orientation is now challenged by methods that are derived from research in socio-linguistics and the humanities.

When compared with the weight of content analytic studies available from mass communication researchers (Krippendorf, 1980; Rosengren, 1981; Weber, 1990), the amount of research available on the content of place promotional materials remains limited and mostly implicit. Lewis (1988), for example, fashioned his analysis of the promotional literature of the American western interior in the 19th century from a content analytic study of 37 guides and 101 promotional publications produced between c.1820–1900 (*see also* Chapter 12). Gold (1974, 1978) applied both quantitative and qualitative analyses to the newspaper and periodical advertising output of one East Anglian and five West Midland overspill towns during the 1971–2 financial year. In a similar manner, Burgess (1982) examined the material found in the promotional packages used by 240 local authorities in mainland Great Britain between 1977 and 1979, producing analyses of both the types of material and the underlying themes employed (see also PEP, 1972). In Chapter 6, Barke and Harrop, revisiting the same territory, hint at the distinctive content and vocabulary of industrial place promotion. Myers-Jones and Brooker-Gross (Chapter 11) systematically studied different editions of a regional newspaper to examine its role in promoting development projects.

Such studies provide a valuable first step in understanding the nature and flow of promotional messages, although they have their limitations (McQuail, 1983:129). In the first place, archived promotional material is rarely complete and available indexing or abstracting services often have their own in-built biases (e.g. see comments by Myers-Jones and Brooker-Gross, Chapter 11). Secondly, there is the danger of investigators imposing their own meaning systems rather than taking meaning from the communicated content. Thirdly, frequency of occurrence is not the only guide to salience or to meaning. Much may depend on the context of an occurrence or the internal relationships between references in texts, which may get overlooked in the process of abstraction.

Pictorial representations

The second step towards comprehending promotional images comes through art historical approaches, in which techniques of iconographic and related analysis are applied to the visual properties of promotional materials. Posters are particularly amenable to such approaches. Throughout much recent design history, the poster has taken its place alongside the record sleeve and the book dust-jacket as an item that is recognised and commodified as art. The place promotional work of poster artists such as A. M. Cassandre, John Hassall, John Held Jnr, Edward McKnight Kauffer, Frank Newbould, Tom Purvis and others particularly comes into this category (e.g. see Hillier, 1969; Hawkins and Hollis, 1979; Holme, 1982; J.S. Johnson, 1983; Green, 1990; Halter, 1992; Hewitt, 1992). As the artistic merit of such work was recognised, dealers and others gained a vested interest in cataloguing and rescuing posters from the general anonymity of most commercial art; an endeavour that was assisted by the willingness of the master poster artists to sign their work.

The main limitation of this approach lies in its elite cultural basis. Although there is much scope for the extension of iconographic analysis to the type of popular culture to which most promotional materials belong (Panofsky, 1970; Cosgrove and Daniels, 1988; Ujlaki, 1993; see also Chapters 13 and 14), current emphases in this research are unhelpful. The approach usually encourages consideration of links between the representation of images and aesthetic movements, graphic and artistic techniques, typefaces and motifs. It also focuses attention on the general evolution of an individual artist's work in representing places (though few advertising artists have worked solely on place promotional themes) and on the artist–patron relationship. While these are useful general directions for research, much place promotional artwork, even that of fine quality, remains stubbornly anonymous and will almost certainly never be reclaimed for posterity by the operations of the art market. At best we might uncover the advertising agency but rarely much more.

The net result makes it difficult to push this approach very far when analysing the distinctive pictorial content of promotional materials. Effectively, there are no taxonomic systems to classify the visual content of promotional materials and classifications, such as those applied in Chapter 6, are necessarily ad hoc. Some progress, however, can be made by using insights available from the practical manual style of publicity literature. To take the example of press advertising, there are, to some extent, broad categories that can be pressed into service (e.g. Dunn and Barban, 1978). These include *inter alia*, 'eye-catchers' (in which more than 50 per cent of an illustration is occupied by a device intended solely to grab attention); 'reminders' (a single graphic device intended to reinforce the key theme of a campaign); and 'logograms' (identifying symbols, *see* Chapter 6). Yet, these too have their deficiencies. They have no conceptual grounding and do not cover perhaps the most distinctive feature of place promotional advertising, namely, the 'collage'.

To elaborate, the collage features between three and six photographs of the place concerned along with a portion of descriptive text. Figures 2.1 and 2.2 show two examples of this genre, respectively placed by Alabama and Telford. Alabama's advertisement contains seven small photographs depicting, clockwise, a post-modern office block, a heritage scene (cowboy riding a horse at the edge of the sea), a port and industrial zone, a hospital operating theatre, a marina, a family group with dog, and a worker in a high-technology industrial environment. Telford's advertisement contains photographs of a yacht in front of a modern factory, a post-modern office block, a heritage scene (the famous iron bridge across the Severn), a multi-ethnic grouping (white scientist, Afro-Caribbean graduate and Japanese female in traditional dress), a modern housing shot, and a family group with dog.

This overlap is not coincidental. Collage-style advertisements are remarkably similar in design, despite the manifest differences in the history and geography of these and other places being advertised. Their recurrent motifs are a scene symbolising high-technology working environments, a workforce grouping that hints at harmony (and sometimes ethnic diversity), a post-modern office building, some new housing, a family group (always with small children and usually with dog), a leisure scene (e.g. yachting, windsurfing, walking) and a picture that hints at the cultural identity of the area. Taken as a whole, this carefully crafted balance means that the collage is more than just a visual summary of the different elements in the selling message. It also indicates the balance between old and new, tradition and modernity, continuity and change, nature and artifice, home and workplace, contemporary image and cultural identity.

Therefore, collage-style advertising is not simply a style of representation; it is also symptomatic of a wider cultural agenda to which place promotional advertising and, indeed, other forms of media-based place promotion belong. Further analysis of this and other typical forms of pictorial representation need to be rooted in that context. Discussion on this theme, however, is postponed until we have formally introduced approaches deriving from cultural studies.

Images and stereotypes

A third set of approaches developed from cognitive-behaviouralism, a broad movement which developed in geography, sociology and environmental psychology (Gold, 1980). From the late 1960s onwards, many researchers examined representations of place as sources of environmental information and as an influence on behavioural decision-making. Place promotion literature proved an attractive area for research, with an important early direction (as noted in Chapter 1) being to consider how the contents of propagandist guidebooks and newspaper advertising influenced the migrational decisions of 19th-century colonists. Later work focused on more contemporary contexts. Gold (1974) and Goodey (1974), for example, examined the presentation of information about British new town schemes; Burgess (1978) considered contemporary promotional representations of Hull; Strauss (1961) and Holcomb and Beauregard (1980) analysed North American urban boosterism; and Ryan (1990) studied stereotypes in official images of Australia.

As noted elsewhere (Burgess and Gold, 1985), most of the theoretical frameworks for these studies drew, implicitly and explicitly, on social psychological research on stereotypes. Defined as highly simplified generalisations about people or places which carry within them assumptions about their characteristics and behaviours, stereotypes are held to be most significant when an individual has little first-hand knowledge of the subject. Once formed, stereotypes are an important category in environmental cognition. They are resistant to change and supply a rapid, if often erroneous, way of coming to terms with environmental complexity, given that individual people or places are all assumed to have the same attributes as the group as a whole.

Stereotypes are relevant in two specific ways for place promotion. On the one hand, promotional materials, like other forms of communicated content, play their part in the maintenance of stereotypes since copy-writers and creative directors frequently resort to stereotypes in communicating with their audience. On the other hand, they also resort to promotional work in an attempt to counter *other* stereotypes.

This latter strategy merits further discussion. Almost all industrial promotion schemes suffer from negative stereotypes in one way or another. Some towns or regions are simply regarded as marginal to their national economy or to the international economy; others are considered bywords for architectural monotony or industrial dereliction; some suffer from labour or civil unrest; yet others are saddled with the image of being in terminal economic decline. Such stereotypes, rightly or wrongly, are felt to be prejudicial to the development process, damaging a town or region's chances of gaining new migrants and perhaps also harming their reputation with resident multinationals that may be contemplating rationalisation of their international activities.

Given the known resistance of stereotypes to change, a popular strategy for dealing with them now is to abandon subtlety and tackle them head on. Brownill (Chapter 8), for example, shows how campaigns were undertaken to boost the sagging image of London Docklands in the face of a severe loss of confidence from industrialists, property developers and corporate investors. Another, longer-term campaign against negative stereotypes has been waged by Glasgow. Once popularly stereotyped as a city with poor housing, worn-out industry, labour discontent and gang violence, Glasgow tried hard to create a new imagery of culture and progress, typified by its successful 'Glasgow's Miles Better' promotional campaign. Superseded by many subsequent campaigns including the current 'Glasgow's Alive' campaign, its advertising continues to hammer away at the past; that this is 'no mean city', that there is vibrant culture, that 'Glasgow's on the move'.

Perhaps the apotheosis of this approach is found in advertising for Northern Ireland. The powerful negative stereotypes of violence and sectarian conflict associated with Northern Ireland make it difficult to attract new industry to an area that has high unemployment. Since 1985, for example, the city of Belfast has attempted a

Figures 2.1 and 2.2   Two recent examples of the collage approach to place promotion. Unlike the traditional approach, which tended to overemphasise details (see Figure 1.3), the multiple images are usually carefully chosen to achieve a conscious overall impression of harmony and balance.

Figures 2.1 and 2.2   (*Continued*)

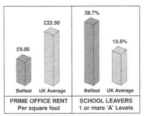

Figure 2.3 Re-imaging a city through place promotion. Belfast's Laganside Urban Development Corporation counterposes the traditional notion of Northern Ireland's 'Troubles' against the ills of urban congestion and high costs on the UK mainland.

're-imaging' process in which planners have promoted 'a critical mass of physical development spearheaded by flagship projects' which, in concept and physical design, 'dilute the backward looking symbolism of the present' (Neill, 1992:8). The redevelopment of the area along the River Lagan waterfront is one such project. In promoting it, Figure 2.3 effectively proclaims the general merits of Belfast without giving prominence to the city's name (a device perhaps intended to intrigue readers and ensure that they read the advertisement further rather than dismissing it out of hand). The creative strategy is not to deny that the area has problems but to suggest that in other respects, such as pollution, other cities might well have worse problems. The advertisement shows a harassed cyclist amid the fumes of heavy traffic adjusting his face mask. This is described as life in the city against which 'Laganside' can offer a breath of fresh air. After that follow a familiar series of advantages – about environment, rent levels, workforce, infrastructure and standard of living – although also claiming that this, like Glasgow, is 'no mean city'.

These examples must suffice to illustrate both a large genre and its underlying approach. Cognitive-behaviouralism helped to establish the fact that place image was a worthwhile object of inquiry and the approach itself suggested tremendous scope for empirical work on how place images were perceived. Nevertheless, it has not proved as productive as its early protagonists had hoped. The prime reason was that much of this work placed heavy emphasis on the individual and on the role of mental imagery. While this is an important dimension of the image communication process, understanding of the full meaning of media messages needs also to be rooted in the cultural context. It is to this question that we now turn.

Cultural studies

The final strand of promotional image analysis derives from the burgeoning field of cultural studies, an area of critical theory and practices that has developed in the humanities and social sciences over the last two decades (R. Johnson, 1983; Burgess and Gold, 1985; Turner, 1990). Cultural studies *per se* have sought to move the focus of inquiry away from elite to popular culture, employing a wide range of different theoretical approaches. Broadly speaking, they are now dominated by the works of the New Left after initial resistance to orthodox Marxism (e.g. Williams, 1958). These vary from structuralism, which sees language as the fundamental structure of social life determining the signifying practices of different cultures (Hall, 1980; Burgess and Gold, 1985:22) to heterodox Marxist-inspired approaches. Prominent among the latter are approaches derived from the theories of Gramsci (e.g. Hoare and Nowell-Smith, 1971; Hall, 1980), which accord more autonomy to cultural practices such as image-making.

Structuralist approaches developed from the linguistics of de Saussure (1915) and the work of structural anthropologists (e.g. Levi-Strauss, 1963) and often make use of semiological analysis (Burgelin, 1972; Gauthier, 1976; Clarke, 1987; Duncan and Duncan, 1992). Structuralism is concerned not only with conventional verbal languages but also with any sign-system which has language-like properties. Structuralists direct their attention less to the sign-system itself than to chosen texts and their meaning in the light of the host culture (McQuail, 1983:130). Such approaches, therefore, focus less on how and by whom specific promotional images were created and more on their ideological significance.

By contrast, approaches deriving from Antonio Gramsci would allow more diverse meanings in such details than structuralist interpretations would allow. Central to these approaches are his ideas on hegemony. Gramsci departed from Althusser and earlier Marxist theorists by arguing that the cultural and ideological relations between ruling and subordinate classes in capitalist societies are less ones of domination than of hegemony (Bennett *et al*, 1986:xiv). The idea of hegemony does not mean manipulation of the world-view of the masses, as is the case under domination, but rather means that, in order for cultural leadership to be achieved, the dominant class has to engage in negotiations with opposing groups, classes and values. These negotiations must result in some genuine accommodation. In this way, hegemony is not maintained through the obliteration of the opposition but the articulation of opposing interests and meanings into the world-view of the hegemonic group (Turner, 1990:213–14). This process may play a part in emphasising cultural distinctions or even reinforcing changes in social attitudes.

These developments have opened the floodgates for a bewildering range of new research, including cultural critique, deconstruction, new linguistic theory, cultural hermeneutics, post-colonial theory, and various brands of post-structural and post-modern analysis. Their great merit lies in the collective desire to shed inhibition, even if, as MacCannell (1992:2) suggested, they are not always successful in doing so. They espouse the desire to be free from the constraints of earlier theorising and claim to refuse to restrict their range of application to particular times and places, to focus on specific subject matters, or to understand themselves historically. Such approaches do have certain drawbacks, notably the plethora of competing schools of thought, the fact that explanations are often overlain with both dense profusions of opaque terminology and, more seriously, the short shelf-life of intellectual fashion. The joys of freewheeling conceptual plurality can too easily become lost in the swamp of fragmentation. Nevertheless, when looked at more positively, they have much to offer in the present context, not least in helping to move understanding beyond the limitations of content analytic, art historical or cognitive-behavioural approaches to consider the ideological and rhetorical meaning of images and messages.

Ideology

Ideology is a contentious and sometimes pejorative term embracing a 'family of concepts' (Plamenatz, 1970:27), but we can define it as the pervasive sets of ideas, beliefs and images that groups employ to make the world more intelligible to themselves. Ideology is thus viewed as an essential part of the process by which people come to terms with the world around them. It is sometimes conceived as being part of a conscious process of manipulation. Others (e.g. Hall, 1977) point out that ideology operates by being openly embedded in commonsense wisdom. Ideology is a frame which helps to make sense of and rationalise experience. Viewed in these terms, the expression and meaning of promotional imagery and messages are therefore seen as being constructed and mediated within the wider ideological context.

Two points follow from this analysis. First, ideology invariably functions as a conservative force. The effect of an ideology even among those, like place promoters, who are each seeking to obtain a competitive advantage relative to rival schemes, is to bring about conformity, contributing to the uncomfortable similarities in promotional material noted earlier. That point is easily verified by even a cursory glance at place promotional literature which oozes a grey homogeneity (see Chapter 1); employing the same terminology, statements of benefits and visual devices to reduce the infinite global variety of place to an insipid sameness.

Secondly, it can be said that a reason for this homogeneity lies in similarities in the ideological outlook of both the producers and consumers of place promotional materials. Although it can be argued cynically that many communicators are happier imitating the best ideas of others rather than innovating, the repetitiousness of place promotion may also reflect the particular nature of their discourse. Seen in this light, a set of shared needs and understandings could be said to contribute to the similarities in the resulting rhetoric: a term which now needs discussion in its own right.

Rhetoric

Like ideology, rhetoric has traditionally had a bad press. Defined as 'the use of discourse, either spoken or written, to inform or persuade or move an audience' (Corbett, 1971:3), it was also long considered as a distortion by philosophers (Baynes et al, 1987:423). Only recently have critical theorists argued that rhetoric is a perfectly normal and rational way of coming to terms with complex reality (Gadamer, 1975; Hartmann, 1981; Blumenberg, 1987; Simons, 1988; Enos and Brown, 1993).

This notion is helpful, since it allows rhetoric to be treated in a non-pejorative manner as a normal part of everyday discourse rather than as a distortion. Rhetoric is part and parcel of ideologically-constructed discourse. It involves presentation of an argument to persuade the audience that a particular scheme or project is worth further consideration, even at the expense of changing their previous position on the matter. That argument is designed to further the interests of the communicator, but to be effective it requires, first, that the audience is convinced that the advertiser is worthy of belief and, secondly, that the advertiser has an accurate sense of the audience and their needs.

We have met one example of rhetorical strategy previously in this chapter in the shape of policies to combat stereotypes. Using a typology derived in part from Andrén et al. (1978:85–110; see also Gibson, 1966), one can identify various rhetorical strategies by which imagery is shaped and presented in its cultural context. Some examples are:

'It's a Man's World'
Unusually for advertising, a genre in which 'sexual incitement is rarely absent' (Inglis, 1972:102), the discourse of place promotion contains remarkably little direct sexual reference. Indeed women, the usual recipients of this treatment, are virtually invisible. They seldom appear in the artwork except as subsidiary and heavily outnumbered figures in board-room scenes or as costumed accessories to indicate multiculturalism. Rather, the discourse addresses the advantages which men would wish to find in a business environment and the living and working conditions which they would seek for

themselves. Immediate expression of this is again found in the artwork. The golfer, the angler, the surveyor in the hard hat, the visionary executive pointing into the far distance, the profile of a face scrutinising a new factory building and the shirt-cuffs and hands of an unseen figure dealing cards are all recognisably male. Text, as Brownill (Chapter 8) shows in her discussion of recent London Docklands advertising, reinforces this rhetoric. Contrasting the virtuous 'docker' against the unenlightened 'knocker', he emerges as someone willing to: 'Take his wife to dinner. In Paris' and would even be prepared to 'Appoint a woman managing director'. Sometimes the rhetoric is more subtle, such as Gwent's invitation to 'you', the reader, to consider what it is like to get home before 'the kids are in bed' – an option that most career women rarely find it possible to contemplate – but the net effect is the same. The dominant impression is of a dialogue that it is man-to-man; male copywriter speaking to middle-aged, male senior executives and company chairmen. Women are almost entirely omitted from the rhetoric of industrial place promotion.

Puns

We noted in Chapter 1 that the communicators' willingness or ability to specify a target audience varies markedly. Nevertheless, place promotion aimed at industrialists is one area in which copywriters normally do have a well-defined conception of the audience that they are trying to reach (even if the design of final copy does not always match the clarity of that conception). The pun, a humorous play on words, is particularly important in this discourse. Given the nature of the audience, the copywriter can predict, with considerable accuracy, their needs, social assumptions, language and vocabulary. In these circumstances, the pun signals communication between intellectual equals, a playful device used to gain readers' attention and intrigue them sufficiently to read further. (For some examples of this gentle art, *see* Chapters 6 and 7.)

Slogans

Slogans are also dealt with in more detail in Chapter 6, but merit brief mention here. A standard way to give identity to a promotional campaign, conveying key ideas in a terse and simplified manner, they have long been recognised as *de rigeur* in the rhetoric of industrial place promotional advertising (Gold, 1974; Burgess, 1982). They can generally be divided into two main types (e.g. Dunn and Barban, 1978:348–50), either emphasising the action to be taken or to stress the rewards offered. Use of slogans, however, poses a problem. While this chapter is not concerned with measuring the effectiveness of advertising, evidence from product advertising would cast doubt on what purpose slogans could possibly serve in the present context. Slogans are found to work best with impulse purchases, which are low in price and bought without much thoughtful consideration and in connection with campaigns that seek to dramatise certain ideas strongly and to do so extensively for long periods of time (Dunn and Barban, 1978:349). None of these conditions apply in the case of place promotion.

In good company

A commonplace feature of place promotion is a series of rhetorical devices through which advertisers seek to give credibility to their discourse by referring to their previous success in attracting migrants. An impressive listing, or some visual representation of internationally famous companies found in the area is a seemingly authoritative and objective test of the town or region's economic performance.

An interesting illustration of this strategy can be found in the response of centres in the English East Midlands following the decision of Toyota to locate at Burnaston (*see* Chapter 1). South Derbyshire, the local authority in which the Toyota factory is located, could trumpet the idea that it was making 'its mark on the international map'. Slightly miffed, its near neighbours made the best of a bad job. The city of Derby claimed in its advertising that Toyota had 'established its £700 million car assembly plant just outside the city'. The borough of East Staffordshire used a drawing of a Toyota car passing a road-sign to show that its boundaries lay just two-and-a-half miles from Burnaston. This reflected glory, it claimed, showed that the area had 'a central location, excellent communications' and the usual litany of other positive features.

Various other rhetorical techniques are related to this strategy. One example is the 'appeal to authority'. This comprises quoting the opinion of independent surveys or a reputable sounding authority to say that a particular town or region scores more highly than its (unspecified) competitors on one or more indices. Hence, in recent advertising Denmark presented scores from the impressive sounding *World Competitiveness Report* to show that it had moved from fourth to first place on the Executive Opinion Scoreboard and from eighth to fourth place on the Report's World Competitiveness Scoreboard. (The actual authorship of the Report, the number of countries entered, or the criteria used are not stated.) In another instance, Wallonia claims the support of a US Labour Force Report (undated) to show that the region's productivity is one of the highest in Europe. Merseyside, too, is keen to emphasise labour productivity, stating that a 'recent Government report by the National Audit Office' shows that office staff are over 20 per cent more productive than their London counterparts. Quite often a sense of independent assessment of worth is given without the actual source being cited. Hence, again in recent advertising, North Carolina claimed that it has 'led the US in new manufacturing plant locations four out of the last five years', while Alsace claims that it 'scores first in France for exports per head, after Paris for turnover per head.'

Yet another technique of providing a seemingly independent appraisal of worth is the testimonial. This idea features as an element in the collage-style advertisements placed, for example, by Alabama (Figure 2.1), but at times also supplies the main element in advertising copy. Instead of selected quotes from sources that sound impressive but cannot easily be verified, these advertisements print statements from senior executives of nationally or internationally known companies who express their satisfaction with the town. The result is effectively an endorsement from a satisfied client and has the added bonus of hinting at partnership and cooperation between industry and municipality.

Transports of Delight
It is widely believed that transport is psychologically as well as economically important in locational decisions and that a move to a location regarded as isolated is equated with becoming uncompetitive. One way to assuage doubts on this score is to claim centrality through superior communications. In Great Britain, this now means

good access to the motorway network – widely considered to be the heart of the British transport system; in France, prominence is given to access to the high-speed rail network; and in the USA, distance from regional and national airports (*see also* Chapters 6 and 7). Other advertisers use cartography to convey their centrality to a specific region, whether or not that centrality has any conceivable importance. Recent advertisements show Bedfordshire is 'beautifully connected' because it lies at the heart of a triangle between London, Cambridge and Milton Keynes. Whether any firm actually wishes to be placed at the centre of that triangle as opposed to one of its vertices is another matter. In the same vein, Finland argues that as part of 'an integrated Europe', a suspect notion in itself, it is a 'unique gateway' to Russia and the Baltic nations. More improbably, Madeira's cartography renders the island central to the 'Atlantic economy' of Europe, North America and Africa. The Var (on the south coast of France) is shown positioned at a 'strategic European crossroads', and Hamburg is in the 'middle of Europe'. There are few limits to what can be argued with selective cartographic devices or concentric circles expressing distances in flying time.

Natural symbols

Nature and naturalistic concepts have a powerful hold in contemporary promotional work. This is partly because of the general value assigned to nature in Western society (Williamson, 1978), but also because naturalistic symbols can be readily used to communicate complex or abstract ideas. In the present instance, these include growth, expansion, and the suitability of industrial premises. The Scottish new town of Irvine, for instance, displays bird's eggs of varying dimensions to draw attention to the availability of different sized factory 'shells' which, in an organic fashion, exactly fit the firm's needs (Figure 2.4). Other examples from recent promotional material include a picture of six different types of fruit growing on the same tree branch ('extraordinary growth in Vienna'), drawings of oysters opened up to reveal double pearls (Merseyside, 'it must be something to do with the water'), and drawings of caged and uncaged birds to represent an escape from the constraints of present location (Rural Wales).

Growth and Enterprise

Growth is not only related to naturalistic rhetoric, but became enmeshed during the 1980s in the pronouncements of the 'New Right'. To elaborate, Conservative administrations in the UK, USA and elsewhere took steps to revitalise the spirit of free market economics. In particular, the four UK administrations headed by Margaret Thatcher assiduously tried to inculcate the notion of a new 'enterprise culture' to replace the social welfare consensus that had characterised political debate since World War II. Given the Conservative disposition of most businessmen, it was not surprising that a new lexicon of specialised terms and phrases quickly entered the global discourse of industrial place promotion.

An international sample shows the extent of its diffusion. Grenoble–Isère commends itself for offering 'enterprise, innovation, training, recruitment . . . competition, efficiency and partnership'. Flanders has 'an enterprise spirit that's open to foreign investment', Connecticut contains 'leading-edge enterprises', Quebec extends 'the driving force of partnership' to incoming migrants and, most improbably, Madeira

Figure 2.4 Natural symbols or analogies sometimes feature as part of promotional messages, often in quite subtle ways. A particularly explicit example is this by Irvine New Town Development Corporation.

claims the advantages of 'some of the most favourable and competitive conditions available today'.

Life-style

Times change, however, and advertising reflects the changing mood of the business community. While 'lifestyle' has long been part of the rhetoric of place promotion, it has recently taken on renewed vigour as part of the reaction to the cruder cultural excesses of Thatcherism and Reaganomics. It is widely believed that businessmen in the 1990s have become sensitive to the appeal of life-style. With this in mind, advertisers increasingly add the virtues of life-style to their promotional message. Mobile industrialists are promised wholesome suburban family values laced with vague hints of metropolitan delights, even in the most unlikely settings.

The cultural cachet

As with the presence of large and prestigious companies, there is perceived to be selling virtue in the cultural associations that a place might possess, not least because they imply permanence and the presence of a social elite. Peterborough trades on its Roman origins, Connecticut invites migrants 'to enjoy America's richest cultural life', Goerlitz (Lower Silesia) and Lausanne market themselves as major 'cultural centres'. For others, culture is the key selling point, with direct allusion to economic arguments distinctly muted. In this way, Glasgow lauds its new café society, Spain trumpets its 'passion for life' and Cologne hails both the city's heritage (a '2000-year history', art galleries, cathedral, 'unique Romanesque churches') and a vibrant new cultural area that symbolises the region's post-war renaissance.

Conclusion

This discussion of rhetorical strategies is no more than an indicative first step in demonstrating the potential of culturally-grounded approaches to place promotional messages. Many other areas of place promotion commend themselves as subjects for future analysis, but space does not permit further exploration on these lines. In this chapter, we have briefly surveyed the four different sets of approaches currently available for the study of the messages communicated in place promotion. Each has its limitations but, equally, each has a contribution to make towards an understanding of the nature and construction of such messages.

Content analytic approaches supply a basic building block for textual analysis, but their prime application is to manifest content. Study of pictorial representations remains a neglected area, given the failure of conventional art historical approaches to deal convincingly with this area of popular culture. More analysis of the typical forms of representation, especially collage-type advertising, was identified as an area that would make a valuable addition to research. Cognitive-behavioural research was considered historically important in exploring the role and significance of image and stereotypes, but has subsequently proved conceptually limited due to underplaying of the cultural context. Cultural studies overcome that deficiency by analysing the meaning of communicated materials within the full cultural cycle of production-message-consumption. Such perspectives have much to offer in the present context, not least in helping to move understanding beyond the limitations of other approaches to consider the ideological and rhetorical meaning of promotional imagery and messages. Whether or not that promise is realised may well depend on researchers' willingness to move beyond experimentation and overcome the associated problems of conceptual plurality and fragmentation.

References

Andrén, G., Ericsson, L.O., Ohlsson, R. and Tännsjö, T. (1978) *Rhetoric and Ideology in Advertising: a content analytic study of American advertising*, Stockholm: LiberFörlag.

Baynes, K., Bohman, J. and McCarthy, T.M., eds. (1987) *After Philosophy: end or transformation?*, Cambridge: MIT Press.

Bennett, T., Mercer, C. and Woollacott, J., eds. (1986) *Popular Culture and Social Relations*, Milton Keynes: Open University Press.

Berelson, B. (1952) *Content Analysis as a Tool of Communication Research*, Glencoe, IL: Free Press.

Blumenberg, H. (1987) 'An anthropological approach to the contemporary significance of rhetoric', in K. Baynes, J. Bohman and T.M. McCarthy, eds., *After Philosophy: end or transformation?*, Cambridge: MIT Press, 429–58.

Burgelin, O. (1972) 'Structural analysis and mass communications', in D. McQuail, ed., *Sociology of Mass Communications*, Harmondsworth: Penguin, 313–28.

Burgess, J.A. (1978) *Image and Identity*, Occasional Paper in Geography 23, Department of Geography, University of Hull.

Burgess, J.A. (1982) 'Selling places: environmental images for the executive', *Regional Studies*, 16, 1–17.

Burgess, J.A. (1990) 'The production and consumption of environmental meanings in the mass media: a research agenda for the 1990s', *Transactions of the Institute of British Geographers*, 15, 139–61.

Burgess, J.A. and Gold, J.R. (1985) 'Place, the media and popular culture', in J.A. Burgess and J.R. Gold, eds., *Geography, the Media and Popular Culture*, London: Croom Helm, 1–32.

Clarke, D.S. (1987) *Principles of Semiotics*, London: Routledge and Kegan Paul.

Corbett, E.P.J. (1971) *Classical Rhetoric for the Modern Student*, second edition, New York: Oxford University Press.

Cosgrove, D. and Daniels, S.D., eds. (1988) *The Iconography of Landscape*, Cambridge: Cambridge University Press.

Davis, H. and Walton, P., eds. (1983) *Language, Image, Media*, Oxford: Blackwell.

de Saussure, F. (1915, 1960) *A Course in General Linguistics*, London: Peter Owen.

Duncan, J.S. and Duncan, N.G. (1992) 'Ideology and bliss: Roland Barthes and the secret histories of landscape', in T.J. Barnes and J.S. Duncan, eds., *Writing Worlds: discourse, text and metaphor in the representation of landscape*, London: Routledge, 18–37.

Dunn, S.W. and Barban, A.M. (1978) *Advertising: its role in modern marketing*, fourth edition, Hinsdale, IL: Dryden Press.

Enos, T. and Brown, S.C. (1993) *Defining the New Rhetoric*, London: Sage.

Gadamer, H.G. (1975) *Truth and Method*, trans. G. Barden and J. Cumming, New York: Seabury Press.

Gamson, W.A., Croteau, D., Hoynes, W. and Sasson, T. (1992) 'Media images and the social construction of reality', *Annual Review of Sociology*, 18, 373–93.

Gauthier, G. (1976) *The Semiology of the Image*, London: British Film Institute.

Gibson, W. (1966) *Tough, Sweet and Stuffy: an essay on modern American prose styles*, Bloomington: Indiana University Press.

Gold, J.R. (1974) *Communicating Images of the Environment*, Occasional Paper 29, Centre for Urban and Regional Studies, University of Birmingham.

Gold, J.R. (1978) 'Towns get the marketing blues', *Urban*, Sept–Oct., 14–16.

Gold, J.R. (1980) *An Introduction to Behavioural Geography*, Oxford: Oxford University Press.

Goodey, B. (1974) *Images of Place*, Occasional Paper 30, Centre for Urban and Regional Studies, University of Birmingham.

Green, O. (1990) *Underground Art: London Transport posters, 1908 to the present*, London: Studio Vista.

Hall, S. (1977) 'Culture, the media and the "ideological" effect', in J. Curran, M. Gurevitch and J. Wollacott, eds., *Mass Communication and Society*, London: Edward Arnold and the Open University Press, 315–49.

Hall, S. (1980) 'Cultural studies and the Centre: some problematics and problems', in S. Hall, D. Hobson, A. Lowe and P. Willis, eds., *Culture, Media, Language*, London: Hutchinson, 15–47.

Halter, A. (1992) 'Paul Dermée and the poster in France in the 1920s: Jean d'Ylen as "Maître de l'affiche moderne"', *Journal of Design History*, 5, 39–52.

Hartmann, G.A. (1981) *Saving the Text: literature, Derrida, philosophy*, Baltimore: Johns Hopkins University Press.

Hawkins, J. and Hollis, M. (1979) *The Thirties: British art and design before the war*, London: Arts Council of Great Britain.

Heath, R.L. and Bryant, J.B (1992) *Human Communication: theory and research. Concepts, contexts and research*, Hillsdale, NJ: Lawrence Erlbaum Associates.

Hewitt, J. (1992) 'The "nature" and "art" of Shell advertising in the early 1930s', *Journal of Design History*, 5, 121–39.

Hillier, B. (1969) *Posters*, London: Spring Books.

Hoare, Q. and Nowell-Smith, G., eds. (1971) *Selections from the Prison Notebooks of Antonio Gramsci*, London: Lawrence and Wishart.

Holcomb, H.B. and Beauregard, R.A. (1980) *Revitalising Cities*, Resource Publications in Geography, Washington, DC: Association of American Geographers.

Holme, B. (1982) *Advertising: reflections of a century*, London: Heinemann.

Inglis, F. (1972) *The Imagery of Power: a critique of advertising*, London: Heinemann.

Johnson, J.S. (1983) *The Modern American Poster*, New York: Museum of Modern Art.

Johnson, R. (1983) *What is Cultural Studies anyway?*, Stencilled Occasional Paper 74, Centre for Contemporary Cultural Studies, University of Birmingham.

Krippendorf, K. (1980) *Content Analysis*, Beverley Hills, CA: Sage.

Levi-Strauss, C. (1963) *Structural Anthropology*, New York: Basic Books.

Lewis, G.M. (1988) 'Rhetoric of the western interior: modes of environmental description in American promotional literature in the nineteenth century', in D.E. Cosgrove and S. Daniels, eds., *The Iconography of Landscape: essays on the symbolic representation, design and past use of past environments*, Cambridge: Cambridge University Press, 179–193.

MacCannell, D. (1992) *Empty Meeting Grounds: the tourist papers*, London: Routledge.

McQuail, D.B (1983, 1987) *Mass Communication Theory*, London: Sage.

McQuail, D.B. and Windahl, S. (1993) *Communication Models for the Study of Mass Communications*, Harlow: Longman.

Neill, W. (1992) 'Re-imaging Belfast', *The Planner*, 78(18), 8–10.

Panofsky, E. (1970) *Meaning in the Visual Arts*, Harmondsworth: Penguin.

PEP [Political and Economic Planning] (1972) *Advertising Overspill: can advertising prevent urban ghettoes developing in Britain?*, Research Monograph 5, London: Advertising Association.

Plamenatz, J.P. (1970) *Ideology*, London: Pall Mall Press.

Rosengren, K.E., ed. (1981) *Advances in Content Analysis*, Beverley Hills, CA: Sage.

Ryan, K.B. (1990) 'The "official" image of Australia', in L. Zonn, ed., *Place Images in the Media: portrayal, meaning and experience*, Savage, MD: Rowman and Littlefield, 135–58.

Simons, H.W., ed. (1988) *Rhetoric in the Human Sciences*, London: Sage.

Smith, A., ed. (1968) *Communication and Culture: readings in the code of human interaction*, New York: Holt, Rinehart and Winston.

Strauss, A.L. (1961) *Images of the American Life*, Glencoe, IL: Free Press.

Turner, G. (1990) *British Cultural Studies: an introduction*, London: Unwin Hyman.

Ujlaki, G. (1993) 'The logic of representation', *British Journal of Aesthetics*, 33, 121–31.

Weber, R.P. (1990) *Basic Content Analysis*, second edition, Newbury Park, CA: Sage.
Williams, R. (1958) *Culture and Society*, London: Chatto and Windus.
Williamson, J. (1978) *Decoding Advertisements: ideology and meaning in advertising*, London: Marion Boyars.

3 Marketing and place promotion

GREGORY J. ASHWORTH AND HENK VOOGD

From place promotion to place marketing

There is nothing new about places being promoted by those likely to profit from their development. Since Leif Ericson sought new settlers in the 8th century for his newly discovered 'green' land, the idea of the deliberate projection of favourable place images to potential customers, investors or residents has been actively pursued. Few British 19th century seaside resorts (Brown, 1988) or suburbs developing on south-east England's expanding commuter railway network in the early decades of this century would have had much to learn from modern local authorities about the skilful creation and transmission of favourable images to potential markets. Indeed places in recently settled nations were so obviously in competition with each other for populations and enterprises that civic 'boosterism', (as described in the 'Zenith' novels of Sinclair Lewis), was expressed almost automatically through place names, slogans, postmarks and the like.

It is self evident that cities and regions have always existed within markets of one sort or another: they compete for resources, activities and residents with other places and equally each service offered within the city competes with others for users or consumers. This would be the case regardless of the dominant prevailing philosophy of political economy. It is no more than just the recognition that many activities, including those provided by government agencies for social rather than economic reasons, operate within a 'market' – whether or not this is made explicit – and that the operation of such markets have important effects upon each other. Intervention to influence this operation is not only both possible and desirable, it is also largely unavoidable.

What is new, however, is the conscious application of marketing approaches by public planning agencies not just as an additional instrument for the solution of intractable planning problems but, increasingly, as a philosophy of place management. This fundamental reappraisal of the relationship between places and their markets at various spatial scales is part of a series of fundamental shifts that have become apparent recently both generally in western economies and societies and also in philosophy and methods of planning: in how places are used and how they are managed. This chapter argues, first, that promotion designed to sell towns and regions is just one of many marketing techniques and, secondly, that it needs to be seen as only one aspect of a much wider approach to place management. Failure to do so at best underutilises its full potential as a management instrument and, at worst, can lead to costly errors.

To explain this wider context, it is first necessary to review briefly the changes in public planning that have resulted in the adoption of marketing, for otherwise selling places is little more than the fashionable substitution of an imported terminology. Secondly, we will explain the developments in marketing science that have allowed this to occur in order to place the promotion of cities and regions in the wider context of marketing as both a set of instrumental techniques and, more fundamentally, a philosophy of place management.

The recent interest in the market context of places, especially in Europe, stems from shifts in the character of cities and regions, together with changes in the attitudes of governments to these changes, at national as well as local level. Within local economies, the three fundamental shifts are in what is produced and how and where it is produced. These result in the increasing importance of services in general and higher-order personal quaternary services in particular. Moreover, they have blurred the distinction between public provision for social goals and private production for individual profit. Finally, they have increased the locational freedom of activities. It is not that space is no longer important in locational decisions but rather that a new set of place attributes and fresh definitions of the accessibility of places have become prominent locational determinants for a new set of economic activities. This has thrust cities and regions into new relationships with their external and internal markets which present both threats and opportunities.

The novelty of the situation and much of the explanation of the relevance of place marketing approaches lies not in the existence of competition as such, but in the abruptly changing rules of the competitive struggle between places. The criteria for likely success are place characteristics such as environmental quality or, more broadly, the way in which cities are now valued as places in which to live, work, enjoy leisure or invest. Amenity and service quality, however difficult to assess, are now active determinants in maintaining, attracting or repelling economic activities. Moreover, because these attributes are potentially ubiquitous, access to the competitive arena is relatively easy for all places. This is doubly so since many of these attributes are locally determined, so that participation in that competitive arena through place marketing becomes possible and attractive.

In turn, these manifest shifts in the economic dynamics of localities are reflected in equally far-reaching social and cultural changes. The individual's relationship to work, the structure of households, patterns of consumption, residential choice and much else have altered, often drastically. Meanwhile, there have been important conceptual and policy shifts in the role of governments and public planning. In a more direct way, this has encouraged local authorities to react by themselves becoming players in the business of marketing places.

In the years between 1945 and 1965, most western European governments sought to guide the processes of local development and influence economic and social changes at the local level (e.g. see Burtenshaw *et al.*, 1991). To this end, these nations instituted a system of planning legislation, regulations and working procedures, operated by a rapidly increasing professionalised bureaucracy in the late 1940s and 1950s. This was subsequently elaborated and refined in the light of experience during the next two decades.

By the 1970s, however, there was increasing dissatisfaction with the operation of this system which was perceived to be cumbersome, complex and unresponsive. Most seriously, it had failed to solve the intractable problems of urban economic regeneration. In short, there was an ill-defined feeling in many western European nations that the public planning system had failed. Significantly, this disillusionment coincided with the economic recession in the late 1970s and early 1980s. A planning system that had been designed to constrain and control the demands on developers' space was now singularly ill-suited to reacting to the failure of those demands by stimulating them. In addition, the rise to power of political parties with a 'radical right' agenda in several countries encouraged an interest in bringing back 'the market' into local government for reasons of political ideology (Jossip *et al.*, 1987; Weiss, 1989).

Severe constraints on public finance coupled with disillusionment about the efficacy of traditional practices contributed towards a willingness to contemplate new attitudes to the role of markets within public planning activity, especially at local government level. Local planners and politicians searching for new sources of finance turned increasingly to a range of techniques drawn from marketing, important among which is promotion. A succinct means of describing the very varied results of this new attitude and the policies, structures, instruments and practices stemming from it is place marketing.

Yet the term and the imported marketing techniques it incorporates are deceptively straightforward. The new practices are beset by an intrinsic difficulty that accounts for most of the problems raised in the rest of this chapter. Quite simply, there was a mismatch between the realities of places as products and established marketing practice. Marketing had evolved largely among commercial firms in the inter-war period, as a means of selling physical products to paying customers for short-term financial profit. By contrast, place marketing can be defined as a process whereby local activities are related as closely as possible to the demands of targeted customers. The intention is to maximise the efficient social and economic functioning of the area concerned, in accordance with whatever wider goals have been established. This definition significantly shifts the secondary definitions of product, customer and goals compared to conventional marketing. To achieve this, it has been necessary to evolve three new marketing concepts.

The first is the idea of 'marketing in non-profit organisations' (sometimes expressed as 'marketing in non-business organisations'), which attempts to address the problem of goals (Kotler and Levy, 1969). The assumption is that both the objectives of private firms as well as the means of monitoring success are different from those of public or semi-public agencies. In practice, those who usually market places have goals other than a direct financial profit for the organisation conducting the marketing. The absence of a direct financial nexus between customer and firm accordingly renders it difficult to measure the effects of such marketing (Fines, 1981). Thus a different form of marketing is required, such as that developed by Kotler and Zaltman (1971), Kotler (1982), and Lovelock and Weinberg (1984). This incorporates the broader- and longer-term goals of public authorities and accommodates the absence of a direct financial link between producer and consumer, which is achieved by extending the concept of what constitutes a market. The differences in objectives lead to differences in marketing strategy, analysis of customer groups and operation of the exchange concept, but not to a rejection of marketing as such (Capon, 1981).

Secondly, marketing 'aimed at enhancing the consumer's and society's wellbeing' (Kotler, 1986:16) rather than selling a specific product to an individual customer is usually called 'social marketing'. The idea was popularised in the 1970s (see Kotler and Zaltman, 1971; Lazer and Kelley, 1973; Rados, 1981) to accommodate a number of distinctly different trends. These included concern for longer-term as well as immediate profits and broadening the idea of marketing to include attempts to influence other aspects of the behaviour of targeted groups besides their direct purchasing behaviour. Such 'attitudinal marketing' was intended to alter or reinforce sets of attitudes held by targeted individuals or groups. These social attitudes were part of the collective responsibilities usually assumed by public authorities, which thereby gained experience and confidence in marketing in general. Moreover, the concern with longer rather than shorter term effectively redefined the term 'profit' to include many indirect and less easily measurable social benefits. It also demonstrated the efficacy of marketing in general, while familiarising public agencies with its techniques.

Finally, it became increasingly apparent in the course of the 1970s that images could be effectively marketed while the products to which they related remained vaguely delineated or even non-existent. 'Hearts and minds' campaigns, for all sorts of objectives, not only gave public sector organisations another demonstration of marketing but also showed that a diffuse, complex and vaguely defined product did not rule out the application of marketing techniques. Such 'image marketing' tries to manipulate the behavioural patterns of selected audiences for political or social as well as economic goals. Obviously, when such a rationale was applied to places it meant they could be marketed through their generalised images even though the actual goods and services that were being sold were difficult to specify and the overall goals were equally varied and non-economic.

The evolution within marketing science of these three concepts taken together paved the way for an integrated concept of place marketing which could be applied by public place management authorities as the demand for it arose.

Elements in a place marketing process

We have argued above that local authorities discovered a need for market approaches, among which promotion was the best known technique, at a time when marketing science had also developed sufficiently to allow a distinctive place marketing to be practised. The various elements involved in such place marketing as a procedure must now be described so that the role of promotion within such a process can be appreciated. In the words of marketing's most widely read theorist: 'marketing is a process of planning and movement of a product from the supplier to those who are to use it . . . and the marketing process is incomplete unless all of its functions are performed' (Kotler, 1986). The main elements in this process are summarised in Figure 3.1. As in any marketing system, the market brings together customers and products in a free exchange of value. Our contention, however, is that each of these elements in place marketing is significantly different to those in more traditional marketing. Moreover, these differences determine the distinctive character of place marketing, making it more than a simple transfer of a known and tried set of techniques from one set of products to another.

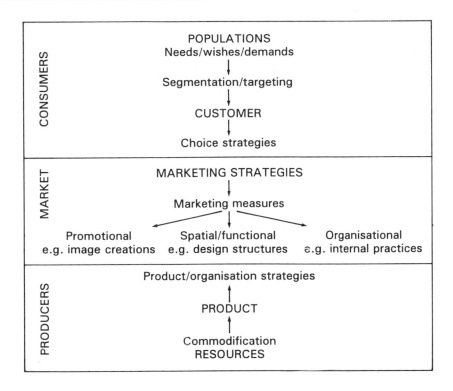

Figure 3.1 Elements in a place marketing process.

The place product

Places are peculiar products and these peculiarities have important consequences for their marketing. They can be defined in terms of the facilities and activities they accommodate or more broadly as an entity. Thus, the place is both a container or stage for activity-based products as well as being a product in itself. Place promotion, therefore, may be the selling of a selected package of facilities or the selling of the place as a whole through images composed of various attributes associated with it. Either is possible but needs distinguishing from the other as each requires a quite different sort of promotion.

Places are locations and areas. The place product as consumed may not correspond to the place product as promoted. Indeed, there is little reason why the jurisdictional boundaries (and thus the boundaries of the area for which the promoting authority is responsible), should coincide spatially with the place consumed by visitor or resident. Similarly places exist at particular spatial scales and nest within spatial hierarchies. This opens up the possibility of many forms of discrepancy. Different levels in the hierarchy may be promoted quite differently for different purposes to different consumers. Promotional shadow effects of one level upon others may be positive or negative. The specific scale promoted may not correspond to that consumed, and neither may be coterminous with any particular governmental jurisdiction.

Finally, places are sold as products to many different groups of consumers. Precisely the same physical space and, in many circumstances, the same facilities or attributes of that space are sold simultaneously to different customers for different purposes. This 'multi-selling' is possible because trading in places does not involve the transfer, or even usually the temporary hire, of exclusive property rights. The sale of the product does not diminish the stock of it held by producers, nor does its consumption by one consumer limit its consumption by another. These theoretical assertions are valid unless, or until, conflict occurs between consumers who have been sold the same finite space. None of these characteristics disqualify places as products, but do make their promotion more complex.

The place-product producer

One consequence of the peculiar characteristics of place products mentioned above is that it is frequently unclear who is the producer and who the promoter. The variety of possible place-product packages that can be produced for the same place is paralleled by fragmentation of possible producers. Local governments have no monopoly of this function, which they may share with other public, semi-public and private organisations. Even different departments of the same authority may be simultaneously engaged in promotion that could be mutually supportive, irrelevant or even contradictory. Equally the promotion element of the marketing process may well be conducted by quite different organisations from those concerned with managing the facilities that comprise the product being promoted.

The place consumer

Two main complications arise in answering the seemingly simple question, 'who consumes the place product?', or more accurately, 'when does a place-product consumer become one?. First, demand cannot safely be equated with participation. Place-product demand contains a particularly large element of latent and option demands. Secondly, an intrinsic characteristic of places means that the same facilities and attributes are being used simultaneously by different groups of customers for different reasons: in marketing terms, they are purchasing different 'buyer benefits'. This in turn underscores the importance of identifying and segregating specific potential customers that can be targeted. Unfortunately, the variegated and vague nature of the place-product does not encourage this to occur. It is not surprising, therefore, that the same, very generalised, place-products are often promoted simultaneously to extremely varied consumer groups.

The place market

The market is obviously the essential arena within which free exchange occurs. 'Free' in this context implies the freedom of choice of customers between comparable products, free access of producers to potential customers and a free exchange of product for some measure of value. The mechanism allowing such freedoms to operate is the pricing system. It is not that place products cannot be priced, for if that were so then place marketing would be an impossible 'marketless marketing'; it is that the pricing of places is usually indirect, intangible, and often only expressible in non-monetary units. The operation of the market is therefore often difficult to discern, complicated to calibrate and sluggish in response. A serious implication of this for place promotion is that the monitoring of its effectiveness in intervening in the market is very difficult and in practice rarely performed.

The place-marketing measures

The range of techniques and instruments available for intervention in place markets includes all those well known methods of promotion that have been developed and refined over this century for selling commercial goods and services. Almost all these techniques have been employed in the selling of places at one time or another, but the particular nature of places suggests that two cautionary points should be made. First, advertising is only one sort of promotion. There are other ways of projecting images and influencing customer behaviour through promotion, such as public relations. Equally, promotion as a whole is only one of many possible sets of marketing measures. Places are particularly amenable to spatial and functional measures, such as the use of physical design. Meanwhile, place-management organisations, especially local governments, often find internal organisational restructuring of working methods and approaches particularly effective. (See Ashworth and Voogd (1990a) for a detailed account of these and many other measures available for the 'marketing mix'.)

Secondly, the choice of measures of intervention is dependent upon the prior choice of both marketing strategies and the wider goals of the place management organisation. In traditional commercial marketing the financial survival goal of the enterprise and the sales maximisation strategy of its marketing are often so dominant as to be self evident and thus not worth considering. By contrast, place-marketing organisations are usually presented with a very wide set of goals. Similarly, the precise purpose of the marketing exercise is often far from self-evident. It can seldom be reduced to a calculation of unit sales. There are in fact many possible strategies, ranging from maximising customer satisfaction, conserving product stocks, maximising capacities or even reducing 'sales' (e.g. by deterring visitors to congested sites at busy times). Each, and more than one strategy may be pursued simultaneously, will require a different mix of marketing measures.

Two conclusions can be drawn from this brief review of the nature of place marketing. First, it is necessarily a distinctive form of marketing, requiring an equally distinctive form of promotion. Secondly, although it occupies an important role, promotion is only one part of a much broader process of marketing and can only be appreciated within that context. Failure to do so will almost certainly lead to a failure of the promotion. It is to the question of outcomes that we now turn.

Promotion: conditions for success or failure

Promotion needs product development

If the quality of the product is poor or has no potential market then promoting it will be a waste of resources. Promotion may even be counter-productive in that it makes public what is better concealed, at least until such time as the product can be improved. Of course, promotion can be used to modify attitudes and thus the purchasing behaviour of the consumer. This purchasing behaviour includes different stages, from the recognition of an existing problem or need by a potential purchaser. Behaviour then moves to a search for solutions and their evaluation, actions are likely to be reiterated, until the final purchase decision and resulting action (e.g. *see* Figure 3.2).

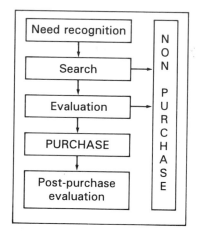

Figure 3.2   A purchase decision-making path.

The point made here is that the 'non purchase' decision not only depends on the quality of the product, but also on the quality of competing products. However, the wider the quality gap between the promoted place and the alternatives, the less effective its promotion will be.

One of the oldest admonitions in marketing mythology concerns the saying that, 'if you want to kill a poor product, advertise it'. Therefore, quality improvement by product development is an essential ingredient of any place marketing approach. The most obvious question in relation to product development is in general, 'what business are we in?' In public sector management operations in particular this question is too often assumed to be self-evident. Public organisations frequently define their task, and thereby the nature of the product they offer, as the effective management of existing facilities through the efficient operation of current working practices for vaguely defined objectives. By the same token, they tend not to review constantly the extent to which their services satisfy actual requirements and expectations of existing or potential customers. To take two analogous examples, the business of a public transport undertaking is not the efficient management of a vehicle fleet, nor is the goal of a public parks authority the management of a stock of green spaces. Rather, they are in the business of satisfying demands for accessibility and recreation respectively, something which may very well lead to quite different management practice.

Product development is strongly related to the perception of its qualities, in other words, its image. At least three sorts of situations can be distinguished:

- Poor facilities with a favourable image require product improvement not promotion. Indeed some de-marketing may be required and customers diverted so that shortcomings are concealed and the undeserved favourable image preserved until product improvement has occurred.
- An existing favourable image combined with good facilities hardly requires marketing and promotional effort beyond that needed to maintain this beneficial situation would be wasted.
- A set of good facilities with an undeservedly poor or non-existent image requires promotion either to correct the former or create the latter.

Therefore understanding the market, including the criteria and product characteristics that will affect consumer choice, is essential in place marketing.

Promotion needs knowledge

Place promotion must be based on a sound knowledge of the city or region under consideration, but places should not be examined simply on an absolute basis. Rather, they should be studied in relation to the characteristics of competing alternatives. The key questions here are: 'which choices do people have?' and 'how might people with a choice between several competing alternatives trade off the various characteristics against each other?' Careful place-market analysis will reveal that different market segments make different trade-offs. For instance, priorities of consumers in a housing market may differ considerably from priorities set by consumers in a recreation market. This demonstrates the importance of performing an accurate and relevant market segmentation and a careful analysis of the potential alternative facilities within each segment, an exercise known as 'product positioning'.

Neighbourhoods, or even smaller building blocks within a city, can be compared with respect to their potency, or attractiveness for a certain target group, by means of a *potency analysis*. This information can be extremely helpful in developing new market-oriented spatial policies. It may also form the basis for a *competition analysis*, in which the competitive situation, as viewed from one or more target groups, is compared with the actual situation existing in the city.

Table 3.1 illustrates this with reference to a competition analysis of seven small- and medium-sized towns in the northern Netherlands, which are effectively rivals in attracting new economic activities. The towns have been assessed on a number of criteria, such as the qualities of site, transport infrastructure, land cost, residential amenity and labour market. This resulted in so-called potency scores (for more details, see Ashworth and Voogd, 1990b). These potency scores aim at providing a normative description of the factual situation. Equally important, however, are the opinions of the regional 'captains of industry' about the towns and criteria under consideration. This was investigated by interviewing a large number of entrepreneurs, which resulted

Table 3.1   Potency and image scores for seven Dutch towns.

Town	Potency	Image
Zwolle	0.398	0.441
Hoogeveen	0.463	0.439
Heerenveen	0.206	0.000
Drachten	0.307	0.423
Assen	0.274	0.239
Emmen	0.114	0.136
Meppel	0.000	0.159

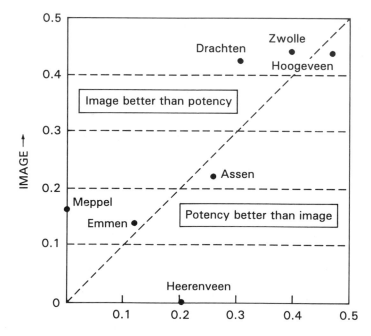

Figure 3.3   Image versus potency of Dutch towns.

in the calibration of image scores. These do not reflect the actual situation in the manner of potency scores, but the situation as perceived by the entrepreneurs. Both kinds of scores are standardised to the same measurement unit in Table 3.1 for purposes of comparison.

Figure 3.3 is based on the scores of Table 3.1 and provides a way to draw simple conclusions. The towns are represented as points in a two-dimensional space. A dotted line divides the points into two groups. The lower part includes towns which have a greater potential for economic activities than their image suggests (Hoogeveen, Heerenveen and Assen), whereas the upper part includes towns with a better image than might be expected on the basis of their potencies (Zwolle, Drachten, Emmen and

Meppel). In addition, the distance of the points from the origin of the graph shown in Figure 3.3 provides information on the absolute quality of the town, in that the larger the distance, the greater is the town's 'enterprise quality'. Figure 3.3 shows Hoogeveen and Zwolle to be the most attractive towns in this part of the Netherlands.

Competition analysis can also focus on a single town. Thus, by comparing the various scores for Hoogeveen, marketing suggestions can be made about the aspects of the market segment under consideration. Such a process could be repeated for different markets using relevant sets of criteria. Equally promotion would appear to be an effective strategy in Heerenveen or Assen but counter-productive in Meppel or Drachten, where product development would be more appropriate.

Promotion needs communication

Although promotion is a communication activity, not all communication is necessarily promotion. Almost all actual or potential users of particular places have an enormous existing store of information, feelings and expectations about them, without necessarily having had direct experience of them. This store of information is continually supplemented by a myriad of sources, very few of which are intended to influence specific consumer behaviour. Promotion, in the specific goal-directed sense used here, applies only to that which is undertaken with clear intent to influence the behaviour of target groups in a predetermined way and, hence, makes only a small contribution to this store of information.

An essential part of communicating place information concerns the transmission of place-images. Transmission forms the link between the images held by individuals and those projected by places. It is the aggregate of the various and diverse channels for communicating information, which may be composed of clearly identifiable publicity media established for this purpose and other less formal sources. The medium of communication, however, is not a neutral conduit but is itself selective both in terms of what, to whom, and to what effect information is communicated. It can act as a transformer influencing the nature, strength and credibility of the message. An important question is: 'how is the information which is used by individuals to shape their images of places obtained?' A proper answer to this question is needed in order to assess the effectiveness of promotional policies. This involves research into the transmission of received place-images, as has been carried out for images of tourist destinations by writers such as Goodall (1988).

However, the transmission of images can equally be investigated from the point of view of their projection. Burgess (1982), as noted in Chapter 2, examined the chosen marketing mix of British local authorities in the late 1970s and discovered a spectrum of communication channels ranging from weakly targeted public media advertising, through more directed exhibitions and promotion to enquirers and other identified potential users, to closely targeted public relations exercises aimed at specific firms, decision-makers, and intermediaries. Many different information media have been investigated. These include public press advertising at various spatial scales (Pocock and Hudson, 1978), slogan advertising on car bumper stickers propagating the names and nicknames of states and cities (Montalieu, 1988), official letters from public authorities (Van der Veen and Voogd, 1987), film (Gold, 1985), television (Gould and

Lyew-Ayee, 1985), news reporting (Brooker-Gross, 1985), and popular music (Jarvis, 1985).

The information must not only be transmitted to reach potential customers so as to be actually received by them: it must also be accepted. However, most of the information that continually bombards individuals is ignored or rejected. If information is to be incorporated into the cognitive map of a place, it must be credible (*see* Chapter 2). Much of the credibility stems from the user's evaluation of the medium of transmission as much as the character of the information itself. How information is transmitted is as important as what is transmitted in establishing the acceptability of the message to the recipient: an issue investigated, *inter alia*, by Nolan (1976), Crompton (1979) and Gitelson and Crompton (1983).

Conclusion

Many of the difficulties of analysing the various sorts of received and transmitted place images also occur in the study of projected images. Consequently, studies of such images have concentrated principally upon promotional images – those deliberately promoted to an envisaged market with the intention of altering consumer attitudes and behaviour. What is termed 'brand recognition' in the marketing of a physical product has a counterpart in place marketing in terms of the association of potential users of a place with its promoted attributes. The amount of success achieved in this respect, in relation to the resources devoted to it, needs continuous monitoring. The complaint that this is not performed adequately, or at all, by many organisations engaged in place marketing does not detract from the fact that such 'market research' has generated an enormous quantity of useful information on the characteristics of place images. Unfortunately, such information has a definite monetary value to the organisation and its competitors. Considerations of commercial secrecy make access to it understandably restricted, which makes comparative research difficult but also challenging.

An organisation contemplating place promotion faces a number of fundamental questions about product definition, market targeting, and how to promote the chosen place attributes. This implies choices which, in turn, depend on the purpose of the promotion and the appropriateness of the message to the phase of decision-making reached by the recipient. Slogans, and indeed much general advertising, attempt to convey an uncomplicated impression of a single place attribute or even just the place's existence.

The conflict here is between effectiveness of communication, which demands compression, and the filtering out of distinctiveness which results from such terseness. At one end of the spectrum, the aim of promotion is no more ambitious than to assert the existence of the town or country which might otherwise have remained unconsidered by an undifferentiated potential market. Effective promotion will attempt to move along this spectrum in parallel with the potential user's changing requirements for information at the different stages of decision-making as illustrated in Figure 3.2. The frustration of the business executive whose specific question is answered by a 'glossy', or the casual tourism enquiry which is answered with a thick town guide, results from a failure of promotion to match the content of the image being projected with the stage of decision-making in the particular market being reached.

There are reasons to suggest that place promotion is particularly prone to such errors in image content. This is not only because of the multi-faceted nature of the product and its simultaneous use for many different purposes, but also because most of the public authorities have neither sufficient funds nor expertise to carry out thorough monitoring of the consumer.

The success of the promotion of place images cannot be assessed only in terms of achievement of congruence between the promoted and received images. This would be too simple. Place images are promoted by organisations concerned with achieving particular management goals in the area concerned and success must be measured against such predetermined goals. Place-image promotion should be seen as one planning instrument within the market-planning process as a whole, and used in preference to or in combination with other non-market oriented place-management techniques as appropriate. This means that there is always a need for selectivity within public planning agencies whether to apply a place-marketing concept or to refrain from it. Many so-called NIMBY (not in my back yard) issues, for instance, would be difficult to resolve through market planning. Consequently, the skill of professionals in reaching a judgement to use such techniques or not is itself a major precondition for the success of place marketing.

References

Ashworth, G.J. (1992) 'Marketing of places: what are we doing?', paper to Marketing Urbano, Turin: COREP.

Ashworth, G.J. and Voogd, H. (1990a) *Selling the City*, London: Belhaven.

Ashworth, G.J. and Voogd, H. (1990b) 'Can we sell places for tourism?' in G.J. Ashworth and B. Goodall, eds., *Marketing Tourism Places*, London: Routledge.

Ashworth, G.J. and Voogd H. (1992) 'Marketing of tourism places', *Journal of Consumer Marketing*, 8.

Brooker-Gross, S.R. (1985) 'The changing concept of place in the news', in J. Burgess and J.R. Gold, eds., *Geography, the Media and Popular Culture*, Beckenham: Croom Helm, 63–85.

Brown, B.J.H. (1988) 'Developments in the promotion of major seaside resorts: how to effect a transition by really making an effort', in B. Goodall and G.J. Ashworth, eds., *Marketing in the Tourism Industry*, London: Routledge.

Burgess, J. (1985) 'News from nowhere: the press, the riots and the myth of the inner city', in J. Burgess and J.R. Gold, eds., *Geography, the Media and Popular Culture*, Beckenham: Croom Helm, 192–228.

Burtenshaw, D., Bateman, M. and Ashworth, G.J. (1991) *The European City: western perspectives*, London: Fulton.

Capon, N. (1981) 'Marketing strategy. Differences between state and privately owned corporations: an explanatory analysis', *Journal of Marketing*, 45, 11–18.

Crompton, J.L. (1979) 'Motivation for pleasure vacations', *Annals of Tourism Research*, 6, 408–24.

Fines, S.H. (1981) *The Marketing of Ideas and Social Issues*, New York: Praeger.

Gitelson, R.J. and Crompton, J.L. (1983) 'The planning horizons and sources of information used by pleasure vacationers', *Journal of Travel Research*, 21(3), 2–7.

Gold, J.R. (1985) 'From *Metropolis* to *The City*: film visions of the future city, 1919–1939', in J. Burgess and J.R. Gold, eds., *Geography, the Media and Popular Culture*, Beckenham: Croom Helm, 123–43.

Goodall, B. (1988) 'How tourists choose their holidays: an analytical framework', in B. Goodall and G.J. Ashworth, eds., *Marketing in the Tourism Industry*, Beckenham: Croom Helm.

Gould, P. and Lyew-Ayee, A. (1985) 'Television in the third world: a high wind on Jamaica', in J. Burgess and J.R. Gold, eds., *Geography, the Media and Popular Culture*, Beckenham: Croom Helm, 33–62.

Jarvis, B. (1985) 'The truth is only known by guttersnipes', in J. Burgess and J.R. Gold, eds., *Geography, the Media and Popular Culture*, Beckenham: Croom Helm, 96–122.

Jossip, B., Bonnet, K., Bromley, S. and Ling, T. (1987) 'Popular capitalism, flexible accumulation and left strategy', *New Left Review*, 165, 104–22.

Kotler, P. (1982) *Marketing for Non-Profit Organisations*, Englewood Cliffs, NJ: Prentice Hall.

Kotler, P. (1986) *Principles of Marketing*, third edition, Englewood Cliffs, NJ: Prentice Hall.

Kotler, P. and Levy, S.J. (1969) 'Broadening the concept of marketing', *Journal of Marketing*, January, 10–15.

Kotler, P. and Zaltman, G. (1971) 'Social marketing: an approach to planned social change', *Journal of Marketing*, July, 3–12.

Lazer, W. and Kelley, E.J. (1973) *Social Marketing: perspectives and view points*, London: Irwin.

Lovelock, C.H. and Weinberg, C.B. (1984) *Marketing for Public and Non-Profit managers*, New York: Wiley.

Montalieu, J.P. (1988) 'Les macarons sur les automobiles', *Annales de la Recherche Urbaine*, Lyon: Image et Memoires.

Nolan, D.S. (1976) 'Tourist use and evaluation of travel information sources', *Journal of Travel Research*, 14, 6–8.

Pocock, D.C.D. and Hudson, R. (1978) *Images of the Urban Environment*, London: Macmillan.

Rados, D.L. (1981) *Marketing for Non-Profit Organisations*, Boston: Auburn House.

Van der Veen, W. and Voogd, H. (1987) *Gemeentepromotie en Bedrijfsacquisitie*, Groningen: Geopers.

Weiss, M.A. (1989) 'Planning history: what story? what meaning? what future?', *Journal of American Planning Association*, 55 (1), 82–4.

4 Time and place: key themes in place promotion in the USA, Canada and Britain since 1870

Introduction

We have already seen something of the ubiquity of place promotion in the 1990s. In this chapter we look backwards to explore aspects of its history and geography since about the 1870s. This allows us to see that place promotion is far from being the great late-20th century innovation that many of its current practitioners, especially in Britain, believe it to be. It also helps us to understand and conceptualise place promotion as an activity, adding depth to the inevitable and understandable pragmatism of today's promoters.

Our initial concern is to identify foci of promotional activity over time and space, whereby locally-based agencies 'sold' their towns, cities or regions to attract the attention of potential investors or visitors. We concentrate particularly on the contrasting experiences of three rather different countries: the USA, especially the South, Canada, especially Ontario, and Britain.

Conscious promotion in these areas reflected two distinct though closely related impulses: a 'boosterist' desire for growth or a more defensive 'regenerative' desire to avoid decline. Both were basically animated by structural instabilities within urban and regional systems, as new space economies emerged and older ones decayed. Yet, though it was fundamental, the structural dimension was never the whole story. Economic pressures, however powerful, were always mediated and sometimes substantially shaped by a series of local, regional or national political and institutional factors. It was through these institutional and political dimensions that promotional agencies were actually created and sought legitimacy and resources for their actions. Moreover, it was these which actually defined the limits and possibilities of effective campaigns to sell places.

These two sets of forces – the structural and the institutional and political – provide a basic analytical framework for this brief review of the development of place promotion. In order to set the scene for this later discussion, however, we start with a brief chronological overview of promotional activity in each of the three case studies since about 1870. We begin with the country and the part of that country where place promotion has been practised in the most sustained and committed fashion.

A tale of three countries

The USA: the selling of the South

Place promotion had played a significant role in the development of the North American continent throughout the 19th century and earlier (Holcomb, 1990: 5–15). A great deal of early activity was focused on attracting settlers or selling potential town sites as real estate ventures. This continued through into the 20th century, especially in the less populated west. More importantly for our present purposes, the beginnings of a more modern, organised and urban-based form of promotional activity are identifiable from about the middle of the 19th century, geared towards the encouragement of a non-agrarian way of life. No systematic surveys exist, but it was a trend that seems to have emerged first in the North Eastern USA as the main industrial and urban regions of the country began to take shape. By the later decades of the 19th century, this promotional practice was spreading to Canada and the Southern and Western states of the USA. There was also a growing and parallel concern with place promotion for tourism from about the same period.

These tendencies became particularly apparent in the South in the aftermath of the Civil War. Throughout the failed Confederacy there were mounting calls to rebuild a 'New South', based more strongly on industry and urbanisation. This basic strategy was first popularised by Henry Grady, the editor of the *Atlanta Constitution* newspaper, during the late 1880s. Grady and the many other Southern promoters of those years devoted themselves to 'talking up' both the entire South and particular areas within it (Cobb, 1984:11–14). There were important initiatives in individual towns and cities (e.g. Lemmon, 1966). In Richmond, for example, a Chamber of Commerce was established in 1867 and by the 1880s was issuing promotional pamphlets for the city, targeted largely at northern investors (Morrison, 1888:44). Its neighbour, Manchester, went further and offered liberal tax exemptions to new industries (Engelhardt, 1902–3:162). Yet compared to what we will find in Canada, the Southern promoters of this period were long on rhetoric but somewhat shorter on real municipal (or state) assistance for new productive investment (e.g. RCC, 1907). Only five Southern states allowed tax concessions to industry, though several others offered assistance to new railway developments.

By the 1920s, 'New South' boosterism had become allied to more reformist municipal and state policies (e.g. Tindall, 1963; Brownell, 1972). These sought to reinforce the campaign for industrialisation and urban growth by improvements to the social and physical fabric. There were, for example, important initiatives throughout the South in education, public health, road-building and electricity. This shift was associated with a marked strengthening of earlier promotional efforts. Such was the extent of this that one commentator wrote, of the whole urban South: 'There is no God but advertising, and Atlanta is his prophet' (cited Tindall, 1963:95). That city's Chamber of Commerce established an Industrial Bureau in 1924 to intensify promotional activity (Garofalo, 1976:190). Two years later a major advertising campaign was launched with the creation of the Forward Atlanta Movement. A similar trend was apparent in Richmond (Figures 4.1 and 4.2), where an impressive amount of promotional literature was produced through the decade (e.g. RCC, c.1923, 1927, 1929). Meanwhile there was more action at state level as Alabama, North

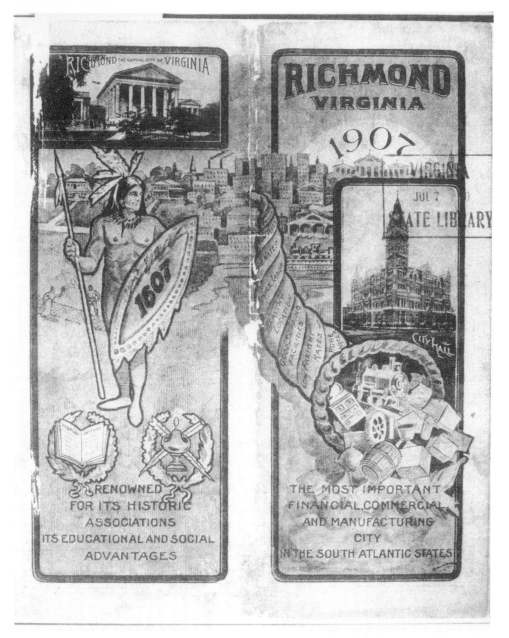

Figure 4.1 Richmond, Virginia, 1907. Typical of Southern advertising at this time, this brochure produced by the Chamber of Commerce emphasised the many advantages of locating in a well-established centre.

Carolina, Florida, Virginia and other states established commissions and agencies designed to advertise their advantages and attract potential investors.

The advertising rhetoric soon began to be supplemented by more direct assistance. Georgia, for example, legalised local tax exemptions for new industries in 1924. The

Figure 4.2 'Down Where The South Begins'. A 1927 promotional brochure for Richmond, showing clearly how the traditional idea of the plantation South continued to be invoked even well into the era of industry and technological progress.

1930s became 'a decade of frenzied plant-buying' (Cobb, 1982:6). Urban, and increasingly rural, communities attracted new industries by a variety of subsidy mechanisms, many of them of dubious legality. Municipal bonds were often used to provide soft finance for factories, particularly in Tennessee. Large local and state tax exemptions were usual, especially in Arkansas, Alabama and Louisiana. Free or heavily subsidised sites, water and power were often offered. In some cases workers were directly covenanted to finance factories or tax breaks by regular wage deductions (for example, in the Tennessee towns of Manchester and Dickson). There were other, even more dubious, practices. Hence Lewisburg (Tennessee) built a shoe factory under the pretence that it was a new town hall and Ellisville (Mississippi) misused federal education funds to build a 'training' hosiery factory, using child labour.

Against this background of desperate expediency came the most significant initiatives of the decade in the shape of Mississippi's Balance Agriculture With Industry (BAWI) Program of 1936. This created the first coherent policy for the subsidised attraction of industry (Cobb, 1982:6–34). As well as intensifying publicity, it legalised the direct municipal provision of factories and the extensive use of municipal bonds to finance industrial development. From the industrialist's viewpoint, this had the double advantage of giving new factories the tax-exempt status of public buildings.

This pre-war experience set the pattern for much that was to follow. After 1945 the whole South embarked on a sustained drive to sell itself, still mainly for industrial development (Perry and Watkins, 1977; Cobb, 1982:35–95; Goldfield, 1982). New state promotional organisations were created in the 1940s and local development agencies multiplied. By 1966 twelve of the thirteen Southern states were each allocating six-figure sums annually for industrial promotion, with Georgia, Kentucky and South Carolina each spending over one million dollars. The Southern states provided seven of the top ten spenders on press and broadcast advertising in 1964. Meanwhile the number of local promotional organisations had also multiplied. In 1966, at least 1811 local communities in the South boasted such organisations, including a growing number of local development corporations.

The scale of local promotional action also increased apace, especially in the main Southern cities. Another 'Forward Atlanta' movement was established in the early 1960s, raising 1.6 million dollars, about half of which was spent on advertising. This huge and highly competitive promotional effort was accompanied by massively increased expenditure on inducements, still mainly by local governments. By the early 1950s, BAWI-type municipal bond funding was prominent particularly in Mississippi, Tennessee, Kentucky and Alabama. Ten years later, this same mechanism was explicitly being used in nine Southern states to attract investment and it had become virtually universal in the South by the late 1960s. Nor was it the only incentive; other promotional instruments included tax exemptions, used both with, and independently of, bond funding. From the mid-1960s through to the early 1980s, this state–local pattern of place promotion was modified, though not substantially changed, by an increased federal involvement in area economic development.

By the late 1970s, however, more fundamental changes had begun to occur in place promotional practice, though they affected the South less immediately than other parts of the USA. The overwhelming emphasis on industrial development which had long underpinned mainstream town and city promotion gave way to a more diverse approach. Commercial and above all service activities began to be more directly promoted than formerly, when city boosters had assumed that services would follow industry. Associated with this, place promotion came increasingly to mean the promotion of property development opportunities. The work of the American developer James Rouse in older American port cities like Baltimore and Boston became a model for this kind of approach (Hall, 1988:347–51; Harvey, 1989; de Jong, 1991). As such examples showed, tourism promotion was moving beyond the traditional resort and holiday areas as industrial towns and cities sought new sources of economic development and industrial dereliction was recycled into heritage. At the other end of the spectrum, there were also growing attempts to attract or stimulate higher level quaternary activities, particularly research and development and higher level management, activities which were increasingly international in their orientation.

In turn, this latter concern was associated with increased attention to quality of life matters, including cultural and recreational facilities. Cultural promotion itself also became an important element of this more recent phase of promotional activity. This bolstered more than just tourism, because it could be used internationally to enhance and demonstrate the attractiveness of cities as locations for higher level economic activities. Although much of the South remained heavily committed to old style industrial promotion, these new concerns became increasingly evident. They were apparent in promotional rhetoric as 'lifestyle' place advertising displaced the functional emphases of earlier years. They were also given more tangible form in the realities of sleek new Research and Development (R & D) concentrations, notably the prototypical Research Triangle Park in the Raleigh-Durham-Chapel Hill area of North Carolina (Goldfield, 1988).

Perhaps the ultimate demonstration of the changing character of place promotion in the 1980s was the intensified competition to host the Olympic Games. It offered a unique way for the candidates to demonstrate their credentials as world cities. The triumph of Atlanta's bid in 1990 to host the 1996 Games underlined how much the South had become a successful player in the new global game of place competition. Although it was heralded as a triumph of the second, post-civil rights, 'New South', it also showed how the accumulated lessons of its past development and promotional experience had not been lost (e.g. AOC, 1990).

Canada: from bonusing to planning (and back again)

While Henry Grady and his disciples were relying on rhetorical flourishes to spread the gospel of the original post-bellum 'New South' in the 1880s, another peripheral part of the emergent urban-industrial economy of North America was vigorously promoting itself in a more direct fashion.

Throughout late-19th-century Canada, but especially in Ontario and Quebec, communities were actively giving large amounts of material assistance, including monetary payments, to railways and factories to locate in their areas. This so-called 'bonusing craze' (Naylor, 1975:130) was characteristic of early Canadian industrialisation, seemingly without any contemporary parallel.

By 1894 Ontario's municipalities had accumulated nearly 5.4 million dollars of debt, nearly 11 per cent of the total municipal debt, on bonuses to assist the development of

Figure 4.3 Changes in Ontario legislation gave more encouragement to promotional advertising in the 1890s. This was an early example, dating from 1898, produced for a town which had a very active industrial policy.

railways and manufacturing in their areas (Ontario, 1896). The city government of Toronto alone had a one million dollar debt for railway bonuses. There was also a great deal of other non-loan assistance that was not included in these figures in the form of tax exemptions, free or subsidised sites and buildings and other concessions. The pattern was broadly similar in other provinces as Canadian municipalities attempted to put (or keep) themselves on the map by high spending promotional initiatives. Like Toronto, the well established city of Montreal felt obliged to give heavy subsidies to railways to ensure it was not left behind. Further west, Winnipeg, with only 1600 population in 1873, secured its future role as a gateway metropolis to the prairies by railway bonusing (Morris, 1989).

Within Ontario, the factory centres of Berlin (later Kitchener), Oshawa and Port Arthur/Fort William (later Thunder Bay) were all active bonusers (Figures 4.3 and 4.4). All managed to promote for themselves a scale of industrial growth that went well above what can be explained by their 'natural' advantages (Bloomfield, 1983a; Ward, 1991). Oshawa, for example, gave successive bonuses to the McLaughlin Carriage Company, the future General Motors of Canada, that helped keep it in the town. Meanwhile as an essential accompaniment to this expenditure, the towns were being 'talked up' in the rhetoric of local newspapers and, increasingly, business directories and promotional brochures.

Provincial government opposition to the wasteful character of bonusing increased significantly during the 1890s, especially in the west. Saskatchewan had legislated

ADVERTISEMENTS—BOARDS OF TRADE   439

STRATFORD

The Hub of Rich and Fertile Western Ontario

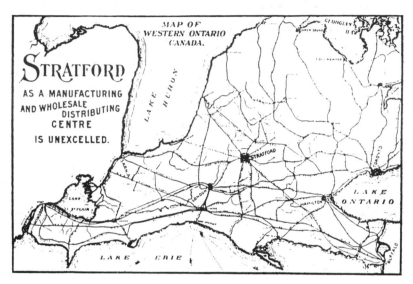

Stratford's Industrial Policy is Filling This Thriving City with Busy Factories

We offer excellent shipping facilities, Niagara power, a plentiful supply of skilled artisans, especially wood and iron workers, and generous civic assistance, including low fixed assessment.

We Shall be Pleased to Furnish Details
See description of Stratford on page 323

WRITE TO-DAY TO

The Secretary, Board of Trade
P. O. Box 353

STRATFORD, ONTARIO

When answering advertisements, please mention Heaton's Annual.

Figure 4.4   Place advertising was routine by the early 20th century. This example dates from 1910 and was typical of advertising in Ontario during the period of early industrialisation.

against it in 1908 and Alberta in 1913 (Bloomfield, 1983b:63). It survived rather longer in Ontario and Quebec. In Ontario an (unsuccessful) ban on bonusing operated from 1892 to 1900. Many of the centres which had been amongst the most active bonusers, like Berlin, exercised voluntary restraint after 1900. Finally, between 1922 and 1924, bonusing and virtually all comparable forms of assistance in kind were made illegal in the province unless there was specific local legislation (Bloomfield, 1981). The only exception to this was the fixed assessment, a limited form of local tax exemption. In Ontario, however, a slight reversal of this trend was evident as municipal powers to provide sites, commonly exercised without specific authority in the past, were formalised in 1929. Some municipalities went further but were reliant on privately organised initiatives. Oshawa, for example, was refused factory building powers in 1928, but the city's new American-style Chamber of Commerce launched its own industrial development company the following year (Ward, 1991:25).

None of these reductions in municipal powers altered rights to create local promotional agencies or advertise. Such functions were often fulfilled by local business organisations like Boards of Trade or, increasingly, Chambers of Commerce that were not in any case subject to such provincial directions (Bloomfield, 1983c). Accordingly, place advertising remained an enduring form of promotional action throughout Canada (and indeed had always been the more dominant element in the western provinces). The individual provinces also began to acquire a significant advertising-based promotional role (e.g. Ontario, 1927). It was this mixture of advertising, modest local tax breaks and land and building initiatives which was to dominate 1930s promotion in Ontario.

After 1945, Canadian local promotion retained the pattern established in the interwar years (Rea, 1985:217–21). Local advertising and promotional action accompanied by site provision and modest tax breaks remained common, though falling well short of what was typical in the Southern USA. In common with the individual American states, a mounting provincial dimension was also evident. In Ontario regional development councils were set up, bringing together local promoters and provincial planners. The hope was to link promotion and regional planning objectives, such as taking the pressure off Toronto and encouraging more peripheral development. The reality, however, fell rather short of the intention, and by the 1960s promotional initiative shifted more decisively to a higher level of government.

A stronger federal interest in area promotion and development became apparent (Bliss, 1982:32–40). Specific area-based incentives for new industrial development began to appear from 1960. Regional promotion and development agencies were created such as the Manitoba Development Fund, Nova Scotia Industrial Estates and Saskatchewan Economic Development Corporation, armed with a wide range of incentives. Meanwhile provincial promotional efforts were also strengthened. Ontario set up its own Development Agency and in 1973 this became the Ontario Development Corporation with subsidiary regional bodies for Eastern and Northern Ontario.

Taken overall, post-1960 promotional action was essentially federal or provincial in orientation and the local dimension was trimmed. Indeed Ontarian municipalities lost the last of their fiscal inducement powers, the fixed assessment, in 1962. In contrast to the Southern USA, where there was a similar growth of federal concern over roughly the same period, Canada managed to subsume much of the inter-urban competition for investment into the wider planned approach. Promotion was subordinated to area development policies.

The victory of the planners was short-lived. Canada was soon affected by the world-wide resurgence in competitive place promotion that we noted in the previous section (Richardson, 1991). Bonusing began to creep back on to the local government agenda as local economies faltered. In Ontario, for example, municipal powers to assist small businesses were introduced in 1986. There was also a growing interest in tourism and cultural promotion appropriate for the post-industrial age. Toronto became the outstanding Canadian example of this, as its harbour front and railway lands were redeveloped in the 1970s and 1980s. By the early 1990s, the new CN Tower and Skydome and a very credible bid to stage the 1996 Olympics had firmly established its promotional credentials as a post-industrial, world city.

Britain: contrary to precedent

When Ontario's provincial legislators were engaged in one of their periodic attempts to curb municipal bonusing in 1899, one of their number opined that the practice was 'contrary to British precedent and practice' (Ward, 1991:1). He had a point. The only 19th-century instances of British places being 'sold' were the new mass holiday resorts. Similar tendencies had already been clearly apparent in North America since the 1870s. The difference was that the tourist promotion of, say, the Muskoka Lakes region in Ontario, or Niagara or Florida remained a secondary, specialist element in North American promotional activity (e.g. Goodrum and Dalrymple, 1990:137–47). In Britain, resort promotion was for many years the primary focus (Ward, 1988b).

The pace was set by railway companies, just as it was across the Atlantic (e.g. Lidster, 1983; Wilson, 1987:15–25, 65–9; Yates, 1988), but there was also an important local element of resort boosterism. This was led by Blackpool, which secured the municipal power to advertise using local tax income in its 1879 Local Act. After 1900 a few more resort authorities were able to secure local powers, though others were forced to rely on rather uncertainly funded publicity associations. Promotional campaigns became more common, usually relying on posters and literature and involving a mixture of railway company and local initiatives.

Other important developments were also occurring by this time. Railway companies and private developers were advertising the new residential suburbs that were growing around London and other big cities, using a combination of booklets, posters, postcards and press advertisement. More importantly, there were also the first glimmerings of the type of town and city promotion that we have identified in North America. The first such campaign occurred in Luton, where a New Industries Committee was set up by the Chamber of Commerce and the Town Council in 1899 (Ward, 1990). The following year the Committee issued Britain's first non-resort promotional brochure, *Luton as an Industrial Centre*. Other towns and cities soon followed suit, including Derby, the new garden city at Letchworth, West Ham, Worcester, Cardiff, Wolverhampton and Warwick (Figure 4.5). Activity, however, remained modest and, even more than resort publicity, was heavily curtailed by central government refusal to sanction advertising expenditure.

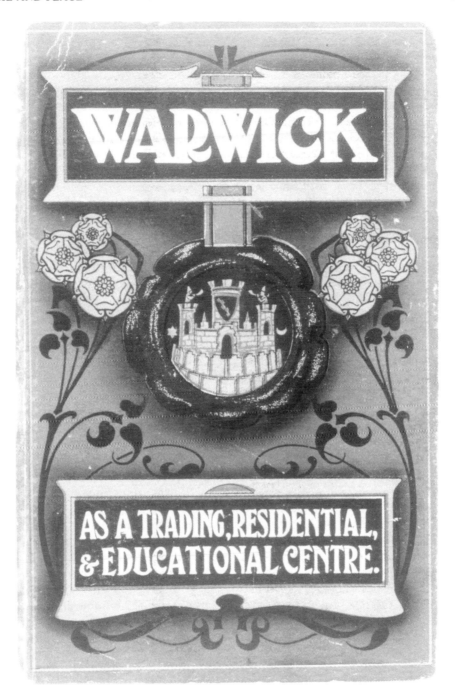

Figure 4.5 The promotional brochure was a later arrival in Britain. This was an early example dating from about 1910. The cover reveals the diverse objectives of this promotional campaign.

Place promotion by public or quasi-public agencies remained mainly tourism-oriented in interwar Britain, though there was a growth in the largely private promotion of suburbs (Jackson, 1973:201–11; also *see* Chapter 5). As earlier, both resort and suburban promotion were widely practised in North America, but were never as dominant as they were in Britain, where the conscious promotion of 'ordinary' towns and cities, so typical in North America, did not become a routine activity until the 1930s. By contrast the resorts finally secured general advertising powers in 1921 (Ward, 1988b), enabling their councils to work in legitimate partnership with railway companies and later the Travel Association, a new central government-sponsored organisation created in 1929 to promote the UK to foreign tourists.

Significantly, the role of this latter body was widened to include industrial promotion under the 1931 Local Authorities (Publicity) Act, which gave general municipal advertising powers to non-resort towns and cities for the first time (Ward, 1990). These powers could only be applied to overseas publicity and channelled through the Travel and Industrial Development Association (TIDA), as it was now renamed. Yet they provided a considerable encouragement for industrial promotion (which had been growing steadily in importance through the 1920s in spite of the absence of municipal powers). Accordingly, the 1930s saw a belated blossoming of North American-style town and city advertising. By 1939, 85 per cent of county boroughs and 35 per cent of other urban authorities were engaged in some sort of promotional activity (Fogarty, 1947:18–19). Regional promotional bodies were also created for Lancashire, Scotland, the north east, south Wales and Cumberland from 1930. Meanwhile, an increasing number of local authorities began to offer specific land- and buildings-based inducements, backed in some cases with soft loans for industrial projects (Ward, 1990:109–11). Much of this was undertaken surreptitiously, most notoriously at Burnley, but Liverpool's 1936 Act brought explicit legal recognition for the biggest local economic development programme of the interwar years.

A very marked change of direction occurred in the following decade as British central government largely superseded non-resort local promotional initiative by the creation of a nationally-based distribution of industry policy (Parsons, 1986:60ff). Although limited local and regional promotion continued, the Board of Trade, the key central ministry, kept a tight grip on such activity (Ward, 1990:113). In some respects local powers were enhanced, for example to spend on promotion (in the 1948 and 1972 Local Government Acts), or to undertake land and factory development (in the 1963 Local Authorities (Land) Act and various local acts) (Collinge, 1992:66–68). Yet throughout these were employed within centrally defined parameters of regional policy.

One of the main exceptions, as always, was tourism, which continued to be the only consistent aspect of competitive place promotion in Britain. Another exception arose from government planning policies for the creation of new and expanded towns after 1946. Much promotional effort was devoted first to selling the generic concept in the 1940s and then to promoting individual towns to both potential migrants and investors during the following decades (Gold, 1974; Gold and Ward, 1994). Occasionally this merged with more conventional promotional concerns, as in the successful efforts at Swindon (Harloe, 1975). Generally, though, Britain had returned to its more traditional pattern, in which place promotion was the exception rather than the rule.

As elsewhere, the pattern has shifted in recent years. The traditional marginalisation of place promotion in Britain has meant that these changes have been all the more dramatic. Since the late 1960s, there has been a marked strengthening of more locally-based promotional action (e.g. Burgess, 1982). This has become much more prominent as national policies to promote or manage regional economic development have been greatly weakened in the 1980s under the Thatcher administration (Totterdill, 1989; Coulsdon, 1986; Collinge, 1992). There was also a multiplication of non-elective local promotion and development agencies, particularly the Urban Development Corporations (Imrie and Thomas, 1993) which rapidly became major players in competitive place promotion, taking their cue from North American cities like Baltimore and Boston. Specific powers to promote local economies were granted to inner city areas in 1978 and effectively extended to all British local authorities in 1989. By the early 1990s they were engrossed as never before in self-promotional endeavour. Yet the lack of experience (and a certain lack of conviction) was all too apparent (*see* Chapter 6), nowhere more so than in the ignominious defeats of successive Olympic bids by Birmingham and Manchester in 1986, 1990 and 1993. Britain's place promoters still have much to learn.

Interpretation

The structural dimension

We can understand a good deal of the diverse histories and periodic convergence of promotional actions in the three countries by reference to the changing structures of their economies and urban systems. The relatively late and limited emergence of place promotion in Britain essentially reflected its early and, by international standards, remarkably spontaneous industrialisation and the creation of a highly stable urban and regional system during the early 19th century (Morris, 1989). This stability was apparent not just in the rank–size hierarchy, but also in functional relationships within and between regions and between individual towns and cities. This meant that representative bodies of local business were largely concerned with problem-solving within the functional niche that their individual towns or cities already occupied, rather than consciously seeking to create a new industrial identity. Moreover, the municipal agenda was largely concerned with managing the wider consequences (e.g. public health or transport) of a capital accumulation process that worked spontaneously, without any fundamental problems.

Thus the railways, which occasioned such intense promotional activity elsewhere, were in Britain inserted into an already established urban system. The main exceptions, largely created by railway development from the later 19th century, and much the most dynamic elements of the late-19th- and early-20th-century urban system in Britain, were the holiday resorts and the residential suburbs. It was here, of course, where new places were jockeying for position in emergent and unstable urban sub-systems, that the most significant British place promotional activity was taking place before 1914. They were the exceptions which proved the rule.

Such promotion was essentially growth-oriented 'boosterism', concerned with the primary accumulation of urban economic functions. By contrast, the more tentative

Figure 4.6 Following the 1931 Publicity Act, promotional brochures became much more common. Derby, a city with a great deal of earlier experience of promoting itself, issued this in about 1933. The cog wheel motif, industrial and civic skylines were typical elements of the period.

emergence of industrial promotion in Britain from 1899 increasingly reflected fears that the growth would no longer be as spontaneous and self-sustaining as it had been in the past. Hence, it was crises in, respectively, their established straw hat and railway engineering staple industries that propelled Luton and Derby into early prominence as promoters (Bonsall, 1988; Ward, 1990:100–101). These first initiatives (*see* Figure 4.6) signalled a general 'regenerative' pattern for British industrial promotion, concerned with preventing urban decline by fostering economic transition as the established industrial base began to falter.

This was radically different from the essentially boosterist focus of early promotional efforts in Canada and the Southern USA. In the context of late-19th-century North America, both were areas of peripheral industrialisation and urbanisation. Canada, though it had the considerable advantage of nationhood, was an economy relying on agriculture and natural resources, with very limited industrial development and a few small trading towns and cities. The Southern USA was a backward agrarian region, traditionally dependent on slavery, a failed nation which had lost the Civil War and suffered serious physical destruction. Its two main cities, Richmond and Atlanta, had largely been destroyed. The spontaneity of the British model of industrialisation and urbanisation had depended on the abundance of mainly local capital and entrepreneurship. By contrast, both Canada and the Southern USA were very short of local capital and successful industrialisation in such circumstances depended on the pursuit of external investment and entrepreneurship.

In addition, there was in Canada a growing national commitment to economic development and industrialisation especially after the 1867 British North America Act, that created the modern Canadian State (Bliss, 1982; Drummond, 1987). More specifically the 1878 tariff on manufactured goods gave Canada the opportunity to develop an industrial base by protecting its embryonic industries from American imports. This growing sense of Canada's destiny as an industrial nation added the specific impetus for the 'bonusing craze'. In the absence of any higher authority preventing such action, industrialisation took the form of intense inter-urban competition for scarce and highly mobile capital, much of it American. Bonusing was a means of attracting and supplementing scarce mobile capital and encouraging local entrepreneurship. The resultant railways and industry became in turn the determinants and symbols of urban success (Morris, 1989). They were seen as providing the secure basis for self-sustaining growth within a highly unstable, emergent urban–industrial system.

The boosterism of the Southern USA in the pre-1914 period can be understood within the same model. The doctrine of the 'New South' provided a similar kind of trigger for a promotional strategy, though it was, as we will see, rather less firmly rooted in Southern society at this time than the equivalent desire for industry in Canada (Cobb, 1988). Moreover, the South was not a separate nation and could not therefore emulate Canada's protectionist trading environment. It took the complete evaporation of the Confederate ideal of the South as an agrarian utopia to create the kind of widespread determination to industrialise that had characterised late-19th-century Canada. This occurred in the interwar years as the scourge of the boll-weevil in the 1920s was followed by world depression in primary product prices in the 1930s. Federal agricultural policies added their own imperatives by encouraging farm modernisation, reducing the need for workers and creating a massive labour surplus in the rural South. It was against this desperate background that the fine words of the boosters were reinforced by incentives and a widespread determination to 'sell' the South and buy industries for its towns and cities.

The world depression of the 1930s produced the marked convergence of promotional practice noticeable in the three case studies. Ontario had achieved a degree of maturity and stability in its urban system by the 1920s, when bonusing was curbed, giving way to a less intensive phase of inter-urban boosterist competition (e.g. compare Heaton and Robinson 1910; 1920). The depression, however, encouraged a more defensive, regenerative approach as the economic bases of (by now) established industrial towns suffered from both cyclical and structural unemployment. Similarly in Britain, where there had been mounting economic problems since the 1920s, the 1930s saw the widespread emergence of regenerative promotion. As in Canada in the 1870s, the ending of free trade (1931–2) was important, precipitating many enquiries from foreign firms seeking to operate within the new tariff walls (Law, 1981:176–77).

The long wartime and post-war boom quickly allowed the majority of British towns and cities to abandon completely their localised regenerative promotional preoccupations of the 1930s. New regional policies subordinated such sentiments to a centrally-led approach in the less favoured areas. Canada also experienced something of this, though boosterist promotion continued to find a role in what was still a less mature urban–industrial system than that of Britain. By contrast, boosterist policies finally triumphed in the Southern USA, spurred by the continued weakness of the traditional rural economy. The industrial base of the South surged ahead under these boom conditions, attracting a wholly disproportionate number of the new jobs, especially low paid manufacturing jobs, created in post-war America. It also benefited from job transfers from the traditional manufacturing heartlands of the North Eastern states.

With the onset of increasing world economic problems in the 1970s and 1980s, there was again convergence. Indeed, the differences narrowed rather more than in the 1930s because the pronounced globalisation of economic activity brought everywhere into more direct competition with everywhere else. This effect was compounded because western de-industrialisation destabilised even the most highly stable urban systems, such as that of Britain. Traditional place identities were undermined so that it was no longer tenable to think, for example, about tourism promotion being the sole prerogative of the resorts and established holiday areas. We can detect the same tendencies in Canada and the Southern USA, though the more recently created urban–industrial system of the latter has been, to date, less drastically affected than in Britain (or the North Eastern USA). Yet nowhere can any longer be immune.

The institutional/political dimension

These structural changes were, however, mediated through political processes and institutional traditions. Particularly important in Britain was the early erosion of local government autonomy, so that central government was able to limit the legalisation of local promotional aspirations.

Superficially the position of municipalities in Canada and the Southern USA was similar to that in Britain. There was, however, a much less confining tradition of state or provincial control of the locality in the early years, compared with the relative centralisation of Britain's unitary state. The reconstruction of government in both Canada and the Southern states in the late 1860s meant that the municipalities were actually the more established form of government, rather than being the legal creation of the new provincial or state legislatures. This meant that local government tended to define its own policy agenda rather than be constrained by a higher framework and manifested itself in many ways. In Ontario, for instance, local Acts authorising bonuses, if necessary, could be obtained with relative ease, even where, as in the 1892–1900 period, they directly contradicted the intent of general legislation

(Bloomfield, 1981). In matters of subsidy at least, Canadian and American authorities were rarely challenged as acting beyond their powers.

After 1900 and especially after 1920, the institutional traditions of Canada and the South began to diverge. Canadian provincial governments imposed considerable moderation of the intense local competition of the bonusing phase. In the South highly competitive local promotion was encouraged to persist and expand during the depression years. In states such as Tennessee 'blind eyes' were turned to many illegal local inducements on a scale that made the 'creative accounting' of British municipal promoters look puny. Moreover, by the late 1930s, local place promotion was beginning to be institutionalised within a state-orchestrated BAWI-type approach that continued to be based on local place competition. This unwillingness to go down the planning road followed by Britain and Canada from the 1940s reflected a stronger American belief in the virtues of competition. It also embodied some rather distinctive Southern US political beliefs in locally-based boosterism.

Politically, this enduring boosterist spirit depended on the existence of a strong and overpowering local ethos of growth and a willingness to commit large amounts of local money, public and private, to such ends. Typically such an ethos was created and sustained largely by local business elites. It also depended on the absence of significant opposition, particularly to the huge costs of promotional agencies and subsidies. The highly conservative nature of Southern society and politics meant that agrarian interests delayed the triumph of 'New South' boosterism, exhibiting some partial opposition to inducements in the later 19th century. Then, as the inevitability of industrialisation was accepted during the interwar years, this same conservative tradition became firmly incorporated within boosterist sentiments.

Throughout the South, promotional strategies came to rest on familiar elements. The planter and the industrialist could find common cause in keeping wage costs as low as possible, in preventing unionisation, in limiting workers' rights, in sustaining institutionalised racism (which inhibited the development of wider class consciousness) and in ensuring that as much as possible of the costs of incentives fell on groups other than themselves. These enduring themes gave Southern promotion much of its distinctively conservative character and go some way towards explaining why the dynamic of boosterism was sustained, especially in the pre-civil-rights era.

It is inconceivable, for example, that strong labour unions would have allowed such high levels of subsidy to low-wage employers, paid for mainly by taxes on the less affluent. (There were though some vain objections from North Eastern unions to the loss of their jobs to the non-union South; see Cobb, 1982:41–42). Similarly, it is inconceivable that the leaders of existing businesses would have sustained their enthusiasm for a boosterist campaign subsidising new industries if they themselves were paying for it. Another potential objection, of subsidising firms competitive with those already established in a community, was directly addressed in legislation under BAWI and tax exemption schemes. Local business leaders were also careful to shun firms which recognised unions – 'inviting the devil into the dining room', as one business leader in Greenville, South Carolina put it (Sloan and Hall, 1979:89).

Even in the 1990s, with institutionalised racism banished, the overall position has not fundamentally changed. The South remains notorious for its anti-union regimes and poor protection for workers rights and, increasingly important, the environment. As his critics have recently reminded us, Bill Clinton's impressive record of boosting the Arkansas economy while he was State Governor rested on these dubious foundations.

The Canadian experience, where comparable boosterist sentiment was much less enduring, serves to support this notion that a local growth alliance could only be sustained for a long period under unusual political circumstances. Thus, although it proved difficult to ban bonusing until the 1920s, the way in which increasing controls were introduced in Ontario showed particular concern for securing local popular and business support. The legislation demonstrated an early recognition of the inequities of subsidising new at the expense of established firms, especially when they were in direct competition. There were occasional early glimpses of labour opposition to financial assistance to notorious employers, for example in Hamilton in 1893 (Weaver, 1982:88–89). Even where support for boosterism remained strong, as in early-20th-century Berlin, there was mounting popular disquiet at the extent of subsidies for industrialists (English and McLaughlin, 1983:93–102). The less affluent particularly were now looking for more action to manage and make tolerable the urban consequences of capital accumulation, rather than further subsidising it.

If it could prove difficult to sustain political support for boosterist policies, even when their contribution to growth was palpable, the politics of locally or regionally self-funded regenerative promotion could be altogether more painful. Communities and businesses which were facing the threat or the reality of decline could easily agree a need for economic promotion, as the near universality of local promotional strategies during the economic downturns of the 1930s and 1990s indicates. Decisions to allocate worthwhile funds to stimulate or restart the processes of capital accumulation, however, needed to be set against the equally important need to protect local populations and perhaps ease the local tax burden on the very industries that were faltering.

The British depressed areas of the interwar period faced exactly these dilemmas, particularly since poor relief, still a major component in maintaining the unemployed, was at that time funded from local taxation. In the worst cases, the relief of poverty could account for about half of municipal spending, drawing on local tax bases that were themselves declining (Ward, 1988a:155–231). Significantly, the Federation of British Industries opposed even the modest proposals that became the 1931 Publicity Act when they were first mooted in 1928, on grounds of extra local tax burdens on industry at a time of stress (PRO, 1928). The Act was only passed after this issue had been avoided by 75 per cent industrial de-rating (i.e. mandatory local tax exemption) under the 1929 Local Government Act.

By the 1980s and 1990s there was greater national funding that eased some of the fiscal burdens of depression on local authorities compared to the 1930s. Yet the political dilemma of finding the correct balance between the priorities of stimulating capital accumulation or funding social consumption remains a very familiar one to many would-be local regenerators today. Indeed, there is a new, even more serious, twist brought on by de-industrialisation and the consequent de-skilling of former workforces: what kinds of job would regeneration provide, and for whom? In the late 1930s it was quite possible for the Lancashire cotton town of Burnley to attract new industries that would readily employ former workers from its closed mills and weaving sheds. This was crucial to the formation of a powerful all-party local regeneration consensus, embracing labour and business, behind a policy that, though effective, turned out to be entirely illegal (Ward, 1984:37–43; 1990:110). By the 1980s it was clear that the possibilities of promoting new jobs that would directly re-employ those shed by older industries were remote indeed.

All too often regenerational promotion in the 1980s used public funds to subsidise developers and create jobs, homes and social facilities for 'yuppies' (young, upwardly-mobile professionals – very much a 1980s term). Employment for the less skilled and de-skilled was scarce and generally menial, low paid service work such as cleaners and security guards. Such tendencies were clearest in schemes that were outside local control, most notably the London Docklands (*see* Chapter 7). Yet the same outcomes were also being increasingly pursued by politically progressive local administrations in both Britain and North America. It was as if they were unable to envisage a more socially sensitive alternative that they could act upon, given the prevailing hegemony of market ideologies, enforced by generally market-oriented higher governments. Those British cities which tried alternative strategies, based on higher public spending and direct council employment, soon found the ground cut away beneath them by central government financial controls. Whether by conscious choice or *force majeure*, the new local promotional style of urban regeneration quickly caught on, even in the most unlikely political settings.

The solidly Labour-controlled city of Glasgow, for example, had done much to change the perceived character of its central city by the early 1990s, building on its famous 1980s slogan, 'Glasgow's Miles Better'. Nevertheless, its bid to promote its cultural role and attract developers, entrepreneurs and tourists has inevitably diverted attention and funds away from its poorest citizens. Despite rehabilitation pro-grammes, its outer estates remain sinks of appalling desolation and poverty. In Sal-ford, another Labour stronghold, the contrast between the gleaming 'mini-Docklands' promotional showpiece of Salford Quays and the neighbouring run-down estate of Ordsall, recently affected by riots, remains stark. In short, the political question of who benefits by contemporary local promotional strategies shows no sign of going away.

Conclusion

We have therefore sketched the key trends of promotional activity in Britain and parts of North America over a period of well over a century. Naturally, there is much more that could be said. We have examined little about the exact nature of promotional action and incentives or their effectiveness in stimulating private business activity. Instead, we have outlined an analytical framework resting on the twin dimensions of economic structure and the agency of institution and politics. It is an approach that certainly has the potential to be applied to other areas, or taken further and used, for example, to help decode promotional messages.

In addition to these matters of analysis, we can also point to some more practical conclusions. Historical experience suggests a simple truth: that the successful manage-ment of place promotion depends on being able to address the need to change local or regional economies at times when it is not a necessity. Although place promotion has certainly boomed during depressions, the more successful strategies have been those which have been conceived or sustained during conditions of general economic growth. We can point here to Ontarian boosterism in the late 19th century or Southern US boosterism in the post-1945 period and occasional British examples, such as Luton before the 1930s depression or Swindon after 1945. Such promotional episodes benefited by generally favourable conditions for new investments and reduced competition from otherwise more favoured locations. Furthermore, all these places had something 'real' to sell often involving, though not relying solely upon, special inducements.

The pro-cyclical notion of promotional success also applies to managing the politics of promotion. This has invariably been a much less painful process if conducted when communal backs are not against the wall. Very significantly though, this has depended on far-sighted leaders being able to establish sufficient political momentum for growth (in the case of boosterism) or change and diversification (in the case of regeneration) at just the point when the existing economic base was performing at least adequately. Such shifts in perception have not normally been easy to accomplish. The inertia of those with vested interests in the status quo has often been a powerful force constraining such re-inventions of place identity at otherwise auspicious times. In addition, wider communities have often been profoundly cautious about the idea of positively seeking such fundamental changes in their collective destinies. Overcoming such understandable objections to change has therefore been a crucial pre-condition of the more successful promotional campaigns. While the conservative and narrow politics of the American South achieved and sustained this without need for fully democratic consent, in the other instances it rested on a wider and credible promise of real benefit for the whole community. There is certainly scope for this historical lesson to be re-learned.

References

AOC [Atlanta Organizing Committee] (1990) *Welcome to a Brave and Beautiful City*, Atlanta: Committee for the Olympic Games.

Bliss, M. (1982) *The Evolution of Industrial Policies in Canada: an historical survey*, Discussion Paper 218, Ottawa: Economic Council of Canada.

Bloomfield, E. (1981) 'Municipal bonusing of industry: the legislative framework in Ontario to 1930', *Urban History Review*, 9(3), 59–76.

Bloomfield, E. (1983a) 'Building the city on a foundation of industry: the industrial policy in Berlin, Ontario, 1870–1914', *Ontario History*, 75, 207–43.

Bloomfield, E. (1983b) 'Community, ethos and local initiative in urban economic growth: review of a theme in Canadian economic history', *Urban History Yearbook 1983*, Leicester: Leicester University Press.

Bloomfield, E. (1983c) 'Boards of Trade and Canadian urban development', *Urban History Review*, 12, 77–99.

Bonsall, M. (1988) 'Local government initiatives in urban regeneration 1906–1932: the story of Derby's Borough Development Committee', *Planning History*, 10(3), 7–11.

Brownell, B. A. (1972) 'Birmingham, Alabama: new South city in the 1920s', *Journal of Southern History*, 38, 21–48.

Burgess, J. A. (1982) 'Selling places: environmental images for the executive', *Regional Studies*, 16, 1–17.

Cobb, J. C. (1982) *The Selling of the South: the Southern Crusade for Industrial Development, 1936–1980*, Baton Rouge, LA: Louisiana State University Press.

Cobb, J. C. (1984) *Industrialization and Southern Society, 1877–1984*, Lexington, KY: University Press of Kentucky.

Cobb, J. C. (1988) 'Beyond planters and industrialists: a new perspective on the new South', *Journal of Southern History*, 44, 45–68.

Collinge, C. (1992) 'The dynamics of local intervention: economic development and the theory of local government', *Urban Studies*, 29, 57–75.

Coulsdon, A. (1986) *The Future Role and Organisation of Local Government*, Functional Study 6: 'Economic Development', Birmingham: Institute of Local Government Studies, University of Birmingham.

Drummond, I. (1987) *Progress without Planning: the economic history of Ontario from Confederation to the Second World War*, Toronto: University of Toronto Press.

Engelhardt, G. W. (on behalf of Richmond Chamber of Commerce) (1902–3) *Richmond Virginia – the City on the James: the book of its Chamber of Commerce and principal business interests*, Richmond, VA: Engelhardt.

English, J. and McLaughlin, K. (1983) *Kitchener: an illustrated history*, Waterloo: Wilfred Laurier University Press.

Fogarty, M. P. (1947) *Plan Your Own Industries*, Oxford: Blackwell.

Garofalo, C. P. (1976) 'The sons of Henry Grady: Atlanta Boosters in the 1920s', *Journal of Southern History*, 42, 187–204.

Gold, J.R. (1974) *Communicating Images of the Environment*, Occasional Paper 29, Centre for Urban and Regional Studies, University of Birmingham.

Gold, J.R. and Ward, S.V. (1994) '"We're going to do it right this time": cinematic representations of urban planning and the British new towns', in S.C. Aitken and L. Zonn, eds., *Place, Power, Situation and Spectacle: a geography of film*, Savage, MD: Rowman and Littlefield.

Goldfield, D. R. (1982) *Cotton Fields and Skyscrapers: Southern City and Region 1607–1980*, Baton Rouge, LA: Louisiana State University Press.

Goldfield, D. R. (1988) 'The future of the metropolitan region', in D. Schaffer, ed., *Two Centuries of American Planning*, London: Mansell, 303–22.

Goodrum, C. and Dalrymple, H. (1990) *Advertising in America: the first 200 Years*, New York: Abrams.

Hall, P. (1988) *Cities of Tomorrow: an intellectual history of urban planning and design in the twentieth century*, Oxford: Blackwell.

Harloe, M. (1975) *Swindon: a town in transition*, London: Heinemann.

Harvey, D. (1989) *The Condition of Postmodernity*, Oxford: Blackwell.

Heaton, E. and Robinson, J. B. (1910) *Heaton's Annual: the commercial handbook of Canada and Boards of Trade Register*, sixth edition, Toronto: Heaton.

Heaton, E. and Robinson, J. B. (1920) *Heaton's Annual: the Commercial Handbook of Canada and Boards of Trade Register*, sixteenth edition, Toronto: Heaton.

Holcomb, B. (1990) *Purveying Places: past and present*, Working Paper 17, Piscataway NJ: Center for Urban Policy Research, Rutgers University.

Imrie, R. and Thomas, H. (1993) eds., *British Urban Policy and the Urban Development Corporations*, London: Paul Chapman.

Jackson. A.A. (1973) *Semi-Detached London*, London: Allen and Unwin.

de Jong, M. (1991) 'Revitalizing the urban core: waterfront development in Baltimore, Maryland', in J. Fox-Przeworski, J. Goodard and M. de Jong, eds. (1991) *Urban Regeneration in a Changing Economy*, Oxford: Clarendon, 185–98.

Law, C. M. (1981) *British Regional Development since World War I*, London: Methuen.

Lemmon, S. M. (1966) 'Raleigh – an example of the "new South"?', *North Carolina Historical Review*, 43, 261–85.

Lidster, J. R. (1983) *Yorkshire Coast Lines*, Nelson: Hendon.

Luton New Industries Committee (1900) *Luton as an Industrial Centre*, Luton: Chamber of Commerce.

Morris, R. J. (1989) 'The reproduction of labour and capital: British and Canadian cities during industrialization', *Urban History Review*, 18, 48–63.

Morrison, A. (1888) *Richmond, Virginia and the New South*, Richmond and Chicago: Engelhardt.

Naylor, R. T. (1975) *The History of Canadian Business 1867–1914: II: industrial development*, Toronto: James Lorimer.

Ontario, Government of (1896) *Return Shewing Municipal Indebtedness*, Published Sessional

Paper 68.

Ontario, Government of (1927) *On the Tide of Prosperity*, Ottawa: Ontario Government.

Parsons, D. W. (1986) *The Political Economy of British Regional Policy*, London: Croom Helm.

Perry, D. C. and Watkins, A. J. eds. (1977) *The Rise of the Sunbelt Cities*, Beverly Hills, CA: Sage.

PRO [Public Record Office, Kew, London] (1928) *Local Authority Publicity – Legislation: Suggesting Amended Legislation – "Come To Britain" Movement*, HLG 52/116, Minute: May.

RCC [Richmond Chamber of Commerce] (1907) *Richmond, Virginia: the most important financial, commercial and manufacturing city in the Southern Atlantic States*, Richmond, VA: Richmond Chamber of Commerce.

RCC [Richmond Chamber of Commerce] (n.d. c1923) *Industrial, Commercial and Financial Advantages of Richmond, Virginia*, Richmond, VA: Richmond Chamber of Commerce.

RCC [Richmond Chamber of Commerce] (1927) *Down Where The South Begins*, Richmond, VA: Richmond Chamber of Commerce.

RCC [Richmond Chamber of Commerce] (1929) *Some Facts about Richmond*, Virginia, Richmond, VA: Richmond Chamber of Commerce.

Rea, K. J. (1985) *The Prosperous Years: the economic history of Ontario, 1939–75*, Toronto, University of Toronto Press.

Richardson, N. H. (1991) 'Reshaping a mining town: economic and community development in Sudbury, Ontario', in J. Fox-Przeworski, J. Goodard and M. de Jong, eds. (1991) *Urban Regeneration in a Changing Economy*, Oxford: Clarendon, 164–84.

Sloan, C. and Hall, B. (1979) ' "It's good to be home in Greenville" . . . but it's better if you hate unions', *Southern Exposure*, 7, 83–93.

Tindall, G. B. (1963) 'Business progressivism: southern politics in the twenties', *The Southern Atlantic Quarterly*, 62, 92–106.

Totterdill, P. (1989) 'Local economic strategies as industrial policy: a critical review of British developments in the 1980s', *Economy and Society*, 18, 478–526.

Ward, S. V. (1984) 'Local authorities and industrial promotion 1900–1939', in S.V. Ward, ed., *Planning And Economic Change: an historical perspective*, Working Paper 78, Oxford: Department of Town Planning, Oxford Polytechnic, 25–49.

Ward, S. V. (1988a) *The Geography of Interwar Britain: the state and uneven development*, London: Routledge.

Ward, S. V. (1988b) 'Promoting holiday resorts: a review of early history to 1921', *Planning History*, 10(2), 7–11.

Ward, S. V. (1990) 'Local industrial promotion and development policies 1899-1940', *Local Economy*, 5, 100–118.

Ward, S. V. (1991) 'Municipal policies and the industrialization of Ontario 1870–1939: the example of Oshawa', *Canadian Studies Research Award End of Grant Report*, CSRA 90/36.

Weaver, J. C. (1982) *Hamilton: an illustrated history*, Toronto: James Lorimer/National Museums of Canada.

Wilson, R. B. (1987) *Go Great Western!: a history of GWR Publicity*, second edition, Newton Abbot: David and Charles.

Yates, N. (1988) 'Selling the seaside', *History Today*, 38, August, 20–27.

5 'Home at Last!': building societies, home ownership and the imagery of English suburban promotion in the interwar years

JOHN R. GOLD AND MARGARET M. GOLD

In an advertising poster produced before the outbreak of World War II by the London-based Hearts of Oak Permanent Building Society (Figure 5.1), a man strides up a winding garden path to be greeted by an ecstatic welcome from his family. Carrying a briefcase and wearing pinstripe trousers, black overcoat and trilby hat, he is clearly part of the new army of commuters who travelled daily to clerical jobs in the City of London. His small daughter runs down the path to meet him and his wife waves from an open window. Above them the caption reads 'Home at Last!'.

This poster symbolises the new opportunities for home ownership lately available in interwar Britain. The rapidly growing professional middle classes were now presented with the possibility of home ownership as an alternative to the traditional pattern of rented accommodation. Building societies like the Hearts of Oak were eager to lend money to promote this shift in housing tenure and actively advertised their services and finance for this purpose. In doing so, they allied themselves with other organisations with which they shared goals, namely, underground railways, builders, municipal authorities and estate agencies. Previously (Gold and Gold, 1990), we identified the restricted repertoire of imagery used by this broad coalition of interests when promoting the new suburbs. In this chapter we return to this context, but specifically examine the rhetoric used by the building societies to entice tenants into the realm of home ownership.

Rhetoric, as noted in Chapter 2, is a normal part of everyday discourse rather than a distortion. It involves presentation of an argument to persuade the audience that a particular proposition is worth accepting, or perhaps just considering further, even if this means that the audience must change their previous position on that proposition. Experience, however, suggests that rhetoric has greatest impact when the communicator is considered worthy of belief and the discourse is characterised by some basis of shared needs and understandings.

When applied to the present instance, it is also helpful to recognise that rhetoric is

Figure 5.1 'Home at Last', Hearts of Oak Permanent Building Society.

not confined to the medium of written or spoken language. Rhetoric, as Jarvis (1987) showed, can just as easily be applied to the graphic depictions of environments and people used in product advertising.[1] Developing this argument with respect to the city, for example, he argued that a series of urban settings (e.g. high-rise downtown skylines or mazes of cavernous streets) have become emblematic; the routine background for communicating images of cultural sophistication and affluence, or triumph over stress, or reliability in the face of environmental menace. Rhetoric, therefore, refers to a language of images and symbols, expressed in both lexical and graphic forms, by which the advertiser addresses the target audience about a product or service and attempts to persuade them of its worth. These images and symbols are selected from reality by the advertisers but fashioned to meet the audience's needs. The frequency with which they occur and recur strongly implies that the language is shared by both parties.

Building on this conceptual basis, this chapter has five sections. The first provides background to the explosive growth of English suburbia between the wars. It maps out the key historical trends, the accompanying changes in housing tenure, and the role of the building societies in the process of expansion. The second section considers the reasons why the building societies turned to promotional work, and highlights the use that was made of poster advertising. The third turns to the depiction of suburban environments and society shown in these posters, identifying the key imagery to be found. The next section then highlights three recurrent symbols found in the visual representations of suburbia. The concluding section summarises the main findings of this chapter, noting the enduring success of the building societies' campaigns regardless of the gap between rhetoric and reality.

Suburban growth and tenure change

Until relatively recently, knowledge about the development of suburbia was sparse. This was fuelled in no small measure by the general distaste for the subject among writers on the urban environment, for whom suburbia then, as now, represented both an aesthetically and socially impoverished living environment (Gold and Gold, 1989; Neiman, 1991; Carey, 1992). However, the situation has greatly improved over the last decade. A wave of new research,[2] emanating from both sides of the Atlantic, has done much to improve our understanding of the basic processes contributing to the formation of suburbia and suburban society.

Full discussion of the growth of English suburbia lies outside the scope of this chapter, but a brief summary helps to locate the significance of the imageries discussed here. The initial point to note is that social character of suburbia has changed dramatically over time. The suburbs of medieval towns were literally considered *sub*-urban, in that they consisted of the poorest, most squalid and ramshackle dwellings (Thompson, 1982:2). They were far removed from the planned and spacious upper-middle-class suburbs that grew around London in the second half of the 18th century, in Birmingham from 1780 onwards, and around cities like Liverpool, Manchester, Leeds and Sheffield in the early 19th century. These latter developments were designed to meet the demands of wealthy merchants and industrialists who wished to leave the increasingly unattractive city centre for a healthier and greener living environment (Carter, 1983:138). They brought in their wake a cultural reappraisal that now accorded high status to places distanced from the city centre. No more the dumping ground for the city's poor, suburbia became a desirable residential environment.

The first significant moves towards mass suburbanisation consisted of 'walking suburbs' (Weightman and Humphries, 1984), such as London's Islington and Camberwell. Intended for the lower middle class, they comprised terraced or row houses built for rent to city clerks. Subsequent suburban expansion took advantage of transport improvements to develop at greater distances from the city centre and provide the benefits associated with larger plot size, although these were still for rental. It was only in the 20th century, and particularly during the interwar years, that owner occupation became a significant form of tenure, with the rise of the new 'semi-detached' suburbs.

This development was linked with profound changes in the property and housing markets. In the 19th century the greatest profits to be made from property came from speculative land development and from building houses for rent. Small investors could expect a return of five per cent on loans to builders, and the resulting housing was bought as an investment, often with borrowed money. The new permanent building societies[3], which emerged in the latter half of the century, had relatively little impact on levels of owner occupation since, in many areas, they loaned money to prospective landlords. Houses were generally rented out with an annual rent of ten per cent of the purchase price, which yielded a return on investment of between four and seven per cent for middle-class property or ten per cent for working-class property (Muthesius, 1982).

After 1900, the rented housing market slumped and the level of new house-building fell, subsequently collapsing completely when rent controls were introduced in 1915 to combat the worst excesses of housing problems for the urban poor. Passed under wartime conditions, the measure was intended to be temporary, but its retention after the war ensured that private rented accommodation was no longer an attractive investment.[4] Moreover, the combined impact of the rising population, ever smaller households, and a rise in the rate of household formation[5] led to an acute housing shortage after World War I which could not be met by the private rented sector.

Initially, the government responded by encouraging council housing, but the impetus soon left the municipal house-building programme (Swenarton, 1981). For most of the interwar period, therefore, it was the private house-building sector, increasingly building for owner-occupation, that took up the strain. The extent of their efforts is shown by the statistics on housing tenure. In 1914, only ten per cent of the housing stock was owner-occupied (Ball, 1983:23), with rented accommodation the norm throughout society. By 1939, this figure had risen to 32 per cent.

The main area of housing expansion lay in the suburbs, especially in the London region which physically doubled in size during the interwar period. London experienced a peculiar set of economic circumstances that boosted its housing market. Housing costs were falling given the decreasing wholesale prices of building materials, low labour costs among building workers and depressed land prices. At the same time, disposable incomes rose substantially in the region, especially among the professional middle classes.[6] It is not surprising, therefore, that housing demand remained buoyant (Bellman, 1949).

However, buoyancy of demand can also be attributed to the fact that a different type of house was now available. Whatever the continuity suggested by the pastiche of traditional building styles used in the external construction of the house, in reality the new semi-detached or detached houses were very different kinds of house to own. Their interiors were lighter, more comfortable and convenient than comparable Victorian or

Edwardian suburban housing. They came equipped with the latest in labour-saving devices including indoor plumbing, hot and cold water, electric light, electric power and associated consumer durables,[7] sometimes even central heating (Barrett and Phillips, 1987; Rybczynski, 1988). Larger plot sizes allowed sizeable private gardens, off-street parking, or even a garage for those who required and could afford one. Ownership bought all this in addition to a mere roof over one's head.

The building societies were keen to capitalise on actual and latent demand for houses, not least because it provided a way out of their own problems. They were awash with funds, given the paucity of industrial investment opportunities in a depression-hit world and the societies' own image as a safe haven for liquid assets. The situation reached the point at which some societies even took steps to staunch the influx. The larger London building societies, for example, tried to repel investors by reducing interest rates to depositors and insisting on a £50 minimum deposit (Jackson, 1991:155), but their efforts were to no avail. Increased lending to potential home owners offered the only realistic way out of their dilemma.

Promoting suburbia

Two broad tactics were used to help bring about this goal. The first was to expand the building societies' presence in middle-class urban areas. The larger building societies rapidly consolidated their networks by increasing the numbers of their branches and agencies. The Halifax Building Society, for instance, tripled the size of its network between 1919 and 1939 (Pawley, 1978:66). With expansion came an increased geographical spread. Before World War I, most societies were locally based, with very little competition between societies. The interwar period saw societies based in northern cities (e.g. Halifax, Leeds, and Bradford) extending their operations into south-east England and, in the process, effectively changing themselves from local to national institutions (see Price, 1958:401).

Second, the building societies instituted promotional campaigns to persuade more people to purchase houses; people who previously had seen themselves as being outside the owner-occupier class. This was new territory for the building societies. Most had not had advertising budgets before and only started to earmark money for this purpose for the first time in the 1920s. To take an example, the Cooperative Permanent Society spent only £410 in 1913 on 'printing, stationery and advertising' combined. By 1931, the size of the advertising budget had swelled this amount to £28,000 and it continued to rise steadily thereafter (Pawley, 1978:66).

At first their efforts were regarded as amateurish and ineffective. Sir Harold Bellman, Chairman of the Abbey Road Building Society, for example, complained in 1923 that: 'advertising is weak . . . (m)any Building Society advertisements are crude in design and overcrowded with matter' (quoted in Cleary, 1965). Later commentators told a different story. Price (1958:399), for instance, identified a 'bold advertising policy' aimed at potential home owners as a key to the building societies' success in the interwar period.

Their promotional campaigns made use of a wide variety of media. Local handbooks were printed, containing a mixture of local topographic information, details of housing developments and guidance about the services offered by the building societies. Extensive advertising was placed in national and local newspapers, as well as relevant periodicals. Considerable use was also made of posters, particularly versions measuring approximately 20 × 30 inches which were meant to be exhibited in the windows of building-society branches and estate agents. Consisting of brightly-coloured lithographed paintings and graphic designs rather than photographs, these posters were intended to be eye-catching at a time when high-street office and commercial facades were overwhelming drab.

These posters are interesting both for their design and rhetorical content. They emerged at a time of considerable innovation in poster design and production (Hillier, 1969). As such, they were models of simplicity, distilling complex selling messages down to their essence. In the following section, we examine a small sample of these posters, drawn from archive sources,[8] as a means of interpreting the imagery being conveyed.

Imagery

The four posters shown in Figures 5.1–5.4 help to locate the interwoven images presented by building societies in the 1930s. The centrepiece of each poster is a painting. While these are in different styles and were commissioned by three different building societies, they share certain design properties. In particular, they each use the exteriors of houses to sell the 'internal' qualities of the home and the personal and family benefits that flow from home ownership.

The Hearts of Oak poster (Figure 5.1), which we introduced earlier, consists of a eight-colour photo-lithographed base on to which an endearingly erratic lettering has been subsequently painted in oils. The bright colours, the theatricality of the welcome, the exclamation mark in the caption and the simulated sprocket holes on the panel on which the building society's name appears seemingly allude to a cinema poster.[9] If so, it would have been seen as a mildly amusing presentation of characters in an everyday occurrence acting as the stars of an epic drama – the return of the wanderer to the safe haven of the home.

The poster itself is unsigned but was most probably drawn by a commercial artist either working freelance or for the firm which printed the poster. The design is loosely modernist in its sparsely-stated design and sharp lines and angles. While the pitched roofs and chimney stacks indicate that modernism did not extend to house design in any strict sense,[10] it is clearly a modern suburban setting. The houses and gardens do not try to convey tradition, age or vernacular longings. Rather they suggest cleanliness, fresh air, and uncluttered space – enhanced by the unusual absence of planting. Housing density is clearly low, given the extent of open space, but there is the suggestion of other similar, yet different, houses in the distance, to indicate that the house is not isolated. Indeed, smoke rising from the chimney of the neighbouring house suggests the family within.

In terms of giving visual clues as to socioeconomic status, the design is equivocal. The vagueness in the depiction of clothing, the absence of signs of material possessions, and the lack of fencing or hedges to indicate plot sizes make it difficult to make judgements. However, that may well have been deliberate policy. Removal of the obvious signs of class or status permitted the advertisement, and its message about the joys of home-ownership, to apply to the widest possible audience. This impression is reinforced by the way in which the houses are portrayed. By drawing them so that they overlap the edge of the picture, the artist conceals their actual size and extent. For example, is the family's house a large detached villa with a single-storey extension or merely a glorified bungalow? Is the neighbouring house detached or semi-detached? There is no way to tell from looking at the poster.

The posters shown in Figures 5.2 and 5.3 were part of a long series which the National Building Society contracted out to Greenlys Ltd, a London-based design and printing house. Both examples embrace similar creative concepts. The artist has used oils to produce a facsimile painting, complete with frame and a plate on which a slogan could be written by an in-house calligrapher. There is also sufficient space left for insertion of the National's standard rubric, overall campaign slogan and reference to the estate agent. The paintings are broadly in picturesque tradition, perhaps illustrating Richards's (1946) subsequent comment that the picturesque tradition was an essential part of the attractiveness of the suburban idea to the English.

In Figure 5.2 the observer was invited to view a painting entitled 'Their happiness can be yours . .' and presumably to identify with the transparent contentment of the small nuclear family depicted there. Composed of the same triad of city-worker father, housewife-mother and small daughter as in Figure 5.1, we see them sitting in the evening sun. The father, still wearing his city suit, has just returned from work but, instead of the public welcome, we now spy on the private realm of the back garden. The postures of the figures and the objects that they clutch show that they are relaxing. The man lounges, pipe in hand, in a deckchair on the terrace with the family dog, a Scottish terrier, at his feet. His wife, immaculate in a sleeveless yellow dress and elegant bobbed hairstyle, reclines across the table, absent-mindedly clutching a pair of red knitting needles in her left hand. Their curly-headed daughter is at the table attending to her doll.

Other features of the composition confirm the basic themes of the painting. The family is viewed through an almost complete circle of summer foliage and flowers; young trees frame the group above and larkspur (delphiniums) engulf them from below. The garden table, covered with a white cloth, is illuminated by bright sunshine softened by the dappled shadow from the luxuriant garden around them. There are glasses containing drinks and straws on the table, along with a discarded book.

Interestingly, very little of the house itself can be seen and certainly nothing that gives any clue as to the size of the dwelling. The one significant detail that is included is the open French windows. It is these that give access to this private and controlled realm, to which one can attribute access to other valued benefits such as peace and quiet, relaxation, refuge, beautiful surroundings, fresh air and sunlight. The slogan suggests that the happiness which this brings can be achieved by others too if only they would follow the final injunction, namely, to buy their houses through the National Building Society.

The companion poster (Figure 5.3) shows a comparable scene in spring. Within the oval picture frame, we again see the family enjoying the privacy of their garden, only in this instance there is a three-generational grouping. The father leans against the back doorway of the house. His rolled-up sleeves and garden implements propped up against the wall suggest that he is taking a break from gardening chores. His wife is seated at his side, wearing a demure yellow dress that suggests Sunday-best.[11] Beside

Figure 5.2 'Their happiness can be yours', National Building Society.

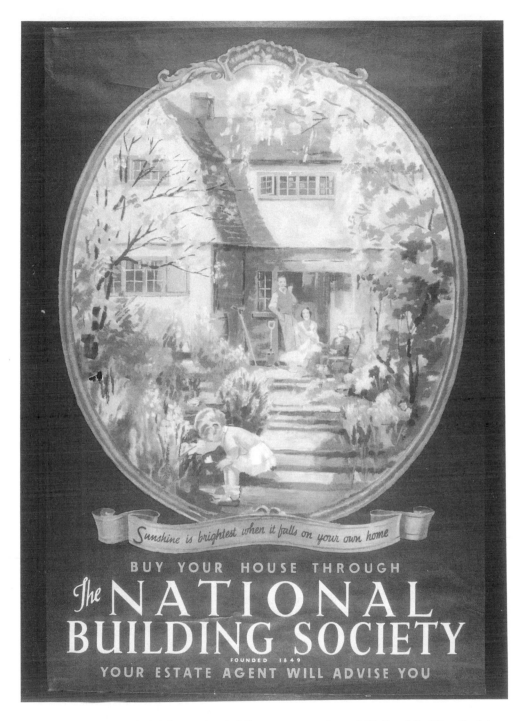

Figure 5.3   'Sunshine is brightest when it falls on your own home', National Building Society.

her, in a purple dress with lace at the neck, sits the grey-haired grandmother. All three gaze admiringly down the terraced garden to where a small fair-haired girl is being allowed, somewhat improbably, to pick the flowers. The positioning of people and their facial expressions convey pride in parenthood and bonds of familial affection.

The garden itself is bursting into life. Cherry blossom and laburnum, which Ferguson (1986:91) describes as the 'eye-catching, springtime sight in British suburbs', frame the scene, while the cottage-style garden is full of yellow spring flowers. More of the house is visible here than in Figure 5.2. The red-tiled gabled mansard roof, lime-rendering, casement windows, wooden shutters and rain butt are features that allude to the vernacular architecture of the country cottage. Their presence, coupled with the smoke rising from the chimney stack signifying the warmth of the family hearth within, intimate that sense of tradition and solidity that suburban promoters so desperately wanted their new estates to acquire.

As such, it can be argued that this impression is complemented by the presence of the three generations; social continuity to match design continuity. Arguably also, it implies that the security of property can pass from one generation to the next, something which was previously only the prerogative of the upper classes. Finally, the scene is bathed in bright sunlight and completed with the multi-layered caption: 'Sunshine is brightest when it falls on your own home'.

Before passing on, it is worth noting a representational theme that emerges consistently in all three posters considered so far. In each case, the artist has taken care to make the size of the house ambiguous. In the first instance, this was done by overlapping the edge of the frame, in the second by showing only a tiny segment of the rear of the house. In this instance another strategy, long used by promotional illustrators of suburbia, was employed. A heavy screen of trees and foliage blocks out the right-hand edge of the picture so that unwanted detail is screened out. The 'unwanted detail' here, judging from the house's design, is the neighbouring, and overlooking house to which it is attached.

The reason for these strategies, as we have shown elsewhere (Gold and Gold, 1990:173) lay in the links between environment and social status. The great English country-house in its spacious grounds represented, and for many still represents, the acme of desirable housing. Such houses were beyond the wildest dreams of the vast majority of the population, but dreams could be built around the nearest practical alternative, the detached suburban house. One therefore sees the paradox that the semi-detached house, the staple of suburbia, was almost never shown in the building societies' promotional posters. Instead what were depicted were either pictures of detached houses or villas, with their connotations of greater social exclusiveness, or carefully-crafted portrayals which disguised semi-detached houses to look detached.

Figure 5.4 illustrates a poster that specifically shows a detached dwelling. Issued by the Woolwich Equitable Building Society, its centrepiece is a standard chocolate-box painting by Guy Lipscombe of a large, hybrid white-walled, irregular detached villa. Detailed scrutiny suggests that the artist was not painting from accurate field sketches. An enormous red-brick chimney stack of industrial proportions dominates one wall. Windows come in two different styles (latticed on the ground floor, square-paned on the first floor), and are positioned at levels which suggest a remarkable interior room layout. The centrally-situated dormer window would seem to have little function given the size of the roof area, and the diminutive doorway has no surrounds.

Figure 5.4 'Our England—Our Home', Woolwich Equitable Building Society.

Authenticity, however, was not the point. The house is used as a vehicle to convey the treasured imagery of the cottage and the English rural vernacular. The red-tiled roof has acquired the patina of age. There are leaded lights in the windows and weather-boarding on the dormer. The house is set amid mature trees and the garden is ablaze with traditional plants – larkspur of various colours, marguerites and golden rod. Wisteria creeps up the external walls in several places. Unlike the three previous posters, no people are seen, but the emblems of their occupancy are everywhere. Many of the windows are open and smoke is coming from the chimney, suggesting that people are in the house. A garden seat waits for anyone wanting to enjoy the summer sunlight.

The poster essays at a somewhat more sophisticated tone than the three previous posters. Unusually, the painting is prominently signed by its artist. The slogan 'Our England – Our Home' parodies Shakespeare. The quote beneath the picture, 'This my house my castle is, I have my own four walls' is slightly paraphrased from Thomas Carlyle's poem 'My Own Four Walls', written in the 1830s. The original reads:

> My whinstone house my castle is,
> I have my own four walls.

The house in the picture is far removed from the dark whinstone of Scottish towns but the sentiments could easily be applied here, given the long acceptance of the motif of the home-as-castle in British society.[12]

So far there is no exhortation to purchase, but these images of an idyllic, sun-bathed paradise of colour and fragrance, oozing traditional values of the independent yeoman and a solid vernacular style, are images of *our* England, *our* home. Those who saw the poster were informed that this England belonged to them. If they wanted to purchase *their* 'piece of England', there was a simple way to do so, namely, to contact the agent whose name would have been inserted into the blank space at the foot of the poster.

Symbols

The use of symbols is a familiar part of the rhetoric of suburban promotion contained here. Derived from the Greek word *symbolon* meaning a 'mark' or 'token', symbols are things that stand for something else and, as such, have both manifest (surface) and latent (hidden) meaning. In the examples of posters that we have examined, three elements have clear symbolic properties. They are the threshold, the figure of the small girl, and sunlight.

Threshold

The notion of threshold is a significant element in each advertisement. Owning your own threshold is depicted as a vital step because it is far more than just the place where one walks in or out of a building. Rather, it is here the meeting place of three conceptually distinct worlds.

The first is the enclosed space of the interior. As noted, interiors are seldom shown in building society posters, but there are always strong *external* signs of life within – the open window, the glimpse of curtains and furnishings, and smoke rising from the chimney. This last aspect is particularly interesting. In many such posters, it is patently summer and even by the 1930s the new, cleaner forms of heating (gas, electricity and gradually central heating) were being installed in new housing. Yet the plume of smoke was irresistible to the poster artist because it is so rich in associations. At a stroke, it signifies the hearth, the heart of the home, and the associations of domesticity connected with it – warmth, comfort, cosiness and security. With so much apparently at stake within, it is not surprising that, following the house-as-castle analogy, several observers likened the front door to a drawbridge that can be shut to repel the outside world (Gloag, 1945).

The second world bounded by the threshold is the public space of the street. The front of the house represents the 'face' that is presented to the outside world and it can be argued that the way in which front gardens are presented reflect the urge to project self-image (Cooper, 1974). The neat presentation of planted borders, carefully clipped hedges, shrubs in pots, and newly swept paths are an occasional feature of building society posters. Surrounding external public space was normally handled by the poster artist in one of two ways; either left out of the picture completely or shown as a neutral setting against which to offset the new suburban idyll. Perfectly logical alternative promotional strategies, such as portrayals of vibrant neighbourhood life, were not the order of the day.

The third world bounded by the threshold is the semi-private realm of the back garden. The garden was a space over which the family had control. Small children could play in safety, coming and going as they pleased through the ever-open back-door or French windows. Informal hospitality could be offered to visitors and the *paterfamilias* could relax after a day spent in a city office. Gardens did imply work: their maintenance was popularly assigned to the husband, just as it was the wife's responsibility to keep the inside of the house in order.[13] However, as depicted here (e.g. Figure 5.3), gardening was a labour of love. Although gardens could have the utilitarian function of growing vegetables for the table, the gardens shown in these posters are flower-strewn cottage gardens that harmonise with the atmosphere of rurality suggested by the house's neo-vernacular trimmings. Gardening here was an individual creative activity to be savoured at the time and to be contemplated from afar. Many would have empathised with the spirit underpinning Sir John Betjeman's (1958:212) gentle evocation of a London commuter wistfully musing on the garden of his home in a Middlesex suburb:

> And all that day in murky London Wall
> The thought of RUISLIP kept him warm inside;
> At FARRINGDON that lunch hour at a stall
> He bought a dozen plants of London Pride

As such, the suburban garden could be seen as a refuge not just from everyday cares, but also from the sense of uncertainty that hung like a pall over trouble-torn 1930s England (Richards, 1946).

The small girl

It is argued by some observers (e.g. Cherry, 1982:33) that this was the 'most family-minded and home-centred (generation) in history'. Whether or not this is true, there is no denying that these illustrations provide a thought-provoking insight into the advertisers' notion of the ideal family relaxing or reunited in their suburban home. The husband is shown as a man of substance, as befits one who had both the income and the security of employment to secure a loan. The wife is depicted as demure and welcoming, the traditional housewife and mother.

Yet perhaps the most interesting symbolic element is the figure of the young girl. Building society posters rarely showed more than one child in the family and that is invariably a daughter (Gold and Gold, 1990). Pedantically, it can be argued that these representations of a small nuclear family merely expressed the demography of the interwar years, accurately reflecting the low birth rates among the middle income groups, and depict the target audience for the advertising – married couples with young children or perhaps wanting to start a family.

Nevertheless, there are deeper meanings implied. The small girl was intended as a symbol of gentleness and defencelessness. The sight of her playing happily and safely in the back garden symbolised the opportunities available to provide children with a secure and healthy environment in which to grow and flourish. It also subtly reinforced the idea that it was the responsibility of the father, who would normally be the sole bread-winner, to provide such an environment in order to give a child 'a decent start in life'. In return, he would receive the emotional security which came from meeting that responsibility.

Sunlight

The final symbolic element that merits further consideration is sunlight. The choice of sunlit scenes in these advertisements may be seen as more than just the artist's preference for bright colours. The 1930s were an era in which great emphasis was placed on the regenerative and recuperative powers of sunshine and fresh air (King, 1984). New houses were built with sun lounges and terraces for *alfresco* eating. Outdoor pursuits such as countryside rambling, sunbathing, even naturism thrived. Preventative medicine started to gain favour, stressing the value of the healthy rays of the sun. Sanatoria offered 'sunray' treatments, both natural and heat lamp, for many ailments.

These positive associations found expression in many aspects of contemporary design, including product advertising,[14] commercial product design and packaging, and domestic fitments. Interestingly, too, references to sunlight were much favoured by builders of suburban housing schemes. Front doors and gates acquired sunburst motifs. Sunrays in stained glass were incorporated into the leaded lights of windows (Oliver *et al.*, 1981). In short, sunshine and its emblems were an ingredient in the selling of suburbia itself.

Seen against this background, therefore, the sunlit tableaux of the building societies' advertisements take on an enhanced meaning. The scenes of families enjoying the opportunity to sit outdoors, windows open to allow fresh air to waft through the house, are making statements, contrasting the situation with older areas of housing which, by comparison, were dirty, lacked open space and in some cases were near manufacturing plant. The dappled spring and bright summer sunlight can be read as symbols of elemental approval for the better and brighter life that home-ownership could bring. Such references would not have been lost on the contemporary observer.

Conclusion

'Advertising', noted Jerry Goodis, Benetton's advertising manager, 'doesn't always mirror how people are acting, but how they are dreaming . . . In a sense what we are doing is wrapping up your emotions and selling them back to you' (Back and Quaade, 1993:65). Much the same sentiment applies to the poster advertising examined in this chapter. Starting from a position in which they scarcely conducted advertising activity worthy of the name, the building societies quickly built up large-scale campaigns. In doing so, they articulated and endlessly reinforced a rhetoric that drew upon a carefully selected repertoire of environmental and social depictions to communicate, simultaneously, the idea of home ownership and the desirability of the new suburbs to their audience.

The reality of suburbia back in the 1920s and 1930s, of course, was rather different from the rhetoric of the advertisements. It would be many years before the newly-built streets and garden plots, surrounded by bare plots and young trees, could look anything like the mature landscapes of the advertisements. Moreover, as we have noted, while advertising showed or suggested distinctive detached villas, the reality for most people was the relative uniformity of semi-detached housing estates, often with quite small gardens. The semi-detached house, which could have any variety of superficial external decoration within a standard relatively low cost design (Edwards, 1981), was ideal for this purpose. The advertisements suggested a rural idyll with cottage gardens and only a hint of nearby neighbours, whereas the reality was that these were urban developments of significant density (albeit with easier access to open countryside at that time than many such districts have today).

Yet, as we argued at the beginning of this chapter, the gap between reality and rhetoric does not mean that the latter should be dismissed pejoratively as a distortion. The building societies had accurately grasped and given expression to the housing dreams and aspirations of the middle classes. Their artists and graphic designers clearly identified a set of values relating to family and property that English society held most dear (Fishman, 1987) and incorporated them into their selling message. In doing so, they produced a language of images and symbols that were neither an exact reflection of reality nor a *Zerrspiegel* – a fairground distorting mirror (Gold and Gold, 1990:178) – but rather a mirror that distorted, selected and enhanced. The historic success of that rhetoric, as measured by the unprecedented growth of suburbia during the interwar period, strongly suggests that the audience fully understood and, indeed, supported the underlying message. Moreover, despite all endeavours to encourage movement of population back to the city and the continued carping of urban commentators about the inadequacies of suburbia, there are good reasons to suggest that its power remains undiminished to this day.

Notes

1. Jarvis, in turn was drawing insights supplied by Williamson (1978), Williams (1980) and Dyer (1982). For other treatments of the subject of rehetoric and advertising, see, *inter alia*, Andrén *et al.* (1978), Sinclair (1987) and Wernick (1991).
2. *Inter alia*, see Forrest, 1985; Horsey, 1985; Jackson, 1985; Barrett and Phillips, 1987; Fishman, 1987; Sies, 1987; Stilgoe, 1988; Cervero, 1989; Pepper, 1989; McKenna, 1990; Ben-Ari, 1991; Stanback, 1991; McGrath, 1992; Wagenaar, 1992.
3. It is not possible to supply a full background on the development of the building societies movement. For more information, see Pawley, 1978; Boddy, 1980; and Holmans, 1987.
4. Although the legislation did not apply to new houses built for rent, initially high building costs made house building prohibitively expensive. Even when costs fell it was virtually impossible for landlords to build for rents which were comparable with the controlled rents (Cleary, 1965) or competitive with the levels of mortgage repayments being paid by the new owner-occupiers (Hamnett and Randolph, 1988, cited in Saunders, 1990).
5. Caused by marriages deferred during the duration of the war.
6. This statement may seem odd given the general economic circumstances of the 1930s. Disposable income, however, increased for those in work and south-east England had unemployment rates which were appreciably lower than elsewhere in the country.
7. It is perhaps fairer to say that the advent of new consumer durables provided the promise of a reduction in the hard graft of domestic chores at this stage rather than the reality.
8. These posters, now part of the authors' private collection, originally came from the archives of George Holland and Sons, estate agents in West London, 1877–1972. Further examples of these posters are depicted in Gold and Gold (1990).
9. It is worth noting that film posters, with the wealth of creative talents employed by production companies to advertise films during this golden age of the cinema, would have been a profound influence on graphic designers in many fields.
10. For example, in the sense of the International Style. While this was used sparingly in the design of suburban housing in interwar Britain, the International Style was surprisingly well-known given the controversy that often occurred when houses in this style were proposed. See Gould (1977).
11. An element of artistic licence here: if this was a Sunday in most parts of London's suburbia, gardening would have been frowned upon.
12. Indeed, these lines themselves echo Sir Edward Coke (1552–1631): 'For a man's house is his castle, *et domus sua cuique est tutissimum refugium*'.
13. The suggestion that the suburban home is divided into gendered domains has been taken up by a variety of commentators. (See, for example: Miller, 1983, 1991; Spain, 1992; Spigel, 1992; Vaiou, 1992.)
14. A good example being Eric Fraser's long-running sunray-starfish figure, Mr Therm. This was devised for gas-industry advertisement around 1935 and was used for more than a quarter of a century to give continuity to the industry's campaigns.

References

Andrén, G., Ericsson, L.O., Ohlsson, R. and Tännsjö, T. (1978) *Rhetoric and Ideology in Advertising: a content analytic study of American advertising*, Stockholm: LiberFörlag.

Back, L. and Quaade, V. (1993) 'Dream utopias, nightmare realities: imaging race and culture within the world of Benetton advertising', *Third Text*, 22, 65–80.

Ball, M. (1983) *Housing Policy and Economic Power: the political economy of owner occupation*, London: Methuen.

Barrett, H. and Phillips, J. (1987) *Suburban Style: the British home, 1840–1960*, London: Macdonald.

Bellman, H. (1949) *Bricks and Mortals: a study of the building society movement and the story of the Abbey National Society, 1849–1949*, London: Hutchinson.

Ben-Ari, E. (1991) *Changing Japanese Suburbia: a study of two present-day localities*, London: Kogan Page International.

Betjeman, J. (1958) 'The Metropolitan Railway: Baker Street Station Buffet', in *The Collected Poems*, London: John Murray, 212–13.

Boddy, M. (1980) *The Building Societies*, London: Macmillan.

Carey, J. (1992) *The Intellectuals and the Masses: pride and prejudice among the literary intelligentsia, 1880–1939*, London: Faber and Faber.

Carter, H. (1983) *An Introduction to Urban Historical Geography*, London: Edward Arnold.

Cervero, R. (1989) *America's Suburban Centres*, London: Routledge.

Cherry, G.E. (1982) *Leisure and the Home*, London: Sports Council and Social Science Research Council.

Cleary, E.J. (1965) *The Building Society Movement*, London: Elek.

Cooper, C. (1974) 'The house as a symbol of the self', in J. Lang, C. Burnette, W. Moleski and D. Vachon, eds., *Designing for Human Behaviour*, Stroudsburg, PA: Dowden, Hutchinson and Ross, 130–46.

Dyer, G. (1982) *Advertising as Communication*, London: Methuen.

Edwards, A.M. (1981) *The Design of Suburbia: a critical study in environmental history*, London: Pembridge Press.

Ferguson, N. (1986) *Right Plant, Right Place*, London: Pan.

Fishman, R. (1987) *Bourgeois Utopias: the rise and fall of suburbia*, New York: Basic Books.

Forrest, J. (1985) 'Suburbia – the myth of homogeneity', in I. Burnley and J. Forrest, eds., *Living in Cities: urbanism and society in metropolitan Australia*, Sydney: Allen and Unwin, 71–87.

Gloag, J. (1945) *The Englishman's Castle*, London: Eyre and Spottiswoode.

Gold, J.R. and Gold, M.M. (1989) 'Outrage and righteous indignation: ideology and the imagery of suburbia', in F.W. Boal and D.N. Livingstone, eds., *The Behavioural Environment: essays in reflection, application and re-evaluation*, London: Routledge, 163–81.

Gold, J.R. and Gold, M.M. (1990) '"A Place of Delightful Prospects": promotional imagery and the selling of suburbia', in L. Zonn, ed., *Place Images in the Media: portrayal, meaning and experience*, Savage, MD: Rowman and Littlefield, 159–82.

Gould, J.H. (1977) *Modern Houses in Britain, 1919–1939*, Architectural History Monographs 1, London: Society of Architectural Historians of Great Britain.

Hamnett, C. and Randolph, W. (1988) *Cities, Housing and Profits*, London: Hutchinson.

Holmans, A. (1987) *Housing Policy in Britain*, London: Croom Helm.

Horsey, M. (1985) 'London's speculative housebuilding in the 1930s: official control and popular taste', *London Journal*, 11, 147–59

Jackson, A.A. (1991) *Semi-Detached London: suburban development, life and transport*, Didcot: Wild Swan Publications (originally published 1973, London: George Allen and Unwin).

Jackson, K.T. (1985) *The Crabgrass Frontier: the suburbanisation of the United States*, New York: Oxford University Press.

Jarvis, R.K. (1987) 'The next best thing to being there: the environmental rhetoric of advertising', *Landscape Research*, 12(3), 14–19.

King, A.D. (1984) *The Bungalow: the production of a global culture*, London: Routledge and Kegan Paul.

McGrath, B. (1992) 'Suburban development in Ireland, 1960–80', *Planning Perspectives*, 7, 27–46.

McKenna, M. (1990) 'Municipal suburbia in Liverpool, 1919–1939', *Town Planning Review*, 60, 287–319.

Miller, R. (1983) 'The Hoover in the garden: middle-class women and suburbanisation, 1850–1920', *Environment and Planning D: Society and Space*, 1, 73–88.

Miller, R. (1991) 'Selling Mrs Consumer: advertising and the creation of suburban socio-spatial relations, 1910–1930', *Antipode*, 23, 263–306.

Muthesius, S. (1982) *The English Terraced House*, New Haven, CN: Yale University Press.

Neiman, M. (1991) 'What, me hate the suburbs? the irrelevance of anti-suburban orthodoxy', *Social Science Quarterly*, 73, 490–500.

Oliver, P., Davis, I. and Bentley, I. (1981) *Dunroamin: the suburban semi and its enemies*, London: Barrie and Jenkins.

Pawley, M. (1978) *Home Ownership*, London: Architectural Press.

Pepper, S. (1989) 'John Laing's Sunnyfields Estate, Mill Hill', in B. Ford, ed., *The Cambridge Guide to the Arts in Britain*, volume 2 'The Edwardian Age and the Inter-War Years', Cambridge: Cambridge University Press, 294–305.

Price, S.J. (1958) *Building Societies: the origin and history*, London: Franey.

Richards, J.M. (1946) *The Castles on the Ground: the anatomy of suburbia*, London: Architectural Press.

Rybczynski, W. (1988) *Home: a short history of an idea*, London: Heinemann.

Saunders, P. (1990) *A Nation of Home Owners*, London: Unwin Hyman.

Sies, M.C. (1987) 'The city transformed: nature, technology and the suburban ideal', *Journal of Urban History*, 15, 81–111.

Sinclair, J. (1987) *Images Incorporated: advertising as industry and ideology*, London: Croom Helm.

Spain, D. (1992) *Gendered Spaces*, Chapel Hill: University of Carolina Press.

Spigel, L. (1992) 'The suburban home companion: television and the neighbourhood idea in postwar America', in B. Colomina, ed., *Sexuality and Space*, Princeton: Princeton University Press, 185–217.

Stanback, T.M. (1991) *The New Suburbanisation: challenge to the central city*, Boulder, CO: Westview Press.

Stilgoe, J.R. (1988) *Borderland: origins of the American suburb, 1820–1939*, New Haven, CN: Yale University Press.

Swenarton, M. (1981) *Homes fit for Heroes: the politics and architecture of early state housing in Britain*, London: Heinemann.

Thompson, F.M.L., ed. (1982) *The Rise of Suburbia*, Leicester: Leicester University Press.

Vaiou, D. (1992) 'Gender divisions in urban space: beyond the rigidity of dualist classifications', *Antipode*, 24, 247–62.

Wagenaar, M. (1992) 'Conquest of the centre or flight to the suburbs? Divergent metropolitan strategies in Europe, 1850–1914', *Journal of Urban History*, 19, 60–83.

Weightman, G. and Humphries, S. (1984) *The Making of Modern London, 1914–1939*, London: Sidgwick and Jackson.

Wernick, A. (1991) *Promotional Culture: advertising, ideology and symbolic expression*, Newbury Park, CA: Sage.

Williams, R. (1980) 'Advertising: the magic system', in R. Williams, *Problems in Materialism and Culture*, London: Verso, 170–95.

Williamson, J. (1978) *Decoding Advertisements: ideology and meaning in advertising*, London: Marion Boyars.

6 Selling the industrial town: identity, image and illlusion

MICHAEL BARKE AND KEN HARROP

Perhaps the greatest contribution made by the industrial town was the reaction it produced against its own greatest misdemeanours. (Mumford, 1966:540)

Introduction

The chapters of this book demonstrate the widespread nature of place promotion in the west and the work begun in earlier chapters is now furthered by examining the messages conveyed in place promotional activity, as revealed by a study of UK experience, and commenting on the marketing processes involved. In particular, we look at the ways in which traditional manufacturing towns have projected themselves for promotional purposes in a changed economic climate.

This activity frequently means that new identities are sought and efforts made to represent existing places in a different guise. In the more extreme cases, a place may even seek to become somewhere else: thus South Tyneside becomes 'Catherine Cookson Country', Swansea 'Dylan Thomas Country', Dover 'White Cliffs Country', Durham 'Land of the Prince Bishops', and Doncaster 'England's Northern Jewel' (Figure 6.1). Inevitably, the media in all their forms play the most prominent role in such representations and reconstructions of place (Burgess, 1990). As will be demonstrated, these attempts can create many difficulties.

Attempts to 'sell' the industrial town derive largely from efforts to combat the long-term decline in British manufacturing industry and to adjust to economic structural change (Cooke, 1989). Between 1971 and 1989, 2.8 million jobs were lost in manufacturing industry in Great Britain, some 35.5 per cent of the total. Over the same period, total employment increased by 304,000 or 1.4 per cent. This modest growth and the massive structural shift that it implies is explained by the growth of the service sector. Between 1971 and 1989 some 3.69 million jobs were created in that sector, a growth of 32.4 per cent. Such figures, of course, continue longer term trends. In 1911, manufacturing employment accounted for 55 per cent of the total jobs in Great Britain; by 1989 this was 23.2 per cent (Champion and Townsend, 1990). However, over both the long term and more recently there has been growth in some manufacturing industries. In the past decade, for instance, high technology industry and dynamic small manufacturing firms have frequently been cited as characterising the new face of British industry.

It is against this background that many industrial towns in Britain, as elsewhere (Watson, 1991), have tried to replace negative images of dereliction, decline and

Figure 6.1   Although Doncaster's slogan may raise a few eyebrows, the attempt to associate a powerful industrial image with precious jewels is cleverly thought out and well presented.

'smokestack' industries with images that stress change of function, modernity, and locational advantages which are often environmental in nature as well as economic.

The meaning of place: identity and image

A primary function of place promotion in relation to industrial towns is to change the conceptions of such places that are held by a variety of individuals and organisations. However, before examining how the promotion of place has been attempted, we must address certain issues of definition. In particular, it is necessary to make a clear distinction between 'identity' and 'image'. 'Every individual, every business, local authority or nation, has an identity' noted Fedorcio *et al.* (1991:24): for an organisation, 'it is the projection of who you are and what you stand for, what you do and how you do it'.

Places also have identities. The 'identity' may be regarded as an objective thing; it is what the place is actually like. Identity though is not the same as 'image', which defines how an organisation or a place is perceived externally. Naturally, image may be strongly influenced by 'objective' identity and image makers will seek to structure the perceptions of others but cannot finally control them. Images may exist independently of the apparent facts of objective reality.

There is another dimension to any consideration of place in the context of marketing. The term 'place' may be interpreted in a variety of ways and take on one of several meanings (Agnew, 1987). First, it may refer to a specific location, in the sense that it has x and y co-ordinates on a map and is a certain distance from other places or features such as airports, docks, motorways and National Parks. Secondly, in addition to possessing a precise location and measurable proximity to other phenomena, places also have internal sets of characteristics. They are locales with assemblages of phenomena, such as types and qualities of housing, schools, commercial and industrial sites. Thirdly, there is the more abstract 'sense of place', usually construed as deriving from some deeper level of meaning, associated with an emotional reaction to place. This may be related to significant personal or more collectively recognised events or simply to the imperative to have a sense of identity with a particular place (Cox, 1968). There is a further element of complexity in any conceptualisation of place. The perception of the previous two dimensions – identity or image; location, locale, or sense of place – vary in an individual, group or community, and a mass basis. We therefore need to be aware of the level of resolution being attempted in any analysis of place; are we concerned with individual, localised group, or mass perceptions?

If we accept that places can be sold – and all the resources and efforts which go into such attempts suggest that many believe that they can be – then the preceding discussion leads to another important question: can they be sold as they are (identity) or do they have to be turned into, or more accurately, represented as, something else in order to be sold? That is, does their image require attention or at least a different, highly selective, identity presented in order to encourage a change of image? As we are dealing with towns whose past *raison d'être* has been based upon manufacturing industry, it is perhaps not surprising that the evidence we shall be examining in this chapter suggests this to be the case. Logically therefore, it follows that, in the selling of places, there has to be a distortion of reality or of identity.

Place promotion in the past

The historical development of place promotion was discussed in Chapter 4, but some brief analysis of past British place promotion is worthwhile here because it helps us to understand, first, the ways in which images of place have been formulated and re-formulated over time and, secondly, the conflict and contradiction that may well arise from ill-founded attempts to change the image of places.

Perhaps the first attempts to promote urban places can be found in town directories in the early 19th century (Corfield and Kelly, 1984). For example, the editors of the

Staffordshire General and Commercial Directory (Parson and Bradshaw, 1818) drew attention to the 'population, opulence, and knowledge' of the Pottery towns which 'present a scene of animation truly interesting to the patriotic observer'. This enthusiastic embrace of an 'industrial' image and the association of wealth, size and patriotism with industrial growth and effort is significant. Nineteenth-century Britain was fascinated with the 'magic of industry' (Briggs, 1968), symbolised by Gladstone's description of the rapidly-expanding town of Middlesbrough in 1862 as: 'this remarkable place, the youngest child of England's enterprise . . . an infant Hercules' (quoted in Briggs, 1968).

Yet even in the mid-19th century, the open embrace of industrialisation as a positive feature of the urban image did not preclude attempts to associate industrial towns with other images. Efforts to make the most of 'modernity' in the form of recent growth in local trade and industry while also emphasising the continued existence of environmentally attractive areas, were commonplace in directories and other local publications for much of the early part of the 19th century. A Preston historian's attempt to have the best of both worlds was typical:

> Preston is generally and deservedly recognized as one of the cleanest and most pleasantly situated manufacturing towns in England. The cotton factories are chiefly erected to the north and east of the old aristocratic borough and do not as yet materially interfere with the more 'fashionable' or picturesque sections of the district. (C. Hardwick, 1857, quoted in Vickery, 1988:58).

The message was clear: progress, wealth creation, vigour and excitement were interrelated with growth and industrialisation.

These early attempts at place promotion concerning the industrial town, whether based on the printed word or more visual symbols, were strong and positive. Yet it was not long before the predominant image of the industrial town became more negative, even hostile (Coleman, 1973). Accordingly, it became necessary to portray the town in a different light and to engage in other forms of place promotion.

The most significant feature of this change was emphasis on the opportunities for economic development possessed by certain locations with a view to enhancing local economic strength or, more frequently, offsetting economic decline. As Ward notes in Chapter 4, it was in periods of decline that promotional activity tended to reach a peak. In North-East England, for instance, the early years of the 20th century witnessed a shift in promotional emphasis towards more practical issues such as the provision of information on sites and infrastructure (Tyne Improvement Commission and North-East Railway Company, 1905; Shaw, 1908). Another example is provided by Derby, where growing concern with over-reliance on railway engineering led to the formation of an economic regeneration committee (Bonsall, 1988).

In general, most promotional activity took the form of publicity and information, although legal problems limited its effectiveness (Ward, 1985). The provision of land and buildings was also attempted by a few local authorities (Ward, 1990). Some areas additionally promoted specific, large-scale events, for example the great North-East Coast Exhibition in Newcastle-upon-Tyne in 1929 which, allegedly, attracted 4.5 million visitors (Baglee, 1979). By the late 19th century, the emphasis shifted from celebrating industry to trying to attract it, yet what remained significant were the straightforward and authentic representations of place. Industrial towns were presented as such rather than wrapped up in some disguise. In the words of Asa Briggs (1968:70): 'even the smoke might be defended'.

Content of promotional literature

In contrast to the indirect and limited promotional activity that characterised the past, most industrial towns now engage directly in promotional activity (Ashworth and Voogd, 1990). Indeed Mills and Young (1986) estimate that well over 70 per cent of all local authorities undertake some form of promotional activity. To gain an impression of the promotional strategies now employed and the authenticity of the 'places' that are being projected, we took a sample of their promotional literature. This was done by contacting a large number of district councils in mainland England and Scotland in summer 1992 to request copies of their literature aimed at promoting economic activity, whether in terms of attempting to attract investment in industry, commerce, or leisure and tourism activity. A total of 148 responses containing promotional material were received from English local authorities and 32 from Scotland.[1]

Undertaking her survey in 1977, Burgess (1982) found the typical constituents of a promotions package to be: a town guide; glossy brochures aimed at industrial and commercial clients; loose-leaf fact sheets giving details of sites or premises available, grants, and rents; and sometimes photocopies of industrial and commercial information. These are broadly comparable with our findings, although booklets giving factual information about the town's existing business services and suppliers are now a common part of the promotions package. Tourist information was also a common element in the 1977 survey, along with material relating to issues such as local housing opportunities and to the local authority and its services.

It is clear from Table 6.1 that, with the single exception of the use of slogans, every

Table 6.1 Comparison of 1977 Survey and 1992 Survey: content of Local Authority Promotions Packages.

	% of Local Authorities	
	1977	1992
Guide	42.6	84.2
Glossy	29.7	56.2
Fact Sheets	20.3	37.7
Industrial/Commercial information	20.9	69.9
Tourist	28.4	84.9
Other	42.6	85.6
Slogan	43.9*	45.2
Magazine/Newspaper	—	32.2
Coat of Arms	—	36.3
Logo	—	73.6

* This reflects the number of cases tabulated by Burgess and is not necessarily the sum total of her sample of local authorities using slogans in 1977.

other type of promotional activity has markedly increased. It is also likely that there have been important qualitative changes. For example, Burgess (1982) noted the 'dour' character of town guides in 1977. Some still deserve that description but many do now attempt to present a livelier image as well as containing more practical information.[2] The growth and continued popularity of town guides owes much to the fact that they involve the local authority in limited expenditure as the costs of publication are borne by advertisers. Well over half of the 1992 sample produced glossy brochures aimed at potential investors and also booklets giving information on local commercial and industrial services whilst over a third included fact sheets. A significant proportion of authorities now also produce some form of magazine or newspaper. Such publications may serve a variety of functions, but a primary one is usually to help promote and develop a sense of local identity.

Over 80 per cent of local authorities now include tourist information in their promotions packages as opposed to 28 per cent in the 1977 sample. In one sense, this might have been expected, given the much publicised efforts to develop tourism in once unlikely places such as Bradford, Wigan and Halifax (Buckley and Witt, 1985, 1989; Law, 1992). In view of the problematic relationship of urban tourism to local economic development (Jeffrey, 1990; Law, 1991), however, it is tempting to interpret this major shift as evidence that local authorities are desperate for any form of economic development and stand open to accusations of jumping on board any bandwagon.

Another interesting feature is to compare the strategies of towns in the 'industrial' and 'non-industrial' categories. Table 6.2 provides some preliminary information on these issues. The classification of industrial towns used below is based on the simple criterion of more or less than average manufacturing employment at the 1981 census.

As Table 6.2 shows, use of slogans on promotional material and production of glossy brochures are more common in the industrial group than the non-industrial. The former are slightly more likely to produce magazines and newspapers, fact sheets, and specific commercial and industrial information than the latter, although the differences are hardly dramatic. Over 60 per cent of 'non-industrial' towns, however,

Table 6.2 Content of Local Authority Promotions Packages, 1992: comparison of 'Industrial' and 'Non-industrial' towns.

	Non-industrial		Industrial	
	No.	%	No.	%
Slogan	17	30.4	49	54.4
Guide	45	80.4	78	86.7
Glossy	21	37.5	61	67.8
Magazine/Newspaper	12	21.4	35	38.9
Fact Sheets	18	32.1	37	41.1
Industrial/Commercial Info.	34	60.7	68	75.5
Tourist Info.	49	87.5	75	83.3
Other Promotional	50	89.3	75	83.3
Logo	41	73.2	68	75.5
Coat of Arms	17	30.4	36	40.0
Total	56		90	

also produce promotional material which provides commercial and industrial information for potential investors. Furthermore, 'industrial' and 'non-industrial' are equally likely to produce tourist-related promotional material.

Thus, despite the marginal differences that do exist, we must conclude that, in terms of the type of content, the promotional packages of 'industrial' towns are not distinctive. We can suggest, therefore, that there has been a convergence of strategies, if not necessarily of textual content, in the promotion of places, regardless of their intrinsic character. Such convergence strongly hints at uniformity in at least one dimension of the promotion of places and could be argued to be a significant step in the 'commodification' of place (Relph, 1976; Mills, 1988) – the techniques and packaging of selling are much the same everywhere. As Burgess (1982:6) reported, one public relations officer observed: 'many of the things I have said about this town, I have said about elsewhere. And that applies to other people too.' Despite the attempts to create a distinctive image for places, no authentic sense of place is likely to emerge from the advertising copywriters. This is all the more likely if the packaging and the type of content is uniform.

Two other common features of promotional literature are their adoption of slogans and logos. It is argued, as in Chapter 2, that these implant images in the minds of readers and, especially in the case of the logo, aid in the recognition of some form of corporate identity. Given that the objective of much of the promotional literature is to change the image of place, one would have thought that the images and symbolism used in the logos employed by 'industrial' towns would reflect these objectives. Table 6.3 shows the results of an analysis of the logos of 95 'industrial' towns.[3]

It should be noted that one logo can contain several 'symbols' or 'images', for example, Sandwell (West Bromwich) has a cog-wheel motif (suggestive of an industrial heritage), within which is a lake scene complete with yacht (environmental/quality of life), and in the background is a silhouetted townscape with a 'traditional' outline on one side (heritage) and a high-rise office skyline on the other (modernity). Some elements are intended to be productively ambiguous, for example, the sun is used in both an environmental sense (fine weather) and as a symbol of re-birth. The various elements in the 95 logos have been classified as shown in Table 6.3.

What is most surprising about the symbolic content of logos is the limited number which directly aim to create a modern, hi-tech or futuristic atmosphere. The majority appear to prefer the rather more traditional elements which highlight environmental or heritage characteristics. Those elements can, of course, be represented in a futuristic or abstract way in order to give a more dynamic image. What is surprising is that so few are. It is also clear from Table 6.3 that many local authorities are promoting similar images through their logos, another element which ill accords with the marketing strategy of stressing uniqueness and difference in order to promote places more effectively.

Similar conclusions apply to an analysis of slogans. These draw attention to features such as quality of life, locational advantages or business opportunities. Perhaps inevitably, there is a considerable degree of similarity between the slogans used. Burgess (1982; also Gold, 1974) indicated that places as far apart as Bedford and Bolton claimed to be at the centre of England! Locational advantages are still stressed in a number of slogans, for example, Barnsley 'our location is our excellence', and 'well connected Wellingborough', but such themes are less prominent and stated more

Table 6.3 Symbols/elements used in promotional logos in 95 'industrial' towns.

Symbol/Element	No. using	% using
Environmental	62	65.3
animals	16	
water	16	
trees	11	
hills/fields	9	
sun	5	
Heritage	48	50.5
historic townscape/landscape	22	
place specific heritage symbol	19	
churches	9	
Figurative	29	30.5
arrow/triangle	19	
circle	10	
Geographical	24	25.3
map/location	9	
bridge	9	
Motorway/routeway	6	
Name/Initial	19	20.0
Modern/Futuristic	11	11.6
abstract/futuristic motif	6	
modern hi-tech townscape	5	
Financial	2	2.1

modestly than before. Thus Boothferry (Goole) claims to be 'the gateway to Humberside', and Preston 'the commercial heart of Lancashire', whilst Middlesbrough's role as 'Gateway to Captain Cook Country' serves to obscure both the real functions and character of that town and other locational advantages it may possess, not to mention the problems that may be associated with being the gateway to somewhere that does not exist.

A specific type of locational advantage claimed by some districts is concerned with proximity to, or ease of links with, Europe. Although Europe is frequently mentioned within the general promotional packages, it is surprisingly absent from slogans, with only eight out of one hundred slogans specifically concerned with Europe. The exhortation to 'be closer to Europe – come and grow in Ashford' is understandable, but Wallasey's appellation as 'EuroWirral' is less so. Similarly, Hull's claim to be 'the northern gateway: serving European business' appears appropriate but Crewe's assertion that it is 'a great place to grow . . . into Europe' could equally be claimed by several hundred localities.

The linking of past and future, in the context of industry and business development, is among the most frequently occurring type of slogan. These range from Blackburn's unimaginative 'Blackburn: the place with a past and a future' and Dudley's 'Tradition in progress', to puns such as Stoke-on-Trent's 'The City that fires the imagination' (Figure 6.2) and Burnley's 'Cotton on to Burnley', in which industrial heritage is linked with latching on to something progressive. Rather different are Calderdale's 'Sorry we

Figure 6.2 In a strategy similar to that of Doncaster, Stoke-on-Trent's undoubted industrial character is combined with an imaginative slogan and a presentation which draws attention to the best of the industrial past, but is also equally representative of the future and modern technology.

started without you' and Crewe's 'If only you knew what we know': ambiguously referring to the past and implying that potential inward investors are missing out on something (*see also* Chapter 2).

A significant facet of slogans is the conflict, if not downright contradiction, apparent between those intended for external consumption and those aimed at the local, resident population. As will be argued subsequently, this is one of the most problematic issues in the whole arena of place promotion. A good example of conflicting messages is provided by Chesterfield. Their external promotional literature makes the assertion that it is 'The place to grow', whereas material aimed at the local population uses the slogan 'Defending jobs and services'. Slightly different but also more than hinting at an uncomfortable reality, at least in the recent past, is Knowsley's 'The way forward. Turning the tide'.

Industrial towns: directions of change and image marketing

Various directions of change for former or existing industrial towns may be identified, directions which it may be felt necessary to 'market' and promote. These include the following:

(a) It is theoretically possible that, despite the major decline in manufacturing industry already outlined, certain places have maintained a relatively high level of adherence to a traditional industrial function. Whether such places may wish to promote this fact in the economic and social climate of the 1990s is somewhat questionable.

(b) More likely, is the case where a traditional (often heavy) industrial base has been replaced by a different type of industry. Thus the town persists as an industrial community but that industry is very different from its previous orientation, as, for example, where light industry such as food and drink manufacture has replaced heavy industry such as steel manufacture (Robinson and Sadler, 1984a).

(c) A variant of this trajectory of change is where older industry has been replaced by so-called hi-tech manufacturing (Garrahan, 1986).

(d) A common direction of change, and one which has created significant opportunities for marketing and place promotion in the past decade, occurs where the former industrial structure of an area is marketed in heritage terms, usually, of course, as part of a tourism promotion strategy (Falk, 1985; Clarke, 1986; Martin and Mason, 1988; Karski, 1990).

(e) Finally, the industrial town may cease its traditional function but seek to replace it with service sector activities based on offices and retailing (Bassett et al., 1989).

Some of these changes in economic orientation remain possible rather than probable and are unlikely to be as clear-cut as described here, but they illustrate ways in which one particular functional type may evolve into another and present the urban area with a different marketing problem. The main point here is that while a wide variety of directions of change are theoretically possible, in place marketing, some offer greater opportunities than others.

It may be thought unlikely that any industrial town would wish to market itself directly as such, but recent efforts to promote industrial tourism do precisely that (Steven-Anian, 1988). A number of famous British firms have long welcomed organised visits by groups, most notably Pilkington Brothers at St Helens with 200,000 visitors annually, Wedgwood (Stoke-on-Trent, 177,000), Boots (Nottingham, 10,000) and Ford (Dagenham, 27,000). Recently, however, a number of towns have sought to promote industry tourism on a co-ordinated basis. Nottingham, for example, held an 'Open to View' week in October 1989 involving 37 private sector organisations (Robinson and Hind, 1992). More ambitiously, Stoke-on-Trent has promoted a 'Do China in a Day' scheme, in which 8 museums, 10 factories and 29 ceramics shops are involved. An hourly bus service between sites is included. Even more wide-ranging was the 'Sheffield Works' scheme in the summer of 1991, 'intended to provide Sheffield with a new visitor experience which built on the city's image as a manufacturing centre' (Speakman and Bramwell, 1992:1). Sixteen firms participated in the scheme, ranging from the manufacture of stainless steel, cutlery and woodworking tools, through textiles, brewing and paper-tissue making, to the manufacture of snuff and toy soldiers. Visits were booked in small parties and a 77 per cent of capacity level achieved (Speakman and Bramwell, 1992:18). Similar schemes exist on Tyneside and Teesside, the latter under the slogan 'The Valley at Work'.

The promotion of this type of activity may be regarded as a kind of celebration of local identity, of local industry and the men and women who work in it. In many other cases, however, marginal shifts in the economic structure of a particular place may be presented in promotional terms as something much greater. This is exemplified by the experience of Consett (County Durham). The combined closure of the steelworks and a ball-bearing manufacturer made 4900 workers redundant and produced male unemployment levels of 35 per cent in the town. A number of much heralded replacement industries have developed, most notably Derwent Valley Foods, trading under the Phileas Fogg label. Yet that firm employed only 90 workers in 1985 and other newcomers are also low employers. Despite the promotional image of successful attraction of new economic activity to Consett, the fact remains that the overwhelming core of unemployment is, as yet, little reduced (Robinson and Sadler, 1984; *Sunday Times*, 22 September 1985).

One of the more determined attempts to change the image of a former industrial town concerns Hartlepool in Cleveland, a town which had grown on the basis of shipbuilding, docking and steel manufacture (Figure 6.3). Hartlepool retains a significant industrial base, the designation of an Enterprise Zone and a variety of measures aimed at assisting small businesses contributing to this continued role. However, this case demonstrates that, even with the most sophisticated promotion, old images die hard. Economic decline in the traditional industries began in the 1950s and, even in the generally economically peripheral north-east of England in the 1960s and 1970s, Hartlepool was recognised as a significant black spot (Morris, 1987). In the mid-1980s the unemployment level stood at 22.3 per cent. Yet, Hartlepool's general promotional literature concentrates on leisure, life style and community issues, and focuses especially – under the banner headline 'Hartlepool Renaissance' – on the Marina scheme: 'A Major Centre for Leisure, Living and Tourism'.

> The Hartlepool Renaissance is now under way. It consists of a massive waterfront redevelopment that will take seven years to complete. The result will be a 400 berth marina, 1500 houses and flats, plus specialised shops, restaurants, bars, a hotel, a business park and a Maritime Heritage Centre.

The well-produced general promotional booklet issued by the Director of Economic Development contains 42 photographs, not one of which is of an industrial site. There

Figure 6.3 Hartlepool uses images of life-style, leisure and recreation as the main promotional tool for its 'renaissance'.

is a clear thrust to stress the attractions of the locality and region in terms of quality of life. Given Hartlepool's traditional image this is entirely understandable, but the fragility of this type of place reconstruction is evidenced by the events of spring 1992 when a casually-written but damning attack on Hartlepool and its people's work ethic appeared in the *Wall Street Journal*. Once having embarked on the image reconstruction route such a challenge could not be ignored, whether it was right or wrong, and the Borough Council had no option but to take out an expensive quarter-page advertisement in that newspaper on 17 March 1992 under the heading 'Hartlepool – The positive place to relocate your business', with a series of rebuttals of the original article. Despite that, it was recognised locally that foreign business confidence in Hartlepool was likely to be adversely affected (Hartlepool Borough Council, 1992). It appears then that, even if an expensive and successful campaign is launched to change the image of a particular locality, that place can remain, ironically, at the mercy and perhaps at the whim of the image communicators.

It is clear from the images communicated in much of the promotional literature that many industrial towns seek to represent themselves as attractive to technologically advanced industry. Stockton-on-Tees, for example, contends that:

> As industry progresses, the innovation continues. The world's first biodegradable plastic was invented in the Borough, and hi-tech centres like the Belasis Hall Technology Park lead Stockton into the next century.

A significant component of this strategy is the liberal use of post-modern architecture in the brochures, either in the form of photographs or of artist's impressions. There is, of course, a considerable literature on post-modernism but there is widespread agreement amongst critics that an essential feature of post-modernism is the way it represents a 'culture of the image' (Jameson, 1984). Post-modern architecture, whether it be in factories, offices or housing, offers considerable attractions for place promotion, representing, as it does, vigour, flexibility and, above all else, newness.

The most obvious examples of industrial towns marketing themselves as centres of high technology are in the new towns of post-war Britain. Even in the late 1960s, long before terms such as 'Silicon Glen' had become current, the Scottish new town of Livingston was selling itself as a location for 'science based industries', although at that time using modernist rather than post-modern architecture as an important symbol (see Livingston Development Corporation, 1971). Other places advertise their hi-tech expertise and opportunities more directly. For example, Swindon's main economic development brochure is 'bullish' in the extreme: 'As you'd expect from a town leading the way in technology, Swindon benefits from the availability of some of the most sophisticated telecommunication services'. It then proceeds with a quite detailed account of the digital telephone exchange, the Integrated Services Digital Network and draws attention to the fact that many sites enjoy access to the Kilostream and Megastream digital private circuits.

Perhaps the most interesting high technology development is Crewe's eco-business park where 87 acres have been developed in liaison with the Royal Society for Nature Conservation who appraised the ecological features of the site and made suggestions for its future management. The aim is to demonstrate that a high-tech site can be developed in harmony with wildlife and its natural habitat in deliberate contrast to the 'disappointing business parks of the high-density pagodas and clipped lawns variety . . . along the M4 corridor' (Griffiths, 1990). In the case of Crewe, there is far more than a mere attempt to present a green image; there is also an authentic strategy to create such an identity. The ratio of buildings to total site area is only 25 per cent, which may be perceived as unacceptably low by many developers, but it has generally won critical acclamation. 'Perceptions of Crewe as a dull railway town were dispelled by the strong environmental bias of the business park', noted the *Daily Telegraph* (28 November

1990) and the first three firms, all technologically based, singled out the environment as the main reason for locating there.

In some ways, the trajectory of promotion chosen by a number of industrial towns, which is based on their manufacturing and commercial heritage, is quite the opposite in character (Alfrey and Putnam, 1992). While there are obvious dangers in the 'museumisation' of places, there is growing evidence that a number of towns have been able to combine the promotion of heritage and the development of contemporary economic activities. 'The Borough of Calderdale has set the pace in Britain for showing what can be achieved when conservation is not simply treated as an add-on, but is fully integrated with economic planning' (Alfrey and Putnam, 1992:149). The principal element in this strategy has been the 'Fair Shares/Inheritance' programme running since 1985 (Figure 6.4). This is based on the recommendations of the Civic Trust which identified the area's stock of 18th- and 19th-century buildings as a major resource for promoting new economic activity. Their report recognised the benefits brought by the restoration of the historic Piece Hall. Renovation and re-use of this building stock is a key concern, along with a marketing strategy that seeks to improve the image of the area as well as establishing its 'historic worth'. Since 1985 the project has attracted direct total investment of £3.5 million for a capital outlay of £0.25 million (Patten *et al.*, 1989).

Though structural antecedents may differ and patterns of change vary, many urban authorities have adopted remarkably similar strategies. This is especially the case with the promotion of tourism and the attraction of visitors; for a limited number of former industrial towns, probably the most successful direction of change. Martin and Mason (1988) have described the usual approach which borrowed heavily from major redevelopment programmes in Baltimore and Boston. Ideally and typically, there are three principal components to the package:

- the development of a major new physical facility (concert hall or museum, for example) in order to provide a focal point and catalyst for developers, media coverage and locals and tourists alike;
- the upgrading of existing facilities and buildings, usually highlighting any heritage elements, and the associated production of systematic and comprehensive thematic interpretation for publicity and marketing; and
- the projection of the urban centre concerned as the ideal starting point for visiting and exploring surrounding geographical areas.

The strategy can be seen, although not always in its full-blown form, throughout the UK – for example, in Bradford, Bristol, Cardiff, Glasgow, Hull, Liverpool, London, Manchester, South Shields, Stoke-on-Trent, Swansea and Wigan. The list might also include Cheltenham, Lancaster and the Isle of Thanet towns in Kent, whose efforts to reconstruct ailing economies provide still further evidence of the extent of the strategy's spread (Cooke *et al.*, 1989).

The celebrated early pioneer was Bradford. The city, which has become a model for marketing the industrial town and for demonstrating the contribution of tourism to the reconstruction of struggling local economies, is now a market leader in short-stay and weekend-breaks, attracts some 6 million domestic and overseas visitors annually and has succeeded in injecting £56 million each year into the local economy as a result

Figure 6.4 Calderdale strongly emphasises industrial heritage imagery, but also features reconstruction and pictorial messages about leisure and lifestyle.

of its efforts to promote tourism. Its success has been recognised by the award of prestigious honours including the Sir Mark Henig Award for tourism development (1983), the Sir Mark Henig Award for Flavours of Asia (1987), an RIBA Award for the Alhambra Theatre, and Museum of the Year Awards for the National Museum of Photography and for the Colour Museum. A little over ten years ago, all this would have been inconceivable.

The origins of Bradford's enterprise are to be found in the economic recession of the late 1970s. Its traditional industries, especially textiles and engineering, had shed some 63,000 jobs. Unemployment rose to 16 per cent. In addition to these economic difficulties, the city's image was only serving to compound the problems:

> To make matters worse, Bradford was losing out on much needed investment to other West Yorkshire towns and cities, chiefly because of its poor image. Investors were reluctant to commit money to what they believed was a grimy, backward, industrial area. Meanwhile, Bradford was making headlines on a daily basis as television documentaries reported high levels of social deprivation and the Yorkshire Ripper stalked the streets. (City of Bradford Metropolitan Council Economic Development Unit, undated)

Accordingly, the decision was taken in 1979 to create an Economic Development Unit (EDU), the first in the UK. Its tasks were to enable the generation of employment by encouraging the expansion of existing companies and by attracting new business. Of necessity, the EDU was charged with improving the city's image. Analysis of strengths and opportunities quickly identified potential selling points, including the home of the Brontë sisters at Haworth, Titus Salt's model village at Saltaire and proximity to the Yorkshire Dales, as well as a good stock of hotel accommodation, under-utilised at weekends. The strategy then began to take shape with the launch of the first two themed short break packages – 'In the Footsteps of the Brontës' and 'Industrial Heritage'. Sceptics and cynics mocked:

> The announcement that Bradford was entering the holiday market was for both press and public alike, the best joke of 1980. The idea that a northern, industrial area, particularly one with a 'dark, satanic mills' image, could successfully market itself as a visitor destination, attracted international comment. (City of Bradford Metropolitan Council Economic Development Unit, undated)

Nevertheless, the strategy paid dividends. Two thousand holidays were bought, national and international media focused on the city, and Bradford was firmly established as a visitor destination in the minds of the travel industry. Awards followed and by 1984 over 30,000 visitors were holidaying in the area. New elements were successfully developed, including mill-shopping, art-lovers' Bradford, television themes and the popular Flavours of Asia package. By the end of the 1980s, Bradford had succeeded in improving its image to such an extent that, in a survey of the country's 38 biggest cities, it came out sixth on the quality-of-life indicator, 21 places above its West Yorkshire neighbour and rival, Leeds (City of Bradford Metropolitan Council Economic Development Unit, undated).

Marketing the industrial town: a critique

Despite the success of Bradford, a number of other towns have had less fortunate experiences in attempting to promote themselves. Before turning to a critique of the marketing of industrial towns, though, it is first necessary to recognise that the concept of marketing as a benign or neutral activity is itself questionable. Marketing is inherently competitive. While there may be new and untapped markets to open up, the very survival of the producer firm or organisation depends on promoting its product, normally at the expense of the competition.

One crucial issue, then, is that of marketing effectiveness. It must be recognised that there is a widespread consensus among students of marketing that the 1970s saw considerable over-optimism concerning the effectiveness of advertising (Beaumont *et al.*, 1989). In one of the few studies of effectiveness of place promotion, Burgess and Wood (1988) report that the advertising campaign in London's Docklands directly stimulated some companies to seek locations there but, significantly, was especially important in boosting the confidence of small investors. The respondents also noted the significance of rate relief, suitable premises and proximity to contacts as important reasons for moving into Docklands. However, it would be interesting to know whether those same companies retain their former optimism nearly a decade after the advertising campaign. Perhaps more importantly, as Brownill (Chapter 8) makes clear, the Docklands were and are a special case, being located in London, possessing a high political profile, and with a well-endowed budget.

More typical authorities, without these advantages, view matters in sceptical terms; for example, many promotional officers and economic development officers at other authorities contacted by our survey commented that: 'We do it because everyone else does it'. In the specific context of local economic development, several officers commented, off the record, that they were not really aware of any significant direct gain to their authority from its promotional activity in the recent past. An officer in an authority where over twenty companies had moved in during the last seven or eight years was quite sure that none had been influenced by promotional material. Empirical research points to a similar conclusion. A survey of Japanese inward investment in the UK, for instance, stressed factors such as reliability and quality of suppliers, availability of skilled labour, good labour relations, communications with other countries, and accessibility to markets as the most important factors in choosing a site (Anon., 1986:4). In other words, they emphasised factors which relate to the identity of places rather than their image. The fact is that when significant inward investors are interested in moving to a particular place, the norm is for a specific response to be made or special package prepared – activity which is scarcely place marketing at all. It may be argued that it was the general place promotion material which excited interest in the locality in the first place, but that hypothesis remains unproven.

Some may argue that the interpretation of place marketing implied here is too narrow:

> If city marketing is no more than the competitive hunting of the small number of possible mobile investors by a large number of increasingly desperate local authorities, with a zero sum result for the region or country as a whole, then disillusionment will quickly follow as diminished returns to promotional effort ensue. A much wider view of the market and the relationship of the city to it must be taken (Ashworth and Voogd, 1988).

However, in taking this wider view of marketing, a set of new problems presents itself. Unlike many or most marketed items, a town is not and never can be a homogenous product. Towns are bundles of different communities, environments, services and facilities, yet it has been argued that 'it makes no difference . . . that only a selected portion of the town, a particular set of facilities and services, is being purchased'

(Ashworth and Voogd, 1990:7). To that point, it can be said that it might make no difference to the purchaser but precisely what it is being sold as certainly makes a difference to the place. As we have seen, particularly in the promotion of industrial towns, the strategy is to attempt to present a uniform image and identity, but image is not the same as identity and, in the case of a town, the two are likely to be in conflict with each other. Problems therefore result from the fact that 'towns are both the product and the container of an assemblage of products' (Ashworth and Voogd, 1990:7). For example, we can then ask what is it then that is being marketed?

Inevitably, in a phenomenon as complex and multi-faceted as an urban environment there will be elements of the 'product' which are in tension, if not in outright conflict, such as social welfare issues versus free market economic criteria. Moreover, unlike most other commodities which are marketed, those doing the marketing have considerably less direct control over the assemblage of products of which the totality of the town is constituted. There is even a strong probability that the representatives of the different 'products' of which the town is composed may pull in different directions. This is spectacularly demonstrated in North Shields on Tyneside where the Royal Quays development, the second largest property investment in the country, lies less than a hundred yards from the Meadowell estate, one of the most deprived estates in the UK and the scene of major riots in September 1991.

Related to this issue is the question of who are the targets for promotional and marketing activity. In the case of local authority place promotion, there are the two broad sets of intended recipient noted earlier, inward investors and the local residents. In marketing terms, attempting to reach these two audiences simultaneously may be problematic because they may be fundamentally incompatible, yet a number of authorities appear to wish to face several directions at once, e.g. Chesterfield. Such a bi-polar promotional strategy cannot be seriously sustained for long. The difference between image and identity once again lies at the heart of this dichotomy. For local people the identity of a place may be defined and symbolised largely in terms of the past but such representation may be bad news in marketing terms for those anxious to attract inward investors. On Tyneside or Teesside, the Tyne Bridge or the Transporter Bridge may be entirely acceptable and meaningful symbols of identity to local residents; to potential inward investors they are more likely to represent an image of an outdated industrial past. That such conflicts amount to much more than small contradictions over local representations of place is witnessed by the furore over the designation and subsequent representation of Glasgow as 'European City of Culture' in 1990 (Boyle and Hughes, 1991).

A further difference between specific places and other marketed commodities is that, for the latter, the vast majority are repetitive purchases. Even expensive items such as motor vehicles have a relatively frequent turnover. However, a place simply cannot be equated with commodities in this way unless the utilisation of that place is essentially and fundamentally a transient one. Thus, arguably, place marketing may be applicable to places as tourist destinations (Goodall and Ashworth, 1988; Ashworth and Goodall, 1990), as the case of Bradford so spectacularly demonstrates, but for most other considerations marketing approaches are appearing in an environment where their contribution may be very limited. For the inward investor, however 'footloose', the choice of a particular location is a major commitment; the 'brand' or 'product' is unlikely to be changed next week or even next year. For a wide variety of reasons there may be a degree of inertia. Furthermore, it is clear that choice of location is not an exact science and that, in reality, many locations differ only marginally and are highly substitutable. While it may be tempting to assume that this is precisely where place promotion plays its crucial role in creating preference for one place over another, the reality of the process points to another conclusion.

It is clear from the responses of most economic development officers to our survey that for most significant inward investors with an interest in selecting a location a specific package will be produced. As Hughes (1992) has noted: 'The commodification of places, involved when marketing precepts are applied . . . shifts the focus from simply "selling places" to the production of what will sell'. This process says much about the nature of place promotion – if special packages are being produced for different clients interested in the same place then we can fairly ask what is happening to 'place' during this process? While that place continues to have an objective, tangible physical identity, it is being represented as something potentially quite different to different clients in image terms. Not only is there likely to be a clear divergence between identity and image, there is also considerable potential for divergence between different kinds of image.

Under such circumstances the concept of place as an identifiable and authentic phenomenon becomes increasingly meaningless. What is really being promoted is a kind of placelessness, in the sense that claims made for a specific place may bear only a limited relation to reality or be equally applicable to many other places (Figure 6.5).

Figure 6.5 An interesting variation on the theme of placelessness in the shape of this cheerful item of place promotion from Alloa in Scotland. However, the fact that the product was made in Italy and imported by the Cornish Match Co., located in Dorset, may give rise to speculation about the authenticity of place and questions of precisely where and what is being promoted.

This is especially likely in the context of the industrial town because in many cases what is really being promoted is not the actual place so much as the various inducements found there. This is quite different from most other marketable commodities but, more fundamentally, it suggests that, given the richness, complexity and immense range of phenomena within any particular place, it is oversimplistic to assume that its identity can be promoted within the confines of a marketing strategy. Only few such images may be so promoted and these may be but a pale and distorted reflection of reality. Such images tell us more about the promotion industry and their clients than about place itself.

Notes

1. However, the latter are largely discounted in the following analysis due to the special role that the Scottish Development Agency plays in the promotion of economic activity north of the border. In addition, a significant number of Scottish local authorities – mainly the smaller ones – produce very little promotional material aimed at industry and commerce. The 148 responses from the English local authorities do compare favourably with the 158 obtained by Burgess (1982:2) in 1977 'requesting the information that would normally be sent in response to a commercial enquiry' (although Burgess only reported results from 148 named local authorities in her Table 1).
2. Many, for example, now contain industrial and commercial information in a Business Directory section.
3. Scottish examples are included in the sample on this occasion, plus some responses from local authorities which did not include a full promotions package but whose letterheads contained logos.

References

Agnew, J. (1987) *Place and Politics*, London: Allen & Unwin.

Alfrey, J. and Putnam, T. (1992) *The Industrial Heritage*, London: Routledge.

Anon. (1986) 'Japanese direct investment in the United Kingdom, 1986–1987', *The Economic Development Briefing*, 10(1).

Ashworth, G.J and Goodall, B., eds. (1990) *Marketing Tourism Places*, London: Routledge.

Ashworth, G.J. and Voogd, H. (1988) 'Marketing the City', *Town Planning Review*, 59, 65–79.

Ashworth, G.J and Voogd, H. (1990) *Selling the City*, London: Belhaven Press.

Baglee, C. (1979) *The North-East Coast Exhibition of Industry, Science and Art*, Newcastle upon Tyne: Graham.

Bassett, K., Boddy, M., Harloe, M. and Lovering, J. (1989) 'Living in the fast lane: economic and social change in Swindon', in P. Cooke, ed., *Localities: The changing face of urban Britain*, London: Unwin Hyman, 45–85.

Beaumont, C.D., Geary, K., Halliburton, C., Clifford, D., and Rivers, R. (1989) 'Advertising assessment – myth or reality?', *Environment and Planning A*, 21, 629–41.

Bonsall, M. (1988) 'Local government initiatives in urban regeneration 1906-1932: the story of Derby's borough development committee', *Planning History*, 10, 7–11.

Boyle, M. and Hughes, G. (1991) 'The politics of the representation of the "real": discourses from the Left on Glasgow's role as European City of Culture, 1990', *Area*, 23, 217–28.

Briggs, A. (1968) *Victorian Cities*, Harmondsworth: Pelican.

Buckley, P.J. and Witt, S.F. (1985) 'Tourism in difficult areas: case studies of Bradford, Bristol, Glasgow and Hamm', *Tourism Management*, 6, 205–13.

Buckley, P.J. and Witt, S.F. (1989) 'Tourism in difficult areas: case studies of Calderdale, Leeds, Manchester and Scunthorpe', *Tourism Management*, 10, 138–52.

Burgess, J.A. (1982) 'Selling places: environmental images for the executive', *Regional Studies*, 16, 1–17.

Burgess, J.A. (1990) 'The production and consumption of environmental meanings in the mass media: a research agenda for the 1990s', *Transactions of the Institute of British Geographers*, 15, 139–61.

Burgess, J.A. and Wood, P. (1988) 'Decoding Docklands: place advertising and decision-making strategies of the small firm', in J. Eyles and D.M. Smith, eds., *Qualitative Methods in Human Geography*, Cambridge: Polity Press, 94–117.

Champion, A.G. and Townsend, A.R. (1990) *Contemporary Britain: a geographical perspective*, London: Edward Arnold.

City of Bradford Metropolitan Council Economic Development Unit, (undated) *Developing Bradford's Tourism Industry*, Bradford: City of Bradford Metropolitan Council Economic Development Unit.

Clarke, A. (1986) 'Local authority planners or frustrated tourism marketeers', *The Planner*, 72, 23–6.

Coleman, D.C. (1973) *The Idea of the Town in the Nineteenth Century*, London: Routledge and Kegan Paul.

Cooke, P. ed. (1989) *Localities: the changing face of urban Britain*, London: Unwin Hyman.

Corfield, P.J. and Kelly, S. (1984) 'Giving directions to the town: the early town directories', *Urban History Yearbook 1984*, Leicester: Leicester University Press, 22–35.

Cox, H. (1968) 'The restoration of a sense of place', *Ekistics*, 25, 422–4.

Falk, N. (1985) 'Our industrial heritage – a resource for the future?', *The Planner*, 71, 13–16.

Fedorcio, D., Heaton, P. and Madden, K. (1991) *Public Relations for Local Government*, Harlow: Longman.

Garrahan, P. (1986) 'Nissan in the North-East of England', *Capital and Class*, 27, 5–13.

Gold, J.R. (1974) *Communicating Images of the Environment*, Occasional Paper 29, Centre for Urban and Regional Studies, University of Birmingham.

Goodall, B. and Ashworth, G.J., eds. (1988) *Marketing in the Tourism Industry*, London: Croom Helm.

Griffiths, D. (1990) 'Case study – "Green" pastures for Crewe', *Estates Gazette*, 9026, July, 138.

Hartlepool Borough Council (1992) *Business Update*, 2.

Hughes, G. (1992) 'Tourism and the geographical imagination', *Leisure Studies*, 11, 31–42.

Jameson, F. (1984) 'Postmodernism, or the cultural logic of late capitalism', *New Left Review*, 146, 53 92.

Jeffrey, D. (1990) 'Monitoring the growth of tourism related employment at the local level: the application of a Census based non-survey method in Yorkshire and Humberside, 1981–1987', *Planning Outlook*, 33, 108–17.

Karski, A. (1990) 'Urban tourism – a key to urban regeneration', *The Planner*, 76, 15–17.

Law, C.M. (1991) 'Tourism and urban revitalization', *East Midland Geographer*, 14, 49–60.

Law, C.M. (1992) 'Urban tourism and its contribution to economic regeneration', *Urban Studies*, 29, 599–618.

Livingston Development Corporation (1971) *Livingston – the Kirkton Campus. For Science Based Industries*, Livingston: Livingston Development Corporation.

Martin, B. and Mason, S. (1988) 'Current trends in leisure', *Leisure Studies*, 7, 75–80.

Mills, C.A. (1988) ' "Life on the upslope": the postmodern landscape of gentrification', *Society and Space*, 6, 169–89.

Mills, L. and Young, K. (1986) 'Local authorities and economic development: a preliminary analysis', in V. Hausner ed., *Critical Issues in Urban Economic Development*, Vol. 1, Oxford, Clarendon Press, 89–144.

Morris, L. (1987) 'Local social polarization: a case study of Hartlepool', *International Journal of Urban and Regional Research*, 11, 331–50.

Mumford, L. (1966) *The City in History*, Harmondsworth: Pelican.

Parson, W. and Bradshaw, T., eds. (1818) *Staffordshire General and Commercial Directory for 1818*, Stoke on Trent.

Patten, R.H., Whelan, J., Dixon, M. (1989) 'Some economic consequences of heritage conservation: the case of Calderdale', in Council of Europe, *Heritage and Successful Town Regeneration: Report of the Halifax Colloquy*, Strasbourg: Council of Europe.

Relph, E. (1976) *Place and Placelessness*, London: Pion.

Robinson, F. and Sadler, D. (1984a) 'Return to Consett', Special Report for BBC North-East.

Robinson, F. and Sadler, D. (1984b) *Consett after the Closure*, Occasional Publications, (New Series) 19, Dept of Geography, University of Durham.

Robinson, M. and Hind, D. (1992) 'Quality North – open to view: a case study in developing industry tourism', unpublished paper presented to Tourism in Europe Conference, Newcastle-upon-Tyne Polytechnic.

Shaw, D. (1908) *The River Tyne: its advantages and possibilities, Newcastle upon Tyne*, Newcastle: Newcastle and Gateshead Chamber of Commerce.

Speakman, L. and Bramwell, B. (1992) *Sheffield Works: an evaluation of a factory tourism scheme*, Occasional Paper 1, Centre for Travel and Tourism, Sheffield City Polytechnic.

Steven-Anian, T. (1988) 'Work watching – the growth of industry tourism', *Leisure Management*, 8(12), 40–43.

Tyne Improvement Commission and North-Eastern Railway Company (1905), *The Tyne as an Industrial Centre*, Newcastle-upon-Tyne.

Vickery, A.J. (1988) 'Town histories and Victorian Plaudits', *Urban History Yearbook 1988*, Leicester: Leicester University Press, 58–64.

Ward, S.V. (1985) 'British Boosterism: An area of interest for planning historians, 1899–1940', *Planning History Bulletin*, 7, 30–38.

Ward, S.V. (1990) 'Local industrial promotion and development policies', *Local Economy*, 5, 100–18.

Watson, S. (1991) 'Gilding the smokestacks: the new symbolic representations of deindustrialised regions', *Society and Space*, 9, 59–70.

7 City make-overs: marketing the post-industrial city

BRIAVEL HOLCOMB

One of the more entertaining diversions while standing in the supermarket check-out queue is to peruse women's magazines for 'make-overs.' Before her cosmetic transformation the woman's skin is blotchy and wrinkled, her hair limp and drab, her eyes tired and careworn. She is usually overweight. After her make-over, she is a portrait of health, vitality and happiness. Her clear skin, sparkling eyes, and bouncy, shining hair make her almost unrecognisable from Ms Before. While she still has that crooked tooth and a little too much chin, she exudes a new confidence. Her image is transformed. At the beauty salons where such metamorphoses are achieved, a final service is sometimes available – full colour portraits of the new you. These permanent representations of the ephemeral conversion can serve as promotional material for potential employers or mates. Perhaps the transformation of the surface induces change within.

Applying this analogy of cosmetic 'make-overs' to cities is far from perfect but serves to introduce some themes of this chapter, which explores the ways in which the transformation of traditional manufacturing cities in North America into 'post-industrial' service centres has necessitated a remaking of the built environment and a re-imaging of the city. I argue that there is a certain tautology between image and reality, that the city is remade to fit a promotable image while the promotional image reflects a highly selective reality. Competition between places and the growth of place marketing has led to many 'cosmetic' changes. Parts of cities are cleansed and beautified and their images used in promotional brochures and press releases. Yet just as the made-over woman returns to her drab, exhausting life, so life for most residents of remade and re-imaged cities remains unchanged.

A second theme of this chapter concerns the paradox of parity marketing of North American cities. As discussed later, many cities today have major marketing campaigns to attract and retain businesses, investments, consumers, tourists and new residents. Considerable effort and resources are put into the creation and projection of urban images reflecting vibrant, growing places with accessible locations, reconstructed downtowns, and sunny business climates. However, an examination of these marketing materials reveals striking similarities in the images projected. Cities which are, in reality, distinctly different, become homogenised and virtually indistinguishable in their images. This, in turn, creates the problem of parity marketing. If your 'product' is essentially the same as that of your competitors (as are those of detergent or cornflake manufacturers) the challenge is to create distinctiveness and a separate but highly recognisable identity for your product. So cities claim both generic 'good business' qualities and distinctive, 'unique' assets (Sack, 1988; Watson, 1991).

This paradox is reflected in the built environment. Most redeveloped cities acquire several of the standard accoutrements of late-20th century revitalisation – a pedestrian mall, a Portman mega-hotel convention centre, a Rouse festival retailing fair, Philip Johnson or I.M. Pei post-modern office blocks, and a sprinkling of Victoriana, Art Nouveau or Moderne restored containers of culture. This standard repertoire underscores the aesthetic cloning of American downtowns. The parts of many US cities which have been redeveloped in the last two decades present the visitor with a remarkable uniformity of appearance and feeling (Frieden and Sagalyn, 1990). Conversely, cities strive to create landmarks and symbols which will put them on the nation's cognitive map. It has been 15 years since Melbourne, Australia offered a prize of 100,000 US dollars to the winning design of a symbol for the city which would have an equivalent recognition as Sydney's Opera House and so establish a place for the city in the international psyche (a project which has apparently been unsuccessful!). A recent advertisement for a satellite paging system features a composite urbanscape with the symbols of various cities (New York's World Trade Centre, St. Louis's Arch, Seattle's Space Needle, San Francisco's Transamerica pyramid, and Chicago's Sears Tower). The slogan reads 'Only Skypager can reach you here.' While some cities adopt symbolic icons, such as New York's Big Apple, Cleveland's Plum, Glasgow's Mr Happy or Portland's Rose, others seek to build their marketing symbols into their physical landscape. Such 'superstar architecture' or 'cover-shot buildings' (Knox, 1993) are often corporate cathedrals, simultaneously imaging the corporation and the city.

This marketing marriage was perhaps never better exemplified then in the 1986 'pop up' ad for Transamerica in Time magazine. The four-page, three-million-dollar advertisement started with a plain, black page on which was written: 'Would the most innovative insurance company in America please stand up.' Flipping the page, readers found the two-page pop up spread of San Francisco's skyline with the Golden Gate bridge, various anonymous buildings, and centrally dominant, the trophy Transamerica building. 'The Power of the Pyramid is working for you', and, presumably, for San Francisco. The advertisement, which was printed and assembled by hand in Colombia and Mexico took 560 workers a total of 17 weeks to complete the 5 million copies, but was judged cost-effective and made marketing history. So, as in parity marketing, as cities become more alike marketeers strive to create distinctive images for their 'products'.

Urban economic developers are increasingly adopting the marketing ideology which distinguishes selling (trying to get the consumer to buy what you have), from marketing (trying to have what the consumer wants). 'Selling focuses on the needs of the seller, marketing on the needs of the buyer' (Schudson, 1984:29). However, urban marketeers may be offering something consumers are not aware that they want, so part of the process, as in advertising perfume or racing cars, is to both stimulate want and to commodify the city. Wernick (1991:35) comments on the invasive and pervasive role of marketing in contemporary life:

> The consumerist address imprisons the subjectivity it projects in a totally commodi-
> fied ontology. Being is reduced as having, desire to lack. No needs or desires are
> speakable without a commodity to satisfy them: no commodity without at least an
> imagined place for it in our affections.

So, I argue here, cities have entered the realm of this commodified culture and are being
produced as commodities to be marketed rather than as vessels of society. As Wernick
(1991:15) illustrated by using the example of Wedgwood china, when crafts gave way
to industrialised mass production, the 'goods left the factory gate and were already
imaged to give them sales appeal . . . Rather than produce, then sell, promotional
requirements were taken account of before production ever began'. Today, frequently,
city homes are sold and office space leased even prior to construction. The product is
sold through advertising imagery before it is produced in reality. Cities are rebuilt to
reflect their marketing imagery.

The post-industrial city

The dramatic economic restructuring of North American cities in the post-
World-War-II period has been well documented (e.g. Holcomb and Beauregard, 1981;
Fainstein et al., 1983; Gale, 1984; Porter and Sweet, 1984; Teaford, 1990). Most cities
experienced the suburbanisation of retailing and middle class residents, the loss of
manufacturing and associated jobs, a growth in the minority and low income
population groups, and fiscal crises as tax revenues declined while the demand for city
services grew. These trends were particularly evident in the old industrial cities of the
north and were exacerbated by the flight of industry to the 'sunbelt'. The causes of
these changes were various but include the search for cheaper (non-unionised) labour,
lower taxes, less regulation (of environmental and workplace standards), and cheaper
and more reliable energy supplies (*see also* Chapter 4). Explanations also include the
deterioration of urban services (especially public education), increased congestion and
crime, and a reduction in the quality of urban life as disinvestment proceeded.

Government policies facilitated this disinvestment and out-migration both by
federally subsidising home mortgage insurance (which enabled millions of people to
buy their suburban dream house) and by constructing Interstate Freeways which
speeded commuter accessibility to the outer suburbs while demolishing inner city
neighbourhoods. Technological innovations were contributing causes.
Mechanisation and automation reduced labour requirements while the horizontal
production line increased ground space needs. Containerisation and the improvement
of road transportation reduced the locational advantages of ports and railway
centres. Advances in telecommunications and computerisation reduced the
advantages of central locations. While the relative importance of these explanations is
debated, and is probably different for each city, the decline of industrial cities was
widespread.

The 'revival' of these cities, which began in the 1970s, has been both patchy and
sporadic, but virtually all have pockets of redevelopment and gentrification. Just as the
causes of urban decline are numerous, so too are the explanations for revitalisation.
The energy crisis brought on by oil embargoes increased the cost of living in, and

commuting from, a suburban single family home. The entry of more women into the workforce, decreasing family size and growing numbers of two career couples made centrally located, small housing units more attractive and the quality of schools less significant in residential location decision making. High home mortgage rates and recession made deteriorated housing in which sweat equity could be invested attractive to some buyers. The rent gap made parts of cities ripe for reinvestment.

The turnaround in the fortunes of cities was much heralded by the media and the academy alike. Headlines and books proclaimed an urban rebirth and a return to the city. In reality, the revival was limited in most cases to relatively small sections of the central business district and adjacent residential neighbourhoods, while large sections of the remainder of the city continued to suffer disinvestment. The 1980s have seen a withdrawal of Federal government support for urban needs ranging from housing to welfare, and from redevelopment to public transportation. During the twelve years of Republican administration, funding from such programmes as Urban Development Action Grants (which had leveraged significant new investment in some cities) ended and the main Republican urban proposal, Enterprise Zones, has not been enacted. With the withdrawal of federal support for cities, urban governments increasingly turned to the private sector to effect change. Numerous cities have established public–private partnerships to plan and implement redevelopment.

Typically, these non-profit organisations are self-appointed, rather than elected, and include business and institutional leaders as well as government officials. Their central tasks are to improve the business climate, the quality of life, and, critically, the image of the city. To regain the momentum of revitalisation, the city must be marketed to potential investors, residents, retirees, employers and tourists. Perhaps unfortunately, the supply of these 'place consumers' is limited, while the 'supply' of cities remains quite stable. Unlike product marketing, which can stimulate increased consumption for mineral water or cigarettes for many brands, cities must compete with each other for their 'market share' of jobs and investments. As capital becomes increasingly mobile, this competition heats up. Cities are increasingly investing public monies and raising private funds to fight these 'place wars' (Kotler *et al*, 1993). While once the main role of planners was to regulate development, now it is to promote it. Planners become 'urban sales agents' (Fainstein, 1991:24) who negotiate deals with private sector developers in order to stimulate growth. Local government has become entrepreneurial using the methods of business (Harvey, 1989). Lake (1992) argues that 'public' planning increasingly involves direct participation with private capital in economic development ventures and that city agencies are behaving like private real estate developers. Not surprisingly, then, the 'business' of urban development increasingly uses the strategies and tactics of the profit making sector.

The growth industry of place marketing

Place marketing is not new, but civic boosterism has evolved from the purview of local businesses, newspapers and politicians into a multi-billion-dollar industry. Early explorers and settlers of the continent were often hyperbolic in their praise of its economic potential. In his analysis of this early promotional literature (the 'literature of persuasion'), Jones (1946:153) noted that:

> Perhaps the commonest element in the promotion literature is the allure of
> economic plenitude. The sober prose of the discoverer becomes as gorgeous as the
> verse of Spenser in enumerating the endless commodities of the New World, and the
> catalogues of the vegetable, animal and mineral kingdoms are as encyclopedic as
> the Polyolbion.

As the continent was settled in the 18th and 19th centuries, many towns and cities
boasted of having the cleanest water, the most elegant residences, the most vigorous
businessmen (and they were mostly men), the most enterprising entrepreneurs, the
healthiest climate and the best location. Boorstin (1965), Glaab (1967) and others
argue that the settlement pattern of much of the continent is as much the consequence
of boosterism as of 'natural' locational advantages. Although on the East coast a
natural port or a fall-line location for water power often were assets explaining the
growth of cities, in the South and West an enterprising businessman, an enthusiastic
editor or an influential politician were often more critical advantages:

> In upstart cities the loyalties of people were in inverse ratio to the antiquity of their
> communities, even to the point of absurdity . . . Promise, not achievement,
> commanded loyalty and stirred the booster spirit' (Boorstin, 1965:122).

Local elites from various sectors of the community joined forces in the competition
between places since success, as Logan and Molotch (1987) recognised, brought wealth
to those leaders of the booster movement who invested in land and property which
increased in value with growth.

I have discussed the historical development of the place marketing industry in more
detail elsewhere (Holcomb, 1990), but a brief summary is helpful here. In the late-19th
and early-20th centuries cities and towns began to institutionalise their promotional
activities by such strategies as establishing Chambers of Commerce, commercial and
industrial associations, holding trade shows and industrial expositions, and placing
advertising in newspapers and magazines.

An early review of the methods of promotion entitled 'The Era of Civic Advertising
and the Chamber of Commerce' (Weir, 1910) clearly shows that smokestack chasing
and the contemporary paraphernalia of economic development are not new. Press
releases, telegrams of invitation to site factories, advertising buttons and promotional
magazines were standard fare. Weir quotes a Municipal Journal editorial: 'It has
become a more or less universal opinion in most sections of the country that any city
which does not make some active effort at direct advertising is dead, and sure to fall
behind the times'. He was enthusiastic about the benefits which promotion can bring for
citizens. He claimed that civic advertising: 'quickens municipal efficiency, eliminates
political rottenness and broadens individual patriotism: for a city of dirty streets or
dirty sewers or dirty politicians can profit little by presenting a glittering circular of its
advantages to the prospective resident or investor' (Weir, 1910:675). Weir thus
assumed that the image projected in place advertising must reflect reality, or at least that
reality will change to fit the image, an argument posited earlier in this chapter.

Glaab (1967) described shifts in the emphasis and strategy of place promotion in the
20th century. Increasingly more elaborate promotional and developmental
organisations were formed to augment Chambers of Commerce and in the 1930s local
government took over the management of development programmes. The repertoire

of inducements to potential investors was widened to include a variety of tax concessions, industrial parks, loan programmes and other lures. In the 1950s numerous cities established local development corporations.

The contemporary place marketing industry, while rooted in a long tradition, is distinguished both quantitatively and qualitatively from the past. It has become a 'professionalised' big business. While traditionally the job of marketing a city was the province of local businesses and governments, today it is increasingly done by advertising agencies and public relations firms under contract to the city. As Guskind wrote, Madison Avenue is selling Main Street. He estimated that in the USA 'somewhere between 3–6 billion dollars was spent in 1986 to sell cities and states' (Guskind, 1987:4). Haider (1992) noted that estimates on the amount places spend on marketing are unreliable. Using data from the *Directory of Incentives for Business Investment and Development in the United States* and other sources, he estimated that states alone spend 20 billion dollars a year on economic development programmes, although only a portion of that is spent on marketing. He cites an 'expert' estimate that 7500 places in the United States now publicly advertise and notes that state government spending on tourism exceeds 200 million dollars in the nation's second largest service industry and employer. 'An estimated 255 cities in the United States and abroad spend $250 million annually for destination marketing and advertising in the highly competitive convention business' (Haider, 1992:130). Added to this public sector marketing expenditure are the considerable funds spent by place-dependent businesses, such as utilities, certain financial institutions and local newspapers. As Cox and Mair (1988) pointed out, such firms have significant infrastructural investment (utilities), local financial investment (savings and loans), or reliance on local markets (newspapers) and thus have considerable vested interest in local growth. Utility firms in particular have aggressive marketing programmes seeking to lure new consumers and retain existing ones.

Guskind (1987) attributed the first 'fully-fledged image-building promotion campaign' to New York State which, in 1977, began its now many-times-cloned 'I ♥ New York' orgy. Today the gift shops of airports around the world carry 'I ♥ X' T-shirts. There are 'I ♥ Bamako' (Mali) postcards, and, a 1981 cartoon in the *New Yorker* depicted with unforseen irony a horse-drawn peasant carriage with a bumper sticker proclaiming 'I ♥ Bosnia and Herzegovina'. New York State's advertising budget grew rapidly from 200,000 to 5.4 million dollars a year and was so successful in attracting visitors that it was credited with helping save New York City from fiscal collapse.

Bailey's study of the urban economic development programmes in 23 cities ranging from large cities such as Chicago and Baltimore to small Spartanburg, South Carolina and Mesa, Arizona concluded that marketing 'is the principal driving force in urban economic development in the 1980s and will continue to be so in the next decade' (Bailey, 1989:3). His analysis indicated that the 1980s saw a shift from 'first generation smokestack chasing' programmes predicated on reducing operating costs to a second generation of programmes with greater target marketing and an emphasis on retention. There was also increased investment in making the community more attractive, in which:

> 'third generation' of marketing programmes is emerging, in which community investment, or 'product development' activities in education, technology, capital

> access and infrastructure are being undertaken to support long-range strategies aimed at the jobs of the 1990s and the 21st Century . . . The logic that more jobs make a city better is giving way to the realisation that making a city better attracts more jobs (Bailey, 1989:3).

Once again, it is asserted that marketing enhances not merely the image, but the reality of a city.

Nevertheless, Bailey argued that despite the increase in expenditure on urban marketing, cities remain distinctly 'undermarketed.' Although advertising constitutes the largest share of the marketing budget the largest current budget for advertising in his sample of 23 cities (for Atlanta and Cleveland), was only in the 0.6 million dollar range – minuscule by advertising standards and probably only marginally effective. In fact, all economic development advertising expenditures in all United States media totals only about 46 million dollars, a little more than half the current annual budget for Miller Lite Beer alone (Bailey, 1989:4). The selling of cities is still in its infancy.

Despite the rapid expansion of place marketing in recent years, most of the work is still done 'in house' by government employees. Marketing firms and consultants are commonly commissioned for particular projects, but with certain notable exceptions (such as International Development Counsellors of New York or Hill and Knowlton of Cleveland), there are still very few firms specialising in place marketing. One explanation for this is probably that more local governments hire local firms and agencies, often on a *pro bono* or reduced-fee basis, and that such firms have local knowledge lacking in the generic expertise of national firms. Moreover, the market for place marketing is dispersed among thousands of local governmental units whose budgets are too small for professional public relations. A 1986 Growth Strategies Organisation survey of 1200 Chambers of Commerce found that 75 per cent of Chambers responding reported a total annual economic development budget of under 100,000 dollars – a figure below a typical annual retainer fee by prominent Madison Avenue firms (Ward, 1989). Hence, much place marketing is still done by people trained in planning, public administration or economics (Ryans and Shanklin, 1986). Small wonder, then, that a commentary based on discussions on place marketing by the National Council for Urban Economic Development concluded that: 'many, if not most, places do not have a well thought out marketing plan or strategy . . . place oriented marketing is a rather undeveloped art in our mass market society' (Haider, 1989:10–11). While considerable resources of time, money, skill and energy are being expended on marketing places, the efficacy of the methods and the effectiveness of the campaigns are seldom scrutinised or evaluated in more than a cursory manner. As we shall see, the marketing of cities tends to be generic and repetitive.

While the cost/benefit ratios of urban marketing campaigns are debatable (and debated), that they comprise a significant component of contemporary economic development is not. The argument could be made, as Goodman (1979) did about tax abatements, that a city is damned if it does and damned if it doesn't. Just as, when every city offers tax abatements, both the comparative advantage and the tax revenues are lost, so too, if a city has a marketing campaign it may merely equalise the competition with other cities, but all cities bear the costs of marketing. If cities elect not to offer tax breaks or engage in promotion, they risk losing investments and residents to competitors who do. City governments are increasingly acting as entrepreneurial competitors in a market economy and the emerging conventional wisdom seems to be that the public sector is thus becoming more efficient (Osborne and Gaebler, 1992). It is hardly surprising, then, that as education vouchers generate competition between public schools, as public housing tenants become owners of their units, and local governments own luxurious convention centres and sports stadia, so the business of public relations, advertising and promotion also becomes a significant public sector activity.

Urban promotional imagery: from production to consumption

As the economies of cities turn from heavy industry and manufacturing to reliance on services or high tech industries, so too do their appeals to potential investors and residents change. The older virtues of central location, cheap labour or low taxes are not abandoned, but much more emphasis is put on 'quality of life' issues. The city is sold as a great place to live, as well as a great place to do business. As firms increasingly rely on recruiting and retaining highly paid managers and, with technological innovation, are less dependent on the supply of unskilled or semi-skilled workers, so must the city be seen as 'habitable' or consumable by upscale executives and middle-class professionals.

As noted earlier, the marketing of the post-industrial city has certain generic themes, some of which are perennials in the history of boosterism. Commonly, the time is future, the direction is up. This is apparent in slogans and titles. New Brunswick *Tomorrow*, the public–private partnership planning the revitalisation of this small New Jersey city, produced a film entitled 'Partnership for a Bright *Tomorrow*' (emphasis added). Nearby Paterson, New Jersey, advertises itself as an 'Emerging Arts Community'. New Britain, Connecticut, is 'Growing Strong'. 'For a Step Toward *Tomorrow*' go to Fairfield, Connecticut. Joliet, Illinois, is 'Breaking *New* Ground,' while New Milford, Connecticut, has 'A Great Past, and a Greater *Future*,' but remains silent on its present. Cleveland has its '*New* Cleveland Campaign'.

Perusal of city advertising in *Expansion Management*, the magazine for 'business mobility decision makers', reveals other common themes. Despite the declining significance of location with innovations in transportation and communications, many places continue to claim central locations. 'Put your Business in the Centre of the World' in Atlanta. Corona, California, claims 'We're in the Middle of Everything'. 'Ever Notice that the Good Stuff is Always in the Middle?' asks the caption of a picture of a lollipop oozing a delectable filling and noting that 'Newport News is in the Middle of it All'. Cuero, Texas, is labelled on a map as 'Centrepoint' while cities several times its size – Houston, Corpus Christi, Austin and San Antonio are peripheral. Hempstead, New York, is also 'At the Centre of the World'. Business has made Sunrise, Florida the 'Centre of Attention' (Figure 7.1). If a place does not claim centrality, it is at least a gateway, as Tracy, California, is to the San Joaquin Valley or Brownsville, Texas – 'Your Doorway to Mexico'. In an earlier advertisement, Brownsville claimed to be the 'connecting point of Northern Mexico, South Texas, and (for good measure) the world!' (Ryans and Shanklin, 1986:15). However, perhaps the prize for locational promotion should go to a locally-dependent power company

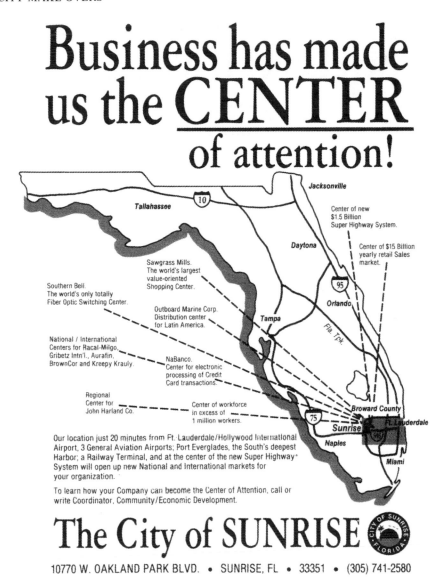

Business has made us the <u>CENTER</u> of attention!

Center of new
$1.5 Billion
Super Highway System.

Center of $15 Billion
yearly retail Sales
market.

Sawgrass Mills.
The world's largest
value-oriented
Shopping Center.

Southern Bell.
The world's only totally
Fiber Optic Switching Center.

Outboard Marine Corp.
Distribution center
for Latin America.

National / International
Centers for Racal-Milgo,
Gribetz Intn'l., Aurafin,
BrownCor and Kreepy Krauly.

NaBanco.
Center for electronic
processing of Credit
Card transactions.

Regional
Center for
John Harland Co.

Center of workforce
in excess of
1 million workers.

Broward County

Sunrise Ft. Lauderdale

Naples

Miami

Tallahassee
Jacksonville
Daytona
Tampa
Orlando
Fla. Tpk.

Our location just 20 minutes from Ft. Lauderdale/Hollywood International
Airport, 3 General Aviation Airports; Port Everglades, the South's deepest
Harbor; a Railway Terminal, and at the center of the new Super Highway
System will open up new National and International markets for
your organization.

To learn how your Company can become the Center of Attention, call or
write Coordinator, Community/Economic Development.

The City of SUNRISE

10770 W. OAKLAND PARK BLVD. • SUNRISE, FL • 33351 • (305) 741-2580

Figure 7.1 Sunrise, Florida: one of many peripheral locations that maintains that it is central.

supplying parts of Arkansas, Louisiana and Texas. Illustrated by a drawing of Adam and Eve, the text reads:

> There is only one location better than ours. The Garden of Eden has a talking snake, tempting fruit and the tree of knowledge, but the ARK-LA-TEX is fast becoming the choice for business opening, expanding or relocating.

$13/square foot.

Right now, your business can get a home on the range for a song.

Metro Denver's average cost for prime office space is only about $13 per square foot. Compare that to $36 in New York, $35 in Chicago, $30 in Los Angeles, and $26 in Boston.

You'll find similar savings on warehouse and manufacturing space, too – but you should move fast because rates are on their way up.

You'll also find a workforce that's 63% above the national average in college-educated adults. And a community that's making a multi-billion dollar investment in what will be the world's largest international airport.

With numbers like that, Denver is every inch a bottom-line value and a golden opportunity.

Playground included.

Photo Credit: Andrew Photography/Keystone Resort

Of course, the numbers only begin to tell Denver's story.

Look closer and you'll see the rest written in sunny days (300 a year), a surprisingly mild climate and an active lifestyle.

The Rockies west of Denver are a playground of world-class ski areas, national parks, dazzling scenery and some of the most picturesque golf courses in North America.

It's a built-in benefits package that makes recruiting and keeping good people easy.

To get a closer look at Denver, call the Metro Denver Network today: (303) 534-8500.

Denver.
Take a closer look.

Figure 7.2   Denver: reasonable rates and outrageous recreation!

Many cities, not unexpectedly, cite such standard attractions as cheap space and low taxes. 'At only 65c Per, We have all the Square Feet a Business will Need' claims Independence, Missouri. Denver's '$13/ square foot. Playground included' combines the average cost of prime office space with a photograph of mountain skiing (Figure 7.2). Readers are urged to 'Consider the Less Taxing Environment' in Orlando, Florida, while Omaha, Nebraska, urges one to 'Look Again!' at the list of tax advantages offered.

Despite the changes in labour force needs in post-industrial economies, numerous cities continue to tout the quality, and sometimes the cheapness, of their labour force, often mentioning if they are in a 'right to work' state (which prevents unions from calling all workers out in times of strike, thus reducing work stoppages and union demands). Quality is documented by productivity. 'Emporia: Working for You' includes testimony from a very serious looking plant manager claiming that 'the workforce of this plant is most productive in terms of work pace and effort within the Modine system'. It is also documented by skill: 'The biggest crowd of polymer scientists hang around Cleveland' (illustrated with a rack of white laboratory coats). 'Twin Fall Idaho Works' while in Eugene/Springfield, Oregon, 'Our Workers Work Out' (Figure 7.3). The latter's claim that 'Eugene is ranked one of the Top 10 Workout Cities in the Nation', is embellished by a photograph of a muscular man, but the derivation of the ranking is not given. One assumes it is not physical strength but health which is being promoted.

Finally, numerous cities claim a high quality of life, claims that are at once often grandiose and vague. 'Riverside (California) has it all together'. Louisville is 'A City Without Limits'. Chicago is 'The City that Exceeds Expectations'. Santa Maria, California is 'A Livable Place to Work' (Figure 7.4). In Greensboro, North Carolina: 'You can have it both ways with the New American Metropolis. The convenience of mid-sized city and the warmth, friendliness and unspoiled beauty of a vibrant community'. Pittsburgh remains, since its 1985 baptism by Rand McNally, the '#1 Most Livable City'.

The promotional repertoires of many cities thus bear significant similarities to each other. Indeed, the standard claims of economic development – good location, workforce, environment, tax climate, land values and so forth – are to be found to a greater or lesser extent in all cities. A few places, grappling with this problem of parity marketing, seek to carve out a different image or to create something more distinctive. The caption of photos of attractive locales asserts: 'This should fill in the blank about Tulsa' (Figure 7.5). The advertisement goes on to say: 'When someone says "Tulsa", some people draw a blank. So the next time you're looking for a perfect business location, we hope this ad will help you draw a better Tulsa picture – not a blank'. Tulsa thus confronted its non-image directly. Portland, Oregon, published a nostalgic advertisement with a misty floral background and a long text which begins in bold print 'Was it a man or a woman . . .' and with Proustian remembrances ends by admonishing that: 'True, you have lived a virtuous life, resisting temptation and all, but this patience thing can only go so far', so you should check out the advantages Portland has to offer your firm. Willoughby, Ohio, also appeals to the past with a sepia photo of a horse-drawn ice delivery cart and the caption: 'In Willoughby, the way we do business may change with the times. But not the reasons why'. Several cities use puns. With a photo of steel bearings: 'Get your business rolling in Cincinnati: Armco

OUR WORKERS WORK OUT!

Employers in Eugene/Springfield, Oregon, find that their workers really work out:

▶ **They're productive.**
The Fantus Company rated "Work Force Productivity" a community asset.

▶ **They're well-educated.**
One-third of Eugene's adult population has a college degree.

▶ **And they're fit.**
Eugene is ranked one of the "Top 10 Workout Cities" in the nation.

Test our mettle. Call to find out more about the strength of our work force.

Eugene/Springfield
Metropolitan Partnership
PO Box 10398 Eugene, OR 97440
(503) 686-2741

Eugene/Springfield
Fit for Business, Fit for Living

Figure 7.3   Eugene/Springfield: selling a fit workforce.

Steel Has' (Figure 7.6). Illustrated with bananas comes the advice: 'Peel out to Cincinnati. Chiquita Brands did' (Figure 7.7). Birmingham, Alabama is 'A Site More than you Might Expect', and superimposed over a photo of building cranes is the question: 'Why are the Cranes flocking to Birmingham?' Exclamation marks are favoured punctuation, as in Bartlesv!lle, Oklahoma, where more than 70 years ago Frank Phillips started Phillips Petroleum and where, today, 'we're looking for more good companies'. Nevertheless, few places have gone as far as Hamilton! Ohio which, on the advice of a public relations firm hired to improve Hamilton's image passed a resolution unanimously in the city council to order legislation to add the 'attention getting' punctuation (*New York Times*, 1986). Perhaps my favourite recent advertisement is for Louisville which juxtaposes a photograph of a multiracial group of elementary school children of both sexes with the caption 'Meet Our Founding

Figure 7.4   Santa Maria: marketing livability in California.

Fathers. In greater Louisville we know our every generation is a new generation of leaders. So we're placing major emphasis on education . . .'

Numerous other examples of efforts to distinguish a city from others, to claim a unique quality that sets the place apart from its competitors could be cited. Yet it could also be argued that parallel contradictory trends of homogenisation versus distinctiveness in image is apparent in the built environment. Cities want the standard apparatus of revitalisation referred to earlier (or what Frieden and Sagalyn (1990) refer to as the 'trophy collection' of the downtown mall, new office towers, atrium hotel and convention centre, restored historic district, with maybe an aquarium, a domed stadium or a waterfront park). That, apparently, is now not enough. One also needs, perhaps, a stadium with a retractable roof (Toronto), the biggest freshwater aquarium in the world (Chattanooga), or the biggest downtown retail mall (Pasadena).

This Should Fill In
The Blank About Tulsa.

When someone says "Tulsa," some people draw a blank. So the
next time you're looking for the perfect business location,
we hope this ad will help you draw a better Tulsa picture – not
a blank.

Find out even more about Tulsa by writing or calling Mickey
Thompson, Metropolitan Tulsa Chamber of Commerce,
616 South Boston, Tulsa, OK 74119, 800/624-6822.
Or better yet, visit Tulsa in person. And draw your
own surprising conclusions.

Tulsa. For Any Business State of Mind.

Tulsa's Out To
Change Your State
Of Mind.

Circle Information No. 83

JANUARY/FEBRUARY 1991 **103**

Figure 7.5   Tulsa: creating an image where none existed previously.

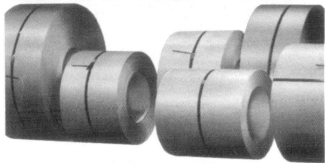

GET YOUR BUSINESS ROLLING IN CINCINNATI.

Armco Steel Has.

Making more than 3 million tons of steel a year takes a strong commitment.
Moving it takes a strong supply of alternative methods of distribution. From river
and rail to interstates and airways, the transportation hub of Greater Cincinnati
gives Armco strength. Call The Cincinnati Gas & Electric Co., Regional
Development Department at 1-800-448-0416 to learn how.

Figures 7.6 and 7.7 Punning promotions used for Cincinnati in association with Cincinnati Gas and Electric Regional Development Department and Chiquita Brands.

As the old industrial city transmogrifies into the post-industrial city of consumption and service production both its built environment and its image metamorphose. Former factories and warehouses become residential condominia. In Pittsburgh the former Homestead steel works, which once employed 15,000 workers, has become a waterside amusement park, while downtown the post-modern, Victorian-Gothic, plate-glass PPG Place houses the corporate command of an industry whose production function is elsewhere (Holcomb, 1993). In Cleveland, memorabilia of the industrial waterfront are preserved in juxtaposition to trendy jazz clubs and expensive eateries. In Boston, New York and Baltimore the bustling docks of a century ago have become equally fervid

PEEL OUT TO CINCINNATI.

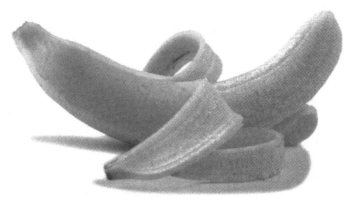

Chiquita Brands Did.

With the opportunities of three states - three tax structures, three incentive plans, three economic development departments - Chiquita found that Greater Cincinnati offered bunches of flexible choices. Call The Cincinnati Gas & Electric Co., Regional Development Department at 1-800-448-0416 to learn more about them.

Figures 7.6 and 7.7   (*continued*)

scenes of conspicuous consumption in festival markets. Remnants of the industrial past are likewise seen in the claims of central location, hard-working labour force, and low tax rates promoted in the contemporary marketing materials of cities, but more significant are the images of high quality lifestyles, unique attractions and distinctive ambience by which cities seek to appeal to footloose capital and to be 'consumed'.

References

Bailey, J.T. (1989) *Marketing Cities in the 1980s and beyond: new patterns, new pressures, new promises*, Cleveland: American Economic Development Council.
Boorstin, D. (1965) *The Americans: the national experience*, London: Weidenfeld and Nicholson.

Cox, K. and Mair, A. (1988) 'Locality and community in the politics of local economic development', *Annals of the Association of American Geographers*, 78, 307–25.

Fainstein, S.S. (1991) 'Promoting economic development: urban planning in the United States and Great Britain', *Journal of the American Planning Association*, 57, 22–33.

Fainstein, S.S., Fainstein, N.L., Hill, R.C., Judd, D.R. and Smith, M.P. (1983) *Restructuring the City: the political economy of urban redevelopment*, New York: Longman.

Frieden, B.J. and Sagalyn, L.B. (1990) *Downtown Inc: how America rebuilds cities*, Cambridge, MA: MIT Press.

Gale, D. (1984) *Neighbourhood Revitalization and the Postindustrial City*, Lexington, MA: D.C. Heath.

Glaab, C.N. (1967) 'Historical perspective on urban development schemes', in L. Schnore, ed., *Social Science and the City*, New York: Praeger, 197–219.

Goodman, R. (1979) *The Last Entrepreneurs: America's regional wars for jobs and dollars*, New York: Simon and Schuster.

Guskind, R. (1987) 'Bringing Madison Avenue to Main Street', *Planning*, (February), 4–10.

Haider, D. (1992) 'Place Wars: new realities of the 1990s', *Economic Development Quarterly*, 6, 127–34.

Harvey, D. (1989) 'From managerialism to entrepreneurialism: the transformation in urban governance in late capitalism', *Geografiska Annaler*, 71B, 3–17.

Holcomb, B. (1990) *Purveying Places: past and present*, Working Paper 17, New Brunswick, NJ: Centre for Urban Policy Research.

Holcomb, B. (1993) 'Revisioning Place: de- and re-constructing the image of the industrial city', in C. Philo and G. Kearns, eds., *Selling Places: the city as cultural capital*, Oxford: Pergamon Press.

Holcomb, B. and Beauregard, R.A. (1981) *Revitalizing Cities*, Washington, DC: Association of American Geographers.

Jones, H.M. (1946) 'The colonial impulse: an analysis of the promotion literature of colonization', *Proceedings of the American Philosophical Society*, 90, 131–61.

Knox, P.L. ed. (1993) *The Restless Urban Landscape*, Englewood Cliffs, NJ: Prentice Hall.

Kotler, P., Haider, D.H. and Rein, I. (1993) *Marketing Places: attracting investment and tourism to cities, states and nations*, New York: Free Press.

Lake, R.W. (1992) 'Planning and applied geography', *Progress in Human Geography*, 16, 414–21.

Logan, J.R. and Molotch, H.L. (1987) *Urban Fortunes: the political economy of place*, Berkeley: University of California Press.

New York Times (1986) 'Hamilton, Ohio, acts to become Hamilton!', 16 May, A17.

Osborne, D. and Gaebler, T. (1992) *Reinventing Government: how the entrepreneurial spirit is transforming the public sector*, New York: Addison Wesley.

Porter, P.R. and Sweet, D. (1984) *Rebuilding America's Cities: roads to recovery*, New Brunswick, NJ: Centre for Urban Policy Research.

Ryans, J.K. and Shanklin, W. (1986) *Guide to Marketing for Economic Development: competing in America's Second Civil War*, Columbus, Ohio: Publishing Horizons.

Sack, R.D. (1988) 'The consumer's world: place as context'. *Annals of the Association of American Geographers*, 78, 642–64.

Schudson, M. (1984) *Advertising, the Uneasy Persuasion: its Dubious Impact on American Society*, New York: Basic Books.

Teaford, J.C. (1990) *The Rough Road to Renaissance: urban revitalization in America, 1940–1985*, Baltimore: Johns Hopkins Press.

Watson, S. (1991) 'Gilding the smokestacks: the new symbolic representations of deindustrialised regions', *Society and Space*, 9, 59–70.

Ward, C. (1989) 'Selling places: the rise of an economic development marketing profession', unpublished manuscript.

Weir, H.C. (1910) 'The awakening of the cities: the era of civic advertising and the chamber of commerce', *Putnam's Magazine*, 7, 673–80.

Wernick, A. (1991) *Promotional Culture: advertising, ideology and symbolic expression*, Newbury Park: Sage.

8 Selling the inner city: regeneration and place marketing in London's Docklands

SUE BROWNILL

London Docklands are the 1980s flagship of urban regeneration which ran aground in the 1990s, but the images associated with the area remain vivid. The steel-clad tower of Canary Wharf, the Docklands Light Railway (DLR) running on elevated track through a high-tech landscape, loft living in converted riverside warehouses. That such images proliferate is more a testament to the power of marketing than a reflection of the reality of Docklands. Yet more importantly it indicates the heightened position of place promotion within inner city policy in the UK in the 1980s.

This chapter explores the relationship between urban regeneration and place marketing by looking at the past decade of development in London's Docklands. It shows how marketing and place promotion became a key strand in the strategy to entice private sector-led regeneration to inner city areas and had an equally key part to play in the boom/slump cycle which resulted. In particular, it looks at how this marketing strategy attempted to refashion popular perceptions of the area and the ideological implications that resulted.

Place promotion and inner city policy

The eight-and-a-half square miles (22 sq km) immediately to the east of the City of London which constitute the Docklands area (*see* Figure 8.1) has been described as the largest redevelopment site in Europe. The area's decline began in the 1960s with the progressive closure of the docks which had formed the core of the local economy since the early 1800s. These closures plus the decline in related manufacturing industry have meant that Docklands have been at the receiving end of inner city policy since the late 1960s, the effectiveness of which has been reviewed elsewhere (see Marris, 1982; Brownill, 1990).

It is the years from 1981, with the setting up of the London Docklands Development Corporation (LDDC), that are of interest here. Since that date, if the publicity is to be believed, £9 billion of private sector money has been invested, 22 million square feet of

134

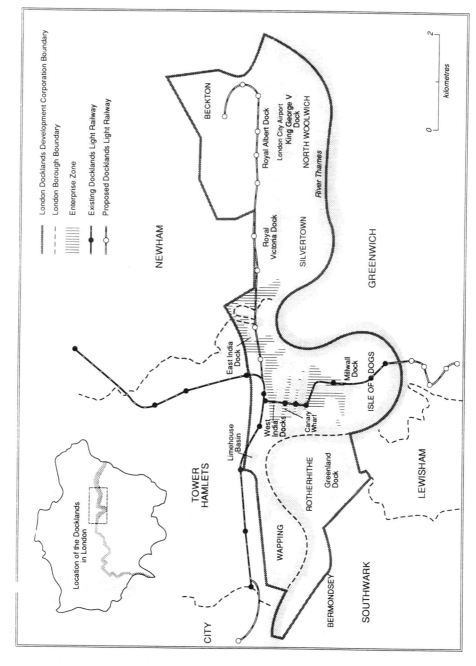

Figure 8.1 Map of the London Docklands Development Corporation Area.

office space built or planned, 17,000 homes completed and around 100 kilometres of roads and railways built or improved. This rapid transformation has been heralded by successive Conservative governments as a policy triumph, yet the transformation ground to a halt with the recession of the 1990s and has been heavily criticised by local residents and planning commentators (ALA, 1990).

Docklands are the epitome of a strategy based on the ideological conviction that only the private sector could provide for the long-term regeneration of the inner city. The government argued that development should be deregulated, by-passing local authorities with the creation of Urban Development Corporations (UDCs) and Enterprise Zones run by boards of government-appointed directors. The red-tape of planning, which was seen as a cause of decline, had to be swept out of the way and the private sector allowed to get on with the job. A UDC was established in Docklands in July 1981 and within the Urban Development Area (UDA) the Isle of Dogs Enterprise Zone was set up in April 1982.

Nevertheless, the private sector needed some help with the regeneration task. Brindley et al. (1989) have referred to the approach used as 'leverage planning' – the use of public investment and activity to underwrite the risks of location in areas more marginal to the market. While the rhetoric of UDCs was that redevelopment stemmed from private sector initiative, the reality was that little would have happened without the substantial public sector expenditure and activity that has gone into Docklands. These represent 'subsidies by any other name' (Massey, 1990). To date public spending in Docklands has been over £1.5 billion by the LDDC plus spending on other public initiatives, mainly transport and the Enterprise Zone tax allowances, of up to £3 billion (ALA, 1990). The powers of UDCs to make compulsory purchases and reclaim sites before selling them on to the private sector ensured land assembly. The removal of local democracy speeded up the process.

Place promotion has to be seen as part of this 'pump-priming' strategy. If the aim was to attract private sector investment from developers, homeowners and office tenants, Docklands had to be sold – preferably to the highest bidder. Far from Docklands' development being 'demand-led', that demand has been created. What better way to create demand than through changing the image of the area through the marketing and publicity tactics associated with place promotion?

A second and related factor which prompted place marketing is what Klausner (1987) has referred to as the 'property value hype'. He argued that the LDDC's pump-priming did not stop at assembling and servicing land but aimed at ensuring that property values increased in an effort to benefit both investors and the LDDC itself due to its own substantial land ownership. As the LDDC literature stressed: 'the returns are dramatic and dynamic' (LDDC, 1988). It was hoped that an upward trajectory would increase confidence, investment and supposedly make regeneration self-sufficient. Indeed rising land values were from the start seen by the LDDC as one of the primary indicators of regeneration. One of the surest ways of hyping up the value was to promote an up-market image of the area.

With the rise of place promotion, policy was also responding to wider processes. As many writers have stressed, the globalisation of capital investment has forced areas to compete nationally and internationally (Cooke, 1989; Harvey, 1989). Coupled with the abandonment of interventionist strategies for 'free-market' approaches such as that of the LDDC, this has led to the place marketing and urban boosterism to which poster hoardings and television advertisement worldwide bear witness. If, as in the case of Canary Wharf, developers play off London, Paris and Frankfurt as potential locations, public authorities including the LDDC have responded by promoting the conditions for investment and marketing the area to catch that elusive footloose capital.

Before looking at the LDDC's marketing strategy in more detail, it is important to appreciate that changes have occurred over time in the LDDC's basic strategy. Three phases can be distinguished. Initially the LDDC was concerned solely with initiating development. The pump-priming in this phase included establishing an identity for the LDDC and the area in the minds of investors and carrying out basic infrastructure and land assembly. In the 'second wave' (1985–8), land and property prices in the area boomed and, with the coming of Canary Wharf, Docklands were being promoted as an extension of the City. Social regeneration was added to the list of priorities and various planning gain deals signed. The third phase from 1989 onwards was represented by the property slump and the efforts of the LDDC to counter the negative impact of the recession and criticism of its strategy.

Remaking Docklands

It could be argued that Docklands have always been more of an idea than a place. The name 'Docklands' and the area that they cover today was largely created in 1972 when Peter Walker, then the Secretary of State for the Environment, employed consultants Travers Morgan to initiate a planning study into the area's redevelopment. Docklands have only ever existed as an area demarcated on a planner's map and do not correspond to any sense of shared space or identity amongst the people living there.

Nevertheless, the inherited image of Docklands was a problem for the LDDC. In the minds of property developers, Docklands represented derelict docks (themselves the result, according to some arguments, of the militancy of the dockers), the East End underworld of criminality and gangs, isolation and poor transport links to the City, run-down council estates and bad-neighbour industries. The East End was the City of London's backyard, with its enclosed docks traditionally being a threat to the wharves in the City. In the minds of City politicians and financiers Docklands should neither be the equal of the City nor the location for high-value development. Place promotion therefore depended on remaking Docklands in a different image and creating, through the marketing strategy, the type of place that would attract investors, stimulate demand and create that magic ingredient – market confidence. This was done in a variety of ways as the following section will show.

Local government becomes big business

As part of the pump-priming of the first phase, the LDDC sought to raise its corporate image amongst investors. The aim was both to distance the LDDC from the vilified red-tape of local authorities and to reflect the business world that was envisaged as the saviour of Docklands. The very fact that the LDDC was called a Corporation and not an authority, that it was run by a Board of Directors with a Chairman and Chief Executive indicates the attempt to leave the town hall behind.

The Annual Reports of the LDDC were more in the style of a private company than a public body. Glossy in nature, written by journalists, they were part of the promotional package extolling the developments that had occurred and carrying through the image sought. Thus the 1986/87 report – *The Year of Arrival* – contained a series of photographs with blurred figures and trains implying a place on the move.

Numerous other publications echoed these themes. The LDDC has produced a constant stream of promotional literature aimed at different segments of the market namely, commercial, residential and general. Publicity has been tailored to each of these sectors with the greatest emphasis being on the 'business decision makers in the South East and London' (LDDC, 1992). Subsidiaries have been set up to publish magazines and other promotional literature including *The Docklands Magazine* and *Docklands Business World* and to run tours of the area by coach or helicopter for prospective investors. Local residents also receive *Docklands News*, a free newspaper delivered to every household in the area.

To support its marketing strategy between 1981 and 1992, the LDDC spent £28 million on publicity and promotion and the Corporation budgeted to spend a further £8 million between 1992 and 1994. Running at between 1 and 4 per cent of annual expenditure, the LDDC has regularly spent more on promotion than community and industry support.

Planning as marketing

While raising the profile of the Corporation was one aim of the publicity strategy, another was to incorporate the LDDC's development control powers into the marketing machine. Despite the claims of the LDDC's first Chief Executive, Reg Ward, that 'the era of the grand plan was dead', it has been noted that UDCs and Enterprise Zones were part of a restructuring of planning (Brindley *et al.*, 1989; Thornley, 1991) aimed at facilitating the market, not intervening in it.

Despite the fact that plan-making powers remained with the boroughs, the LDDC undertook, as one of its first tasks, the publication of Area Frameworks. These frameworks covered five areas: Wapping, Limehouse, The Isle of Dogs, The Royal Docks and Surrey Docks. The choice of these areas was not primarily a reflection of the fact that Docklands comprised separate communities, but more the belief that they represented discrete products to be marketed. In this way the 'Future For Wapping' was seen in its proximity to the City with the potential for high-value housing and the growth of commercial development around St Katherine's Dock. The Royal Docks, problematic as they were furthest from the City, were to become 'a new Water City for the 21st Century'.

These Frameworks were in the LDDC's own words 'marketing tools to secure maximum private investment' although they were also 'local plans in all but name' (LDDC, 1982:34). They contained stylised pictures of what developments were possible, desirable or even already proposed in certain locations and indicated where the LDDC would be putting in infrastructure. In an attempt to move away from the idea that they were plans, zones were vaguely indicated, buildings were hesitantly sketched in and transport links shown by crayoned squiggles.

In this way planning ceased to be an activity in guiding development and ensuring debate about the future of Docklands and became another way of selling the area. Although comments were invited, no response was made to local criticisms and views and no alteration to the marketing ideas ensued. This led local residents and organisations to call the consultation both on these plans and other LDDC decisions 'public relations . . . informing people of decisions after they had been made rather than involving them' (Docklands Forum, 1982).

Docklands as a state of mind

Despite the significance of the corporate and planning strategy it is the manufacturing of an image or 'a vision' of Docklands by the LDDC that has had the most significant role to play in place promotion. As place promotion depends on emphasising the uniqueness of the product on offer, it is here that the locality has a key part to play, but what aspects of the locality? Burgess and Wood (1988) drew the distinction between the physical attributes of a location and the cultural and psychological meanings associated with it. While the LDDC was keen to promote and exploit the physical location of Docklands next-door to the City, other less tangible senses of place were addressed. In particular, as we noted earlier, the negative view held by business locators had to be reversed. This did not entail the complete denial of the locality, rather the strategy adopted was of taking selected local features and refashioning them to meet the task in hand. Paradoxically, although the multi-national nature of investment may appear to negate local differences, the attraction of investment is based on promoting the characteristics of particular areas, or at least their manicured images.

The middle of nowhere?

Bearing this in mind, during the first phase from 1981 to 1985 advertising and promotion aimed to raise awareness of the LDDC and the Enterprise Zone as well as stressing the attractions of Docklands as an investment and residential location. Burgess and Wood (1988) showed in their analysis of the early Docklands' advertising campaigns how this was achieved on the level of location and imagery. Three television adverts using animated crows were the main focus of the campaign – a direct analogy to the phrase 'as the crow flies' implying the closeness of Docklands to the City – the factor identified as giving Docklands the edge over other assisted areas (Figure 8.2). Familiar London landmarks were also used such as Tower Bridge and Nelson's Column and at the same time poster and newspaper adverts proclaimed: 'Why move to the middle of nowhere when you can move to the middle of London?'

On the level of imagery, what was of interest in this campaign was how images of the East End found in television programmes such as *Minder* and *The Sweeney* were used to sell Docklands. Cockney accents and the sanitised versions of East End criminality and wheeler-dealing portrayed in such programmes both aimed to use humour and to influence how people thought of the area. These borrowed images of the area began the process of remodelling it for marketing purposes and in the process: 'the richness and diversity of the specific localities of Docklands have been reduced to a commodity to be packaged and sold' (Burgess and Wood, 1988:115).

Figure 8.2 An early Docklands advertisement, emphasising the closeness to the existing business centre of London compared to the regional development areas.

If the LDDC was using second-hand images of the East End to sell Docklands one aspect of reality that was heavily promoted was the 55 miles of waterfront. Hence, the promotional literature stated: 'The vast waterscape environment of Docklands offers a wholly unique potential' (LDDC, 1988). Waterfront development has been called the phenomenon of the 1980s and similar developments in Boston, Toronto and elsewhere had indicated the potential of such large-scale development sites (Hoyte *et al.*, 1988). Its use, of course, was not just a marketing ploy – waterside locations added value to the developments which fronted them. Thus, in the game of 'property value hype', water was an invaluable asset.

The ways in which water was used in selling Docklands were many and varied and contributed to the altered image of Docklands being created. It was not the recent past of the docks that was stressed (although the boom years of the 1950s were referred to from the point of view of thriving commerce), but visual metaphors were borrowed from abroad. Thus the LDDC's own promotional video begins with pictures of Venice at its commercial height accompanied by the following hyperbole:

> Just as the Renaissance heralded the modern world culminating in an outpouring of creative talent and new thought, so now, in its own way a new freedom of expression in London's Docklands is fashioning a wholly new environment which heralds the 21st century. This is the Docklands vision.

Canary Wharf was said to 'Look like Venice, Work like New York' and was also referred to as 'Wall St on the Water'. Publicity photos stressed the attractions of water. The DLR running over the elevated section of its track in the sunset became a favourite as did romantic pictures of the empty Royal groups of Docks.

Architectural styles also reflected the waterside theme. Dutch developers Vom built a housing scheme on the Isle of Dogs which mirrored the style of Amsterdam canal-side houses. Footbridges over the docks also copied Dutch design. In the same way that selected local features were remodelled in promotional campaigns buildings became pastiches of the area's past. Thus the Cascades development designed by fashionable architects CZWG has a triangular shape mimicking a sail, porthole windows and rails on balconies suggesting a ship's prow. The ideal of the flat in a converted warehouse could be approached by new properties trying to look like converted warehouses. The latter were often built in an almost fortress style with gated entrances to keep the locals out. The LDDC even bought redundant dock cranes and used them as landscape architecture. Areas and landmarks were renamed in this remodelling of Docklands' space. For example, Blackwall Basin became Jamestown Harbour, Surrey Docks became Surrey Quays and the British Rail station at Silvertown was renamed London City Airport station. In this way the existing locality was forced out of the new Docklands image.

Where did local people fit into this? Reading much of the literature, investors might well assume Docklands was a greenfield site, but in fact in 1981 there were almost 40,000 people in the area on designation. It was a source of anger and antagonism that the initial strategy paid little attention to local residents and their needs. There was a feeling that the LDDC wanted to replace the existing community with one which was more in keeping with the image being manufactured.

We have already seen how the LDDC saw the local population as part of the image problem. Lacking skills, having a history of militancy, being housed mainly in council housing, the existing population did not fit in with the new Docklands and were represented by crows or television characters in the promotional activities. At the extreme, one proposal suggested local residents could become living exhibits in a proposed Docklands Museum. Their lifestyle was of interest only as a history which could be neatly packaged and sold.

From the policy point of view LDDC initially firmly believed in the miracle of 'trickle-down' – benefits would inevitably spread to the local population from the developments taking place. In the second wave, in response to the failure of trickle-down and to the private sector's criticisms that the LDDC was 'failing to win the hearts and minds of local people' (HC, 1988), a new consensus was forged with partnerships between the public and private sectors at its core. The publicity material began to incorporate pictures of smiling residents enjoying the fruits of 'social regeneration'. However, we shall see later how the unequal benefits remained and such publicity only served to hide the polarising effects of the strategy of selling Docklands to the highest bidder.

Superficially, the LDDC was keen to promote architecture and design as part of its rebuilding of Docklands. We have already seen how developments reinterpreted the Docklands locale as a selling technique. Developers have reported that, far from being *laissez-faire*, when it came to design features the LDDC was strict in its granting of planning permission. This was all part of the attempts to massage the market. Opinion is divided over whether the LDDC has succeeded in this aim, with references to 'the architectural zoo' on the Isle of Dogs alongside acclaim for prize-winning edifices such as Nicholas Grimshaw's *Financial Times* building.

In addition, as a result of attempts to clean up the image of Docklands, at least £47 million has been spent on environmental improvements and more has been contributed to the rehabilitation of housing estates. While this has provided some benefits for local residents, the main aim was to prettify the area. Landscaping and tree-planting in strategic locations and external improvements to housing aimed to repudiate the view of Docklands as a run-down inner city location.

The emerging City?

After 1985 Docklands was caught up in the boom years of the Thatcherite 'economic miracle'. Land and house prices rocketed and the Corporation referred to the 'second wave' of development. Riverside residential sites originally valued at £0.5 million per acre fetched as high as £5–6 million in 1987. Prices for some properties quadrupled over the same period of time. On the commercial side the decision to build the 12 million square feet Canary Wharf development was seen as a triumph for the Docklands approach. The development already followed a decision that 'the sector best able to exploit the space of Docklands' (LDDC, 1985) was financial services, a result of the supposed boost to demand for space unleashed by the 'Big Bang' when City of London's financial markets were deregulated.

Therefore, in the second wave, the aspect to be highlighted in terms of publicity and promotion was the idea of Docklands as a third centre of office location in London after the City and the West End. 'The Exceptional Place', 'the Emerging City', 'the

Example of LDDC Marketing.

Working Lunch.

London Docklands. Right in the heart of London. Next to The City.

And not just another development area in the middle of nowhere. But open space. Not a concrete city jungle, but a whole new concept in living, working and playing; a brand new Water City of the 21st Century, right in the heart of London.

Already set to become the new financial and professional services centre of the UK, and each new development a Work of Art, dedicated to the Art of Work.

To find out more about the State of the Art developments in London Docklands, call (01-) 515 6000 and ask for the Development Showcase.

London Docklands. Dedicated to the Art of Work.

Figure 8.3 The possibilities of Docklands as a 'whole new concept in living, working and playing' feature strongly in this advertisement. Again closeness to the City is an important background theme.

Expanding City' were slogans characteristic of this phase. The pictures accompanying the captions nearly always had the National Westminster Tower as a reference point to show the proximity of the City. Indications of the size and character of Docklands were made by reference to central London. The Royals, for example, were said to equal an area from St Paul's to Oxford Street; Tobacco Dock, a 'festival shopping' centre in Wapping, was likened to Covent Garden.

Transport links were emphasised in response to the view of Docklands as an isolated backwater. One reason that the Canary Wharf developers insisted on a link to the London Underground at Bank station and were prepared to contribute to its costs was the need, in their words, for a psychological link with the City. Water sports were used as another attraction for the business locator. For example, one advertisement showing a windsurfer with a cellular telephone was accompanied by the caption 'Working Lunch' (Figure 8.3). The LDDC was aiming to promote Docklands as a place to live, work and play – the all-round location for the businessman. With this, the imagery moved on from being merely associated with a place to selling a lifestyle.

Residential developments such as Cascades were equipped with tennis courts and saunas. Burells Wharf, by the same developers, Kentish Properties, was built with a health club (open to non-residents at a large annual fee). The developers admitted that they were selling more than a roof over people's heads, it was the lifestyle that went with it. The idea of loft-living by the Thames was reflected in films (*A Fish Called Wanda*) and advertisements (Halifax Building Society's cashpoint machines). Whenever advertisers needed to imply up-market trendiness, Docklands were often used to supply the image. Here was another marketing ploy to get over the negative image of Docklands. What was furthest from a striking docker in people's minds than a Porsche-driving boy in red braces?

Through such publicity Docklands became associated with the mid-eighties phenomenon of the 'yuppie' (young, upwardly-mobile professional). Residential developers saw an easy market for their properties in city workers who might well only want a weekday *pied-à-terre*. Indeed, mirroring the activities of the supposed buyers, a futures market developed in flats whereby they would be sold on at ever-increasing values before being completed or even started. The facts are different. A recent survey showed that although new residents in prestigious developments were high-earners, many were in the arts and media not finance (QMC, 1990). Nevertheless, the image of the City whizz-kid as Docklands resident has prevailed.

Thus in massaging the market, the LDDC left the physical locality of Docklands behind. As the area continued to be remade on the level of culture and imagery Docklands became 'a state of mind' (Davies, 1987), but it was not just the LDDC which was engaged in such activities. Private developers also used design, architecture and the repackaging of Docklands as marketing tactics. It is to this issue that we now turn.

Canary Wharf: a place within a place

No development epitomises the marketing of Docklands within the second wave more than Canary Wharf. Both in size and appearance Canary Wharf was built to be the instant business district (Figure 8.4). A place within a place, it traded on the Docklands

144

Figure 8.4 Canary Wharf, the final conception. By 1993, the grand plan was only partly realised, essentially the core area west of the central tower. It was virtually all empty.

myth and also engaged in its own image building. What distinguishes the marketing of Canary Wharf is the way in which architecture and design, culture and aesthetics were used as marketing devices.

The publicity stated that 'Canary Wharf will be unique: built in a unique place to meet a unique need' (O&Y, 1990). The overall aim was to replicate the squares, circuses and architectural variety of central London, providing immediately the urban fabric that usually takes decades to develop. The unique needs which developers Olympia and York presented themselves as fulfilling were to maintain London as a world financial centre and global city through the provision of such space – neatly covering up the need of developers to make profits.

The unique place is the locality. Yet once again it was not the reality of Docklands which constitutes space here but an area 'near derelict close to the existing business centres . . . we started with a clean slate . . . so we have been able to plan nothing less than a new business district for London' (O&Y, 1990). The inner city is to be transformed to resemble 'St. James Park', 'Bond Street' and 'Trafalgar Square'. The attention to detail that echoes the City has been remarkable. Railings, gates and street lights have all been individually designed and mature London Plane trees were imported from Germany to complete the effect.

Again one local feature is important. To the instant business district just add water: 'water is a priceless asset, and at Canary Wharf it is exploited to the full to create a sense of space, light, exhilaration' (O&Y, 1990). A sense of *rus in urbe* is promoted through the provision of open space, marketed as giving Canary Wharf the advantages of a country town but in the heart of London. The provision of public space, together with the cultural activities sponsored within it including sculptures, a Jazz Festival and classical concerts, again aims to build an image of cultural significance while portraying Olympia and York as providers of the public good.

A sense of place has also been achieved through employing big-name architects such as Cesar Pelli and Skidmore Owings and Merrill, who designed the tower. In the drive for uniqueness in office space, which is itself a fairly standard product, differentiation comes in the secondary features of design and image: the publicity claiming that: '(e)ach building has individuality and character'. Using such architects followed a theme of quality in the development including the marble and stainless steel cladding and the attention to open spaces. The tower in particular was to be 'a sublime statement of confidence in the new district'.

Such marketing not only aims to sell office space but serves a distinctly ideological purpose (Crilley, 1993). The fact that Canary Wharf was a speculative office development is obscured by its promotional image as the saviour of London's place in the world market, an architectural showpiece and a cultural addition to the capital. Development of the inner city could be achieved through benign developers prepared to sign agreements, as in the case of Olympia and York, to secure local employment and training. The aesthetic and cultural validity sought for the development was in reality a marketing tactic, but it served to wrap the development in a cloak of public munificence.

Yet in the end no amount of marketing could make Canary Wharf work. In May 1992, with the building still only 60 per cent let, despite costly deals to secure tenants, the administrators were brought in. Canary Wharf had in some senses been taken over by events. In 1987, when Olympia and York began marketing, rents in the City at

£60 per square foot were twice those envisaged in Docklands. By 1992, a combination of the slump and the relaxing of planning controls in the City in response to the threat of Canary Wharf had created a glut of space in Central London, which brought rents down to little more than the Docklands levels. Moreover, the lack of completed transport links undermined the image of an accessible extension of the City. Canary Wharf was not the only Docklands casualty and as development in Docklands entered a third stage of slump a new marketing strategy had to be devised.

Remaking the image: the docker versus the knocker

From the late 1980s onwards the British economy and property market experienced one of its severest recessions. The Docklands not only followed the trend but were hit earlier and harder than many areas due to the area's association with the contracting financial services sector. Problems for Docklands developers began with the stock-market crash in late 1987. Shares in firms with developments in the area were badly affected and Kentish, the developers of Cascades, became one of the first of a spate of property firms to go bankrupt in the summer of 1988. The impact of the recession on the property market in Docklands was dramatic. House prices fell by 30 to 50 per cent from the peak in 1987. One development was offering new flats at half-price. A conservative estimate put the number of unsold properties in 1990 at 1400 (ALA, 1990). Land was lying derelict, blighted not by planning but by the drop in values. Rents had fallen and 50 per cent of office space was unlet.

Mounting criticism was voiced about the deficiencies in the LDDC's *laissez-faire* approach. At the top of the list came the results of the lack of planning and, in particular, the failure to coordinate infrastructure and land use. For example, when Canary Wharf was announced, there was no strategic inquiry into whether or not the development was appropriate for Docklands. Instead there was an *ad hoc* attempt to put in the transport infrastructure after the event. A major highway, the upgrading of the DLR and a new Underground route in the form of the Jubilee Line extension were planned but would be completed only five years after the first tenants moved in and, significantly, provided that private money was found to finance them. Other criticisms were directed at the lack of attention to local needs, the privatised nature of the space provided, and the lack of facilities such as shops, schools and health care.

As income from land sales dried up and the transport bill soared, the LDDC experienced a financial crisis. In the year 1991–92 it made a nominal loss of almost £55 million due mainly to the writing down of land values. What is fascinating in terms of place promotion is how the marketing tactics associated with the boom years added to this slump, as the very image that had been cultivated – of the financial services sector and 'yuppies' – warned investors off rather than encouraged them. Docklands had become synonymous with the Thatcher years and the excesses that went with them: greed, the disregard of non-market needs, the lack of regulation of markets and the excesses of the private sector. Patrick McCormack, one-time President of the Royal Institute of British Architects, referred to Docklands as Three-Dimensional Thatcherism. Such an image was now a liability.

The strategy of property value 'hype' and the associated remaking of the image of Docklands in effect created a bubble which burst. In an interview with the author, one developer thought Docklands' prices were 25–30 per cent over-valued in 1987 compared with the rest of London. This differential was in some ways a result of the marketing and imagery used. When the slump came, the marketing was a hindrance and the tarnished image had to be discarded. The LDDC's response was not to change its strategy but to engage in a new marketing campaign to remake the image of Docklands for a second time.

A joint campaign by the LDDC and developers already working in Docklands began in 1989. The involvement of developers not only reflected the desire on the part of government to secure private-sector funding but showed the dissatisfaction of the private sector with the LDDC. Developers felt that the Corporation was undermining confidence in their investments by failing to promote a positive image of the area. Initial campaigns centred on a 'Keep the Traffic Moving' slogan, stressing the positive measures being undertaken to ease transport problems. In October 1991 a television and poster campaign aimed at business decision-makers in the South East exhorted them to 'Go With the Flow', again stressing transport, the river and the on-going movement of investors and tenants to Docklands.

However, a campaign mounted in September 1992 had the highest profile (Figure 8.5). Asking people whether they were 'a knocker' or 'a docker', the aim was to counter negative views of the area and those associated with it. Using the 'lead-in' style of advertising where the product, (i.e. Docklands), was not mentioned until later advertisements, the idea of a 'docker' is built up. Thus, in the caring 1990s, he (sic) 'is just as able to change a nappy as well as a tyre'; he is prepared to take risks, 'says the Channel Tunnel's a good idea' and, further appealing to the male executive, 'is a fan of David Gower'. On the other hand, the knocker 'presses his jeans', 'would not have built Concorde' and 'orders steak and chips in an Indian restaurant'. When it comes to Docklands, the knocker thinks 'Docklands is right out in the sticks' and 'has never visited London's Docklands, not even as a tourist', while the docker states 'in fact it's closer to St Paul's than Oxford Street is' and 'knows beyond doubt that London Docklands will be a success'.

The image equates Docklands with major developments such as Concorde, the Sony Walkman and the Channel Tunnel which were all initially seriously criticised but later seen by some as major achievements. With supreme irony, those who support the LDDC are called 'dockers'. In this way, one of the most lasting symbols of the area and its history is remade in the LDDC's favour, symbolically sealing the death of a culture that the LDDC did much to destroy. It remains to be seen how successful this campaign will be, but it is likely that it is the amount of public money put into Docklands which will bring about a change in its fortunes rather than advertising alone.

Imagery and ideology

Place promotion can be seen as serving functions other than just marketing. The ideological nature of such publicity (taking ideology to mean the use of imagery to hide the nature of power relations) has been commented on by several writers (Harvey, 1989; Crilley, 1993: also Chapter 2). There are a number of ways in which place promotion has literally glossed over what is really going on in Docklands.

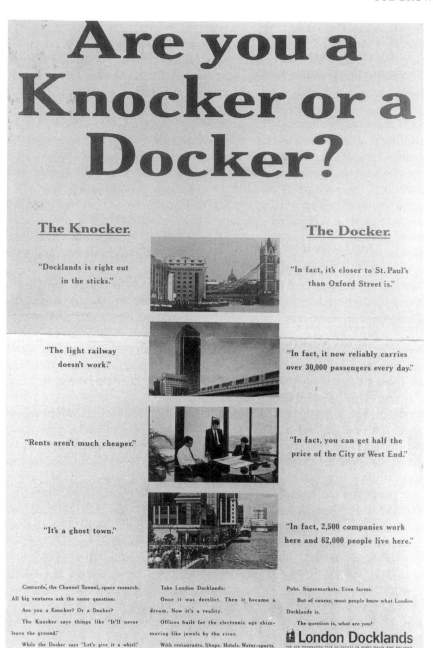

Figure 8.5 The Knocker and the Docker: advertising Docklands in 1992. This was one of several newspaper advertisements that mocked the old-fashioned and blinkered attitudes of the 'Knocker' compared to the smart and progressive thinking of the 'Docker'. Traditionally, the real dockers had been viewed in rather a different light by those who had inspired and facilitated the whole Docklands project of property-led regeneration.

First, the redevelopment of Docklands has always been a point of conflict between those who see the area as an extension of the City and those who argue that it should be redeveloped to meet local needs. Yet the LDDC's approach is presented as the only way forward and it is assumed that this strategy and the socio-economic change that results from such global and local shifts are inevitable, positive and impartial – there is no alternative. Detractors are 'knockers' with no clear arguments and nothing to put in its place while in reality this is not the case. Alternative plans have existed in the form of statutory local plans produced by the boroughs and local community groups, such as the People's Plan and the Limehouse Petition.

Such conflicts are ignored, however, in the Docklands of the publicity brochure. The image projected is one of consensus – all will benefit from the developments. The LDDC has fostered a cosy consensus through the notion of 'social regeneration', but such appearances serve to mask the unequal benefits which result from a private-sector-dominated regeneration strategy. The reality is, once again, different. Since the LDDC began its work, needs in the area have increased and polarisation between those who benefit and those who do not has increased along class, racial, ethnic and gender lines (for a fuller discussion of this, see ALA, 1990; Brownill, 1990). Moreover, once the LDDC lost its independent income from land sales, investment in the social regeneration programme was the first area to be drastically cut.

To take an example, homelessness in the three Docklands boroughs increased by over 200 per cent between 1981 and 1990 at the same time as the LDDC was proudly announcing that it had increased the percentage of owner occupation in the area from 5 per cent to 46 per cent. Given that 80 per cent of new housing has been for sale, new residents are more likely to be better off than their pre-LDDC neighbours and to work in white-collar City employment. A survey carried out in 1984 showed that 30 per cent of new residents were in the professional and managerial categories compared to between 7–13 per cent of the populations of the Docklands' boroughs (GLC, 1984). At the same time the vast majority of residents of the Docklands boroughs cannot afford to buy. The physical juxtaposition of new and existing housing is often taken to be one of the starkest indicators of the 'two nations' in Docklands. As a recent study of new migrants to Docklands concluded: 'rarely have social distances so vast been matched by physical distances so small' (QMC, 1990).

Polarisation has also proceeded along racial and ethnic lines. The 1984 survey showed that 93 per cent of new house purchasers were white compared to 85 per cent of the local population. Similarly, a recent household survey found that Bangladeshi men constituted 6 per cent of the total population of the UDA, 14 per cent of the unemployed and only 2 per cent of the working population (LDDC, 1990). Due to their lower economic power women, black people, members of ethnic minorities and people with disabilities are less likely to benefit from a market-based strategy despite the fact that, because of their greater needs, they have the most to gain.

Secondly, the imagery used reflects and perpetuates gender divisions in the use and development of the built environment. As we have already seen, the marketing was aimed at corporate decision makers and the assumption made was that they are male. Thus, we had the appeals to cricket fans and 'new men' in the Knockers versus Dockers advertisement and the male windsurfer in the earlier campaigns. Ideas of masculinity and feminity also pervade what has appeared on the ground in Docklands. Drawing on the notion of production and reproduction in the built environment and its relation to gender, it could be argued that the space created in Docklands, at least in the Enterprise Zone, reflected the 'productive' world of work, commuting, economic relations, with the tower of Canary Wharf graphically symbolising this fusion of male and corporate power (see also comments on the gendered nature of promotional rhetoric in Chapter 2).

Finally, not only are the unequal benefits of regeneration ignored but the rhetoric also hides the fact that the much-heralded renaissance of the inner city was, as with Canary Wharf, speculative property development backed by large amounts of public investment. The ideology holds that it is private initiative which has pioneered development in Docklands. Again the reality is different, as highlighted by the public sector, in the form of the funding of the Jubilee Line, being seen as the saviour of Canary Wharf. Nevertheless, from the point of view of place promotion, it is the dream which prevails.

Conclusion

The example of the LDDC has shown how place marketing was used as an integral part of a particular inner city strategy, designed not only to attract investors but also to change the image and perception of Docklands. Dream and reality became intertwined and confused in the attempt to market the area. This did not entail obliterating the locality – but a redefinition and a reworking to fit a particular need at a particular time. Moreover, we have also seen how the publicity had a major ideological function both to hide the conflicts and the nature of the processes of change occurring.

In the 1990s, the acres of unlet space, vacant land and empty properties testify to the weaknesses of the strategy. The Docklands of the 1980s were froth blown away by the harsh wind of recession in the 1990s. Yet there are no signs of change. The advertising campaigns instead seek to find another image, one more suitable to present conditions. This process could continue almost indefinitely when, instead, the evidence in Docklands would suggest that an alternative strategy should be sought.

In this respect the counter-position by Thompson (1990) is useful. He argues that regeneration should not just rest on attracting the private sector though inducements and clever photographs but on investing in the local area and intervening in the processes of restructuring. In this way the locality would not remain a picturesque backdrop to developments, but would become an asset in its own right. Place marketing in this scenario may well have its role, but as part of genuine place promotion and not the marketing hype of image over reality.

References

ALA [Association of London Authorities] and the Docklands Consultative Committee (1990), *Ten Years of London's Docklands: how the cake was cut*, London: Association of London Authorities.

Brindley, T., Rydin, Y. and Stoker, G. (1989) *Remaking Planning*, London: Unwin Hyman.

Brownill, S. (1990) *Developing London's Docklands*, London: Paul Chapman.

Burgess, J.A. and Wood, P. (1988) 'Decoding Docklands: place advertising and decision-making strategies of the small firm', in J. Eyles and D.M. Smith, eds., *Qualitative Methods in Human Geography*, Cambridge: Polity Press, 94–117.

Cooke, P., ed. (1989) *Localities*, London: Unwin Hyman.

Crilley, D. (1993) 'The enchanting mountain: Olympia and York and the contemporary megastructure', in P.L. Knox, ed., *The Restless Urban Landscape*, Englewood Cliffs, NJ: Prentice Hall.

Davies, C. (1987) 'Ad Hoc in the Docks', *Architectural Review*, 181 (1080), 30–37.

Docklands Forum (1982) *Consultation? What Consultation*, London: Docklands Forum.

GLC [Greater London Council] (1984) *Housing and Employment in Londons Docklands*, London: Greater London Council.

Harvey, D. (1989) *The Condition of Post Modernity*, Oxford: Blackwell.

HC [House of Commons] (1988) *The Employment Effect of UDCs. Employment Committee Third Report, Vol 2, Minutes of Evidence*, HC 327–11, London: HMSO.

Hoyte, B., Pinder, N. and Hussain, M., eds. (1988) *Revitalising the Waterfront*, London: Belhaven.

Klausner, D. (1987) 'Infrastructure investment and political ends; the case of London's Docklands', *Local Economy*, Vol 1(4), 47–59.

LDDC [London Docklands Development Corporation] (1982) *Corporate Plan*, London: London Docklands Development Corporation.

LDDC [London Docklands Development Corporation] (1985) *Annual Report and Accounts*, London: London Docklands Development Corporation.

LDDC [London Docklands Development Corporation] (1988) *London Docklands*, London: London Docklands Development Corporation.

LDDC [London Docklands Development Corporation] (1990) *London Docklands Household Survey*, London: London Docklands Development Corporation.

LDDC [London Docklands Development Corporation] (1992) *Annual Report and Accounts*, London: London Docklands Development Corporation.

Marris, P. (1982) *Community Planning and Perceptions of Change*, London: Routledge and Kegan Paul.

Massey, D. (1990) *Docklands: a microcosm of wider processes*, Docklands Forum Lecture, London: Docklands Forum.

O&Y [Olympia and York] (1990) *Vision of a New City District*, London: Olympia and York.

QMC [Queen Mary and Westfield College] (1990) *New Migrants in London Docklands*, Dept of Geography, Queen Mary and Westfield College, University of London.

Thornley, A. (1991) *Urban Planning Under Thatcherism*, London: Routledge.

Thompson, R. (1990) 'Economic regeneration: trickling downwards or growing upwards?', *The Planner*, 23 February, 40–42.

9 Art-full places: public art to sell public spaces?

BRIAN GOODEY

Art and decoration have been accepted as integral elements in urban design throughout history, and even though urban design as a process is now seen as something more, or something other, than creating pleasing public places, these places and the works which they contain still epitomise art in the environment. Successful applied art in urban places should be both adopted by the community, and remain functional.

The continuing impetus for art and decoration has flowed from designers themselves (Tibbalds, 1992:46):

> The integration of pieces of art on and around buildings has for centuries enriched public environments . . . . This does not mean dumping a mediocre piece of stereotype sculpture in a square or entrance foyer as a token or afterthought. It means considering art and decoration . . . as part of the design of the building or space. This means that the artist must become part of the design team – ideally as soon after the inception of the project as practicable.

It has also been generated by the community, for art is not just an aesthetic contribution; it is also often a memorial or specific public statement – as with the *Memorial to the Living: 'Why Do You Forget Us?'* dedicated to surviving soldiers at the Minnesota State Capitol in St Paul. If fans have their way, Freddie Mercury will join the figures of Peter Pan, Thomas Carlyle and Dante Gabriel Rossetti in the Royal Borough of Kensington and Chelsea (Marriot, 1992), although a Conservative borough councillor is quoted as stating: 'We are secretly hoping the plan will go away. We're trying to say as little about it as we can in the hope that they forget about it.' In Britain, at least, such a lack of aesthetic interest by elected members reflects, and is reflected in, much public comment. The attitudes and expectations of planners utilising art in environmental improvement are currently (1993) being explored by the Policy Studies Institute. Meanwhile Taylor (1991:7) observes from practice that:

> The obstacles to improvement in public attitude are enormous. The problems lie deep in our cultural make-up. Letters to the local press about a recent attempt by the City Council to introduce street sculpture to Leicester's City Centre have ranged from incomprehension at this use of poll-tax payers' money to 'I told you so' smugness when the sculptures were vandalised.

It has been suggested, also, that a Freddie Mercury statue might generate conflict in the gay community, but then controversy has been the fate of most of public statuary. If figurative or recognisable art is established in a public place, then public response is implicitly sought. Who can forget the symbolic toppling of Lenin and Stalin throughout eastern Europe? Who can remember the destruction, by soldiers on leave, of Prince Albert's Portsmouth statue during the Great War (Darke, 1991:24)? More recent debates over the statue to 'Bomber' Harris relating to the devastation in Dresden, and the complex history of the erection, in London, of a memorial to the massacre at Katyn are indicative of the willingness to engage.

Public statuary and memorials have provided a focus for community identity and, by extension, offer symbols for place promotion. Figurative memorials combine both the image of a renowned individual with local connections, as well as a human-scale indication of heritage and of attractive public places. Clearly informal and formal art in the environment does much more, representing a complex statement of private purpose from within.

This chapter focuses on recent examples of cities which have deliberately chosen to use art in public places as a major element in urban regeneration, and considers the techniques used and their contribution to the quality of public places. First, however, we examine the more traditional use of pre-existing artistic endeavours, especially literature, for place promotion.

Promoting the city as art object

Urban promotion, as represented in advertising and tourist materials, contains both enduring and cyclical elements. Casting far back into history, the excitement, bustle, heightening of the senses, and safety of the city's centre are typically established. Such characteristics are maintained regardless of the particular iconography of the place which may be contemporary or historic, populist or elitist, depending on the prevailing political climate and the market being sought.

Thus Coventry, a significant medieval city, promoted its modern recovery in the post-war era and itemised the intended revolution in urban planning. There was still room, however, for the establishment of a key public place and for the incorporation of traditional Coventry icons (Coventry Corporation, 1959:15):

> The post-war reconstruction was initiated by the laying out of the square, which uses generous gift of plants from the Netherlands (sic). This helped to maintain public interest, at a time when shortages of everything, not to mention building licences, prevented any early start on the permanent buildings. The bronze statue of Godiva was executed by Sir William Reid Dick . . . . Interesting features are the Bridge Restaurant, clockwork figures of Lady Godiva and 'Peeping Tom', the Martyrs' Monument.

As Clarke and Day (1982) reveal, the Godiva story, presumed to have indelible links with Coventry since its Saxon origins, only gained such recognition following the tours of Defoe and Pennant in the 17th and 18th centuries (*see* Chapter 14), and from paintings after that time. The story of a naked rider, of the voyeuristic Peeping Tom, and of tax protest seemed sustainable through its diverse appeal, but by the late 1980s

(English Tourist Board, 1987) the symbolic primacy of Godiva had given way, in Coventry's promotion, to the sculpture of St Michael and the Devil from the nave exterior of Coventry Cathedral. Godiva is now on the brochure's inside pages, relegated by the work of Jacob Epstein, the *enfant terrible* of earlier public art. Godiva was subsequently replaced on city entrance signs by a stylised rural landscape, and in central-area restructuring was all but enrobed by the canopy of a new shopping centre. Clearly Godiva's contemporary correctness is in question!

With the slogan 'A modern face, an ancient heart', Coventry now attempts to combine the images of heritage city and thriving retail centre. This same combination, found for example in the publicity of Saint-Omer – 'The Old French Town', 'Town of Art and History Sited in a Garden', 'Shopping', 'Tourism' – represents a current standard, identifiable in countless other towns and cities (Région Nord Pas de Calais, n.d.).

In effect, though, it is the city as art, usually an assemblage of historic buildings as art, that has now assumed prominence in tourism promotion. In Britain at least, this practice has grown steadily since European Architectural Heritage Year in 1975 when the general tourist potential of urban heritage was realised, and the model town trail, the Austrian *Wiener Spaziergang*, served as a model for such exploratory routes (Stadt Wien, 1975).

Typical interpretations of town as heritage art include the 'Macclesfield Town Trail' (Norris, n.d.) from which all 20th-century reference is banished, and the 'Discover Islington–The *Real* London' (Figure 9.1) programme which appears to set reality in the late 18th century (Discover Islington, n.d.). Another example is 'Tendring is Heritage' (Tendring Borough Council, 1988) in which the once prominent seaside resorts of Clacton, Frinton and Walton are downgraded in favour of village and dockyard imagery. As Sir Philip Dowson (1992) has recently noted:

> . . . we seem to try and rob our cities of their twentieth century reality. There is a regressive instinct which seeks the false security of known historical patterns, even where these may be quite inappropriate, or yesterday's solutions to yesterday's problems, and which merely reflect an 'escape culture' – a dream.

Significantly, though, literary and artistic heritage may form part of this escape culture. Thus Coventry has laid claim to being the city in Shakespeare country, so Tendring manages to stretch beyond its bounds to feature 'Constable Country' in its idealised visitor map. Yet although England has a considerable reputation in landscape painting, the 'Constable Country' (see Daniels, 1992) is something of an exception. Artists and architects have seldom provided the theme for English areas to be marketed. In sharp contrast, consider, for example, the way in which Gaudi's Catalan personality and work have been used since permitted in a democratic Spain. Gaudi's work has formed a foundation for the prolonged city promotion drawing on Picasso, Dali and, currently, Miro, and on the period street furniture of the city. This sophisticated, and highly developed approach, makes an interesting comparison with the Black Country town of Dudley's efforts, pioneering in Britain, to maintain and feature through 'The Tecton Trail', their unique collection of early modern-movement architecture by the seminal Tecton practice of the 1930s (Dudley Metropolitan Borough Planning and Architecture Department, n.d.):

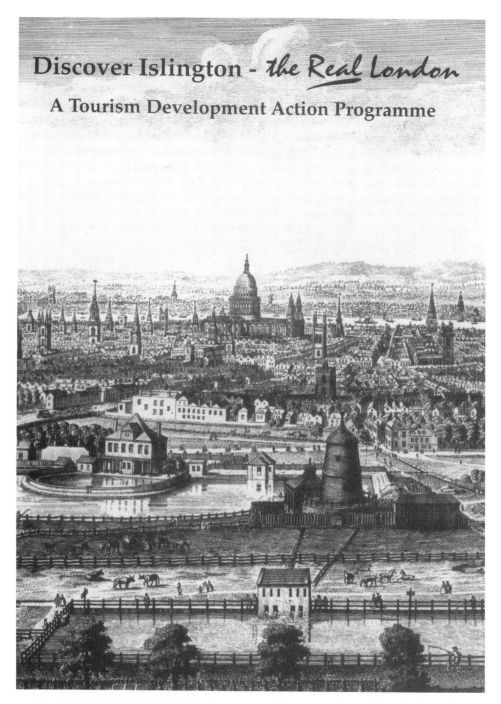

Figure 9.1   Discover Islington – *the Real London* can evidently show nothing after the 18th century.

> The vision for the Tecton Collection is to restore the perception of the buildings which people had when they flocked in their thousands to Dudley Zoo in 1937. The buildings in those days were revolutionary and it was not until the Festival of Britain in 1951 that such an architectural experience was to be repeated.

In Britain, at least, it has been place themes deriving from the literary rather than the visual arts which have attracted visitors and therefore formed the basis for current marketing strategies. One reason for this is alluded to in Rugby's 'Tom Brown Trail' (Rugby Borough Council, n.d.):

> Some 'poetic licence' has been assumed in naming this guide to the town after the novel, because not all the places mentioned have anything to do with Tom Brown's Schooldays. Many of the buildings and landmarks identified in the book have long since disappeared. Some do remain however, and Rugby School, with its beautiful buildings, is still very much in evidence, as is the statue of Thomas Hughes in the grounds of one of the school buildings.

Quite simply, promotion through literary reference allows more flexibility than through historic graphics which often compare unfavourably with contemporary reality.

The saga of Wigan Pier exemplifies the advantages of this flexibility. A 1975 educational trail for Wigan (Keyte, 1975:5) clambers through the detritus of the industrial revolution and halts a little uncertainly at Wigan Pier: 'As you climb a slight ramp on the towpath, rather like a small railway station platform, you are on the site of Wigan Pier. At least, this is the most generally accepted site . . .'. By 1979 the British Waterways Board had decided on demolition of these disused coal staithes (Steed and Arnold, n.d.:13) but just three years later the Pier area had become a 'unique and valuable complex' of industrial buildings. Literature and popular theatre both played their parts in this rapid promotional transformation. A music-hall joke attributed to George Formby Snr., and the social critique, *The Road to Wigan Pier*, by George Orwell were pressed into marketing service. One panel of a recent promotional leaflet from Wigan ('Metropolitan Wigan: We've Got It Right') features the Orwell portrait from the end gable of the dockside pub which is named after this none-too-complimentary author (who had drawn his own pseudonym from a river in Suffolk). The implications of *Animal Farm* or *1984* are hardly explained in the excellent interpretive centre nearby. George Orwell, like the Pier, is reduced to icon (Metropolitan Wigan, n.d.).

The iconography of literature in tourism marketing is most evident in Brontë Country where film and pop-record references are the closest most visitors have come to the authors' work. As Herbert (1991) comments:

> Haworth may be the capital of Brontë Country, but what exactly has Brontë Country to do with the introspective Victorian scribblers whose name it bears? Almost nothing, as far as the traders and trippers are concerned. Seven years ago a survey of the latter revealed that only 8 per cent of visitors to Haworth are drawn by interest in the Brontës. A few come to see the Haworth–Keighley steam railway – where 'The Railway Children' was filmed – but the rest flock in because Haworth has become 'a place to visit', a day out.

With the rapid growth of urban tourism over the past two decades the majority of visitors have been successfully seduced by contained, and largely contrived, indoor attractions or 'experiences' where newer arts of animation and audio-visual presentation, pioneered by Disney, have been exploited to the full. In Britain, the Jorvik Viking Centre in York was both pioneer and exception, being based on an authentic location and remains. A result of cooperation between archaeologists and developers, it offers a ride experience through the sounds and smells of a vividly evoked interpretation of Viking life and, with subsequent related developments, has become the focus of a York visit.

'Cadbury World: The Chocolate Experience' is another signficant example. It moves further from place – Bournville, of great architectural significance as a pioneering garden surburb, is only a footnote to the brochure and exhibition which feature dioramas of the Court of Montezuma and film-clips of corporate advertising. Although featured in Birmingham's promotion, and a popular day-visit destination, 'Cadbury World' exemplifies the antithesis of art as a feature of urban promotion and design, yet it is indicative of a form of urban tourism with broad-based popularity. It offers popular icons – here advertising symbols and fun food – and aesthetic satisfaction in its parallels with both Disney and television image. Here also is convenience, specialist shopping in the form of a dedicated 'Chocolate Shop', a food court, and free, secure parking. Part of Bournville, the model suburb, has been converted into a small, themed, out-of-town shopping centre, the perpetual challenger to promoted towns and cities.

Public art as urban design

To counter the flight to the periphery, cities have turned to more conscious use of public art and featured architecture since the 1970s. Three major tendencies have been evident. The first is the initially spontaneous celebration of 'community art', a product of the 1960s liberation and democratisation of art in student communities:

> Corporate advertisers control the airwaves, printed media, and most city walls. Not only have they painted their inane commercial messages on the sides of buildings, they have also built new walls in the countryside and called them billboards. The lesson of the mural groups is that some exterior spaces can be reclaimed by the community to reflect its own culture. There are many walls still to be painted, a great deal of material for sculpture, but above all, there are creative people who have inherited a thousand years of experience in the use of paint and stone. (Sommer, 1975:cover)

The early American murals owed much to Mexican antecedents (Edwards, 1966) endorsed by government in the early 1920s, and their revival by the Works Progress Administration in the New Deal USA of the 1930s. Their successors sought to increase inner city identity – the Detroit 'Wall of Pride', Chicago's 'Wall of Respect' and New York's 'Arise from Oppression' featuring ethnic achievement. They also drew on the occasional commercial enhancement which had achieved fame for earlier locations – especially the rural hog idyll surrounding the Farmer John Brand meat packing company in Los Angeles.

By the early 1970s American mural painting (see Schmidt-Brummer, 1973) had become locally regulated, professionalised, and internalised by public authorities. The

Figure 9.2   Multi-purpose shrine -religious sculpture, nationalistic red, white and blue framing, popular idols. Liverpool, 1985.

lines were cleaner, the visual japes more complex (especially when deconstructing blank elevations or intrusive objects; see survey by Greenberg *et al.*, 1977). Their news value grew and became more positive for both the local community and civic authority. There has been a 20-year transition from locally produced decorative murals, through the arrival of gallery artists such as Allan D'Arcangelo on New York City buildings by 1970, to the careful colour grading schemes of new Paris apartment buildings and contrived covers for out-of-scale errors. The sequence concludes with the design of blocks as mural structures in a number of major Brazilian cities by Fernando Peixoto (1991).

Community-inspired and -maintained art is, of course, a common characteristic of most cultures (Figures 9.2 and 9.3) but although the image may remain 'amateur', and

Figure 9.3 Dry season community graphics with political additions in Elche, southern Spain, 1992.

all the more attractive for that, permissions and organisation are now commonly required (detailed in Jones, n.d.). In the UK there were antecedents in the much-photographed, sectarian, gable-end paintings of Belfast, the subject of postcards and popular illustrated books. The 'community art' movement formalised rapidly into two artist residencies and programmes of largely figurative, and often polemic or humorous, super-graphics and sculpture. Now often faded, gable-end graphics are evident in the inner city ring of many cities, but programmes such as Swindon's, initiated in 1975, have provided a lively range of colourful memorials, including one to the film starlet Diana Dors. Although never featuring strongly in its promotional campaigns, the Swindon programme is indicative of the way in which accessible art has been used to humanise a town undergoing a rapid physical change and to transfer the image from railway centre to high-tech expanded town. The spirit of 'community art' saw some revival in the early 1990s (Melhuish, 1989, 1990; Carr, 1990). Jones (1993) provides a detailed account of the gradual progress achieved by a local authority with an imageable, traditional sculpture.

What Swindon might have achieved is evident from the internationally recognised example of Chemainus, a town with a population of 3500, 50 miles north of Victoria, British Columbia. In 1983 the only local industry, the sawmill, was closed. In the face of the collapse of the town, five murals were unveiled in 1982, a further seven in 1983, with others following. The town received 300,000 visitors in 1990 (Patty, 1991) and had 70 new businesses including a new sawmill. Chemainus is perhaps unique in its development of public art as a major industry. The range of Canadian artists involved, and the local, regional and national history which they reveal, have put the town on the map as never before. Now the developing Pacific Rim Artisan Village is building further on the arts theme, as a recent brochure suggests:

> The Master Lodge will be an integral part of the Artisan Village. This impressive 120-suite guest facility will pay tribute to the master artists and craftsmen of the world. Each suite will be dedicated to a famous artist: DaVinci, Rembrandt, Raphael, Michelangelo . . .

One might query this eclectic approach, but the fact remains that a town in decline has recovered and diversified around the arts, retaining a strong emphasis on popular arts and crafts, accessible areas for the visitor and consumer.

In the 1970s a number of British programmes attempted to place art more firmly in the public forum. The 1972 City Sculpture project was (Arts Council of Great Britain, 1972):

> . . . an attempt to bring advanced sculpture to the public, to gain interest and patronage for sculpture from the direction it has traditionally come, but which has increasingly been in abeyance.

The nation-wide programme of sculptural contributions continued an international sequence of exhibitions which had focused on abstract, largely hard-edged structures. Paradoxically, therefore, it was Nicholas Monro's five-metre-high fibreglass gorilla erected in Birmingham's Bull Ring, which most engaged public interest. Although accessible, 'Guy the Gorilla' or 'King Kong' (as variously titled by the local press) was rejected by community and civic authorities as a slur on Birmingham's cultural integrity.

A similar fate befell many of the proposals which emerged from the Arts Council's 'Art into Landscape' competitions for artists, architects and landscape architects in the 1970s (Grayson, 1974, 1977; Groves, 1980). Few of the proposals for nominated 'difficult' sites were effected, and some that were reflected imposition rather than adoption. Thomas Meddings' *Brobdingnagian Knot Garden* was erected by the Greater

162 BRIAN GOODEY

Figure 9.4 Typical British approach to public art. A (now) politically incorrect representation of butchery stranded in the market place of the former New Town of Harlow, Essex, 1991.

London Council (a major arts benefactor) by the Thames at Rotherhithe following the 1977 competition; ten years later it had collapsed into a heap of unmaintained rusting hawsers. Adoption by the successor authority was obviously not a priority. Seldom is community recognition alone sufficient to ensure the survival of art in public places. Regular civic maintenance and conservation are necessary, a commitment to public space which has not been accepted (Figure 9.4).

The second main approach is the American use of public art as an integral element of, and benefit from, new development initiatives. This is often characterised by the 'percentage for art' programme (Harney, 1981; Cruickshank and Korza, 1988). The key image here is of the 'Chicago Picasso', a fifty-foot-high, abstract, female head of Cor-Ten steel in what is now the Richard J. Daley Plaza in 1967. The Picasso was a direct attempt to redirect the national image of a corrupt and declining city, focusing interest on new architecture and public places. It was followed by contributions from Calder, Chagall, Oldenburg, Dubuffet and many American artists in the 1970s and early 1980s. While Chicago's works are set within, and often define, their public places, the Seattle percentage for art programme, developed since 1972, represents a much closer integration of site-specific work with new public contexts (Mahler *et al.*, 1991). It includes elements of civil engineering, such as flood-control barriers, and street furniture. This programme was developed further, in 1990, with the Art in Public Transit project which delivered 30 works for the city's underground bus tunnel. Sacramento (California) adopted a more limited programme to its light rail system in the mid-1980s (see Kahn and Worpole, 1992) and has influenced current design thinking in the West Midlands proposed light rail system.

Finally there are the Dutch percentage-for-art programmes tracing their origins to the 1920s (see De Boer, 1977; Benjamin, 1983). Through national and city government sponsorship they have made the most visible contribution to the land and townscape of a nation. Although evident in travel, with a particular emphasis on transport routes and interchanges, this is not a facet of the Netherlands which is widely promoted except in new towns and suburbs now seeking visitors. There are two major reasons for this. The first is that most Dutch centres can build effectively on a heritage market based on the many well known Low Country painters. The second reason would seem to be that the artistic contributions to new architectural, urban and landscape development have become routine – only meriting discussion when they offend.

One can imagine the furore which might have been engendered in some cultures by the decision symbolically to crash and partly submerge an engine unit (Figure 9.5) in an embankment as part of the Dutch railways' contribution to the five-yearly Floriade garden festival, held at the former new town of Zoetermeer in 1992. Yet this was not the first such image to be employed in the Netherlands. As with landscape design, there is a disposability, a regular harvesting of artists' work in the Netherlands, which reinforces the judgement that here, as in no other nation, art has been fully integrated with the public's expectation of the environment, and its ability to renew.

One hundred percent for art?

The featured illustrations for the 1992 catalogue of the Yokohama Urban Design Forum (Tsuchida, 1992) are indicative of the contemporary role which urban design is being encouraged to play in city marketing. Following a series of international visits and interviews, Yokohama mounted a congress which allows the 'world cities' to feature their urban design initiatives. The catalogue is instructive, suggesting the architectural, planning or community orientation of presumed world leaders.

Paris particularly stands out in this group. The past decade of Mitterand-inspired *Grands Projets* in this group has fundamentally altered the iconography of that city's promotion. Yet these are but part of an approach to public art and architecture which runs both broader and wider. Meade (1991:555) suggests that a 'deep-rooted identification of great buildings with civilisation and the glory of the French State' may

Figure 9.5   Part of Dutch Railways' striking contribution to the 1992 Floriade at Zoetermeer.

be traced at least to the early 16th century. Certainly since De Gaulle's Fifth Republic and his appointment of André Malraux as Cultural Minister, major architectural projects have been regularly used to establish public places, albeit with raging political debate which, of course, has ensured further visibility for the product. Thus President Pompidou initiated the competition for the Beaubourg cultural centre, designed by Piano and Rogers, though opposed by Pompidou's successor Giscard d'Estaing. Yet as Banham (1977:277) showed by quoting Sigfried Giedion, Fernand Léger and José Luis Sert's 'Nine Points on Monumentality', it serves as a unique symbol of the Modern Movement:

> . . . re-planning on a large scale . . . will create vast open spaces in the now decaying areas of our cities. In these open spaces, monumental architecture will find its appropriate setting.

'The Pompidou' did much more than keeping its sponsor's memory before the public. Its technological inside-out image, deposition of art collections and library in a new central city setting, and the managed spontaneity of external space all became featured in international journals and texts and provided a new, colourful art object for the city.

Giscard d'Estaing followed with proposals for the Orsay Museum and, just prior to the 1981 presidential elections, selected a further museum scheme for the redundant, De Gaulle-inspired, abattoir site at La Villette. Under Mitterrand, La Villette became one of the most famous of *Les Grands Projets*. A further competition to create 'the park of the twenty-first century' was won by Bernard Tschumi in 1983. Mitterrand also initiated competitions for the Institute of the Arab World, the Bastille opera, the Finance Ministry at Bercy and, most notably, L'Arche de la Défense. The Grand Louvre, I.M. Pei's pyramid at the Louvre, and the Arche have, as intended, become international marketing images.

Before considering L'Arche de la Défense in more detail, it is important to recognise that *Les Grands Projets* represent a sequence of controversial national monuments generated from the presidency. Their immediate promotional impact is national and international in scale; thus global discourse is matched with local political tensions. Conflicts between presidency and Jacques Chirac as Mayor of Paris ensured that art and architecture remained on the public agenda, and as I write (January 1993) over 30 jolly, people-friendly statues by the Colombian sculptor Fernando Botero pace the walker down the Champs-Elysées.

It is, however, l'Arche de la Défense ('Arche') which most clearly embodies the purpose and origins of *Les Grands Projets*. Like the model for all triumphal city arches – the last imperial celebration by Constantine the Great in Rome – the Arche appears to conform to the international language of such structures (Figure 9.6). It seems to provide a gateway, a passage whereby its grandeur is visited on those who pass through, a reaching for the sky, a formal acknowledgement of achievement by its donor, and possibly by its users (*see also* Chapter 10). In reality, however, the Arche is actually few of these things. To Mitterrand it was 'an open window on an unforeseeable future' dedicated as a symbol of the defence of human rights, as a commemoration of the bicentenary of the French Revolution, and the centenary of the Eiffel Tower. Designed by Danish architect, Johan Otto von Spreckelsen in 1983, it is a megastructure, an open monolithic cube with glass lifts carrying the visitor to a rooftop belvedere, hanging gardens and a view of Paris which visitors are drawn to enjoy (Glancy, 1993). A heavily marketed attraction, its development was nearly halted in 1986, and was achieved largely from private investment. A major purpose of the Arche was to draw business to the office centre of La Défense, which though embodying a powerful image of Paris, is outside the mayoralty of the city itself. This it has succeeded in doing and it sits amid the gleaming headquarters towers of major French and international companies. As to place-making value, Paul Andreu (1991: 577) notes, 'there are a lot of high density apartments in the area, and people express their satisfaction at living somewhere that is on the map'.

The Arche is truly monumental public art, a major urban design feature, concluding (for the present) an axis marked by the Champs-Elysées, Place de la Concorde, and L'Arc de Triomphe. Whatever the criticisms, and there have inevitably been many, it addresses the city user at a variety of scales, from the tourist map to the use of the rooftop as viewpoint, the latter a feature of most Parisian landmark structures. While Paris is unique in implicating its newest and most monumental structures with effective place marketing, it provides a model which others have followed. The Civic Centre in

Figure 9.6   La Grande Arche, La Défense, Paris. A dramatic example of the deliberate use of artistic statements to market a place for tourism and investment.

the sprawling suburban community of Mississauga near Toronto (see Arnell and Bickford, 1984), designed by Jones and Kirkland, offers ready interpretation as a symbol for the city and provides its first significant tourist venue (Mississauga, 1987):

> Observers of the building have commented that the cylindrical Council Chamber is the grain silo; the steel-frame clock tower is the windmill; and the high-rise office block the main house with its cottage roof frame. The central building, the most important farm structure of all, is the great shed-roofed barn with its grand doors and rows of smaller doors and windows.

In São Paulo, Brazil, a former inner city industrial site has been developed as the Memorial da America Latina with work by Oscar Niemeyer, doyen of Brazilian modern architects. Here the monumental is taken a step further, with a sequence of concrete, arched, pavilions housing libraries, museums and an auditorium. The scale is vast (78,000 square metres of which 20,000 are under cover) befitting a city which extends to every horizon. In a society where the buildings of Brasilia have established a national role as art objects for those with time to enjoy, this is a further manifestation of the integration of the arts in an urban site. The whole purpose of the Memorial is to establish São Paulo as a visitor destination for Latin America, to stake a city's claim to an international clientèle. Its spirit is now continued in the radical landscape scheme which has, once more, claimed the city's historic core for pedestrian use.

Nowhere has this tendency been more evident than in Barcelona, culminating in the success of the Olympic Games in 1992 when the world saw, at its opening, that even the popular artistic tradition of urban masque could be revived on a massive scale without a hitch (Goodey, 1992b). Elms (1992:45) described with incisive detail the path which the city's Mayor Maragall has taken to achieve what must stand as a model of 20th-century city revival: 'We have a tradition of radical architecture and design to live up to. I believe it is our duty to support exciting, excellent projects, to back talent. This is happening throughout Spain, but most actively here in Barcelona we cannot just live on our past'.

Against an outstanding architectural background (see Woodward, 1992), the city has worked with its neighbourhoods to establish some dozen new parks and 150 new plazas, has achieved the Olympic accommodations and marked the whole by the erection of Norman Foster's Torre de Collserola standing above the city. A programme of public sculpture 'to give dignity to public spaces' engaged the likes of Serra, Caro, Lichtenstein, Oldenburg and Miro at a standard £10,000 fee (Elms, 1992:44) but with materials provided and a licence to create freely. Clearly the visitor is invited to enjoy this city in all its parts. Foreign language, full-colour guide leaflets with clear maps, texts and illustrations offer 'Barcelona – Barri gotic (Cartes, n.d.); Modernisme (Perrmanyer, n.d.); Nou urbanisme (Calzado, v.d.). There are few world cities that can feature their 'new urbanism' in a density which no visitor can avoid, and can back it up with restaurants, galleries and shops which re-emphasise the role of design in everyday life. Barcelona has become the model for effective art and design generation and promotion for at least the next decade (Figure 9.7).

Good of their kind

Examples of new urbanism, and especially of public places dedicated to artists' work are, inevitably, rarer in Britain – a country not known for its contemporary confidence in monumentality but which thrives on its heritage reference. Visitor centres market the safe Victorian streetscape, however contrived (Figure 9.8), or feature the aesthetic merits of a windblown sub-Victorian park alongside the lacklustre design of an indoor water experience at the 'seaside'. Ian Nairn, one of the sponsors of the 'Art into Landscape' programme noted, after a visit to the sculptured public spaces of the French new town of Grigny-la-Grande-Borne, that the British design was faulted as accepting 'the letter but unable to reach the spirit' (Nairn, 1972) and this is an appropriate judgement on what follows.

As we saw in Chapter 6, industrial centres with decreasing population and an urgent need to make contact with the national visitor and international conference-goer have had to work harder, and it is here that some rewarding examples of city promotion emerge. In urban design terms, most of these schemes have involved the making or re-making of urban place, a positive re-statement by the city of its commitment to downtown in the face of out of town retail attractions. The Swansea Maritime Quarter, developed around a former industrial dock area, has pioneered a continuing pro-gramme of Architectural Enhancement, and 'Stony Stories: A Maritime Quarter Trail' which is a key feature in the marketing of both properties and visitor attractions in the area (City of Swansea Tourist Information, n.d.):

Figure 9.7 Parc de l'Espanya Industrial, Barcelona, 1985, by Luis Pena Ganchegui, creates recreational opportunities, architectural creativity and different types of sculpture.

Like the stone panels of the Enhancement programme its function is to remind us of Swansea's maritime–industrial heritage. And by reminding us of the past, add to the sum total of our enjoyment of the present by creating an awareness of history. The architecture, enhancement features and Stony Stories are all layers of meaning and interpretation which help visitor and local alike come to terms with the new. Stony Stories reconstructs in graphic form the missing world replaced by the Maritime Quarter, and repopulates the ghost world of Swansea's heritage.

Figure 9.8 Typical British heritage street scene – medieval route with Victorian sign co-ordination, Lincoln, 1992.

So, it is back to heritage – but with a density of imagery and availability of interpretation which endorses contemporary relevance. Overall the Swansea programme provides sculptural punctuation to a new piece of city, aids orientation, and reclaims heritage in a contemporary style, which allows the visitor to dig deep into the past (British American Arts Association, 1989; Campbell, 1990).

A more modest but singularly imageable project is Sheffield's Tudor Square which shares with out-of-town competitor, Meadowhall Shopping Centre, and Burbage

Moor the cover of the recent 'Sheffield: The Welcoming City' brochure (Destination Sheffield, n.d.). Now freed of parked cars, Tudor Square serves to link the Victoria Lyceum, and modern Crucible theatres, the Art Deco geometry of the Central Library, and the Ruskin Gallery. With facades jostling for dominance, the sculptor Paul Mason worked with the city's Urban Design team and developed a quiet visual language derived from the forms of runes and other precursors of writing. These designs are reflected in metal tree grilles, railings and paving detail. The artist's hand has been present and effective though without ever demanding the attention of the viewer.

The same cannot be said for Birmingham's Centenary Square which provides a major exhibition and performance space fronting the new International Convention Centre (see Knott, 1991) and the existing Repertory Theatre as well as a vastly improved pedestrian link through to the 1970s brutalist Library, and thence to the city's centre past Victoria Square where additional monumental features were revealed in May 1993. Centenary Square is only the most evident of a number of Birmingham initiatives (see Stewart, 1991; Arnott, 1992; Hall, 1992) which must serve to reinforce the city's internal and external visibility. Centenary Square was achieved through the city's urban designers and landscape architects and the Birmingham-based Public Art Commissions Agency which engaged Tess Jarray following her success at Victoria Station, London (Ostler, 1985) to manage this percentage-for-art scheme. To unify the disparate array of surrounding buildings she used an Italian firm to effect an over-complex terra cotta and brick paving scheme which reflected Birmingham's Victorian and Edwardian facades (Harrod, 1991). The very extensive array of street furniture also harks back to Birmingham's industrial heyday. In addition to the existing classical 1930s Hall of Memory, now seen in new light, there are four major sculptural elements which structure vision and movement within the square. The first, a neon impression of birds in flight, marks the Convention Centre entrance; there is a joyful fountain by Tom Lomax dedicated to Enterprise, Industry and Learning, and a timeless memorial to the typographer John Baskerville outside the council office which bears his name (Figure 9.9).

The most imageable element is Raymond Mason's fibreglass *Crowd Scene*, seemingly a barge-borne squad of Brummies of various ages, advancing from smoke-plumed factories (Figure 9.10). Figurative and provocative, Mason's work has served the purpose as a major talking-point in an otherwise artistically complex environment. Unlike Sheffield, Birmingham seems to want resident and visitor to recognise the city as a patron of the arts. Yet although Centenary Square vastly improves the pedestrian experience and provides new insight to surrounding buildings, it has not featured prominently in promotional material which tends to emphasise the interior comfort of the adjacent new facilities. Centenary and Tudor Squares have both been inserted within the framework provided by existing buildings, so the visibility and composition of environmental art may well suffer from being an addition, the icing on an existing cake. Yet, despite similar constraints, Barcelona seems to have avoided this problem (Gayford, 1992).

All this begs the question of how the artist's contribution fares when a novel context is generated: does it, or the new architecture, steal the show? Two London examples are instructive. First, Canary Wharf, with its tower by Cesar Pelli, 800 feet high (*see* Chapter 8). This landmark feature, visible at many points on the M25 orbital motorway around London, is so dominant an image that even other substantial

Figure 9.9   Civic Art in Centenary Square, Birmingham 1992 – from the foreground are visible paving by Tess Jarray, part of David Patten's monument to the typographer, Baskerville, a layer of 'Britain in Bloom' and the inter-war Hall of Memory.

architectural contributions by the likes of Aldo Rossi and Skidmore, Owings and Merrill are dwarfed. Prior to its financial collapse, Canary Wharf featured an arts and events programme which achieved limited recognition, but neither the landscape nor the commissioned elements within the buildings and public spaces received any public attention (for an assessment see Tate, 1991). Unlike the Arche in Paris – for thoughts of monumentality must have touched the reader at this point – the tightness of Canary

Figure 9.10 Characters from Raymond Mason's *Crowd Scene* in Centenary Square, Birmingham, seen against the backdrop of the Alpha Tower, designed by Richard Siefert. Does this account for their expressions?

Wharf offers the visitor no escape from the symbolic dominance of the tower. With a larger area dedicated to public pleasure, and the transport to get there (as at La Défense) this might have been an appropriate place for public art. Instead we are prescribed the tight-rolled umbrella of Cabot Square. Regrettably Canary Wharf has become the enduring symbol of Docklands greed and retreat from urban design.

Fortunately Broadgate, adjacent to the vastly improved Liverpool Street Station in the City of London, has been more effective, raising an important pointer for art in the contemporary city. The development features a central piazza and an array of sculpture, effective planting, and a widely promoted events programme. While Richard Serra's angled rusted steel plates, *Fulcrum*, hark back to an earlier age of imposed sculptural performance, Fernando Botero is represented by a sensuous *Venus*, and George Segal's nearby *Rush Hour* portrays a group of such washed-out commuters that their real-life equivalents raise a smile. Broadgate's design has achieved national recognition, but it is the working urban community which is drawn to the site for lunchtime leisure amid fixed and performance art.

The city as event

Urban marketing and promotion have generated the media city, the urban place composed of televised and advertised districts at local scale, and of symbolic structures at national and international levels. Events and their settings have been both generated and embraced by this process (see Goodey, 1992a). Increasingly, central cities survive and grow from the careful spatial and temporal manipulation of events around which shopper, visitor and tourist programmes can be constructed. Increasingly too, such events occur in privatised or pay-bounded environments. In this regard out-of-town shopping centres and garden festivals share many characteristics affecting the range of art available to the public. Unguarded urban settings are often seen as too dangerous for the casual walker and for most public art. Retreat from the violence and danger of city centres is, to this writer, an unacceptable reality but it has already sorted out the forms of art which appear in the city and elsewhere.

The secure and temporary nature of British garden festivals, and of the Dutch Floriade, have provided settings for some of the most exciting and approachable public art being created today. At Liverpool, then Glasgow, Stoke (Art and Design, 1986; Goodey, 1989), Gateshead (Festival Landmarks, 1990), Ebbw Vale and Zoetermeer the fun environments represented a visitor cropping, to be replaced by urban development (Figure 9.11). At each site the public arts programmes served to illustrate a much wider range of features than could ever be safely incorporated in a public place. It was Andrew Darke's Japanese styled *Threshold* arch which featured most strongly in press coverage of the Ebbw Vale site (see Gilson, 1992; Goodey, 1992a) and Andy Plant's *Newport Clock: In the Nick of Time* (Figures 9.12 and 9.13) which drew most attention on site. Many sculptural features blurred the public vision of art, providing opportunities for climbing, looking through, sitting on, and feeling which would seldom be attempted, or permitted, in an urban setting.

Both Ebbw Vale, where the new village of Victoria is growing around some retained artworks on site, and Zoetermeer, where the Floriade site structure was more clearly established to allow future development (den Ruijter, 1987; den Ruijter and Hinse, 1987) with a sequence of canal-side folly structures which will survive, represent a new first cropping by art. The garden festival, like the sculpture park, provides a controlled setting for innovation, for transaction between the artists and publics (Floriade, 1992):

Figure 9.11   Sculpture as fun – the Dragon water feature at the Gateshead Garden Festival, on Tyneside, 1990.

The Floriade theme park was recognised by the organisers of *Allocations* as a public environment in which the work of art could tell 'another' story than in the 'enclosure' of the museum or in the bureaucratised urban environment.

Allocations means allotment, sharing out. Art's rare product is always shared out through channels designed for it, such as the gallery, museum and the art press. Complicated transfers take place between artist, work of art and public, in which the work of art must serve various interests . . . . The meaning of the work of art is not something that the artist has invested it with, which subsequently survives all of these transfers and displacements. Some works obtain their meanings *precisely* at a certain place, on a certain occasion, or during certain events. The works in

Figures 9.12 (*above*) **and 9.13** (*overleaf*)   Temporary arch, the Newport Clock: In the Nick of Time, by Andy Plant. This was commissioned by Newport Borough Council for the Garden Festival, Wales, 1992. As its creator commented: ' The Newport Clock is a cross between a cuckoo clock and an expresso coffee machine, 31 feet high, lovingly clad in stainless steel, each wobbly weld is the mark of a true craftsman. On the hour, the devil points up to the clockface, doors open and skellies look out, waving their hour glasses . . . smoke starts to ooze out of cracks, there's thunder and lightning and the whole clock tower begins to collapse . . . what will happen next? . . . The only white knuckle clock in the world.'

> *Allocations* refer, in highly diversified ways, to the rich thematic area of the public space and the status and place of the work of art within it. They also deal with the relationship of human beings to the natural and artificial environment in which they live and relax.

Whether, in the commercial buzz and multi-media extravaganzas of the Dutch Floriade, visitors were able to view and contemplate the *Allocations* collection is open to question. This quotation, however, does return us to the essentials.

Figure 9.13   (*Caption on p. 175*)

Conclusion

By incorporating 'art' in the environment, society is allocating a small part of budget, space and time to the contemplation of evidence which is, in part at least, intended to stimulate awareness of the other-than-functional, doing, achieving world. The artist provides stimulus in the choice of material and form, offering comment on circumstance, event or object (Figure 9.14). Whether the majority of city users are equipped, or allow time, to consider such objects will depend on form, location . . . and promotion. As Thomas (1990) noted, 'public art can be difficult to live with, it may not enhance or beautify public space. Like the abstract sculptures sited on some of the main streets of West Berlin it may draw attention to the deficiencies of our public space' and, perhaps, legitimise the retreat from the city. Yet for all these traditional roles of art, beyond or alongside the material imperatives of society, the environment itself has now been commodified. Even chancing upon a woodland sculpture, most visitors will then seek an interpretive panel, guidebook or postcard to validate the experience. So it is that local, regional and national promotion strategies have become an integral part of the artistic statement. Unless recognised by the authority of media, the object is seldom worthy of consideration.

In special cases the art object can epitomise the quality of space. This is in the continuing tradition of lofty markers claiming their surrounding space, but is now extended to the implicit combination of designed space and the events which it is expected to contain. For the future we can expect the redundancy which mass media encourages, to consume art-in-the-environment innovations with increasing speed. A

Figure 9.14 A retreat to ruralism, Howard Bowcott's 'Oak Leaf Seat' at Garden Festival, Wales. This was originally commissioned by the Woodland Trust for Coed Cymerau-isaf, Vale of Festiniog, Gwynedd, 1992.

re-designed square with a century's life may only claim the required media attention for a month. Promotional literature may feature it for two or three years. The dilemma is that the structured space requires regular tending in order to meet its most immediate user-needs. With a continuing corporate necessity to generate new media images for promotional purposes, there is every chance that those responsible will discard such spaces long before the community and its successive generations have had time to adopt and venerate them. As we have noted in other chapters there is inherent tension between the promoter's and the community's requirements of place. The pack-up-and-go garden festival or urban event is, therefore, a more appropriate setting for artistic innovation in this non-place age.

References

Andreu, P. and Lion, R. (1991) 'L'Arche de la Défense: a case study', *Royal Society of Arts' Journal* (August–September), 571–80.

Arnell, P. and Bickford, T. eds. (1984) *Mississauga City Hall: a Canadian competition*, New York: Rizzoli.

Arnott, C. (1992) 'Brum saves itself from the Philistines', *The Independent*, 11 November.

Art and Design (1986) *Sculpture at Stoke*, guidebook reprinted from *Art and Design*.

Arts Council of Great Britain (1972) *City Sculpture*, London: Arts Council of Great Britain.

Banham, R. (1977) 'The Pompidolium', *Architectural Review*, 161(963), 271–90.

Benjamin, L. W. (1983) *The Art of Designed Environments in the Netherlands*, Amsterdam: Stichting Kunst en Bedrijf.

British American Arts Association (1989) *Arts and the Changing City: an agenda for urban regeneration*, conference report.

Calzado, B. (n.d.) *Barcelona: nou urbanisme*, Barcelona: Patronat de Turisme, Ajuntament de Barcelona.

Campbell, R. (1990) *Sites and Enhancement Sculpture Monuments*, Swansea: Special Projects Group, Development Department, Swansea City Council.

Carr, R. (1990) 'Urban renewal can be an art form', *Building Design*, 4 May, 16.

Cartes, F. (n.d.) *Barcelona: Barri gotic*, Barcelona: Patronat de Turisme, Ajuntament de Barcelona.

City of Swansea Tourist Information (n.d.) *Stony Stories: A maritime quarter trail*, Swansea: City of Swansea Tourist Information.

Clarke, R.A. and Day, P.A.E. (1982) *Lady Godiva: images of a legend in art and society*, Coventry: Herbert Art Gallery and Museum, Leisure Services, City of Coventry.

Coventry Corporation Public Relations Department (1959) *Development and Redevelopment in Coventry*, Coventry: Coventry Corporation Public Relations Department.

Cruickshank, J.L. and Korza, P. (1988) *Going Public: a field guide to developments in art in public places*, Washington D.C.: Arts Exhibition Service, Visual Arts Program of the National Endowment for the Arts.

Daniels, S. (1992) 'Reconstructing Constable Country', *Geographical Magazine*, October, 10–14.

Darke, J. (1991) *The Monument Guide to England and Wales: a national portrait in bronze and stone*, London: Macdonald Illustrated.

de Boer, H. (1977) *Kunst en Omgeving: beschouwingen en informatie over de inbreng van beeldende Kunst in de omgeving*, 's-Gravenhage/Amsterdam: Staatsuitgeverik/Stichting Kunst en Bedrijf.

den Ruijter, M. (1987) 'Functional Festivity: Dutch Floriade 1992', *Landscape Design*, June.

den Ruijter, M. and Hinse, T. (1987) 'The Dutch Floriade 1992 – synchronism of landscape design and town planning', *Urban Design Quarterly*, 24.

Destination Sheffield Visitor and Conference Bureau (n.d.) *Sheffield: the welcoming city*, Sheffield: Destination Sheffield Visitor and Conference Bureau, Yorkshire and Humberside Tourist Board.

Discover Islington (n.d.) *Discover Islington: the Real London: a tourism development action programme*: Islington: London Borough of Camden.

Dowson, P. (1992) 'Towards a New Urban Aesthetic?', unpublished paper presented at Charleroi, Belgium, December.

Dudley Metropolitan Borough (n.d.) *A Vision for Dudley Castle and the Tecton Collection*, Dudley: Planning and Architecture Dept, Dudley Metropolitan Borough.

Edwards, E. (1966) *Painted Walls of Mexico*, Austin: University of Texas Press.

Elms, Robert (1992) *Spain: a portrait after the general*, London: Heinemann.

English Tourist Board (1987) *Mini-Guide: Coventry*, London: English Tourist Board.

Festival Landmarks (1990) *Festival Landmarks '90: arts and crafts installations at the National Garden Festival, Gateshead 1990* (Catalogue).

Floriade (1992) *Allocaties/Allocations: art for a natural and artificial environment*, n.p.

Gayford, M. (1992) 'Do office blocks and art mix?', *The Daily Telegraph*, 13 February.

Gilson, M. (1992) *Alchemy: the public art programme at Garden Festival Wales*, Ebbw Vale: Garden Festival Wales Visual Arts Unit.

Glancey, J. (1993) 'That old Paris embrace amid the New Brutalism', *The Independent*, 17 March.

Goodey, B. (1989) 'Landscapes revisited: the Stoke Garden Festival Site', *Landscape Overview*, 2.

Goodey, B. (1992a) 'How green the next valley', *Landscape Research Extra*, 11, Winter.

Goodey, B. (1992b) 'The rain in Spain', *Town and Country Planning*, July–August, 200–201.

Grayson, S. (1974) *Art into Landscape: prize-winning and other entries*, London: Arts Council of

Great Britain.

Grayson, S. dir. (1977) *Art into Landscape: an Exhibition of schemes to enliven public spaces*, London: Arts Council of Great Britain.

Greenberg, D., Smith, K.S. and Teacher, S. (1977) *Megamurals and Supergraphics: big art*, Philadelphia, PA: Running Press.

Groves, J. (1980) *Art into Landscape 3*, London: Arts Council of Great Britain.

Hall, T. (1992) *Art and Image: public art as symbol in urban regeneration*, Working Paper 61, Birmingham: School of Geography, University of Birmingham.

Harney, A.L. (1981) *Art in Public Places: a survey of community-sponsored projects supported by the National Endowment for the Arts*, Washington, D.C.: Partners for Livable Places.

Harrod, T. (1991) 'Bravura answer to brutalism', *The Independent on Sunday*, 2 June, 16–17.

Herbert, S. (1991) 'Wuthering hype', *The Daily Telegraph Weekend*, 29 June, I.

Jones, G. (1993) 'Public Art in Harrow', *The Planner*, January, 22–33.

Jones, S. ed. (n.d.) *Art in Public: what, why and how?*, London: Artists' Handbooks, AN Publications.

Kahn, N. and Worpole, K. (1992) *Travelling Hopefully: a study of the arts in the transport system*, London: Illuminations.

Keyte, V. (1975) *A Canal Trail for Wigan Prepared as a Contribution to European Architectural Heritage Year*, Wigan: Department of Education, Wigan Metropolitan Borough.

Knott, S. (1991) 'International Conference Centre, Birmingham', *Landscape Design*, May, 31–3.

Mahler, D. (1991) *The Official Guide to Seattle's Public Art*, Seattle: Seattle Arts Commission.

Marriott, E. (1992) 'Freddie Mercury or bust', *The Independent*, 23 November.

Meade, M. (1991) 'Glories, past and present', *Royal Society of Arts' Journal*, August–September, 555–60.

Melhuish, C. (1989) 'Street values', *Building Design*, 19 May, 28–9.

Melhuish, C. (1990) 'Public images', *Building Design*, 7 September, 24–5.

Metropolitan Wigan (n.d.) *Metropolitan Wigan: we've got it right* (publicity brochure), Wigan: Wigan Metropolitan Borough Council.

Mississauga, City of (1987) *The Mississauga Civic Centre: official opening July 18, 1987*, promotional magazine, City of Mississauga.

Nairn, I. (1972) 'A fun town we ought to copy', *The Sunday Times*, 2 July.

Norris, J. (n.d.) *Macclesfield Town Trail*, n.p.

Ostler, T. (1985) 'Artistic platform', *Building Design*, 1 March, 22–3.

Patty, S.H. (1991) 'Canadian town brushed itself out of a corner', *Los Angeles Times*, 21 June.

Peixoto, F. (1991) 'Na contramao', *Arquitetura/Urbanismo*, 35, April–May, 86–91.

Perrmanyer, L. (n.d.) *Barcelona Modernisme*, Barcelona: Patronat de Turisme, Ajuntament de Barcelona.

Région Nord Pas de Calais (n.d.) *Saint-Omer: the old French town*, Calais: Région Nord Pas de Calais.

Rugby Borough Council (n.d.) *Tom Brown Trail*, Rugby: Rugby Borough Council.

Schmidt-Brummer, H. (1973) *Venice: California: an urban fantasy*, New York: Grossman.

Sommer, R. (1975) *Street Art*, New York: Links.

Stadt Wien (1975) *Wiener Spaziergang*, Vienna: Presse-und informationsdienst der Stadt Wien.

Steed, E. and Arnold, T. (n.d.) *Wigan Pier: a canal trail*, Wigan Pier: Pier Publications.

Stewart, I. (1991) 'Birmingham urban design studies', *The Planner*, 13 September, 5–6.

Tate, A. (1991) 'London's new leviathan', *Landscape Design*, 205, November, 37–40.

Taylor, M. (1991) 'The art of the environment', *The Planner*, 3 May, 6–7.

Tendring Borough Council (1988) *Tendring is Heritage*, Tendring: Tendring Borough Council.

Thomas, M. (1990) *Public Space and Public Art*, paper to conference on 'Quality Environments', Bristol, May.

Tibbalds, F. (1992) *Making People-Friendly Towns*, London: Longman.

Tsuchida, A. (1992) *Urban Design Report: a city in step with humanity: world urban design 1992*, Yokohama: Yokohama Urban Design Forum Executive Committee.

Woodward, C. (1992) *The Building of Europe: Barcelona*, Manchester: Manchester University Press.

10   Transitory topographies: places, events, promotions and propaganda

BOB JARVIS

This chapter is concerned less with the promotion of permanent places than with the creation and use of temporary places for promotional purposes, transforming streets and spoil heaps, parks and parade grounds, to promote particular ideologies and perceptions of place. This choreography of topographical experience, occupying a mere moment of space and time, has acquired a renewed significance in the service of the larger place promotional game, as already shown in Chapter 9 by Goodey. I argue here that such temporary transformations draw on a rich and diverse tradition of public spectacle. Yet while Goodey sees today's Garden Festivals as the ultimate commodification of place for a throw-away society, I seek to show how the temporary places of the past frequently served to promote somewhat different values and ideologies, frequently overtly political.

Such diversity of purpose has had the effect of fragmenting the research and documentation of individual events. In collecting together the traditions of the temporary public spectacle we step outside the compartmentalisation that characterised the historical literature of spectacles (Strong, 1984:172). Direct comparisons of the kind which follow are rare.

We begin with the princely political pageants of the Renaissance, but earlier public rituals and festival had sought not only 'to massage the senses but also to engage the mind' (Borsay, 1984:237) in the life of small English towns since medieval times. Later, the newly-established French and Russian revolutionary republics used spectacular displays for political messages. By the mid-20th century, the South Bank Exhibition of the Festival of Britain marks something of a turning point, the beginning of the approach to spectacle that dominates today. Finally, we consider the role of spectacles in today's 'Society of the Spectacle' and conclude by looking to the re-establishment of local and vernacular public celebrations, echoing Goodey's call for places that have more than just a promotional purpose.

Unlike the social and art historical backgrounds that characterise many of the sources of this chapter, the focus here is on the environmental effects and intentions of these brief, purposeful transformations, and their relation to the cultures, ideologies and image repertoires of their promoters and designers. In this respect the concerns here are common to many other studies of place and promotion. The decline in the coherence and importance of the outdoor spectacle is matched by the growth of mass media and their powers to communicate and influence, to the extent that television outside-broadcast rights have become a major factor in the staging and character of the spectacular events themselves. At the same time, however, the artistic importance of these events has declined, and leading mainstream artists and designers have turned to other fields, so that outdoor spectacle has been reclaimed for more experimental expressions. Though the subject has begun to attract historically oriented research and documentation, it still, sadly, lies outside the mainstream of the urban design and planning professions – to their loss.

Renaissance and revolution

We can trace the origins of the modern temporary urban spectacle back to the Renaissance, when the whole approach to architecture, permanent as well as transient, was predicated on the notion of spectacle. The connections between Renaissance architecture and theatre design (familiar today in Serlio's *tre scena*, the fixed stagings of Scamozzi in Palladio's *Teatro Olympico*), were united in their command of perspective and stage management; an *integrazione scenica*, of villa and landscape (Van der Ree *et al.*, 1992:25). Yet, a sense of spectacle was also the hallmark of the successful courtier. 'The court becomes a great theatre; an individual's actions, really acting; the ideal courtier the star of stars' (Rebhorn, 1978:23) is a summary of Castiglione's *II Libro del Cortegiano* (1507–1527), one of the courtly manuals of the time.

Such perfections, of course, were aspirations, images and unrealised projects more often than realities. The court itself was a closed and 'sacred precinct', an 'enchanted storehouse' (Bertelli, 1986), set apart from the chaos and squalor of the medieval townscape, politically imperilled by dynastic genealogy, military strategies and shifting allegiances. Dukes, princes and monarchs seized opportunities to impress, imitate and intimidate, in effect to assert their cultural and political hegemony, through the enhancement of public events – the royal *entrée* and the tournament. The images they created, the precedents they sought and mythologies they invoked were classical and antique, however obvious the ephemeral artifice of their triumphal arches: a lath and plaster Rome-in-a-day. As Zorzi (1986:163) noted: 'What people saw through them was a kind of theatrical townscape half dream, half-recognisable, which added to the festival atmosphere the sense of the extraordinary'. Similarly, Strong (1984:86–7) saw in these decorations not only a temporary invocation of Imperial Roman authority but also a foretaste of the architectural expressions of absolutism. This evocation of the architectural and cultural forms of a past military empire supplied legitimacy to a new dominance.

The processional way focused attention on the ruler, through ornament and decoration on key buildings, imaginary perspectives, and statues and reliefs. Public spectacles were the ceremonial developments of courtly pursuits of jousting and tournaments. Classical, mythological themes were played out in public places as well as in the courtyards of palaces to celebrate and elaborate the symbolism of alliances, marriages and coronations. The vast expenditure on these events created an art 'whereby society could be persuaded and transformed' to meet the ideals of power. Such spectacles were essential vehicles in a ritualistic and symbolic society, surrounding rulers with the mystical aura of authority that helped legitimise their power over their subjects (Strong, 1984:40).

The pageantry and especially its *apparati* were recorded in laudatory programmes, diaries and correspondence (often to rival nobles and princes), and have been catalogued (Nagler, 1964; Bonner, 1979). We can judge something of their topographic effect from accounts and engravings of the events themselves, surviving sketches and designs by the artists involved (who included Vasari, Palladio, Antonio Sangallo, Guilio Romano, Tintoretto and Veronese) and commemorative painting and decorations, although evidence is sometimes incomplete (a single arch drawn in isolation) or one dimensional (only a written description).

Yet the aspirations of the designers and the royal clients of such *entrées* are vividly indicated in two paintings, Andrea Mantegna's *The Triumphs of Caesar* (painted for Lodovico Gonzaga between 1486 and 1492), and Antoine Caron's *Augustus and the Sybil* (c.1575). Mantegna emphasises the grandeur of the procession itself: massive and emblematic chariots, seized trophies and treasures displayed, fortresses and towns vanquished depicted on banners or modelled on the backs of elephants. Circulated in woodcuts and engravings these antique images and devices, which Mantegna was able to research from authentic classical sources (Strong, 1984:46), became models for subsequent processions. The background of Caron's painting shows a just recognisable Paris (antique galleys on the Seine) as a Nova Roma replete with triumphal arches, obelisks and temples stretching to the horizon.

Some contemporary prints, though imprecise with regard to setting, give magnificent indications of the scale of the *apparati* and processions. Palladio's arch and loggia for the entry of Henry III to Venice in 1574 stood some 40–48 feet high, the centrepiece of a display of arms, fanfares, fireworks and gondolas against a desolate Lido. Matteo Grenter's print of the entry of Archduchess Maria Magdelena, Bride of Cosimo Medici II, into Florence in 1608 shows the procession of 9 bishops, 48 gentlemen of Florence, 9 monasteries of monks, 13 of friars, a band of 300 knights, 100 knights from Sienna, 10 companies of lancers, and 15,000 foot soldiers as they made its way from the Porta al Prato to the Pitti Palace through 5 triumphal arches (decorated with paintings and statues) and a pair of obelisks at Santa Maria Novella (Zorzi, 1986: 146–7).

Between the columns and capitals, the arches and swags, the putti and the Virtues, the heraldry and the historic references in these engravings, there are occasionally glimpses of the background, the ordinary townscape suppressed into severe perspective and notable by the emptiness and baldness of its presentation. All attention is focused on the triumphal *apparati* itself, on the brief glories of the rulers and their borrowed antiquity.

These scenes contrast markedly with their French Revolutionary counterparts, which contained a new, if equally political purpose. In the words of Jaques-Louis David, himself regarded as the pageant-master of the Republic (Dowd, 1948): 'National festivals are instituted for the people; it is fitting that they participate in these with a common accord and that they play the principal role there' ('Lettre sur les spectacles'; *Oeuvres Complètes*, II:176). The difference is immediately apparent when comparing engravings of Renaissance and French Revolutionary public celebrations; not only are they peopled, but the boundaries of audience and celebrants are not always immediately apparent. The Revolutionary festivals were also carefully choreographed propaganda events on an urban scale, but not only were they educational – they also had to be *re*-educational, to instil, inspire (and often revise) a rapidly changing revolutionary agenda, and redirect attention away from old religious and royalist associations.

Such a model of the Revolution itself as festival required not only a re-inventing of myths and ceremonies, but also of spatial imagery. It needed an arena of absolute equality, endless and undifferentiated, a 'space without qualities' (Ozouf, 1988:127), on which the new order could be written, with no sense of limit other than the vault of heaven. The frontiers of town and country were to be abolished, symbolised by the planting of a young tree under the King's window in the Louvre by the ladies of Les Halles (Ozouf, 1988:128). The boundaries of the crowd itself were the ideal limit to the spectacular event, and the ascent of an aeronaut its culmination in a view of huge, ordered, intoxicating panoramas.

These utopian, bare spaces were solemnised by the Revolution's own monuments and a new symbolic map. Expediency meant these were perishable and temporary. The familiar elements were columns, and square altars, pyramids and mountains and the Tree of Liberty (though even their verticality was suspect: 'What is a mountain if not an eternal protest against Equality' (Mathieu, cited in Ozouf, 1988:137)). Generally, the architecture and the streets of the old city were ignored, avoided or effaced. For some festivals a simulated forest replaced the city; the city's streets and squares were the spaces of ghosts, images of absolutism, tragedy and bloodshed.

The iconography of the Revolutionary festival evolved quickly and in opposition to the cult of reason that sought expression in writing and rhetoric rather than irrational image making (Gombrich, 1989:21–3). The iconography appropriate for these occasions was carefully scrutinised and argued: the sizes of simulacra; the choice of sculptures rather than paintings; the use of plaster rather than paper or bronze; the celebration of the Tree of Liberty; and, above all, the choice of the Antique arose from heated debate and discussion (Ozouf, 1988:Chapter VIII). In building the new nation while abolishing the *Ancien Régime*, in sustaining a sense of the sacred while abolishing the Church, the Antique style offered both a return to origins and avoided recent decadence, in a nostalgic evocation of a golden age (Ozouf, 1988:274). In their scale and grandeur, however, these festivals were transitory rehearsals for the ever greater colossal and permanent monuments and spaces that David and others planned for Paris. Statues, pyramids and a huge domed amphitheatre were realised only in the windy rhetoric of speeches to the Convention, in drawings and in festivals.

Constructing the constructivist spectacle

The political and revolutionary role of the festival was also quickly recognised by the Bolsheviks in Russia. The Decree of the Soviet People's Commissars entitled 'On Monuments of the Republic' (12 April 1918) declared, *inter alia*:

> (1) Monuments erected in honour of the Tsars and their servants and of no historical interest should be removed . . .
> (5) . . . to organise the city's decoration for 1 May and replace inscriptions, emblems,

street names, coats of arms etc, with new ones reflecting the ideas and mood of revolutionary working Russia . . .
(7) The necessary resources will be allocated on presentation of estimates and explanations of time estimates.

Public festivals and spectacular celebrations were not only visible agitation and public propaganda for the Soviets' seizure of power, they were also visualisations of the people's dreams for a real and achievable future. Unlike the vague classical symbolism of the French Revolution, its religious air and its anti-urban settings, the Russian Revolutionary celebrations quickly invented new satirical and abstract imagery rooted in material and secular aspirations and achievements, and transformed the urban spaces bequeathed to the people by the vanquished régime.

Its precedents were not wholly the French Revolution and the Paris Commune. There had been religious processions and elaborate celebrations of Tsarist coronations in the parks and streets (Cooke, 1990a:34–6). Later revolutionary theorists even placed festivals in a world context, but: 'to the Russian workers of the twenties, however . . . most of that was theory. They were out on the streets because it was a traditional thing to do in Russia. The content might be new, but the activity was entirely familiar to them' (Cooke, 1990a:37). However revolutionary the message, First Anniversary celebrations (1919) were predominantly traditional in style, on the swags and banners, arches and flags, tassles and masts the heroes of labour and slogans of struggle displaced kings and classical gods. Only in a few cases were abstraction and Constructivism visible and the whole language of the landscape transformed.

Most striking of these were Nathan Altman's designs for Uritsy Square in Petrograd. He operated: 'not by the laws of harmony but by the laws of opposition and constraint . . . did not vie with old masters but placed next to them something totally new and contrasting . . . angular and disturbing . . . a correct new principle capable of broad application' (Pumpansky, 1919). Yet none of the mass performances which marked the second phase of the Russian festivals achieved the scale of A.M. Gan's plan to enact the Communist city of the future: 'a magnificent drama in which the whole city would be the stage and the entire proletarian masses of Moscow the performers' (NARKOMPOS, 1920). The mass performances organised in Petrograd culminated in *Storming the Winter Palace* (November 1920) with 10,000 performers dramatising and reliving events of only 3 years earlier in the same setting. The massing and movements of the crowds and the Expressionist exaggerations of the sets and properties (giant sacks of Roubles, vertiginous perspectives), the score of aeroplanes, bells, sirens and fireworks were 'more dramatic and damaging to the buildings than the original event' (Cooke, 1990b:122).

Such events, including symphonies of factory sirens (in Moscow 1923), were renowned as avant-garde theatre but they were rarely popular. Later events were realistic, 'accessible to the untutored observers' (Lastockhin, 1926). Processions paraded floats with replicas of factories, reading rooms, telephones and railway engines. When political scenes were used: 'Their aim is to show simply one moment . . . and to portray it with the utmost brightness and conviction. The content is schematic, the characters presented as types' (Lastockhin, 1926). A brief moment of using the city as stage subsided into the political parade.

The themes celebrated in the parades between 1927 and 1933 were the goals and achievements of Soviet industry. Models of blocks of flats were paraded; decorations made from the tubes and pipes of industrial plants overlaid the crumbling facades of Moscow and Leningrad; tractors the size of buildings rose from Sverdlov Square; a vast ball-bearing crowned the Bolshoi Theatre; caricatures of capitalists and fascists were smashed and devoured by Soviet heroes and their industry in a huge composition covering the facade of the Summer Palace. Everything exhorted growth and production 'at a Soviet pace'. The Constructivist artists were still employed, but under the scrutiny of the Party: 'for the first time a political editor worked side by side with the artist on the designs' (Toot, 1931). In 1932 a Central Artistic Commission was set up to regulate the artistic decoration of Moscow, 'qualified political consultants' were to strengthen artistic arrangements (Bulletin of the Central Artistic Commission, 1932).

Artistic skills and techniques were refined and developed; careful consideration of light and scale, monument and movements were rehearsed and planned with great care; simplicity and comprehension tested in models and sketches of the settings organised with military efficiency (Kalm, 1933; Troshin, 1977). The future at least could be delivered in cloth and pasteboard, enemies defeated and production increased in models and floats, but the festivals lost their exuberance. Instead of covering and transforming the old city in red calico and plywood of chaotic 'cubo-futurist' displays, these displays were 'more miserly disposal of decorative emphases', sited at selected points between the 'clean lines of the streets and new buildings' (Andreev, 1933).

Trade fairs and the world expositions

> A cultural experience on the level of that enjoyed by Test Card Appreciation Society (Sudjic, 1992, on Expo' 92 at Seville).

Meanwhile the late 19th-century industrial building technology and production had provided the means and the content, and national pride and expanding markets the motives for a new temporary landscape predicated more on commerce than on political ideology. This was expressed in the form of the international exhibition and the trade fair.

The Great Exhibition of 1851 marks the emergence of the fair as a showcase for the new political economy of industrial capitalism and the wealth of nations. Here, for the first time, was a clear attempt to use the temporary public spectacle for reasons of national promotion based on economic dominance, demonstrating Britain's commercial and industrial supremacy to British subjects and the world as a whole. Paxton's Crystal Palace established a cheap, flexible building that provided a neutral background for the excesses of ornaments on display but, when each nation was invited to construct its own pavilion at the Paris Exposition of 1867, architectural style and taste became part of the potlatch of national displays, a means of gaining prestige and shaming rivals (Benedict, 1983:8). Individual buildings were designed without reference to their neighbours to display national styles and materials and boost the achievements of national arts and sciences. Sometimes these resulting juxtapositions seem staggering in their incoherence. The Rue des Nations (Paris 1900) lined up palaces and fantasias from around the world along the River Seine, yet it was the most popular display. One commentator wrote:

> This is what should remain . . . Hungary is a marvel, Italy blatant in its colours but
> has something of the arabesque, Austria pretty enough to make you go down on
> your knees, Belgium has produced one of these town halls which she alone has the
> secret . . . Monaco has sent us a tower almost as high on the German and Germany
> is gilded and painted like a house in Basel . . . It really is a picture (cited in Julian,
> 1974, 65–6).

Other juxtapositions were more prescient, such as the famous opposition of the
German and Russian pavilions at the Paris Exposition Internationale des Arts et
Techniques dans la Vie Moderne in 1937.

Where a uniform style was imposed on the various exhibition halls, it was
predominantly classical. The 'White City' created for the Columbian Exhibition in
Chicago (1893) was a popular success. Its president claimed that 'a man can feel that he
is in Athens during the age of Pericles', but it was less popular with critics. 'Architecture
died in the land of the free . . . thus works the pallid academic mind, denying the real,
exalting the fictions and false' railed Louis Sullivan. The engineer, Vierendeel, was
equally disappointed: 'we have been profoundly deceived' (Alwood, 1977:84). The
layout of spaces and pavilions, whatever their style, was formal. Grand avenues and
lakes lined with pavilions and hastily planted trees resulted in a scenic repertoire that
aligned the visitor with set pieces and huge vistas along which each pavilion was a
separate message of style, nationhood or theme, a landscape of confectioners' displays.

The sophistication of display technology and the 'for the sheer hell of it' quotient of
modern engineering expertise has increased, but the effect is unchanged. Monorails
and cable cars have accelerated and elevated motion through and around the
cacophony of nations' claims to build the city of the future, but their design remains
'architecture at play' (Slessor, 1992). Some of the landmarks of modern architecture
were exhibition pavilions, notably Gropius and Meyer's Werkbund Exhibition
(Cologne 1914), Le Corbusier's Pavilion de l'Esprit Nouveau (Paris 1925) and Mies
van der Rohe's Barcelona Pavilion (1929), each an achievement of architectural
experiment and innovation (Stamp, 1992). The 140 years of exposition design that led
to Seville in 1992 produced:

> a version of one of these housing estates where everybody sets out to impress their
> neighbours with their lurid architectural dreams . . . it's a bookful of one liners.
> Walking around is an exhausting trip where everything shouts for attention just like
> a trip to a department store (Sudjic, 1992).

Looking back over the recent history of such events, however, the Festival of Britain
stands out as a watershed: at once a glimpse of new approaches yet also belonging to a
more innocent age before television and mass tourism created a society of continuous
spectacle. Like previous festivals, it had an important role in national promotion
though, at the time, it was much more a celebration of a people emerging from the
darkness of war and austerity and a foretaste of more permanent post-war reconstruction. It was all in sharp contrast with the confident demonstration of global economic
hegemony that underpinned the Great Exhibition a century earlier.

The South Bank Exhibition of the Festival of Britain broke away from Beaux-Arts
formal layout to tell the 'interwoven and serial' story of the land and people of Britain
as a 'series of sequences of things arranged in a particular order so as to tell one

continuous interwoven story' (Cox, 1951:8). Yet the message of this 'brief city' was blurred and overwhelming even by the admission of its designers: 'only a fraction of this verbosity (of captions) was read . . . so much was displayed as to make comprehension impossible . . . the exhibition would have been better if the number of exhibits was decimated' (Misha Black, cited in Banham and Hillier, 1976:84–5). The official guide book admitted: 'Visitors who from habit or inclination feel impelled to start with the last chapter and then zig-zag their way backwards . . . will be as welcome as anyone else. But such visitors may find that some of the chapters appear mystifying and inconsequent' (Cox, 1951:8). Though Black observed: 'The magic of the Exhibition was that of place . . . it was the total experiment that was cherished and remembered' (Banham and Hillier, 1976:84). The writers of the *Architectural Review* wrote its urban exegesis. The message on the South Bank was not the content of the displays, but their form, a celebration of the English picturesque in urban (rather than garden) design: 'It demonstrates how successfully the informal principle of town planning can be translated to the English urban landscape . . . stand in the centre of main concourse and . . . you might be in the main square of a modern town' (Anon., 1951:75). The *Architectural Review* offered a route round the exhibition, not as a story, but as a landscape sequence of experiences in space. The visitor:

> might well be exploring a subtly designed town. He is led from point to point and his interest continually renewed by the use of the town designer, as well as the exhibition architect, exploits – or should exploit – in order to heighten vitality and underline the personality derived from the nature of the site (Anon., 1951:80).

In 1951, as in 1451, temporary display hinted at possible urban forms: formal to celebrate the Renaissance prince; picturesque for the common man (albeit still following a pre-ordained route). Gordon Cullen's (1951) suggestions to retain this urban vitality on the South Bank remained unrealised; his own *Townscape* (Cullen, 1961) being perhaps the Festival's most influential survivor.

Spectacles in the society of spectacles

> In societies where modern conditions of production prevail, all of modern life presents itself as an immense accumulation of spectacles. Everything that was directly lived has moved away into a representation (Debord, 1987:para 1.1).

The South Bank Exhibition of the Festival of Britain was one of the last spectacular events of the pre-spectacular society. In the post-war era changes in society and travel, in mass-communications and mass-media have placed the transitory event in a very different context. The spectacular event itself has become one representation among many in the society of spectacles. Chaney (1992:262), examining BBC coverage of Victory Parades (1946), the Festival of Britain (1951) and the Coronation of Elizabeth II (1953), concluded: 'national festivals have become effectively media occasions rather than occasions to which the media have access'. Nevertheless, expositions and festivals continue. Sites are identified, themed and sponsored displays are constructed. Visitors arrive and depart; demolition crews claim the site, the shows are cleared away, debris blows across the landscape.

The series of National Garden Festivals (Liverpool 1984, Stoke on Trent 1986, Glasgow 1988, Gateshead 1990 and Ebbw Vale 1992) were temporary summer (May–October) flowerings of landscape design, horticultural display and public entertainment on sites reclaimed from industrial dereliction and pollution before their re-use and permanent development. Their successes in reclamation, investment and re-use (Holden, 1989:33) were not matched in the creation and design. Though promotions and postcards biannually claimed 'The most spectacular event of . . .' and 'A day out of this world', the shows they presented were disorganised, incoherent, confusing and poorly laid out (Smith, 1984; Holden, 1989; Jarvis, 1990b). The Liverpool Festival, for instance: 'lacked any theme, or had too many themes they muddled together, nothing makes an unequivocal impact on the senses or the intellect. Everything has equal importance since nothing has boundaries' (Smith, 1984:16).

The carefully contrived informality of the South Bank Exhibition had become a post-industrial *laissez-faire* paradise of consumer selection, rewriting industrial history into a hybrid of garden centre and theme park. Garden Festivals, however, were just as didactic as the Festival of Britain: 'a clear ideological message to the people of the north of England and Scotland. Wake up!! You have entered a brave new entrepreneurial world' (Roberts, 1989). The suburban pastoral form of these dreams was the more pointed for being spread over and around manicured fragments of the industrial past (Roberts, 1990).

Accounts by the design teams of Liverpool (Teal and Deeley, 1984) and Stoke-on-Trent (Samworth, 1984) emphasise the technics of construction, visitor through-put and the marketing value of the full day-out package of visitor experiences. There is an uncritical focus on achievements, relishing the debased spectacle: 'a walk through the gardens will reflect English History and in turn contrast with the space age technology of the viewing tower' (Samworth, 1984:25). Whether the one documented attempt to rethink the consumerist philosophy of Garden Festivals, to root their design in a more radical philosophy would have achieved any different result remains speculation (Jarvis, 1990a).

The failure of Garden Festivals as anything more than a 'circus with plants', follows the triumph of things over events, of space over time in architectural and urban design (Jarvis, 1990c). It is a mistaken philosophy that sees buildings as finished at the very point at which their real, inhabited lives begin (Lerup, 1974) and fails to realise that it is human activities, the things that happen over and over again, that give places their character (Alexander, 1979). In post-war architectural theory, attention to transitory events is thin and marginal despite some distinguished starts. From the celebrations of everyday ephemera and popular culture by the 'Independent Group' (whose members and associates also included artists Richard Hamilton, Eduardo Paolozzi, Reyner Banham and Lawrence Alloway) grew Alison and Peter Smithson's ideas of 'transformations of the city' and 'life's decorations of the urban scene' (Smithson and Smithson, 1968). From the research into city image and environmental information by Kevin Lynch and his colleagues at the Massachusetts Institute of Technology in the 1960s came proposals for celebrations of the city in signs and lights, 'counter functional street constructs' and user responsive light and sound Environments (Carr, 1973).

Enough has also been published to outline contemporary possibilities. Derek Walker's (1984:49–51) enthusiastic review of the Los Angeles Olympics illustrated something of the potential that might be realised:

Exploit ephemera. And neutralise nationalistic fervour. Cut out totalitarian graphics and monumental buildings which consciously project sport as a political weapon . . . the city will be transformed overnight as if an invasion of butterflies has descended upon it . . . stay close to the Californian tradition of pop mobility. If you have sun on your side, spectacular landscape and a three week invasion: back your strengths. A city that has Whittier Boulevard and Rodeo Drive might be able to do a hell of a decorating job.'

The Archigram group moved beyond the science-fiction civil engineering of their best known projects, 'Plug-in City' and 'Walking City', back to their original concerns of the city as software of people and their situations, of their Living City exhibition (1963). Projects such as Instant City (Herron and Cook, 1970) extended and developed the mobile technologies emerging from open-air rock concerts (Pawley, 1970). The strength of Archigram lay in their graphic imagination, their extreme and fantastic projections were influential sketches of possibility, which, of course, remained unbuilt.

The full-blown manipulation of spectacular effects of light, sound and visual animation in temporary settings remains something few designers are able to practice. Fisher Park's success, which turns audiences' experience of 'watching a set of small figures performing 100 yards away into a stunningly memorable occasion' (Lyall, 1992a:59) relies on the budgets and market-oriented imagination of the rock music industry (Lyall, 1992b)) but has rarely been turned to civic, urban events. Over-cautious authorities prevented a display to celebrate the centenary of the Statue of Liberty in Hyde Park (London), which would have consisted of a facsimile statue rising above a pyrotechnic waterfall to the sound of Copeland's 'Fanfare for the Common Man' (Fisher and Park, 1986). A one-night, two-million-dollar extravaganza on the theme of mankind's progress from primeval chaos to future world unity was dropped by the organising committee from the opening of Expo' 92 in Seville due to the organisation's shifting politics. Drawing on the exuberant architectural imagery of the local *feria die Avril*, the spectacle would have been visible two miles away (Lyall, 1992a).

Conclusion

The achievements of Fisher Park for the 'peripatetic corporations' of the rock music industry, the brief national and corporate extravagances of Olympic Games and Expos are far removed from the drab and confused reality of the contemporary urban landscape. Nevertheless, they are probably no further removed from their settings than were the princely and regal spectacles of the Renaissance, or the state ceremonies of the French and Russian Revolutions. The intention may have been the same, but their purposes are now very different: diversion and entertainment predominate as part of the larger project of promoting a new, post-industrial, service-based economy. The present spectacle no longer celebrates or illuminates collective futures (however unrepresentative). Rather it promotes the new mass culture of individualism based on enterprise and competition, reified in the temporary and hyper-real topographies of contemporary public spectacle. Yet such messages are read mainly by politically conscious art historians. For the paying public, it is just another 'Day out of this World'.

It need not be like this. There are other versions of the spectacle. Following research into the declining social and public, rather than commercial, functions of town centres, Ken Worple (1992:90) concluded that festivals and carnivals could make the 'invisible web' of local voluntary activity visible and public space could be re-appropriated by the people. Engineers of the imagination are already at work to animate these vernacular celebrations:

> We challenge with humour and offer, for an instance, an image of another world; another world where social purpose and personal creativity are allowed to go hand in hand, and the finished work revitalises the image, myths and aspirations of the community in which it is produced (Welfare State International, n.d.).

The philosophy behind their work (Fox, 1991) challenges the treatment of art as a commodity, and the economy of consumerism. Their celebrations: 'turn landscape into living theatre and audience into community'.

Other commentators on the city and city life today are less optimistic about the revival of spectacle and theatricality. Reviewing debates on the post-modern city as an 'Imaginary Institution', where consumption and leisure are recomposed as 'experience' and the presentation of the self, the look, and a new wave of *flâneurs* are its leading edge, Robins and Wilkinson (1990) see a spurious sense of togetherness being manufactured and manipulated. The fate of 'The Ride of Life' – an ironic presentation of everyday experience commissioned and then abandoned by the developers of Meadowhall Shopping Centre in favour of a wall of electronic billboards, may prove them right. The transitory topographies of public spectacles, always conceived with some ulterior motives, frequently political, have now been appropriated into the tool-kit of the modern place promoter, to re-package and re-image localities, regions and nations. Thus, Spain's bid to become Europe's California was underscored and made plausible by its year of spectacle in Seville, Madrid and, above all, Barcelona in 1992. This was an unusually concerted exercise in promotional public spectacles. More usually, it has been individual cities that have grasped these opportunities. Few have managed to bridge the gap between promotional imperatives and genuine identification with community in any convincing way, but enough positive contemporary examples exist to suggest that this gap can be closed.

References

Alexander, C. (1979) *The Timeless Way of Building*, New York: Oxford University Press.
Alwood, J. (1977) *The Great Exhibition*, London: Studio Vista.
Andreev, A.A. (1933) 'Light, colour and movement', in V. Tolstoy, I. Bibinova, I. and C. Cooke, *Street Art of the Revolution*, London: Thames and Hudson, 225–6.
Anon. (1951) 'The South Bank Exhibition', *Architectural Review*, 110(656), special issue.
Banham, M., and Hillier, B., eds. (1976) *A Tonic to the Nation: the Festival of Britain 1951*, London: Thames and Hudson.
Benedict, B. (1983) *The Anthropology of World's Fairs*, London: Scolar Press.
Bertelli, S. (1986) *Italian Renaissance Courts*, London: Sidgwick and Jackson.
Bonner, M. (1979) *Italian Civic Pageantry in the High Renaissance*, Florence: Biblioteca di Bibliographica Italiana.

Borsay, P. (1984) 'All the town's a stage: urban ritual and ceremony 1600–1660', in P. Clark, ed., *The Transformation of the English Provincial Towns 1600–1800*, London: Hutchinson, 228–58.

Bulletin of the Central Artistic Commission, (Bulletin of the Central Artistic Commission of the Moscow Soviet for the Decoration of Moscow for the 15th anniversary of the October Revolution), 1 October 1932, 6–7.

Carr, S. (1973) *City Signs and Lights: a policy study*, Boston, MA: MIT Press.

Chaney, D. (1992) 'A symbolic mirror of ourselves: civic ritual in mass society', in D. Collins, ed., *Media, Culture and Society*, London, 247–63.

Cooke, C. (1990a) 'The artists are mobilised', in V. Tolstoy, I. Bibinova, I. and C. Cooke, *Street Art of the Revolution*, London: Thames and Hudson.

Cooke, C. (1990b), 'Mass performances and spectacles', in V. Tolstoy, I. Bibinova, I. and C. Cooke, *Street Art of the Revolution*, London: Thames and Hudson.

Cox, I. (1951) *The South Bank Exhibition: a guide to the story it tells*, London: HMSO.

Cullen, G. (1951) 'South Bank translated', *Architectural Review*, 110(656), 135–8.

Cullen, G. (1961) *Townscape*, London: Architectural Press.

Debord, G. (1987) 'Society of the spectacle', (originally '*la Société du Spectacle*'), Paris: Editions Buchet-Castel.

Dowd, D.L. (1948) *Pageant Master of the Republic: Jacques-Louis David and the French Revolution*, Lincoln, NE: University of Nebraska Press.

Fisher, M. and Park, J. (1986) 'Outdoor spectacles: Mark Fisher and Jonathon Park', *Art and Design*, 2, May, 6–12.

Fox, J. (1991) 'A plea for poetry', *National Arts and Media Strategy Discussion Document 3*, London: Arts Council of Great Britain.

Gombrich, E.H. (1989) 'Signs of the time', *FMR*, 39(8), 1–24.

Herron, R. and Cook, P. (1970) 'Instant city in progress', *Architectural Design*, 40, 566–73.

Holden, R. (1989) 'British garden festivals', *Landscape and Urban Planning*, 18, 17–35.

Jarvis, B. (1990a) 'Scratching at the face of reason: a fable of our time', *Landscape Research*, 15(2), 23–6.

Jarvis, B. (1990b) 'How dreams end', *Urban Design Quarterly*, 36, 24.

Jarvis, B. (1990c) 'Mind:body, time:space, things:events – a performance perspective for planning', Paper to fourth AESOP Congress, Reggio, Calabria, November.

Julian, D. (1974) *The Triumph of Art Nouveau: Paris exhibitions 1900*, London: Phaidon.

Kalm, D. (1933) 'Rehearsal of the squares', *Soviet Art (Sovetskoe iskusstve)*, 50, 2 November 1933.

Lastockhin, N.A. (1926) 'Artistic designs for the festivals', in V. Tolstoy, I. Bibinova, I. and C. Cooke (1990) *Street Art of the Revolution*, London: Thames and Hudson, 164.

Lerup, L. (1974) *Building the Unfinished*, Beverley Hills, CA: Sage.

Lyall, S. (1992a) 'Stage management', *Architectural Review*, 190, 59–60.

Lyall, S. (1992b) *Rock Sets: the astonishing art of rock concert design, the work of Fisher Park*, London: Thames and Hudson.

Nagler, A.M. (1964) *Theatre Festivals of the Medici*, New Haven, CN: Yale University Press.

NARKOMPOS (Section of Mass Performances and Spectacles of the Theatrical Department of the Commissariat for Education) (1920) 'A constructive approach', in V. Tolstoy, I. Bibinova, I. and C. Cooke (1990) *Street Art of the Revolution*, London: Thames and Hudson, 125–6.

Ozouf, S. (1988) *Festivals and the French Revolutions*, (trans. A. Sheridan), Cambridge, MA: Harvard University Press.

Pawley, M. (1970) 'Caroline go to canvas city immediately – your friend Linda has been visited: and that's not all', *Architectural Design*, 40, 558–65.

Pumpansky, L. (1919) 'The October Revolution celebrations and the artists of Petrograd', in V. Tolstoy, I. Bibinova, I. and C. Cooke (1990) *Street Art of the Revolution*, London: Thames and Hudson, 81–2.

Rebhorn, W.A. (1978) *Courtly Spectacle*, Chicago: Wayne State University Press.

Roberts, J. (1989) 'Green mantle', *The Guardian*, 17–18 June, 20.

Roberts, J. (1990) 'The greening of capitalism: the practical economy of the Tory Garden

Festivals', in S. Pugh ed., *Reading Landscape: country, city, capital*, Manchester: Manchester University Press, 231–45.

Robins, K. and Wilkinson, S. (1990) 'The imaginary institution of the city', Paper presented at a seminar on 'Property-led Regeneration', University of Newcastle, March.

Samworth, J. (1984) 'NGF 86: Stoke on Trent', *Landscape Design*, 151, October, 25–8.

Slessor, C. (1992) 'When worlds collide', *Architectural Review*, 190(1144), 22–3.

Smith, A. (1984) 'Muddles on the Mersey', *Landscape Design*, 151, October, 16–18.

Smithson, A. and Smithson, P. (1968) 'Triennale die Milano: transformations of the city', *The Shift*, Architectural Monographs 7, London: Academy Editions.

Stamp, G. (1992) 'Exhibitionalistic architecture', *Architectural Review*, 190 (1144), 75–80.

Strong, R. (1984) *Art and Power*, Woodbridge, Suffolk: Boydell Press.

Sudjic, D. (1992) 'The world through kitsch spectacles', *The Guardian*, 20 April, 28.

Teal, F. and Deeley, P. (1984) 'The joys from the blackstuff', *Landscape Design*, 151, 12–13.

Tolstoy, V., Bibinova, I. and Cooke, C. (1990) *Street Art of the Revolution*, (trans. by F. Longman, F. O'Dell and V. Wankov), London: Thames and Hudson.

Toot, V.S. (1931) 'Artistic decoration of October festivals', in V. Tolstoy, I. Bibinova, I. and C. Cooke (1990) *Street Art of the Revolution*, London: Thames and Hudson, 200.

Troshin, N. (1977) 'Personal archive', in V. Tolstoy, I. Bibinova, I. and C. Cooke (1990) *Street Art of the Revolution*, London: Thames and Hudson, 226–7.

Van der Ree, P., Smienk, G. and Steenbergen, C. (1992) *Italian Villas and Gardens*, Amsterdam: Prestel/THOTH.

Walker, D. (1984) 'Ephemeral Olympics', *Architectural Review*, 174, 48–51.

Welfare State International (n.d.) *Engineers of the Imagination*, pamphlet, Welfare State International, Ulverston.

Worple, K. (1992) *Towns for People*, Buckingham: Open University Press.

Zorzi, E.G. (1986) 'Courtly spectacle', in S. Bertelli, ed., *Italian Renaissance Courts*, London: Sidgwick and Jackson, 127–88.

11 Newspapers as promotional strategists for regional definition

HOLLY J. MYERS-JONES AND SUSAN R. BROOKER-GROSS

Like other cities, Roanoke, Virginia, has its share of economic development plans, bolstered by the support of a coalition of civic leaders from business and government. Again like other cities, Roanoke has its downtown redevelopment projects, combining shining new structures with historic preservation and show-casing the arts alongside profit-making. Unlike many cities where the selling of the regional image has been documented, however, Roanoke occupies a lower rung in the urban hierarchy: it is a small city with a relatively recent history. Its urban boosters are equally concerned to revitalise the urban core and ensure an economically healthy centre city through regional prosperity. The functional region identified to achieve these ends extends beyond the city and its immediate suburbs to incorporate outlying growth nodes. In promoting growth, leaders imply that stagnation is itself a result of too small a city. In this chapter, we show how the push to increased size is expressed spatially, to garner new territory, more people and greater prosperity.

In documenting this effort to adopt a larger geography of Roanoke, we examined the presentation of the issues by the city's major daily newspaper, the *Roanoke Times & World-News*. As the dominant print medium of the region, the newspaper offers a podium for both pro-growth and anti-growth activists through its news, letters, and commentary sections, as well as exerting its own influence in direct editorial stances, and less overtly, in the choice of news content. As an active part of the 'growth machine', the newspaper advocates projects which enhance Roanoke's image and which increase its real and symbolic geographical dominance. As an enterprise with its own balance sheet, its trade area reflects its power to earn subscription and advertising revenues. These separate motives for increasing the scale of the region appear compatible, but tension exists between building a region which identifies with Roanoke and serving a territory which has not yet expressed such allegiance.

The study region

The city of Roanoke, population 96,397 (1990), the surrounding county of Roanoke (79,332), and the more rural Botetourt County (24,992) comprise the Roanoke

Metropolitan Statistical Area (MSA) as defined by the US Census. Lying beyond the MSA are two areas of growth. To the west, Montgomery County is the site of Virginia Tech, the state's major engineering and agricultural school-turned-comprehensive university, with over 23,000 students. To the southeast, one of the fastest growing areas in Virginia is the recreation-based development in and around Smith Mountain Lake. Roanoke's pro-growth leaders seek to 'adopt' these two regions through specific development projects.

The *Roanoke Times & World-News* publishes zoned editions for these two markets. The region surrounding the university is served by the New River Valley edition, including a six-day-per-week tabloid supplement, the *Current*; the Smith Mountain Lake area is sent the edition for Bedford and Franklin counties, which has in the past included a summer *Lake Supplement*. These two editions differ in small ways from the other zoned editions – weekly supplements for neighbourhoods within the city and the out-of-town 'state' edition.

Newspapers and local development

Scholarly debate over the importance and independence of locally-based efforts to stimulate growth has been focused on politics and economic development (Jonas, 1993). Is local growth contingent on regional, national, and global restructuring (Logan and Molotch, 1987; Cox and Mair, 1988; Wolch and Dear, 1989), or is it shaped by 'place-specific conditions' (Kirby, 1985; Harloe *et al.*, 1990; Pickvance, 1990)? Despite evidence that local development varies with scale and position in an urban hierarchy (Kirby, 1985), we find few examples of the intermediate scale. In focusing on larger metropolitan areas, studies of common growth strategies – for example, sports facilities, convention centres, art centres and other tourism-based construction (Law, 1992) – typically focus on downtown revitalisation and its competition with suburban interests. Less attention has been paid to strategies of expanding the areal extent of the locality (although for an exception, see Jonas, 1991).

Central to either sort of pro-growth strategy is the creation of an attractive and distinctive image to be marketed to prospective investors, tourists, and migrants. The metropolitan newspaper is one historic vehicle for this marketing, as documented by studies of 19th-century boosterism (Belcher, 1947; Abbott, 1981). While 19th-century newspapers were clearly aimed at that external market of potential investors and migrants, the late-20th century press works to build the image locally. Newspapers can serve the interests of growth coalitions by their purposeful eavesdropping on the discourse of development, thereby extending that discourse to a wider public. In this era of public–private sector partnerships in development projects, newspaper coverage provides an essential link between the wider public and the projects.

Since newspapers are one of the 'clearest cases' of a locally-dependent firm (Cox and Mair, 1988), their economic well-being rests on the successes of development projects. Dependent on the local area for subscription and advertising revenue, the newspaper must mirror that local area. As a key player in the local growth coalition, the metropolitan newspaper has an incentive to portray the region in the best possible light. Focused on the local readership, the image-making often constructs competition between the local community and other communities similarly situated. Local energies and funds must be employed to ensure victory in this competition. By selling the agenda of the growth coalition to local residents, the resulting positive image promotes a sense of well-being among residents and reinforces their own feeling of local dependence (Cox and Mair, 1988; 1989).

While the pro-growth agenda may unambiguously define the overall business interests of the metropolitan newspaper, it is less applicable to the news functions and news values of the press. News values, embedded in anti-big-business muckraking and anti-government investigative reporting, frame any editorial boosterism with a populist attitude of suspicion. Journalistic values require attention to the material, and sentimental losses which may attend growth generally or individual projects specifically. In highlighting the local attachment of individuals, households, small businesses and, in our example, outlying communities, the newspaper underscores both the threats to those attachments and the strength of those ties to fight off unwanted development projects.

A further ambiguity in the newspaper's role in regional growth strategy is a quotidian bias toward the central city, specifically downtown (Kaniss, 1991). This bias is born both of logistical routine (easier news collection from closely spaced officials of a single central city government), and of traditions of journalism (downtown as the 'action scene'). It is reinforced by personnel policies which assign highly valued staff to the city beat while leaving the suburbs to the novice and the exiled. In the case of Roanoke, the outliers include not only the suburban county, but the growth centres lying beyond the MSA's boundaries.

With these varied interests of the metropolitan press, we expect to find equally complex image-making and image-destroying news-handling for three specific development projects in the Roanoke region.

The development projects

Each of the three projects we will discuss was conceived as an answer to the slow economic and population growth experienced by Roanoke during the last decade. This stagnation stood in stark contrast to the economically and demographically booming regions of the state, notably the 'Golden Crescent', an urbanised area stretching from the suburbs of Washington, through Richmond to Virginia Beach. While Roanokers eyed the prosperity to the north and east, they also viewed with alarm the continuing economic decline in the most southwesterly portions of the state, including the coal region to the west which had fed its earlier prosperity as transportation hub. Loss of the headquarters of the Norfolk and Western Railroad after its merger to become Norfolk Southern intensified the threat of stagnation and decline. Fears of even worse economic times resulted in growth coalition members setting their sights on closer links between the two growth areas lying just outside the metropolitan region, the Smith Mountain Lake area and the New River Valley.

Explore

Explore is the project to link Roanoke with the Smith Mountain Lake area. With a total price tag of approximately 185 million dollars, it is the most ambitious of the three projects under study. Explore is envisaged as a living history park designed to highlight the role of Virginia in the exploration and development of the American West. Originally the project was to have included a theme park, restored frontier town, luxury hotel, environmental education research and conference centres, and a large, naturalistic zoo with a collection of North American animals. It is difficult to ascertain the scope of the project at present, but the 1000-plus acre site is currently used as an environmental classroom for local school children and other groups, and a breeding habitat for the endangered North American red wolf. The current emphasis is on environmental education and research.

The roots of the Explore project reflect the merger of three separate ideas. First, and most generally, Explore attempts to improve the economic base of the Roanoke region through tourism. This is a common strategy in post-industrial America as regions re-define their potential for economic development. Explore's planners estimate an annual attendance of one million visitors pumping millions of dollars into the local economy. Related to the tourist theme, a second idea was to build a scenic parkway along the Roanoke River stretching from the Blue Ridge Parkway to Smith Mountain Lake's resort and retirement communities. Explore's promoters hoped that the site's proximity to the junction of the Blue Ridge and River Parkways would encourage interaction between Roanoke and the affluent lake residents. Finally, Explore grew out of the long-range planning done by Roanoke's zoo to escape the constraints of its present cramped city site. The Explore site was originally considered for potential relocation of the zoo.

Explore was the brain-child of former Roanoke city manager Bern Ewert and then-Roanoke banker Doug Cruickshanks. In July 1985, Ewert left his position with the municipality to become the director of the non-profit River Foundation, created to see the project through to fruition. Initial funding for the project came from private and corporate donations, including a large contribution by the *Roanoke Times & World-News*.

Explore is now officially a state park under the control of the Virginia Recreational Facilities Authority, which contracts with the River Foundation to administer the park. The state of Virginia was originally very supportive of the project, allocating six million dollars in 1988, but its financial difficulties, coupled with the River Foundation's inability to raise enough private money, ended additional state funding. The lack of large private donations also resulted in Ewert's replacement in 1991 by Rupert Cutler, a nationally-known environmentalist with impressive credentials in fund-raising. Although backers remain optimistic, the project's immediate goals have been scaled down.

Hotel Roanoke

To the west, two development projects seek to attach the city to the university town in Montgomery County. The first of these projects is physically located within Roanoke and seeks to relocate university-based growth to the city. The Hotel Roanoke is a railway hotel built in the 1880s as a centrepiece for the Norfolk and Western Railroad. In Tudor style, atop a hill overlooking the commercial core of downtown (and inconveniently on the opposite side of the railway tracks from downtown), the hotel was a symbol of elegance and city prestige that was, for many years, the city's main claim to fame. By the late 1980s it was in need of a facelift, having failed to keep pace with newer facilities in Roanoke and elsewhere. Railway officials made reinvestment in the old hotel contingent on the city building an adjacent conference centre to attract major business clients. The outcome, in 1989, was the donation of the hotel from the railway to the university in Blacksburg. This gift was seen as a way to expand the university presence in the Roanoke Valley, a desired, and politically expedient, expansion of the service mission of the university. At the same time, the precious landmark hotel would be preserved – or if it failed, the railway would not bear the blame. The hotel would stimulate additional economic development by bringing in conferences, business meetings, and tourists. By bringing part of the university to the city, the hotel project fosters efforts to 'adopt' Virginia Tech. At the time of writing, the hotel is neither renovated nor reopened, and the convention centre remains a paper plan.

Opposition to the hotel project has centred on Blacksburg. Coming at a time of cutbacks in educational funding, worries emerged on campus over expenditures on the hotel. Reassurances that money earmarked for higher education was not being spent were received sceptically by many Blacksburg residents. There was also fear among Blacksburg business and civic leaders that the university was abandoning the town in favour of the larger city.

Direct Link

In his 1986 'State of the City' address, Roanoke's mayor advocated that the city and the university town of Blacksburg be more directly linked by a highway. From that point, there were many permutations on the proposal, but the major goal of shortening the travel distance between the city and the state university remained. Blacksburg had been passed by in the initial construction of the Interstate highway system. Moreover, as commercial growth occurred along the road corridor between Blacksburg and the Interstate, journey times to Blacksburg lengthened. This time–space divergence coincided with advocacy of closer ties between city and university in the name of economic development. Particularly desired was high-tech industrial growth linking the research expertise of the university faculty and the campus research park with the city's amenities, industries and airport.

Unfortunately, the nature of growth also fed hostile sentiments. The visual blight of new shopping malls, fast-food restaurants, and other strip developments undermined support for construction of any new highways which could have the same detrimental effects. The anti-road sentiment was especially pronounced in the scenic valley through which the road was to run, with ecological issues intermingling with 'not in my back yard' (NIMBY) arguments. The goal of a Direct Link from Blacksburg to Roanoke became confused with the goal of managing the new congestion on the existing roadways. Controversy focused on whether the two goals should be achieved through the same construction project, or whether two separate projects were needed. Moreover, if two were needed, which had the greater claim on scarce resources?

A variation on the theme of the Direct Link came in 1989, when a member of the Roanoke County governing board proposed smart highway technology for the link. A technological vision of better road design, the 'smart highway' was also an expedient tool to garner support for the Direct Link. A compromise position was mediated by a member of the state highway transportation board to treat the road projects separately. The Direct Link/smart highway was to be funded through unusual procedures: public and private funds would be used, and the expertise of the university faculty would be called upon. The improvements to the existing roadways were to follow 'usual' procedures in state highway funding. At the time of writing, the Direct Link between the university town and Roanoke remains a plan, but with commitments for funding from both Federal and state governments.

Data and methods

Our data for examining these issues and their marketing to the local publics came from the *Roanoke Times & World-News* newspaper. Using an index maintained by librarians at Virginia Tech, we used keyword analysis to identify reportage of the three projects of interest between 1988 and March 1992. We also examined all letters to the editor, commentaries, and editorials, which were not indexed for issues before 1 January 1992.

The university library itself receives the New River Valley edition of the newspaper, but microfilm is available of all zonal issues. The microfilm itself contained each day's 'Metro' (city) edition, followed by zoned supplements, and any zoned edition pages which differed from the Metro edition. We noticed only occasional omissions of pages that could not have been identical (because of the way stories were continued from another page). There were also a few stories listed on the index which could not be found in the microfilmed copy. A possible bias in the methodology arises from stories not carried in the New River edition, and thus never indexed. However, it was not felt that these were likely to produce significant distortions.

The Explore project in the press

Due to its enormous price tag, geographic scope, and influential backers, the Explore project has received vast news coverage and elicited numerous opinions, including profound scepticism. There are three sources of this scepticism: the difficulty of conceptualising such a nebulous, large-scale project; inability to convince Roanoke's residents of the area's tourism potential; and serious doubts about the benefits of a tourism-based economy to stimulate real, long-term economic growth. Opposition from Roanoke city representatives was grounded in fears that Explore would divert future development dollars and tourists from downtown, promoting its further abandonment by tourist-oriented establishments.

News about Explore was generally printed in all the zoned editions (*see* Table 11.1). Where omissions occurred, they were from the state edition and were usually on subjects of local concern. Perhaps more interesting are the varied headlines that captioned the same article in different editions (21 per cent of the articles in 1988, 17 per cent in both 1989 and 1990, and 6 per cent in 1991). The zoned editions are not printed simultaneously, accounting for some changes in headlines and changing allocations of space. Nonetheless, some of the differences in headlines give the impression of trying to

Table 11.1 Reportage of key development projects.

Explore

	News features	Opinion	Total
1988	80	91	171
1989	29	33	62
1990	46	68	114
1991	34	20	54
1992*	0	0	0
Total	189	21	401

Hotel Roanoke

	News features	Opinion	Total
1989	28	14	42
1990	30	14	44
1991	32	21	53
1992*	14	4	18
Total	104	53	157

Direct Link

	News features	Opinion	Total
1988	5	3	8
1989	24	32	56
1990	4	13	17
1991	18	33	51
1992*	16	18	34
Total	67	99	166

* January–March only

slant the news. For instance, three different headlines in connection with one article (14 July 1988): 'Regional flood plan gets push: Explore officials speak up in channelisation debate' (Metro); 'Explore seeks flooding study' (New River Valley); and 'Explore disputes city plan: Park officials enter flood controversy' (State). The Metro edition headline has a positive slant, while the state edition is more negative. Different headlines to identical stories are consistent with segmenting the market. Readers distributed over a larger geographic area with differing views on local political relationships can be catered for without readily apparent compromises of journalistic objectivity. Thus differential headlines were most common in 1988, the year of greatest controversy, and least common in 1991, a relatively non-controversial year. These particular headlines also reveal the subtle pro-Explore bias of the paper: even in the Metro edition, Roanoke City's point of view is not portrayed favorably.

Unlike the other two projects under study, Explore is not designed primarily to promote downtown, nor has it raised local opposition to being incorporated into a greater Roanoke. Instead, Explore exemplifies the type of large-scale project that local growth coalitions are fond of developing to re-create the image of their region as it is perceived both externally and internally. The newspaper's role in this project has primarily been one of selling this new image to local residents and the rest of the state.

Plans for the project were already two-and-a-half years old at the start of our analysis (January 1988). News coverage, more than three-quarters of which was written by the same reporter, was also generally positive. Negative news was reported and stories were sometimes written from an investigative perspective, explaining the source of criticism, but never really validating it. Both positive and negative coverage tended to be gathered from key speakers or institutions consistent with the news-gathering process which favours ease of access to sources. During the time study period, newspaper coverage progressed through several phases coinciding with changes in the project itself and shifting levels of support. At the start, most coverage was 'hard' news with a positive slant, although critical news and details of controversy were also in evidence. The next phase of coverage consisted largely of articles commenting on the diminishing level of criticism about Explore. Finally, the newspaper took on almost a pure public relations role, helping to sell the scaled-down, restructured project to the public and keeping it in the spotlight.

The greatest controversy expressed in reporting was in 1988. Explore became the subject of a heated legislative battle over funding during the first three months of that year. The newspaper extensively quoted Explore's promoters as they extolled the benefits of growth for the local economy, emphasising the role that the project would play in stimulating economic development throughout the region. At least one law-maker suggested that Explore and other regional projects might be able to stimulate sufficient regional population growth to help offset the region's shrinking political power in the state. These pro-growth arguments were not restricted to legislative rhetoric. An article quoted extensively from a letter written by the mayor of Blacksburg: 'Roanoke's growth rate has slowed down to almost a trickle . . . and, as the Roanoke Valley goes, so goes the New River Valley' (28 January 1988). He went on to say that 'You (the Roanoke Valley) need to promote image' and that Explore would give Western Virginia a new identity. Explore's organiser Cruickshanks was quoted as saying: 'Among business leaders, you would get pretty broad agreement that this is not a vibrant economy . . . The bright spots in our economy are Blacksburg and Smith Mountain Lake' (27 November 1988).

News analysis of the project was written primarily by the newspaper's best known journalist, Dwayne Yancey, who cast issues in a political frame of reference. In these articles, Yancey developed a class analysis to explain the local political battle over Explore: 'The historic split in Roanoke Valley politics is the natural division in a railroad town between a business-backed establishment energised by visions of civic greatness and a blue-collar citizenry leery of footing the bill for fancy projects it sees no need for' (26 January 1988). The analysis takes no explicit stance, pro or con, and objectivity is achieved by recounting others' views. Yet there were factual comparisons that could, but were not, made. For example, Roanoke's pro-growth lobby was previously allied over the downtown Civic Centre. Now in operation for many years, the Centre and its parallel claims of fostering economic development could have been evaluated. In failing to conduct this or other relevant analysis, Yancey left his readers with the impression that economic development projects are successes and their promoters visionaries.

Another example of a positive slant on negative news came in April 1988 when the authority responsible for Explore purchased a tract of land for an amount 94 per cent greater than its assessed value. Instead of expected scrutiny of this use of state funds, news articles stated, in a matter-of-fact way, that the inflated prices, which resulted from the authority's powers, had been limited to appease Explore's critics. This trend continued, with an article (10 July) reporting: 'Explore opposition seeming to fade as results mount'. The occasion for this article was the third anniversary of Explore, and the content could best be described as a press release from Bern Ewert, project director, documenting the project's successes. Ewert even comments in the article that the newspaper had recently stopped its negative coverage. In the same vein, the headline of a 20 July article was: 'Explore convinces former foes'.

By 1989, stories were written from the growth coalition's perspective. One headline, 'Explore expected to blaze impressive fund-raising trail', is indicative. In the article, Yancey (24 July) wrote: 'Four years after Explore was conceived amid derision and ridicule from hometown critics in Roanoke, the project is starting to be taken seriously by some out-of-town people who matter most – those who can afford to donate the millions necessary to build the proposed $185 million state park re-creating Virginia's role in opening the American west'. In this and similar stories, we can see unquestioning loyalty to the project as well as the not-so-subtle attempt to rework readers' local sense of place by convincing them that Explore can expand and enhance Roanoke's image regionally and even nationally.

Editorials were even more supportive of the project. No editorial during the study period questioned the appropriateness of Explore, or its ability to stimulate local economic development. The purpose of many editorials was old-fashioned boosterism, frequently referring to the need to build a new image for the Roanoke region. The successes of similarly situated regions, examples of growing, future-oriented economies, were used to challenge Roanokers to enlarge their aspirations. One editorial (10 January 1988) quoted extensively from a speech given by a nationally-known North-Carolina-based developer. The developer, Faison, outlined Explore's importance in creating an image of the Roanoke area which could attract young, highly educated workers, and satisfy the lifestyle needs of these workers so critical to high-tech corporations. The editorial concluded: 'Faison says he'd rather have Explore than a new IBM factory. If we do get Explore, maybe we can have both'. Another editorial (10 September 1989) emphasised the importance of Explore in creating a new image for Roanoke, an image of a 'progressive city in a scenic area'. Regionalism and regional image were repeatedly the main editorial themes: 'Explore is of regional and even national significance' (27 July 1990); 'Roanoke gradually is extending its sense of place to encompass a wider region with broader opportunities for growth' (2 September 1990). In 1991, editorial references were made to the importance of increasing the geographic scale of the region, describing the process as 'expanding outward our notions of regional community' (1 January).

In its support for Explore, and for an expanded functional region, the *Roanoke Times & World-News* was accused by politicians and correspondents of threatening the future of downtown Roanoke. In light of the paper's support for downtown revitalisation, notably in support of the Hotel Roanoke, such accusations were ironic. The newspaper, however, consistently argued that Explore would not detract from downtown and presented a positive picture of compromises which were made between Roanoke city officials and Explore backers to ensure the city its fair share of state development funds.

Responses to the newspaper's coverage of Explore reinforced the notion that its acceptance required a massive public relations campaign. Letters to the editor were almost evenly split between supporters and critics of the project. Supporters reiterated the newspaper's own and reported arguments about the importance of stimulating economic growth in the region, taking a regional view, and updating Roanoke's economy and image. Some critics wrote of the threat to their community identity and sense of place which the project posed. These were people in local residential communities who feared their homes or way of life would be threatened by the project. Unlike the case with the Direct Link, however, there were actually very few residents affected (fewer than 500) and the truly rural non-farm nature of their communities, lacking retail or employment opportunities, weakened their defence of local attachment.

Another group of correspondents focused on the newspaper's coverage of the story. These letters reveal the deep-seated opinions held by readers of the responsibilities of a newspaper in properly carrying out its job. Several times, the paper was criticised by Explore's officials for its negative coverage of the project. Others complained of the newspaper's one-sidedness. 'Your newspaper, along with other wealthy and powerful institutions in Roanoke Valley, is so determined to have the Explore boondoggle become a reality that you would never allow the voters of Roanoke Valley or all Virginians vote on a project where so many millions of taxpayers' dollars would be wasted. Never has there been such a blatant show of power pressure on the people of Roanoke Valley' (2 September 1988). One writer even questioned the validity of news stories declaring that opposition to Explore was waning.

Others called for the newspaper to take a more critical perspective on Explore and to represent better the interests of the region. One writer anticipated the thesis of this research, stating that 'your involvement with the Explore project will one day make an excellent case study of just how a newspaper crosses the line between journalism and public relations' (2 July 1991). Supporters of Explore tended to view the newspaper's involvement as a 'good story' that would sell newspapers. Critics of Explore, on the other hand, saw the *Roanoke Times & World-News* as a growth-coalition player, seeking its fortunes in bigger business, printing positive news that would sell the region.

Hotel Roanoke in the press

Coverage of the closure of the Hotel Roanoke, its acquisition by the university, and the long struggles toward redevelopment comprises a smaller set of news and opinion items than the Explore project, in part because of its shorter history (*see* Table 11.1). Interest centred on the city, with a minority of letters to the editor from the New River Valley (4 out of 23). Nonetheless, considerable segmentation of the larger region's market was evident in news coverage between Metro and New River Valley editions. The newspaper presented the city's support for the project, covered the New River Valley's opposition, and largely ignored the opposition from Roanoke County, except at critical junctures.

While the Hotel Roanoke is physically located in the city, the rhetoric of the press portrayed it simultaneously as the city's top economic development priority and an issue of concern to a wider public than the city itself. As with the Direct Link, the hotel is a mechanism to gather into Roanoke the prosperity of the outlying region, specifically that of the university, but unlike the road to Blacksburg, the hotel project intends to relocate some of that growth to the city. A promotional supplement titled 'Virginia Tech-Roanoke Connection' advertised that link to the outlying market of the New River Valley. The news-like text which separated the advertisements spoke of the 'unique opportunities' presented by 'the grande dame of the Star City,' and of the university's mission to the city of Roanoke (24 September 1989).

Early in 1990, plans for the hotel's reopening were outlined in the newspaper, followed later in the year with the 'down-side' about finance. As attention turned to making plans more concrete, the newspaper covered the refusal of Roanoke County to support the hotel project financially, lamenting the county's shortsightedness. Their opposition was painted in a bad light, choosing quotations by county residents apparently concerned only with power and trivialities. One resident of Roanoke County, for example, was quoted as opposing the financing of the hotel because he had received poor service there before it closed (26 September 1990)!

Subsequent editorial resolutions (2 January 1991) focused on the need to work cooperatively across a wider region in order to create prosperity for all. The Hotel Roanoke and the conference centre were a symbiotic focus for several development projects: Explore would provide conferences to use the hotel; the Direct Link to Blacksburg would strengthen city–university ties already forged in the hotel project. Detractors also wrote about that symbiotic relationship, on one hand labelling them all as 'bad eggs' and, on the other, worrying whether Explore and the hotel were more competitive than cooperative (19 June 1991). In the autumn, an editorial again drew on the image of cumulative impact, with benefits to accrue to the entire Roanoke Valley and to the New River Valley as well. A November editorial pointed to the need for large, visionary projects to spur economic development, which was in turn the only way to finance programmes to address social needs. In this response to the criticism of favouring development over people, the paper drew the circle tighter, focusing on the benefits to the city's needy population, not needs in the larger region.

Coverage of the Hotel Roanoke drew on the local attachment of residents, and the symbolic significance of the structure to the community – primarily the city and downtown. Human interest coverage centred on holidays and nostalgia. In its last days of operation in late November, the final Thanksgiving feast featured town-folks' memories of the hotel. News and feature stories were complemented with letters to the editor praising the hotel's charms. Holiday nostalgia resurfaced a year later, with stories of Christmas tree lights on the property commemorating one year of closure.

While early 1991 news largely reported the details of financing and development plans, symbolic support came in reporting on public opinion and from readers' letters. Public confidence was demonstrated in reporting a poll which showed 71 per cent had 'much' or 'some' confidence that the hotel would re-open (31 January 1991). Details of projected plans prompted letters to the editor pleading for preservation of the traditional architecture of the hotel. At the end of the study period, the symbolic attachment to the Hotel Roanoke was again being used to promote its desirability: 'One thing the hotel's planners don't have to do is sell the project. All that most people want to know is when it will re-open. Fewer want to know the cost, and fewer still the way it will be financed' (29 December 1991). Even with its increased pessimism in early 1992, the newspaper feature writers continued to remark on the sentiment attached to the hotel: 'All the emotion and support a community can muster will not guarantee the resurrection of an old friend' (26 January 1992).

The people of the city of Roanoke, so the newswriters wrote, were strongly attached to this local landmark. City government continued to see it as the 'No.1 economic development priority' (26 January 1992). In efforts to gather university-generated prosperity, however, newspaper personnel had to make distinctions between the local attachments of two different places, Roanoke City and the New River Valley (and choosing not to respond to local sentiment in Roanoke County opposition). The New River Valley, in particular the university town of Blacksburg, was threatened by the hotel project. Blacksburg's own desire to construct a conference centre was initially derailed. The Blacksburg Chamber of Commerce president wrote to the paper listing university decisions which had hurt Blacksburg, including accepting the gift of the hotel. The letter was printed only in the New River Valley edition. A news report by New River Valley staff journalist Cathryn McCue noted Blacksburg's mayor's unwillingness to take on the fight. The headline of this July story was ambiguous: 'Plans may not leave Blacksburg out in cold' (26 July 1989). This particular story was carried in all editions, but other opposition was largely relegated to the New River Valley *Current*.

Blacksburg opposition was tied to divergent views of the university's well-being and to the outlook for the town's private sector. The university president attempted to soothe concerns. His reassurances were quoted in the newspaper, stating that the Hotel Roanoke would not siphon funds from teaching and research, 'a sensitive subject on the Blacksburg campus' (31 August 1990). Reader commentary in September 1990 underscored the unpopularity of the hotel in the campus community.

In October 1990, the state governor intervened with accusations of unwise uses of resources in promoting the Hotel Roanoke while the university's finances were so straitened. In one of the most contrasting sets of coverage offered by the *Roanoke Times & World-News* during the study period, the same words were rearranged to tell different stories to Roanoke City and to the New River Valley. The Metro edition opened the story with efforts by the city to inform and persuade the governor of the project's importance to Roanoke. The New River *Current* supplement was headlined 'Criticisms seen as silencer', leading with a discussion of political rifts between the governor and the university, then picking up the Metro version midway through (16 October 1990). In a subsequent editorial, the newspaper supported the university, berating the governor's action in releasing his comments to the press before notifying university officials and reiterating that no state money was being used for the hotel. Two days later, an editorial noted that the governor's comments were intended 'to whip Tech into line' (16 November 1990).

The Blacksburg pocket of opposition posed a dilemma for a newspaper so editorially committed to the project, but also provided two benefits. One arose from the intensity of opposition and the direct threat to merchants and faculty. This intensity of feeling provided a means of securing readership for the New River edition, especially the tabloid *Current*, while reinforcing local loyalty to the community within Blacksburg. A second benefit was to provide a venue for the journalistic value of 'questioning authority!' – although more was generated by letters to the editor and reader commentary than by investigative reporting. Due to public opposition, more straightforward reporting (of, say, Chamber of Commerce reactions) could be interpreted by readers as combative journalism, putting the powerful project promoters on notice. In a similar vein, the governor's opposition fitted the agenda of supporting the hotel while reporting and editorially commenting on the failings of the powerful, in this case, the governor.

These instances, however, were substitutes for critical reporting. The critical stories that were not done may be as telling as the editorial support so clearly behind the Hotel Roanoke. Reporters tended not to question closely the financial standing of the hotel, consistent with Kaniss's (1991) finding that reporters tended to gloss over numbers. Reporting alternative sources' statements about financial viability was the norm, augmented by officials and individual members of the public offering their opinions on feasibility.

The Direct Link in the press

The proposed road to connect more directly the city of Roanoke with the college town of Blacksburg is an explicit move to create a region encompassing both. The goal of the Roanoke growth coalition is to benefit from the growth potential of the university. Synergistic effects are asserted, although with little specific sense of their reality. Blacksburg's support for the proposal similarly talks about the benefits of joint efforts made easier by the road, but the examples focus more on access to Roanoke as a means to depart and enter the region via Roanoke's airport and better access to the interstate highway.

In 1988, at the start of our study period (*see* Table 11.1, page 201), the Direct Link was the subject of various governmental hearings and public meetings. With a wealth of potential news events, both pro- and anti-road, the *Roanoke Times & World-News* coverage mirrored the span of reader and citizen sentiment. By early 1989, however, the editorial position of the paper was clearly in support of the Direct Link: 'The Roanoke Valley is the largest metropolitan area in Virginia – on the East Coast, some say – that has no public four-year college or university' (11 January 1989). The theme was often repeated in position statements. In late January, the proposed road figured prominently in a feature article on economic development. When a lobby was formed to promote the Link, a March 1989 lead editorial reprised: 'Roanoke is the largest city (now in the Southeast) without a state university, the university needs a city, the city needs the research of the university, the link is vital for economic development'.

The Direct Link plan became even more controversial when the grander vision of the 'smart highway' arose. In May 1989, the newspaper reported a Roanoke County official's idea to add technology to the road, making it a 'smart highway', a testing ground for new ideas to computerise traffic flow. The theme fitted in well with the technological promise of tying together city and university in order to create a high-tech, growth environment. Engineers at the university would provide the expertise and businesses in Roanoke would benefit from the research and development and possible production attending the high-tech road project. The gimmick of a smart highway also opened alternative funding sources, and varieties of public support, which were as attractive to many supporters as was the technology itself.

The newspaper continued to support the road project editorially and by its features throughout the time when local authorities were meeting with federal government officials to support the smart road idea. In October, those meetings were front-page news, and profiles of road proponents were feature stories. Editorially, the paper defended the county official against reader accusations: the official had no personal interest, save his commitment to the region's economic base. In February 1990, the county supervisor who had formulated the smart road idea was given commentary space to describe his plan. He took it for granted that there would be a road; only the question of how remained: 'First of all, we are going to build a road that in effect will link one of the nation's leading research universities to our Roanoke Valley, with its emerging presence in various technical fields, especially fibre optics' (11 February 1990).

One lead editorial was entitled 'The yellow brick road to Blacksburg', endorsing the necessity of the road (2 March 1990). Despite the headline, the editorial did not imply the road was a fantasy better left in Oz. Instead the future of the Roanoke region was likened to the established Research Triangle in North Carolina. A feature depicted the road as the way to end the university's 'oft-lamented rural isolation', and placing it in the forefront of smart road technology (25 April 1990). The entire state should endorse the road was the not-too-hidden message, since the research would benefit traffic in the more densely populated areas of Virginia. Against the backdrop of intense local loyalty, this effort to extend the benefits of the road to the whole state parallels the pragmatic region-building that accompanied the Direct Link project, as well as the Hotel Roanoke and the Explore Project: efforts to preserve the growth and prosperity of Roanoke by a hard-headed, realistic yet visionary look at where growth can be found, and appropriating it for the city. The editorial agenda for 1991 was to 'think more regionally' and build the smart road, among other actions (3 January 1991). Yet the focus was, typically, on the well-being of the city. Pro-road advocates tended to be covered in all editions of the paper; anti-road and which-road disputations tended to be in the New River Valley supplement only.

Letters to the editor were the primary source of anti-road comments, and most letters to the editor about the road were published in the New River edition. In fact, no letters were published in any edition from Roanoke Valley residents! With the road truly 'distant', Roanoke residents seemed to care little. Coverage about which road was carried in both the city and the New River edition, but placed more prominently in the New River edition. Anti-road letters to the editor complained of the ludicrously small gains in convenience that the Direct Link would produce, and the high costs it would entail. Opposition letters also detailed the environmental costs that the road would produce. A longer reader commentary appeared in 1991 from a citizens' group leader, warning that the road would spoil the landscape and pave the way for a megalopolis stretching from Blacksburg to Roanoke. This vision is a logical conclusion from the rhetoric of the newspaper's promotion of a growth agenda, although it is doubtful whether the vision of a larger region would involve a continuously built-up area. Although ties to the university are now standard ('for years, it's been widely understood that if the Roanoke Valley is to continue to prosper and grow, it should forge closer ties with Virginia Tech', 12 May 1991 editorial), we rarely read of an urban region of the future that extended all the way to Blacksburg.

In the summer of 1991, a spate of anti-road letters appeared. The writers saw the road as wasteful, harmful and unnecessary. Letter-writers rejected development. An expatriate of the 'ravages of unbridled development in Northern Virginia' wrote of her deliberate escape from that environment to the quiet of rural Montgomery County, a quiet which the Direct Link threatened to shatter (16 June 1991). Urbanisation itself was the issue: an urban refugee pleading to preserve the refuge.

New River Valley opposition to the road finally surfaced in the city edition with a description of a public meeting held in Blacksburg in late September 1991. More detailed coverage was printed in the New River Valley edition, but the meeting was headlined in all the editions as '"Smart highway" called "dumb" idea by citizens' (27 September 1991). One reader's response underscored the possible ways to interpret the newspaper's position on the road. To this reader, the repeated editorials supporting the road project were apparently invisible; the coverage of road opposition forces in the New River edition, including reader letters, was quite visible. This letter to the editor commented that the writer only bothered to attend the meeting because of the prior negative coverage by the paper: 'The anti-road group (with the help of reporter Cathryn McCue and the *Roanoke Times & World-News*) wants us all to believe that this cost to the taxpayers will only result in a savings of six minutes between Roanoke and Blacksburg' (7 October 1991). He answered in rebuttal that the cumulative impact of those six minutes, day-in and day-out, would be a considerable saving of time and transportation costs. To this reader, at least, the newspaper had taken an anti-road position through its routine coverage of road opposition.

While fostering this local attachment to the landscape, to a small town and rural atmosphere, and to anti-development sentiments in the New River tabloid, the newspaper was not above using barbs directed at the intellectual centre up that proposed road. Despite the long-standing argument to promote ties to the university, an anti-intellectual twist is used to dismiss the opposition. In an October Sunday feature, the writer noted 'Road foes turned out by the dozens, many of them Virginia Tech graduate students who had met a few days earlier to plan their strategy' (20 October 1991). Graduate students, presumably, need not be taken seriously, as their sense of local attachment is fleeting, and are hence suspect. That aspersion is furthered by the underlying sense that public opinion should be spontaneous, not planned in advance. Similarly in February 1992, a lead Sunday editorial characterised the 'anti' crowd: 'A small group of Virginia Tech graduate students and Ellett Valley [where the road is to be built] residents are orchestrating most of the ruckus' (16 February 1992). Road proponents were not held to this standard; as leaders of business and government, it is their job to plan. One final letter, expressing a different sentiment, is worth noting. The writer does not attack the road as directly as she attacks the promotion for the road: 'Blacksburg–Roanoke route also strewn with shoppers, kids, moms', read the headline. Not all travellers, said the writer, are 'men in business suits on economic development missions' (27 November 1991).

It may be appropriate to leave the final word on the road as of early 1992 to the newspaper's former higher education writer, now economic writer. The cynicism of the New River Valley is clearly evident in his opening: 'Just ask the backers of Western Virginia's twin 'Trust-Me' projects, the Hotel Roanoke renovation and the Mont-gomery County smart road. By the way, it's probably no accident that you'd find the same power brokers and activist bureaucrats behind both endeavors' (23 February 1992). Yet the major thrust of the column is to stop the in-fighting between the two communities, as he details why opposition is found in Blacksburg (budget cuts in state support of the university), and why Roanokers back such projects (economic health of the valley), and reprises the warnings from leaders to stop jurisdictional in-fighting. In other words, he reiterates the continuing theme of the newspaper to 'think regionally'.

Discussion

It would be mistaken to conclude that the pressure to expand Roanoke's regional extent is inherently related to land size or a territorial imperative. The loyalty evident in the newspaper portrayal is to the city of Roanoke itself, with – as Kaniss (1991) has pointed out – a bias toward the downtown. The strategy to acquire outlying locations arises from the locations themselves: the university town and the lake resort area. These two attractions are awkwardly located for the city and for its newspaper urban boosters – slightly too far away for spillover growth to coalesce into the built-up urban region in a short period of time. The spatial strategy is thus one of building connections, both metaphoric and physical transportation.

The newspaper-as-promotional-strategist has two different stances with regard to Explore and the Smith Mountain Lake region on one hand and to the university-oriented ties on the other, different stances tied to the existence or not of a separate market at the outlying attractions. In the case of Explore, the population not tied to Roanoke is a small but affluent market. Smith Mountain Lake resort and retirement area, as an emerging population centre, is still seen as a potential subsidiary centre with strong ties to the central city. The strategy to incorporate this area by Roanoke is in some ways a classic case of inter-urban rivalry with Roanokers concerned about losing this area to Lynchburg, Virginia. The newspaper's marketing response is a zoned edition, but one that is published irregularly, and that varies little from other editions when one is published. Depending on the success of the development at the lake and the sustained connections to the city, a clearly separate identity may or may not evolve.

Given the tenuous reward of Direct Link with the Smith Mountain Lake community, the newspaper's support of Explore seems to be simple boosterism, emanating from the newspaper's local dependence and pre-eminent position in the growth coalition. The grandiose Explore project is seen as a catalyst for growth, a giant, visible magnet which will draw visitors and dollars from outside the region. It is hoped that such a magnet will alter the regional image, enhancing it and boosting Roanoke up a place in the national urban hierarchy. What locally dependent enterprise could resist promoting such a project?

In contrast, the western attraction, the university town, is a sizeable and separate market, with a vocal anti-growth perspective. Disdain for big-city life is a common Blacksburg theme. Consequently, news coverage for the Blacksburg market tends to reflect the scepticism toward the Hotel Roanoke and the Direct Link or smart road. Letters from Blacksburg – whether in the tabloid or the editorial page – underscore that scepticism. Meanwhile, the editorial stance of the paper continues to support the project through its uniformly positive editorials.

Through its coverage, the newspaper attempted to negotiate a fine line between promoting the coalescence of Roanoke and Blacksburg and not offending its anti-growth Blacksburg market. The newspaper managers either see the contradictions as no serious threat to its future (and no other paper has emerged to rival its New

River Valley circulation) or, as a result of their inherent central city bias, believe that the central city perspective will prevail in the end.

The latter perspective is evident in the newspaper's coverage of the Hotel Roanoke project. While closer ties to the university are an underlying reason for the newspaper's position, the project also reinforces Roanokers' traditional sense of place and attachment to downtown as the core of the region. Even Roanoke residents who are opposed to growth find a restored Hotel Roanoke an appealing way to preserve the status quo.

Conclusion

This study of the newspaper-as-promotional-strategist in local development suggests that the strategies developed by smaller metropolitan areas may be very different from those of larger ones. While large urban regions struggle to hold the centre together and their central city newspapers struggle to retain influence and dominance over an ever-expanding fringe, it is likely that Roanoke's response is typical of a strategy to bring non-metropolitan areas within the region in terms of both sentiment and function. Yet as this study also shows, it is very difficult to incorporate non-metropolitan areas into the urban region especially when residents of those areas pride themselves on their non-metropolitan status. Functional links ranging from shopping trips to newspaper subscriptions may be more easily established than links of sentiment. Yet historically newspapers have played a prominent role in the creation and promotion of local attachment. This is certainly true in the case of the *Roanoke Times & World News*. It is in this regard that the newspaper, as a member of the growth coalition, must perform a careful balancing act in promoting a greater regional attachment while maintaining its credibility as a critical forum for debate.

References

Abbott, C. (1981) *Boosters and Businessmen: popular economic thought and urban growth in the antebellum Middle West*, Westport, CT: Greenwood Press.

Belcher, W.W. (1947) *The Economic Rivalry Between St. Louis and Chicago*, New York: Columbia University Press.

Cox, K.R. and Mair, A. (1988) 'Locality and community in the politics of local economic development', *Annals of the Association of American Geographers*, 78, 307–25.

Cox, K.R. and Mair, A. (1989) 'The politics of turf and the question of class', in J. Wolch and M. Dear, eds., *The Power of Geography: how territory shapes social life*, Boston: Unwin Hyman, 61–90.

Harloe, M., Pickvance, C. and Urry, J., eds. (1990) *Places, Policy and Politics: do localities matter?*, London: Unwin Hyman.

Jonas, A.E.G. (1991) 'Urban growth coalitions and urban development policy: postwar growth and the politics of annexation in metropolitan Columbus', *Urban Geography*, 12, 197–225.

Jonas, A.E.G. (1993) 'A place for politics in urban theory: the organisation and strategies of urban coalitions', *Urban Geography*, 13, 280–90.

Kaniss, P. (1991) *Making Local News*, Chicago: University of Chicago Press.

Kirby, A. (1985) 'Nine fallacies of local economic change', *Urban Affairs Quarterly*, 21, 207–20.

Law, C.M. (1992) 'Urban tourism and its contribution to economic regeneration', *Urban Studies*, 29, 599–618.

Logan, J.R. and Molotch, M. (1987) *Urban Fortunes: the political economy of place*, Berkeley: University of California Press.

Pickvance, C. (1990) 'Introduction', in M. Harloe, C. Pickvance, and J. Urry, eds., *Places, Policy and Politics: do localities matter?*, London: Unwin Hyman, 84–118.

Wolch, J. and Dear, M., eds. (1989) *The Power of Geography: how territory shapes social life*, Boston: Unwin Hyman.

12 Marketing landscapes of the Four Corners States

ERVIN H. ZUBE AND JANET GALANTE

The Four Corners States

There is only one point in the contiguous USA where the boundaries of four states join in an orderly, orthogonal relationship. This distinct phenomenon is responsible for the area being known as the Four Corners Region, comprising the four states that are the focus of this chapter: Arizona, Colorado, New Mexico, and Utah (Figure 12.1). These are among the larger states of the lower 48 states; New Mexico ranking fourth largest, Arizona fifth, Colorado seventh, and Utah tenth. Together they cover approximately 14 per cent of the USA (excluding Alaska and Hawaii).

The region contains widely varying and valued landscapes, with no less than 53 units of the National Parks system. The natural landscapes are the products of three geological provinces (Figure 12.2). The *Colorado Plateau* which occupies the centre of the region and encompasses parts of each of the states lies at an elevation of 1500 metres or higher with scattered peaks rising to 3350 metres. The Plateau contains an impressive variation of scenic wonders, ranging from desert in the lower elevations to coniferous alpine forests at the higher elevations.

The *Basin and Range* province to the south and west consists of dry plains (basins) and highly eroded, raised and tilted, rugged fault block mountain ranges. Perennial streams are rare, but there are some notable water features including the Great Salt Lake in Utah, the Rio Grande River in Colorado and New Mexico, and the Colorado River. The *Rocky Mountain* province to the east and north have their greatest impact on the landscape in Colorado, with 55 peaks exceeding 4300 metres.

Overlain on this physically and biologically diverse natural landscape is more than 10,000 years' history of human occupancy. While much of this history is difficult for the untrained observer to comprehend in physical terms, there are notable examples of human landscapes dating back more than 1000 years. These sites provide vivid, visual evidence of Hohokam, Anasazi, and Mogollon cultures in the forms of pithouses, cliff dwellings, kivas and, for the Hohokam, advanced irrigation systems that allowed for survival in a hot, arid landscape (Lister and Lister, 1983; Haury, 1985).

In the 19th century, this region was little-known. Its states had not yet entered the American Union and their landscapes were classed as part of the 'Great American Desert', a generalised appellation applied to the region that emerged from ignorance and fiction more than from fact. From the mid-19th century, however, continuing

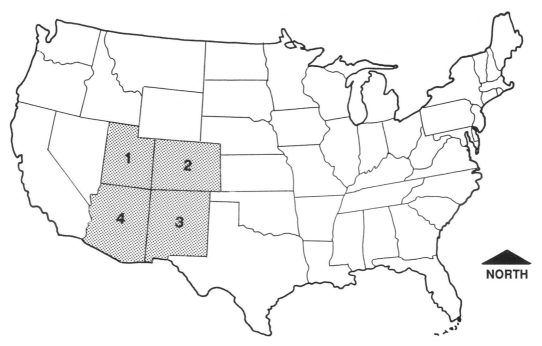

Figure 12.1   The Four Corners States: 1, Utah; 2, Colorado; 3, New Mexico; and 4, Arizona.

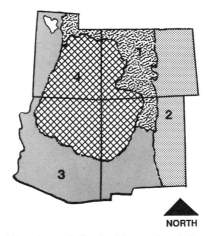

Figure 12.2   Geological Provinces: 1, Rocky Mountains; 2, Internal Plains; 3, Basin and Range; and 4, Colorado Plateau.

efforts were made, in various ways and for various purposes, to market the landscapes of the Four Corners states. In this chapter, we adopt an interactional perspective to explore four dimensions of marketing and their interactions with the fifth dimension – time. The four dimensions are: the *landscape* and its specific attributes; *agents* – who did the marketing; target *audiences* – to whom the agents were addressing their marketing; and, the marketing *media* – primarily books, pamphlets and advertisements.

Marketing beginnings

In the 16th century, Coronado came to the south-west in search of the Seven Cities of Cibola, the mystical seven cities of great wealth. He failed to find them in his travels through Arizona and New Mexico, but the search for wealth in the region continued. As early as 1829 gold had been discovered near Santa Fé, New Mexico. The discovery that attracted the most attention, however, was in California in 1849. That finding was followed by another widely heralded discovery in Colorado in 1858. Several years later the first delegate to the US Congress from the Territory of Arizona addressed that body and extolled the deposits of gold and silver waiting to be discovered in Arizona (Gressinger, 1961). Other minerals, notably copper, lead and zinc were soon found in the Four Corners States and Territories. These discoveries stimulated immigration to the West, notably to California and Colorado.

Following the end of the Civil War in 1864, the first railway reached Colorado in 1870; an event that was accompanied by a rapid population increase and a parallel increase in agricultural production. The first trans-continental rail line had been completed one year earlier, in 1869, when the Union Pacific Railway, starting in Omaha, Nebraska, and the Central Pacific, starting in Sacramento, California, met at Promontory, Utah. That same year the *Great Trans-Continental Railroad Guide* was published (Dadd, 1869), described on its cover as a virtual encyclopedia of information about the resources and attractions to be found along the route (Figure 12.3).

Other trans-continental connections eventually serviced all of the Four Corners Region. In 1881, the Atchison, Topeka, and Santa Fé Railway completed a line running from Chicago through central New Mexico and northern Arizona to Los Angeles. In 1883 the Southern Pacific Railroad completed a line running from New Orleans through Texas, southern New Mexico and Arizona, and then on to Los Angeles, providing the Four Corners States and Territories with, what was for the time, an impressive means of access. The stage was set and the first steps taken in what was to become a continuing series of marketing activities for the landscapes of the Four Corners Region.

The temporal dimension

Three overlapping eras in marketing activities have been identified for the landscapes of the Four Corners Region. The first was an era in which territorial and state governments, along with the railways, played significant roles as marketing agents. The primary targets of their marketing efforts were immigrants to settle the area and persons of wealth to invest in development activities. These agents tended to be most active from the mid-19th to the early 20th centuries. The second era, which overlapped the first, was a period era of transition. Lasting from about 1890 to 1950, it saw the change from the railways being primary marketing agents, targeting wealthy tourists from the Eastern and Midwestern regions of the country, to the emergence of the car and associated changes in patterns of tourism. A new marketing medium, the guide book, began to appear. It was published as a commercial venture by individuals and printers who were independent of the railways and the states and territories. The third era, from about 1950 to the present, has been characterised by a growing diversification

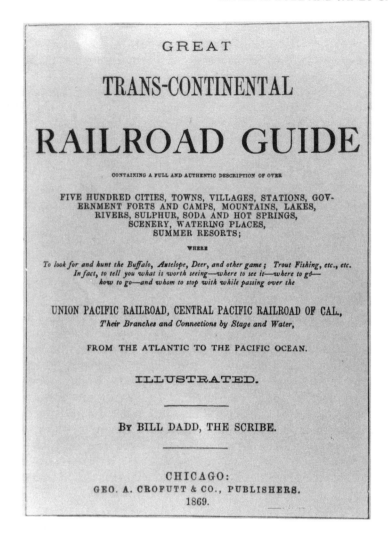

Figure 12.3 *Great Trans-Continental Railroad Guide*, 1869, promoting travel, economic development, land sales and immigration.

of marketing agents, a greater specification of landscape elements and target audiences, and by additional diversification in marketing media.

The first era: immigrants, capital, and health

Predominant among the interests of the Arizona, New Mexico and Utah Territories in the early years of their existence was the attraction of immigrants and economic investors so as to build population and economic bases to sizes that would merit positive consideration by the United States Congress for statehood. This involved marketing mineral deposits, agricultural resources, and a healthy climate.

The Utah Territory, or more accurately the Mormon Church, which was the dominant political and social force in the Territory, was the first to initiate a programme to attract immigrants. Hunter (1946:263) noted that:

> One of the teachings of the Mormon Church was that missionaries were to be sent to the various countries throughout the world to make converts to that religion.

These missionaries were *de facto* marketing agents. In 1849, the Perpetual Immigrating Fund Company was established with donated funds to make it possible for converts to Mormonism in foreign countries to migrate to Utah. Brigham Young, Territorial Governor and President of the Mormon Church, commented on the effectiveness of the Fund in his report to the Territorial Legislative Assembly on 11 December 1854. He stated:

> By the aid of this fund, much good has already been accomplished; many persons have been taken from the depths of poverty and placed where they can, not only sustain themselves, but soon find a competence for themselves and families. Still thousands are anxiously waiting for the time when the Company will be able to bring them, also, to a land where labour finds its reward. The operations of the Company prove doubly remunerative; it not only places the poor in a situation to sustain themselves, but adds to the sum of labour necessary to develop the resources of the territory . . .

The missionaries who carried the message of Mormonism throughout Europe were successful, with 85,220 persons migrating from Europe to Utah between 1840 and 1887 (Hunter, 1946:269).

Among the other three territories, Colorado appears to have been the least aggressive in trying to stimulate immigration. While a Board of Immigration was established by the Territorial Legislature in 1872, it disappeared when statehood was achieved in 1876, to reappear again only in 1909. There is no evidence, however, that these Boards were very active or aggressive. Perhaps this was because a flow of immigrants had started earlier with the discovery of gold and other natural resources by early surveying parties, and because of its great accessibility compared with the other states. (It would be more than a decade before the railways crossed Arizona and New Mexico; see Riegel, 1926.)

In the last decades of the 19th century, the Legislatures of Arizona and New Mexico also established immigration offices. Arizona created a Board of Commissioners in 1871 and subsequently, a Commissioner of Immigration in 1881 for purposes of promoting the Territory, attracting immigrants and capital and, undoubtedly, to increase population so as to enhance prospects for achieving statehood. Between 1871 and 1890, the Board and the Commissioner produced at least ten publications extolling, with sometimes unrestrained hyperbole, the resources and virtues of the Arizona landscape (Zube and Kennedy, 1990). Statements such as 'come if your health is impaired', 'renew the activity and vigour of your youth', and 'the so-called deserts are being transformed into green fields and orchards' created images of a fecund, pastoral, and health-giving landscape, not of a harsh and sometimes unforgiving desert. These publications, which ranged in length from 37 to more than 400 pages, were distributed in response to inquiries about the Territory from the Eastern part of the country and from Europe. In like fashion, Annual Reports submitted by the Territorial Governor to the Secretary of the Interior in the national capital were also distributed by mail to inquirers. In addition to the lengthy publications, shorter pamphlets were printed for mass distribution, frequently accomplished with the assistance of the railways in the Eastern and Mid-western parts of the country, railways that also served the Four Corners Region.

At the same time as the Territory was trying to promote a positive image, a popular Eastern magazine, the *Atlantic Monthly* was printing stories about Apache Indian raiding parties, the murders of more than 1000 citizens (Evans, 1886), and about the three stages of thirst prior to death from lack of water in the Southwestern desert (McGee, 1898). Clearly, a positive and enthusiastic approach to marketing the Territory was required to counter the images created by such articles. One New Mexican publication even included a chapter entitled 'Life and Property Secure' in an attempt to assuage such notions (Ritch, 1885). The brochure stated that:

> While in the past hostile Indians have made frequent raids upon outlying settlements, murders and robberies by white men have been numerous. Since October, 1881, hostiles have not made a demonstration in New Mexico, and 'rustlers' and desperadoes have scarcely made an appearance.

The New Mexico Territorial Legislature created a Bureau of Immigration to promote the Territory in general, entice people to move there, and promote tourism. During the 1880s, William G. Ritch wrote a number of promotional publications similar to those published in Arizona. They ranged in length from a brief 16 pages to more than 250 pages. While complete records are not available, the following partial record provides some indication of the kinds of materials that were produced. *The Resources of New Mexico*, 64 pages, was published in 1881. *Illustrated New Mexico*, a publication of 140 pages was in its third edition in 1883. Expanded editions with new titles were published in 1884 and 1885. *Santa Fé: Ancient and Modern; Including Its Resources and Industries, With Numerous Illustrations, and a Map of the County*, 68 pages in length, was published in 1885. A 1908 publication by the Bureau was targeted more narrowly to a specific audience, *Ho! to the Land of Sunshine: A Guide to New Mexico for the Homeseeker*. The distribution of these publications was probably similar to the pattern followed in Arizona, and was in response to specific inquiries about the Territory and the opportunities it afforded.

The railways, aided and abetted by the federal government, played an instrumental role in marketing and facilitating immigration and regional growth and development. The federal government subsidised the building of trans-continental railways with grants of land along the proposed rights-of-way, lands that the railways then offered for sale. For example, the *Great Trans-Continental Railroad Guide* (Dadd, 1867) contained a full-page advertisement for the Union Pacific Railroad Company. It announced:

> The Union Pacific Railroad Company have a magnificent land grant – of – Twelve Million Acres of *Rich Farming Lands and Valuable Coal and Iron Mines* along the line of their road. 1,500,000 acres of this Grant *NOW OFFERED* for sale in the state of Nebraska.

Similar lands were available in every western state traversed by the railways. In addition to offsetting capital construction costs, the successful sale of these lands could contribute to the development of communities along the rail-lines and provide for potential passenger and freight shipments to sustain the line, be they agricultural produce, the products of mining or, at higher elevations, the products of timber harvesting. These land sales continued for a considerable period of time. The Union Pacific Railroad, for example, spent more than 800,000 dollars over 10 years advertising its land and placed advertisements in 2311 newspapers and magazines in just one year, 1874 (Wheeler, 1973:213).

The railways also recognised the potential impact of tourism for continued growth and profit, always keeping in mind that visitors were potential immigrants. Travel, tourism, and settlement in the American West were interrelated, the result of a complexity of interactions between explorers, conservationists, entrepreneurs, the states and territories, and most importantly, the railways. Even before the trans-continental railway, the West was visited for adventure and pleasure. The earliest tourists were drawn by the variety and abundance of large game animals for sport hunting, and by reports of magnificent landscapes and seemingly unlimited natural resources.

Tourism required not only willing participants with a destination, but also the availability of transportation and accommodation. The earliest visitors must have been very willing because travel, difficult at best, was often a test of sheer endurance. These travellers often began their journeys without a destination and usually depended upon the generosity of ranchers and settlers for food, lodging, and transportation (Borne, 1983). A solution for these problems came in the form of an unlikely alliance between railways and conservationists. Anxious to expand and with support from the National Parks, the railways became instrumental in the establishment and development of National Parks (Shankland, 1970; Runte, 1990).

The designation of Yellowstone in 1872 as the first National Park was largely a result of the efforts of the Northern Pacific Railroad Company. The Northern Pacific vigorously promoted Yellowstone with the completion of a spur line to the park. The successful attraction of tourists did not go unnoticed by other western railways. Recognising the potential attraction of the Grand Canyon, the Atchison, Topeka, and Sante Fé Railroad implemented a stage service from Sante Fé to the Canyon in 1892. The trips were heavily promoted extolling the beauty of the scenery and the Canyon, but not elaborating on the discomfort that the traveller body would endure seated with 17 companions on wooden seats in large wagons pulled along dirt roads in the desert heat for many hours! The Grand Canyon Spur Line replaced the wagons in 1901, connecting Williams, Arizona, to the South Rim of the Canyon in a much more comfortable and convenient fashion (Thomas, 1978). Publicity and accessibility provided by the Santa Fé Railway contributed immeasurably to the designation of the Grand Canyon as a national monument in 1908 (Runte, 1990:33).

Even with the great improvements in transportation, travel was uncomfortable, difficult, and expensive. European vacations often cost less than domestic trips to the West (Borne, 1983:162). Pomeroy (1957:7) reported that a trip to northern California, without stops in Salt Lake City or the Colorado Rockies, would cost about 800 dollars. He pointed out that at the time 'six-room houses rented for eight dollars a month and schoolteachers taught for two hundred dollars a year'. Recognising that only the wealthy could afford trans-continental rail travel, the railway companies provided Pullman cars for travellers to the West, described as 'the most luxurious of sleeping-cars' and that provided 'more comfort and luxury than anywhere in the world' (Pomeroy, 1957:9). With support from the National Park Service, the railways also responded by developing luxurious accommodations with first-class service in the National Parks.

Dining en route to the West, however, was another story. Early on, Fred Harvey, an entrepreneur from Kansas, watched as travellers were subjected to vile meals and hostile service in the few railway stations where meals were available. He approached the Sante Fé Railroad and formed a partnership that would continue to provide innovative services to passengers for many years. The Sante Fé Railroad was aware of the Fred Harvey Company's reputation and often subsidised their projects for the advertising value. By the time of his death in 1901, Harvey operated 15 hotels, 47 restaurants, and 30 dining cars and had acquired a reputation that equated the Harvey name with quality (Thomas, 1978).

Early on the railways recognised the importance of marketing and promotion. One of the first attempts at promoting the West was the previously mentioned *Great Trans-Continental Railroad Guide* (Dadd, 1869) which was sold for 50 cents by the Union Pacific and Central Pacific Railroads. The Guide's cover promised to provide information for over 500 locations on where 'to look for and hunt the Buffalo, Antelope, Deer, and other game; Trout Fishing, etc., etc. In fact, to tell you what is worth seeing – where to go – how to go – and whom to stop with while passing over . . . .' In fact, the Guide concentrated on the economic vitality and liveability of the localities along the route of the rail-line, rarely hinting at recreation or tourist opportunities.

Railway brochures continued to promote opportunities for settlement in the West for many years, but as tourist destinations developed, the railway companies and their passenger agents became more sophisticated in the use of persuasion, becoming true masters in their mission to lure Easterners to the West. The resulting lavishly illustrated publications and brochures provided information on parks, landscape and historic features, economic information, and populations of cities and towns that passengers would see along their journey. The Denver and Rio Grande Western Railroad, a narrow gauge line, published 25,000 copies of *The Tourists' Handbook* each year in addition to many other brochures including: *Health, Wealth and Pleasure in Colorado and New Mexico: A Reliable Treatise on the Famous Pleasure and Health Resorts, and the Rich Mining and Agriculture Regions of the Rocky Mountains* (1881); *Rhymes of the Rockies, or What the Poets Have Found to Say of the Beautiful Scenery on the Denver and Rio Grande* (1887); *The Gold Fields of Colorado* (1896); and *Sights, Places and Resorts in the Rockies* (1900).

The second era: from railways to cars

As we noted above, the second period covers an era from the dominance of the railways to the emergence of the motor car. At the start of the period, the railways were investing substantial sums in promoting National Parks. In 1915 the Santa Fé and Union Pacific Railroads invested nearly one-half million dollars in National Park displays at an exhibition in San Francisco. In 1916, railway companies distributed two million copies

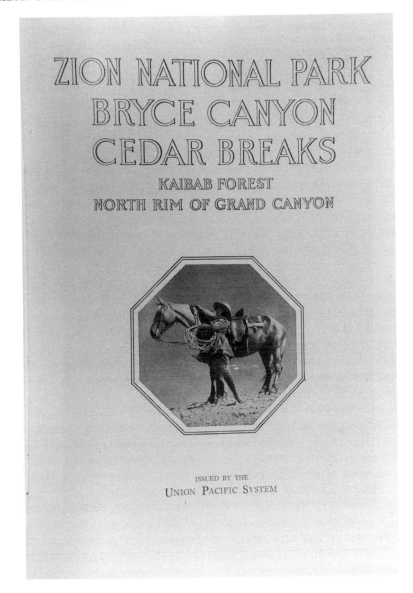

Figure 12.4 Union Pacific Railroad promotion of national parks and forests in Northern Arizona and Utah.

of publications about National Parks (Figure 12.4). The following year, 17 Western railway lines contributed 43,000 dollars to publish 250,000 copies of the first edition of *National Parks Portfolio* (Shankland, 1970:145). The bound portfolio of photographs and text was described by Stephen Mather, first Director of the National Park Service as, 'the first really representative presentation of American scenery of grandeur ever published, perhaps ever made' (Yard, 1921:5).

As well as producing brochures and subsidising National Park Service publications, the railways advertised heavily in a wide variety of popular magazines such as *Holiday*,

Cosmopolitan, *Colliers*, and the *Saturday Evening Post*. The Atchison, Topeka, and Sante Fé Railroad proved to be especially accomplished at 'discovering the powerful and poetic uses of the wilderness' and marketing them 'through a dazzling diversity of advertising themes' (McLuhan, 1987). One particularly innovative approach was the distribution of thousands of lithographs of Thomas Moran's famous painting, 'Grand Canyon' purchased by the Santa Fé Railway in 1914 and followed by invitations to scores of artists to stay at the Canyon to paint (Runte, 1990). The railway companies continued vigorously to promote the National Parks until the popularity of rail travel began to be challenged by the car in the 1920s.

The car was a serious competitive threat to the railways, but also offered new opportunities. Fred Harvey recognised the potential as early as 1899, when the *Flagstaff Coconino Sun* newspaper announced his intention to operate service from Flagstaff to the Grand Canyon using 'horseless carriages'. Unfortunately, technology was unequal to the dream and the effort ended in failure. Years later, however, the Harvey Company did succeed in a similar venture (Thomas, 1978). The railways continued to expand, providing increasingly convenient service to the National Parks, but with the substantial efforts of the 'See America First' movement, the tourist's appetite for the wild, adventurous West intensified. Interest in the 'vanishing American Indian' was stimulated by articles that encouraged Easterners to 'see the old West before it is gone' (Borne, 1983:89), forcing promoters to prove that the West was 'as western as it had ever been' (Borne, 1983:76). Recognising the growing interest in indigenous Western cultures, and railways' inability to reach isolated attractions, the Harvey Company, with the cooperation of the Sante Fé Railroad, began Harveycar Motor Cruises.

The Motor Cruises were devised to offer the rail traveller a diversion of several hours to several days from the 'familiar beaten path of the railroad' (Harveycars, 1928). The most popular and best known of these tours were the 'Indian Detours'. Typically, passengers would alight at the station offering the desired tour and re-board at another station along their route at the end of the motor tour. Although scenic beauty continued to receive attention, Native American Indian cultures and archaeological sites gained promotional prominence. The tours were guided by attractive, young, college-educated women 'trained and examined by an Advisory Board of nationally known authorities on the archaeology, ethnology and history of the Southwest' (Harveycars, 1928:11). Emphasis was placed on the Harvey reputation and the quality of the tours and accommodations, but as rail travel received increasing competitive pressures, budget tours were offered. The Harvey Company sold the Motor Cruise operation in 1931 and it continued to operate in a sporadic fashion until the 1960s.

Even with innovations like the Motor Cruises and significant fare reductions, trans-continental passenger rail travel continued to decline although travel to the West continued to grow. The 'See America First' campaign encouraged domestic travel, World War I made European vacations impossible, the lure of the West was more compelling than ever before, and with the increasing availability of the car, Americans were mobile. The notion of the vanishing West was becoming increasingly prevalent and the search for a real Western experience led some adventuresome travellers to the dude ranch vacation.

Dude ranches originated in the late 1800s when ranchers provided accommodation for the occasional hunter or sightseer. Many of the ranches were near National Parks and eventually, as travel increased, the ranchers began charging a fee for their hospitality and expanded their services to include guided pack trips. Early advertising for the dude ranches was by word-of-mouth from satisfied guests and then by personal visits back East by ranch proprietors to speak at various clubs and organisations. In the early 1920s the Northern Pacific Railroad saw the potential in supporting the dude ranches and began an alliance that would last for many years. Experienced in promotion, the railways advertised heavily and developed marketing materials including brochures, display materials, and even motion pictures. The Sante Fé Railroad promoted dude ranch vacations in the South-west as 'a fine answer to the deep-seated American urge to escape from the hum-drum and drab routine of life in the crowded places' (ATSFR, 1936). The dude ranch or guest ranch vacation maintained its popularity for many years, with some ranches visited year after year by the same families and others gaining notoriety for luxury such as the Tanque Verde Guest Ranch in Tucson, Arizona, which was one of only twenty-two places in the United States listed in the 1945 *300 Best Hotels in the World* (Borne, 1983:183).

The early decades of the 20th century created new marketing opportunities. Both Arizona and New Mexico responded in the 1920s to the growing popularity of the car, with their state highway departments publishing magazines to promote their expanding highway systems and car-tourism. *New Mexico Highway Journal* was launched in 1923 and *Arizona Highways* in 1925. Cars became increasingly popular among the holidaying public, partly because they provided freedom from the inflexibility of both the railway track and the timetable (Belasco, 1979). Just as the railways stimulated a flurry of marketing activity when the cross-continental tracks were completed, these magazines were conceived as trans-continental highways were being improved and subsidiary roads were being built in the states traversed by those highways. Arizona and New Mexico were both traversed by US Highway 66, as were the states of Texas, Oklahoma, Arkansas and Kansas, each of which produced a similar state magazine (Bowman, 1992). An indication of the emphasis placed on marketing of landscapes is found in the use of the Grand Canyon as a cover illustration for *Arizona Highways* 25 times between 1925 and 1972 (Cooper, 1973).

The first issue of *Arizona Highways* set forth a self-perceived mandate in a brief introductory article titled 'To The Public':

> With this issue, ARIZONA HIGHWAYS makes its bow to its public. In its decision to issue a magazine devoted to the interest of good roads, the Arizona Highway Department is following the example of 22 other state highway departments, the American Association of State Highway Officials and the United States Bureau of Public Roads, in disseminating information in regard to its activities of the nation (*Arizona Highways*, 1925:5).

The article indicated that each issue would contain 'interesting and well illustrated articles by authorities on roads and allied subjects' and that 'each issue will contain a travelogue'. The first travelogue guided the car traveller from the California State Line at Yuma, Arizona, to Phoenix, the state capital.

Car sellers also promoted travel to the Four Corners Region. The Nash-Breyer Motor Company, dealer for the Nash Car in Los Angeles, California, published a monthly magazine 'for its Nash owners and friends'. The May 1928 issue, titled the 'Arizona Number', was devoted to a 'Tour to Navajo and Hopi Indian Country', sub-titled 'Nash Sedan Visits Blue Canyon, Pillars of Hercules and Canyon de Chelly on Journey'. Included were a route map, maps of the Navajo and Hopi Indian Reservations, the State of Arizona, and numerous photographs of natural and cultural resources.

Interest in car travel spread across the country. The American Automobile Association was formed in 1902. It published 'Blue Books' which rated hotels and garages and provided maps and detailed descriptions of travel routes (Jakle, 1985:110) including an *Official Manual of Motor Car Camping* published in 1920 (Belasco, 1979:67). Americans were truly adopting the car as a mode of transportation and recreation.

State and regional promotional and guide books appeared at the same time. The Arizona Good Roads Association produced a car-oriented travel guide, *Arizona Road Maps and Tour Book*, as early as 1913. Between 1917 and 1922, impressive guides were produced for each of the states in the Four Corners Region by the Page Company of Boston (James, 1917, 1920, 1922; Baggs, 1918), part of a long list of state and regionally oriented books published by the company. Each was between 300 and 500 pages in length and contained topographic and cultural information and occasional travel hints. They were clearly targeted for the upper-class, intellectually inquisitive reader and traveller and not for the tourist of idle curiosity. The volumes were endowed with illustrations including a fold-out map, reproductions of regional paintings, and photographs of landscapes and places of interest. The title page of the Utah volume (James, 1922; *see* Figure 12.5) described its contents as including:

> The story of its desert wastes, of its huge and fantastic rock formations, and of its fertile gardens in the sheltered valleys; a survey of its rapidly developing industries; an account of the origin, development and beliefs of the Mormon Church; and chapters on the flora and fauna and on the scenic wonders that are a heritage of all Americans.

In the ensuing years, the publication of guide books oriented to the needs of the American car traveller proliferated, particularly following the end of World War II when disposable income and leisure time increased and the pent up demand for outdoor recreation created a significant market for travel information.

The third era: some old and some new ideas

This era is characterised by the continuation of past marketing activities, involving some of the same landscape elements, agents, audiences, and media, and, also by an impressive expansion and specialisation in elements, agents, and audiences. A powerful indication of the kind of transformation that had been occurring during the previous half-century is found in a 1951 report by the University of Arizona Bureau of Business Research about mode of tourist travel to Tucson during the 1950–51 season. The report indicated that only 18 per cent of the winter visitors had arrived by train, while 70 per cent had arrived by car. Unknown at the time was what the 10 per cent that had arrived by aeroplane would portend for the future.

Among the little known consequences of increased access to the Four Corners

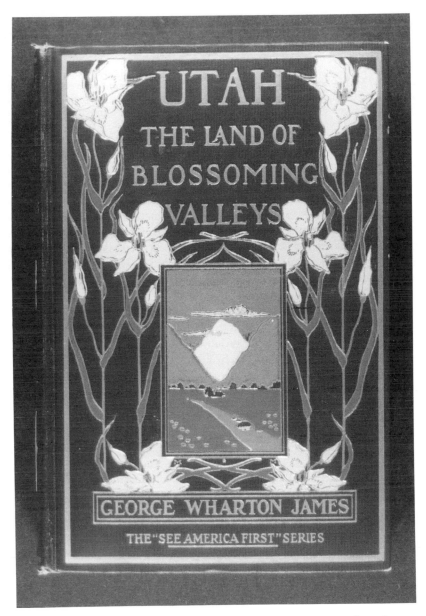

Figure 12.5 A detailed, illustrated introduction to Utah, one of a number of promotional books marketed for the Four Corner States during the first decades of the 20th century.

States, especially Arizona and New Mexico, was their attractiveness to individuals and couples living in the Midwest who were contemplating retirement. After a winter vacation in the southern parts of either state, the long, cold, and snowy winters of the Midwest lost their appeal. In addition, the increased availability of air conditioning in the 1950s ameliorated summer heat.

In the opening paragraph of *Arizona: A Guide to Easier Living*, the author describes an average January day in Midwestern and Northeastern cities in terms of the low temperatures, grey skies and snow, sleet and slush. The second paragraph starts:

> In Phoenix, Arizona, on this average day, the temperature at mid afternoon reached a balmy 72. This book is designed to entice tourists, immigrants *and* retirees to the Southwest. Climate is not the only attribute emphasised, also included are the healthy environment, low cost of retirement, employment opportunities and the extensive opportunities for travel to visit bedazzling natural wonders . . . that aren't farther away than a hop, skip, and a jump (Stocker, 1955).

This image of Arizona, or variations on it, has been used to market each of the four states.

Not all was well with marketing the amenities of the Four Corners landscapes. A variation on the hyperbole expressed in marketing media produced by the Commissioners and Bureau of Immigration in the 1880s and in later promotional literature, emerges with unrestrained enthusiasm, notably in Arizona, New Mexico, and Colorado in the 1970s. This time the marketing focused on land proposed for residential development and was undertaken by agents who represented greed, half-truths, and outright lies. It was not the kind of boosterism associated with the earlier Arizona Commission and New Mexico Bureau or the 1955 'Guide to Easier Living'. A series of articles published on five consecutive days, 26–30 December 1971, in *The Arizona Daily Star* described the sales deception and land fraud in detail. The articles described the practices and behaviour of some of the largest land developers in the state and referred to similar problems in Colorado and New Mexico. The first article (26 December 1971:1) opened with the following warning:

> There is a time-bomb hanging over Arizona. It threatens to explode in 10 to 15 years when thousands of out-of-state residents, who have invested in hundreds of Arizona speculative land developments, come to build their homes in the warm, wide-open beauty of Arizona. Instead of the fully developed, prospering community touted by salesmen, they may find nothing but barren land, without water, power, or roads and suited only for the land's oldest use, ranching.

Subsequent articles provided dramatic illustrations of the hazards that were strewn in the path of the unwary buyers, including statements in the sales documents that the seller 'shall not be responsible or liable for any inducement, promise, representation, agreement, condition or stipulation not specifically set forth herein' (28 December 1971:7). If buyers failed to read the fine print and relied only on promotional literature and real estate sales-people, financial loss and disappointment were just around the corner. The end results were a long overdue revision of state land development laws.

There are, however, both clever individuals who find ways around the law and naive and greedy buyers for land at prices that seem too good to be true. For example, in 1986, fifteen years after the first series of newspaper articles, some of the same desert land that had been involved in fraudulent land sales in the 1960s was again being marketed to the unsuspecting. The lands involved had been declared ineligible for sale by the state because legal access to them was not available. It was a land-locked island surrounded by federal land. Nevertheless, this did not stop an enterprising individual from selling phoney mortgages for lots to unsuspecting buyers (Sitter, 1986).

Marketing activities during this time period involved an ever-increasing array of agents and, frequently, more sharply defined target audiences. This is not to say that broad-scale marketing for tourism and economic development did not continue, but rather that a number of specific target audiences were identified, particularly in reference to recreation landscapes.

National Parks and monuments continue to be marketed with enthusiasm, but the marketing agents are more diverse and the attributes of the parks that are being marketed have expanded. Grand Canyon National Park provides an interesting example of the diversity of marketing agents. The Fred Harvey Company still manages and markets hotel accommodations and restaurants in the park. In the adjacent town of Tusayan, motels and restaurants use their proximity to the park as the primary advertising strategy for highway signs, newspaper advertisements, and promotional brochures. The Grand Canyon Natural History Association, a non-profit organisation, produces educational materials, including books, video-tapes, maps, and brochures that are sold to tourists in the park. More aggressive marketing programmes are pursued by the various businesses that provide guided trips for the thrill seekers through the tumultuous rapids of the Colorado River and, for those who want a bird's-eye view, aerial flight over the Canyon. Eighteen independent groups operate on the river and offer boat trips of varying durations, from three to fourteen days. These groups promote the Canyon and their river trips with full-colour booklets up to 20 pages long, advertisements in national magazines that cater to those interested in sports and the out-of-doors, and with colour brochures that are available in motels throughout the Canyon area. In addition there are at least three companies offering aerial flights. One company has produced promotional literature in both English and Japanese.

There is also growing awareness of public concern for the loss of historic objects and places, as well as the growing appeal of nostalgia. An expression of this is seen in the preservation of narrow-gauge railway lines constructed for mining and timber harvest in the late 19th century (e.g. the Grand Canyon Railway from Williams, Arizona). These are now promoted via highway signs, listings in guide books, and full-colour brochures.

A major factor today in marketing Four Corners landscapes is the role played by state tourism and economic development offices and local town and city Chambers of Commerce or visitors' centres. Most towns and cities with populations of more than 10–15,000 residents are engaged in marketing in some manner. The material provided to inquirers, usually full-colour pamphlets and booklets, resembles the content of material produced and distributed by the various immigration offices that existed in the 19th and early 20th centuries, albeit with less hyperbole. Landscapes remain an important component of these initiatives, as are climate and recreational and vacation opportunities. Equally prominent, however, are local economic activities, cost of living, educational facilities, governmental services, and cultural attractions.

An important innovation that emerged in this era is that of regional marketing. While such marketing had been employed for National Parks and monuments in the 1930s (Southwestern Monuments Association, 1938), the developments of the 1980s bring together the interests of private and public sectors in the establishment of three organisations.

The *Tourism Council* describes itself as consisting of organisations, businesses, and individuals who have banded together to promote tourism in the four-state area surrounding the Four Corners Monument for approximately 200 miles in any direction. It is a non-profit organisation that is 'devoted to the generic promotion of a region rather than the specific promotion of commercially oriented destinations' (Four Corners Tourism Council, 1992).

A parallel organisation, the *Four Corners Heritage Council*, has been formed and has as its mission the forming of partnerships among the states, local communities, Indian tribes, and the private sector. The governors of the four states were instrumental in its formation and the shaping of its mission. A major focus is placed on relationships with the Navajo Indian Reservation and includes providing guidelines for foreign visitors in their own languages, and educating tourists about Navajo customs and need for privacy.

The *Grand Circle Association* provides a contrast. Formed within the last ten years, it is a membership organisation with both subscription-paying and non-subscription-paying members (the former including state tourism and travel offices, cities, airlines serving the area, car rental agencies, tour operators, a narrow gauge railway, and hotels). Their unstated interest is economic development, with the objective of promoting a 1400-mile-long travel route linking 'the incredible landscapes of the Colorado Plateaus . . . America's highest concentration of scenic national parks and monuments, rugged mountains, deep canyons, skyward cliffs, prehistoric Indian ruins, nostalgic villages and other fascinating ruins' (Schlenz, 1988). A large format, full-colour, 48-page publication features the scenic and historic features of the area. It is augmented with a full-colour map depicting the route and location of each attraction along the way and is available for purchase throughout the region. Another free publication, in 12-page newspaper format is *The Grand Circle Adventure* (Figure 12.6). It provides information about 28 landscape attractions as well as transportation, tour services and accommodation. All of the commercial enterprises that are listed are subscription-paying members.

The idea of featuring the resources of the Colorado Plateau is not new. The Museum of Northern Arizona produced a 74-page Colorado Plateau guide in the late 1970s (Trimble, 1979). What is new is the formation of the Grand Circle Association to market actively the natural and cultural landscapes of the region and thereby market their places of business.

Summing up

To suggest that the settlement of the West would not have been possible without the trans-continental railways is not an overstatement. Trains facilitated economic growth, enticed visitors who often stayed and settled, and helped create and perpetuate the myth of the West that exists even today (Arrington, 1969). It is a myth of good and bad, of black and white with no shades of grey, of hero and villain, of cowboy and Indian. It is a myth of the cowboy hero portrayed against 'the most vast and majestic backdrop ever imagined, both in reality and even more in the created images' (Bruce, 1990:11). It is a myth portrayed in film, literature, painting, and sculpture. It is a myth of extremes manifest in the mid-19th century perception of the great American desert which contrasts with the 1897 report on the Arizona Territory that stated:

Figure 12.6 First page of the Grand Circle Association's 'free guide', with information about scenic and cultural landscapes and tourist accommodations and services (reproduced by permission of the Grand Circle Association).

The surface consists of elevated tablelands broken by lofty mountains and interspersed by irrigating canals, dotted with thriving towns, and bright with the green and gold of orchard, field and vineyard. Some of those valleys are . . . more fertile than the valleys watered by the river Nile . . . In a few years the territory will be one vast garden, excepting those portions reserved for grazing.

The marketing of the natural and cultural landscapes of the Four Corners Region contributed to the perpetuation of the myth. Taking a broad view of that marketing, one can argue that impressive changes have occurred over the past 140 years. On the other hand, an equally strong argument can be made that little has changed. The perspective that one takes determines the conclusion at which one arrives.

Many of the changes that have occurred are the result of political, social, and economic transmutations, technological advances, and a shift in the collective consciousness of the USA. The changes are evident over the eras in each of the four identified components of marketing: agents, target audiences, landscapes, and media.

The agents of promotion were in many ways the agents of change. The railways made the Western territories accessible for the population growth necessary to achieve statehood. The resulting changes shifted the responsibility of promotion to the states in the form of Departments of Tourism and Economic Development, to the cities in the form of Chambers of Commerce, and to the regions in the form of organisations and associations.

The railways' stronghold in marketing weakened as technologies changed and the car companies and allied agencies and associations assumed a more predominant marketing role, only to be later usurped by the airlines. The audiences targeted by these agents of promotion were also a reflection of change. The earliest targets were immigrants seeking religious freedom and economic opportunities and wealthy tourists seeking adventure. Travelling west was fraught with difficulty and approached with great trepidation. Marketing agents responded by reducing the emphasis on the roughness and wildness of the West, promoting instead its scenic beauty, natural resources and climate.

As the car became increasingly affordable, greater numbers of tourists could experience what some were calling the 'vanishing West'. Visitors no longer worried about their safety and were in search of the mythical, 'true' Western experience. Marketing agents once again rose to the occasion by reasserting the image of the 'Old West' that they had attempted to negate only a few years before. Native American Indian cultures, archaeological sites, and dude ranches were vigorously promoted with a new array of techniques and media.

Medical advances replaced the inflated claims of a healthy environment with hot springs and spas, and tuberculosis was no longer a threat. Nevertheless, for many people the warm dry climate of the lower elevations in the Four Corners Region still provided soothing relief from arthritis. The 'Sunbelt' attracted a new type of immigrant, the retiree. Families were also attracted by the climate, the prospering economy, employment opportunities, and the availability of relatively inexpensive land. This growth paved the way for the 'new desperado and rustler', the real estate swindler. The airlines were making travel even easier and the Four Corners region more accessible than ever. Tourists, both foreign and domestic, enticed by increasingly sophisticated brochures, advertisements, books, maps, billboards, and video-recordings, came west to capture the nostalgia of the 'Old West' and to enjoy the scenic beauty, historic sites, and recreational opportunities.

Perhaps the most visible change is a manifestation of all of the others: the imposition of an endless maze of railway tracks and highways criss-crossing the landscape through mountains and deserts and ancient pueblos accompanied by the resulting development. Mines and clear-cut mountain sides, urban sprawl, agriculture and cattle have all made their impact. Some things, however, remain constant. Unequalled scenic beauty can still be found and the climate is still dry with enticingly pleasant winters and refreshing mountain summers. The Native American cultures have not vanished and continue their own traditions despite years of interference. With the support of the millions of people who have experienced their beauty and meaning, the national monuments and parks of the West remain protected.

References

Arizona Highways (1925) 'To the public', 1(1), April, 5.

Arrington, L.J. (1969) 'The transcontinental railroad and the development of the west', *Utah Historical Quarterly*, 37(1), 3–15.

ATSFR (Atchison, Topeka & Sante Fé Railway) (1936) *Sante Fé Dude Ranch County*, Sante Fé: ATSFR.

Baggs, M.L (1918) *Colorado: the queen jewel of the Rockies*, Boston, MA: Page.

Belasco, W.J. (1979) *Americans on the Road: from autocamp to motel, 1910–1945*, Cambridge, MA: MIT Press.

Borne, L.R. (1983) *Dude Ranching: a complete history*, Albuquerque, NM: University of New Mexico Press.

Bowman, J. (ed., *New Mexico*) (1992) Personal communication with E.H. Zube.

Bruce, C. (1990) 'The myth of the west', in A. Runte *Myth of the West*, New York: Rizzoli, 11–18.

Cooper, T.C. (1973) *Arizona Highways: from engineering pamphlet to prestige magazine*, unpublished MA thesis, Department of Journalism, University of Arizona at Tucson.

Dadd, B. (1869) *Great Trans-Continental Railroad Guide*.

Evans, R.K. (1886) 'The Indian question in Arizona', *Atlantic Monthly*, 58(346), 167–76.

Four Corners Tourism Council (1992) Report of the Four Corners Development Committee presented at: National Park Service, Navajo area superintendents and the Four Corners Tourism Council meeting, Page, Arizona, 10 April.

Gressinger, A.W. (1961) *Charles D. Poston, Sunland Seer*, Globe AZ: Dale Stuart King Publishers.

Harveycars (1928) *Motor Cruises*, Sante Fé: Harveycars.

Haury, E.W. (1985) *Mogollon Culture in the Forestdale Valley*, Tucson: University of Arizona Press.

Hunter, M.R. (1946) *Utah, the Story of Her People, 1540–1947: a centennial history of Utah*, Salt Lake City, UT: Deseret News Press.

Jakle, J.A. (1985) *The Tourist: travel in twentieth century America*, Lincoln, NE: University of Nebraska Press.

James, G.W. (1917) *Arizona, The Wonderland*, Boston, MA: Page.

James, G.W. (1920) *New Mexico, the Land of the Delight Makers*, Boston, MA: Page.

James, G.W. (1922) *Utah, the Land of the Blossoming Valleys*, Boston, MA: Page.

Lister, R.H. and Lister, F.L. (1983) *Those Who Came Before*, Tucson: University of Arizona Press.

McGee, W.J. (1898) 'Thirst in the desert', *Atlantic Monthly*, 81(486), 483–88.

McLuhan, T.C. (1987) 'Dream tracks: the railroad and the American Indian', *Arizona Highways*, 63(6), 4–11.

Mather, S. (1921) 'Presentation', in R.S. Yard, ed., *The National Parks Portfolio*, Washington, D.C., Department of the Interior, National Park Service, 5.

Pomeroy, E. (1957) *In Search of the Golden West*, New York: Knopf.

Riegel, R.E. (1926) *The Story of the Western Railroads*, New York: Macmillan (University of Nebraska Press edition, 1964).

Ritch, W.G. (1885) *Aztlan: the history, resources and attractions of New Mexico*, Boston, MA: Lothrop.

Runte, A. (1990) *Trains of Discovery*, Niwot, CO: Roberts Reinhart.

Schlenz, M.A. (1988) *Exploring the Southwest's Grand Circle*, Santa Barbara, CA: Companion Press.

Shankland, R. (1970) *Steve Mather of the National Parks*, New York: Knopf.

Sitter, A. (1986) 'Desert lots used in '70s land fraud under new probe', *The Arizona Republic*, 4 October, B1, B3.

Southwestern Monuments Association (1938) *The Guide to Southwestern National Monuments*, Popular Series 1, Coolidge, AZ: Southwestern Monuments Association.

Stocker, J. (1955) *Arizona: a guide to better living*, New York: Harper.

Thomas, D.H. (1978) *The Southwestern Indian Detours: the story of the Fred Harvey/ Sante Fé Railway experiment in 'detourism'*, Phoenix, AZ: Hunter.

Trimble, S. (1979) *The Bright Edge: a guide to the National Parks of the Colorado Plateau*, Flagstaff, AZ: Museum of Northern Arizona.

Yard, R.S. (1921) *The National Parks Portfolio*, Washington, DC: Department of the Interior, National Park Service.

Young, B. (1854) Message of His Excellency Governor Brigham Young to the Legislature of the Territory of Utah; Delivered 11 December 1854, Salt Lake City: Utah State Archives.

Wheeler, K. (1973) *The Railroaders*, New York: Time-Life Books.

Zube, E.H. and Kennedy, C. (1990) 'Changing images of the Arizona Territory', in L. Zonn, ed., *Place Images in Media*, Savage, MD: Rowman and Littlefield, 183–203.

13   Promoting the Forest of Dean: art, ecology and the industrial landscape

GEORGE REVILL

This chapter looks at the promotional role of the Forest Sculpture Trail in the Forest of Dean. It examines the ways in which the sculptures represent changing conceptions of the industrial landscape and the wider role of art in promoting that landscape. It also considers how art can mediate the relationship between nature and industrialisation, showing how the phenomena of de-industrialisation and ecological crisis are brought together in an industrial 'heritage' landscape. Landscape is viewed here as a socially constructed means of imposing order on the world. From this viewpoint, landscape perception both results from and justifies specific forms of economic and social organisation (Cosgrove and Daniels, 1988).

This chapter opens by setting current interpretations of the Forest of Dean's landscape in the context of history, previous interpretations of its landscape, and its geographical location. It then examines the way in which current promotion of the Forest for tourism represents a particular social construct which justifies and reconciles us to the post-industrial landscape.

De-industrialisation and the promotion of tourism

The peripherality of the Forest of Dean to the British economy has contributed to several cycles of de-industrialisation since the 1950s. In 1965 the deep mines in the Forest were closed, along with many other of the UK's smaller collieries, as part of the rationalisation embodied in the *Revised Plan for Coal* (Hart, 1971:424–5). Subsequent attempts to attract industry to the area brought in a number of multinational companies which opened branch plants in the area. These, however, suffered in the recession of the early 1980s, with several plants closing. The result was a dramatic loss of manufacturing employment. Rank Xerox, for example, which accounted for 22 per cent of jobs in the southern part of the Forest of Dean, shed over 3000 jobs in one year leaving the area with high unemployment (Lee, 1990:43). A submission for assisted status in 1983 identified the area as nationally one of the worst hit by unemployment, with a labour market that combined some of the worst attributes of rural deprivation with those of traditional heavy industry (Lee, 1990:49).

Among the strategies to create employment and bring income to the Forest has been a concerted attempt to develop tourism. In 1985 a Tourist Action Programme was established. Survey and analysis of the Forest's tourism potential demonstrated the area's richness in sites of natural and industrial history including the scenic Wye Valley, Tintern Abbey, Symonds Yat, Cannop Ponds, St Briavel's Castle and the ancient iron mines at Clearwell Caves. As part of this Programme, the Forestry Commission established the Forest of Dean Sculpture Project in 1986 in the very centre of the Forest near Speech House, the historic Verderers' Court from which the common rights of the Forest were administered. This now forms the focus of a 'honeypot' development, with a visitors' centre and extensive parking and picnicking area.

The Sculpture Project itself involved collaboration between the Forestry Commission, Bristol's Arnolfini Gallery, a number of charitable trusts that support the arts, and the District and County Councils. Sixteen sculptors of national and international standing were eventually asked to contribute a single sculpture each. They were invited to:

> respond to and interpret the character of the Forest of Dean with its long history of timber production, coal and iron ore mining and charcoal burning by creating works of art for specific places within the Forest (Forestry Commission, 1989).

The resulting Sculpture Trail Project has been constructed over a period of five years, with the sculptors producing a total of eighteen works that are now situated on a four-mile circular walk.

The Trail, as such, constitutes part of a wider collaboration between local people, visitors and artists. There has been a continuing programme using art both to promote and enhance the experience of place. Work in schools and the commissioning of artists in residence to interpret the forest have generated numerous ancillary exercises. For example, Fay Godwin's (1986) photographic record of Dean Forest life, *The Secret Forest*, was commissioned in the project's planning stage and its publication coincided with the launch of stage one of the Trail (Martin, 1990:32).

Art, place promotion and the industrial landscape

The linking of art and place promotion is not new. Since the early Industrial Revolution, the arts have played a part in place promotion and been important for the accommodation of industry in the tourist landscape (Clayre, 1977; *see also* Chapter 14). In the later 18th century the development of theories of the picturesque by writers such as the Rev. William Gilpin taught the new breed of middle-class tourists how to value mines and mills in the landscape as rusticated curiosities with scenic qualities (Ousby, 1990). The evidence of work, traces of smoke on the horizon or evidence of wear, the rustic machinery of a mill, could be visually pleasing. Visual form was distanced from the actual activity of industry by abstracting the picturesque, decayed qualities of industry and, as a result, the physical presence of industry was interpreted out of the view (Rosenthal, 1982:78; Revill, 1989).

The romantic fascination with the sublime provided a somewhat different though complementary perspective, linking the chemical and mechanical energy of industrial processes with the language of classical mythology and an animate nature. Combined with the nationalistic sentiments which coloured the period of the Napoleonic Wars, the alchemical power of industrial processes such as iron founding became both a metaphor for British ingenuity and a symbol of the strength and determination of the British war effort (Daniels, 1992a). Tourists were encouraged to visit industrial centres such as Coalbrookdale and view the works from this perspective. Manufacturers such as Abraham Darby were keen to promote their manufacturing activities and opportunistic artists fostered and exploited a view of industry which both marvelled and recoiled at a view of industry as a theatrical vision of Hades (Daniels, 1992b).

Both complementary and in contrast to the picturesque and romantic views of industry was a cool observational style derived from the draughtsmanship necessary for topographical surveying, cartography, mechanical and civil engineering. It was grounded in the scientific skills necessary to construct industrial machinery and build the infrastructure of the industrial revolution, its canals and railways. Eighteenth-century cartographers, such as Paul Sandby, adopted this style to depict industrial installations and produce urban panoramas specifically for the developing market of middle-class picturesque and romantic tourists (Herrmann, 1986; Christian, 1991). In the mid-19th century this style, which was convenient for mechanical reproduction by lithography, became the medium by which early railway companies promoted themselves both to investors and travellers in volumes which give a pictorial excursion along the line (Rees, 1980).

The self-promotion of the newly-emerging corporate travel industry in the guise of the railway corporations exemplifies this. Engravings and later photographs of railway engineering structures, rolling stock and lineside scenery produced for promotional purposes combined the overt display of industry as new, revolutionary, thoroughly modern with a picturesque sensibility. This mediated the old and the new together as a harmonious unified experience of travel packaged for the customer, and promoted an image of the railway corporation as the engineer of place, bringing towns and cities closer together for industry and private citizen alike (Revill, forthcoming).

The promotion of places subject to economic decline and restructuring since the mid-20th century have also used the arts to sell specific localities and reflected the expectations of industrialised landscapes generated by images in film, painting and television. As Goodey (Chapter 9) shows, visual and literary portrayals of industrialised landscapes, such as George Orwell's Wigan Pier, can be key attractions and marketing aids. Our present culture now values old industrial landscapes as precious reminders of past industrial achievement and symbols of more rooted, less individualistic social values. This is partly the result of a reflective revaluing of life in the old industrial order (Robbins, 1983). During the 1960s, blighted industrial landscapes represented the worn-out Victorian social organisation of exploitation and deprivation. These were regarded as areas ripe for the bulldozer at precisely the moment that the physical remains of 18th- and 19th-century industry became candidates for preservation as monuments to past industrial triumphs, social certainty and security.

The physical remains of the industrial past within the redevelopment of old industrial landscapes has a status similar to that of art and local culture. The origins of industrial archaeology in the 1960s stem not only from the threat of redevelopment, but from engagement with the process of economic and social renewal. In *The*

Industrial Past and the Industrial Present, a record of the pioneering conference of those concerned with the new subject of industrial archaeology, Kenneth Hudson (1965:viii) was keen to assure us that 'an informed, critical awareness of past achievements can be immensely useful as a spur to further creative effort'. Hudson (1965:4) argued that 'to regard industrial remains as mere dead things, mere bits of buildings and machinery, is to miss the point of it all'. In this interpretation, industrial remains have a symbolic status, the study and contemplation of which is an imaginative activity important for psychic health and material well-being. Moreover, it is an activity that brings us closer to the historical past we have lost to modern redevelopment whilst generating a creative energy important for progress.

Industrial archaeology promoted a vision of landscape where industrial sites were islands of industrial history set as individual artefacts within a sea of redevelopment. If an artefact is something adopted or created by people for a current purpose (Katz, 1992), then we should understand the industrial archaeological landscape during the 1960s and 1970s in terms of its symbolic value to contemporary society rather than the past (Thomas, 1992). The current status of the industrial elements in the landscape derives not from their separation from a historical past but from their role in the imaginative constitution of new landscapes of welfare capitalism. The adoption of Coalbrookdale to sell Telford New Town during the 1970s exemplifies this use of the industrial landscape as part of a continuing modernist project: an internationally recognised historical symbol projected to lend Telford credibility as a location for innovative and progressive industrial activity.

Promoting the Forest of Dean

We can find many instances of these general trends in the promotion of the Forest of Dean. Many contemporary tourist publications draw on representations generated within the picturesque, romantic, classical observational, heroic and grounded modernist aesthetics which have informed the accommodation of industry into the landscape since the 18th century. Volumes such as Bick's (1980) *The Old Industries of Dean* and Hart's (1971) *The Industrial History of Dean* contain images of ancient and decayed workings, mellowed by vegetation in the picturesque manner, and gothic scenes of mercurial activity in representations which are both historical and contemporary. There are also closely observed engineering drawings, 19th- and early-20th-century photographs produced by the large joint stock industrial concerns which demonstrate a confidence in industry most evident in corporate publicity. Hart (1971:425), whose book was in the vanguard of industrial archaeology, concluded by considering the success of post-coal mining industrial regeneration:

> Many people bemoaned the passing of the coalfield, but some would have been justified in applauding it because it ended the unnatural underground work, thereby bringing men from the dark, dirty, hazardous (and often hard) jobs to the light, cleanliness and safety of modern factories.

The *Visitors Handbook To The Royal Forest of Dean* (Wright, 1990) reflects the multiplicity of readings available for the interpretation of the industrial landscape. The

Forest is projected within a clearly romantic sensibility as a place of mystery and refuge. The Forest is a land set apart, somewhere with its own special past, while at the same time being a summation of the history of all industrial landscapes.

The use of the image of the Dean Forest miner to advertise Clearwell Caves illustrates this tendency. Here, a complex of natural caves has been mined for iron ore for some 2000 years. Displays of 19th- and 20th-century mining machinery complement the shadowy traces of ancient mine working, the pick marks of pre-history and the soot of 16th-century gun powder to constitute a landscape fabricating the essence of industrial exploitation. The figure of the miner, derived from the 13th-century Free Miners Brass in Newland church, symbolises the particular circumstances of the independent forest free miner, a product of an historically and geographically specific set of property rights. However, like the many national monuments to unknown soldiers, his very anonymity is important. In this case, he represents the ingenuity of all our ancestors, knowledge and familiarity with native soil, their sacrifice and labour on behalf of the present and the never-ending struggle against natural odds.

The Sculpture Trail draws heavily on the same ideas. The Trail is isolated, hidden deep in the woods where one discovers the elemental and communes with nature. Miles Davis's sculpture *House in the Forest* provides a comforting form of solitude as the trees giving shelter from the elements imbue the area with a sense of timelessness (Martin, 1990:83). Similarly, Cornelia Parker's *Hanging Fire* used the symbol of fire cast in iron in order both to refer to the specific history of metal-working in the Forest and to encourage the idea of 'elusive eternity' embodied in the forest as a place of worship (Martin, 1990:89).

The cover of the *Visitors' Handbook To The Royal Forest of Dean* (Wright, 1990) features a watercolour picture depicting a leafy woodland glade in typically picturesque style. Prominently placed inside the cover is a photograph of the redundant New Found Out Mine. Its disused headstocks and piles of pit props emerge from the encroaching woodland in an organic assembly which reduces industrial exploitation to an extension of natural vegetative growth. In the picturesque manner, we are distanced from the actual processes of industry by the overall harmony of the composition and the evident disuse of the industrial plant. The Sculpture Trail is also conceived with a picturesque aesthetic. Many of the sculptures which represent industry, like *Black Dome* by David Nash which represents charcoal burning, are designed to decay into the landscape (Martin, 1990:21). Throughout the whole Trail we are told that the sculptures are not finished objects. Rather, each work of art results from the observation of an interplay of textures and colours through the seasons and during the ageing process such that 'their appearance alters according to the season, the time of day and the weather conditions, making it worthwhile to revisit them at different times of the year in order to see them in a new light' (Martin, 1990:61). The Trail is conceived as an engagement between object and place. Unlike many sculpture parks such as Grizedale or Portland, every piece was commissioned for its final resting place. Each piece has a relationship with its environment such that its visual appeal derives from a dialogue between pictorial elements 'not as an inert gallery but as a living active engagement between work and setting' (Martin, 1990:9).

The adjacent Wye valley was important to the historical development of middle-class touring during the 18th century. It was associated, for example, with

William Gilpin, and numerous artists and writers including Wordsworth and Turner. Symonds Yat and Tintern Abbey, the latter with its industrial appendages, were important locations for the definition of tourist taste, and recent reworking of the industrial landscape has not surprisingly employed the visual codes developed at that time (Ousby, 1990:117–19). New Fancy viewing point situated on top of a former colliery spoil tip at the centre of the Forest, reflects many of the codes of the 18th-century tourist spectator. The spoil tip with its viewing platform rises high above the forest, its slopes covered in wild verdant growth. It provides a deep valley perspective across the carefully managed forest. An information board points out individual 'important landmarks'. Like an 18th-century tourist standing on a synthetic Symonds Yat, we are awestruck at the sublimely elevated prospect, delighted by the precisely composed view with its textural and chromatic variety and informed by knowledge objectified in cartographic form.

Just like the landscape of 1970s industrial archaeology, the Forest is promoted as a collection of artefacts which derive status from their modern utility in a re-invigorated landscape of leisure and recreation. The Forestry Commission's Tourist Map advertises an eclectic arrangement of historical attractions: Newent Shambles, a mock Victorian shopping street; Litteldean Hall, one of the most haunted houses in England; Clearwell Caves, ancient iron mines; Jubilee Park; Symonds Yat, with its museum of Mazes. Framing a tourist map of the Forest which portrays landscape features, leisure activities and historical sites in the uniform typeface for tourist sites, each is outlined in black as independent and free standing. These artefacts are integrated into a greater whole only by representations of the seasons in each corner of the map, suggesting for the visitor the experience of the Forest at various times of the year.

Promoted in this way the Forest becomes simply a collection of settings, with the purpose of each being to generate a particular type of imaginative experience. Godwin informed us that the contents of her photographic study *The Secret Forest of Dean* 'are the result of rambles and visits . . . They are not intended to be taken as a guide book' (1986:7). They comprise individual snapshots of various aspects of the Forest environment, industry, agriculture, tourism, unsociable fly-tipping and congenial community life, linked only by their current availability as images by which to recreate the life of the Forest past and present.

The Sculpture Trail is also landscape constructed from individual artefacts. The original title of the Project, 'Stand and Stare', was derived from the principle that the sculptures were there to arrest attention (Martin, 1990:16). They were to act as catalysts for the imagination, each artefact represents a specific element of natural or industrial history, mining, quarrying, forestry, transport, primitive settlement. Like the isolated elements of industrial archaeology each exists to encourage visitors to reconstruct an entire industry, activity or way of life from the individual passive object. The artefactual approach to the history of the Forest adopted in the Sculpture Trail uses this history as a set of found objects, a folk culture to be taken as the raw material for an abstract modernism grounded in the specific history of place. An assembly of sawn logs, representing the craft of the forester, becomes an exploding star of geometrical timber shapes; a mound of charred larch poles refers to the local skills of the charcoal burner but translates this artefact of the past into a purely formal statement of modernist minimalism.

Heritage, ecology and the industrial landscape

There are now at least 464 museums in the UK possessing collections of industrial material, of which a third have been founded since 1970. The increasing concern for the past has been closely linked by many commentators to the failure of Britain to develop and sustain its industrial position in the world (Sked, 1987:42). Writers such as Hewison (1987) and Wiener (1981) have related the interest in industrial history to the decline of an industrial ethos and to the decline of industrial capitalism itself as part of a culture which is increasingly anti-technological and anti-industrial. Hewison (1987:91) stated:

> Now that time has eroded their function, industrial monuments, defined as 'any relic of an obsolete phase of an industry or transport system, ranging from a Neolithic flint mine to a newly obsolete aircraft or electronic computer' can be accommodated into the safe and pleasing past.

The industrial heritage landscape of the Forest of Dean forms part of this movement and it is easy to trace links between the de-industrialisation of the Forest and the growth of tourism as the alternative to an industrial economy.

If such landscapes are associated with the decline of industrial capitalism, they have been closely associated with the rise of an economy of symbolic capital, driven by the technology of manipulating information, computerisation and the mass media. Critics of the heritage industry attribute the desire 'to experience the past' to a technological culture with great resources where the spatially and temporally distant can be brought into the present. In this context Harvey (1989:284–307) wrote about 'time–space compression', where the modern concern with time and space, and the perceived ability to manipulate them through technology, has resulted in the believed ability to live history, to inhabit different times and places in one moment. Similarly, Lowenthal (1985) considered 'heritage' not just as a quality present in museums or a matter of preservation, but part of an entire culture of 'creative anachronism' where past, present and future appear freely available through modern media.

The metaphor of Disneyland is most commonly applied to themed environments, the synthetic and eclectic forms of which appear to bring an exotic or anachronistic symbolism to a specific locality. Much theory would locate a whole range of heavily promoted environments, from Meadowhall Shopping Centre in Sheffield and Alton Towers Leisure Park to Coalbrookdale, as a set of free-floating signs and symbols bearing little relationship to the present 'reality' of their locations (Bell, 1976; Jameson, 1984; Jencks, 1984; Chambers, 1987). In this manner, the Forest of Dean also brings together diverse histories, collapsing time and space in a heritage landscape which juxtaposes red telephone boxes and Roman iron foundries.

Naturally, it would be easy to interpret the imagery in art and advertising which promotes tourism in the Forest of Dean as Disneyesque, merely a collection of past styles, reused images and unreflected romantic stereotypes deployed for the purpose of generating tourist revenue. However, the Forest of Dean Sculpture Trail not only serves as a microcosm for the various layers of interpretation to which the history of the Forest has been subjected. Here, the heritage industry can now offer new

dimensions, particularly expressing the infiltration of ecological ideas into current
thinking on tourism economy and the presentation of history:

> New museums are about interconnections: the links and parallel histories of our
> social and natural environments. Such places are one of the legacies of the diffusion
> of ecological ideas in the culture (Wilson, 1992:245).

It is to the promotion of this issue that we now turn.

Symbiosis, decay and the definition of productivity

From its time as a Royal Hunting Forest, the Forest itself has represented as much of
an industrial landscape as did those areas associated with the mining and metal-
working industries. In 1904, for instance, the first British Forestry School was
established here and subsequently Dean has been a landscape manicured with the
pioneering techniques of scientific woodland management. Wilson (1992) has suggested that contemporary tourism involves a massive conceptual reorganisation of the
landscape as lands once productive in a traditional industrial or agricultural sense are
reclassified as recreational zones. Seen in this light, the Sculpture Trail is indicative of
the redefinition of the role of the Forestry Commission away from being a national
timber reserve and a producer of timber on a commercial basis towards that of
managing recreational woodland.

To elaborate, as keepers of a national heritage, changing economic, political and
social priorities have altered the emphasis in the Forestry Commission's mission from
the maintenance of a strategic reserve of timber for building and manufacturing purposes during times of national crisis to the maintenance of a strategic reserve of 'natural' woodland to relieve the social and psychological crisis of urban living (Gilg,
1978:31–4; Watkins, 1983:39–45; Forestry Commission, 1984). Historically, this can
be traced to the establishment of the Forest of Dean as one of Britain's first National
Forest Parks on the eve of World War II in 1939 (Watkins, 1983). However, the greatest
impetus for the Forestry Commission to diversify has emerged in the last 15 years.
During this period, the extension of more sophisticated accounting procedures within
governmental organisations has also redrawn the boundaries of productivity so that
internal efficiency is defined in terms of more immediate and tangible forms of profit-
ability (Forestry Commission, 1984:8). In this way the Sculpture Trail, with its associations of social welfare, productive of national health and vitality, also serves the
promotional concerns of big business in the same manner as the visitor centres now to
be found at many industrial and manufacturing plants (*see* Chapter 6). These not only
earn revenue from previously unproductive or redundant plant, but act also as corporate advertising. The Sculpture Trail may be regarded as 'explaining' the importance of
commercial forestry and justifying the continuing role of the Forestry Commission. In
the words of the Trail's co-organiser Rupert Martin (1990:9), its function is to open
visitors' eyes to the 'sense of beauty of a living and productive environment':

> Since Forestry Commission forests are a national heritage, their foresters are happy
> to encourage visitors and would like to see them experiencing a deeper enjoyment

than just fresh air and exercise. Such a wish is not wholly altruistic. There is a belief that if visitors go away with a greater understanding they will be more likely to conserve the forests for the future.

As such, it forms part of a dialogue with what is often called 'green tourism' and reflects the hostility to the monoculture of conifers amongst certain classes of ecologically sensitive tourist (Urry, 1990:99).

The designers of the Trail (Martin, 1990:12) openly admitted that they were not working with a truly natural environment but with a productive commercial woodland:

> Naturally, long term placements of sculpture could bring constraints to forest management. The Forest is a crop and trees have a natural life span. To keep crops standing after this may cost money, so in selecting from the artists' proposals, future forest management had to be borne in mind. The team were not planning an interpretation of an urban park but a living, producing forest.

The idea of the productive forest adopted in promoting the Forest of Dean includes more than just the processes of modern commercial forestry. Modernist conceptions of productive activity are bound together with romantic and historicist notions of work and craftsmanship in an ecological language. The Sculpture Trail becomes, therefore, not something new or imposed on the forest, but a continuation of the long-standing practices it purports to depict:

> The sculptures could be seen as an intrusion into this history, but the work of carving, moulding and constructing is in essence a continuation of the history of workmanship and craftsmanship in the forest (Martin, 1990:61).

Martin argued that such work is not just productive in the manufacturing sense, but also 'in a more spiritual sense, since it meets the needs of our increasingly secular and materialistic society to find something in nature that is absent from our urban culture'.

Parallels were drawn between the forest as an ecosystem and human society. The former was seen as a role model for the latter and the valued qualities of society, communality and constructive energy were the qualities that humans share with the physical world. Industry is the highest achievement of humanity when it replicates nature: 'the sculptures of the forest, as with other vestiges of man's (sic) labour, are part of the same creative spirit which points to the particular character, at once congenial and sublime, of that society of trees which we call a forest' (Martin, 1990:18).

To a certain extent this echoes the modernist aesthetic which claims that the best scientific and technological achievement follows functionalist forms derived from the natural world. Yet it does more than this because rather than privileging human industry as an improvement of natural fecundity it draws the two together. This is more than an expression of romantic empathy, the physical and the social are one single ecological system in which the two components are fused in symbiosis.

Ecological metaphors also act as a means of explaining the effect of industrial cycles on the landscape. The Forest is a landscape which shows the traces of human activity like layers of organic material which provide a culture out of which grows the next generation of productive activity. According to the organisers of the Sculpture Trail (Martin, 1990:61):

Nothing is permanent in the forest, and these artistic interventions are no more than the latest marks left by man on the land. From the first excavations, the forest has been inscribed with lines of passage – paths, railways and watercourses; dug into and sculpted by mines; or cut down and replanted along avenues and in well-defined plots.

This is much more than the picturesque conception of decay as a means of coming to terms with industry as already worn out, it is seen as a positive and inevitable stage in the process of renewal and reinvigoration. Many of the works of art are themselves designed to decay and eventually disappear within the encroaching undergrowth. Several including the *Bracken Ring, Bracken Knot* have already decomposed, but they are not lost without purpose. The Trail itself is translated into an organic stimulus, an economic and cultural nutrient by which the Forestry Commission is 'giving something back to the forest' (see Orrom in Martin, 1990:10).

The organisers' concern to include local people both in the initial decision-making process, through work with school and adult groups, illustrates the concern both to ground contemporary sculpture in the concerns and interests of local society and also to use the art work as a social medicine, concepts common to forms of grounded modernity. The works of art provide merely another set of marks in the landscape and like the previous marks of industrial activity they are productive. This is because they encourage both an imaginative response to the Forest and a physical and intellectual means of engaging with and entering the Forest, participating in its life and understanding the processes at work. In addition to this dimension of social welfare, they are also productive because they bring tourists generating income and, through specific ecologically sensitive management practices, result in a richer flora and fauna:

> The valley has now taken on a new lease of life with its designation as a National Nature reserve, and the sculptures have become a part of the regeneration of the forest and forest life which is taking place in the Dean today (Martin, 1990:61).

Discussion

The concern with ecology that is expressed in the Sculpture Trail and elsewhere in the Forest of Dean is a powerful marketing tool in the hands of the area's promoters. Its appeal is particularly great to those who Urry (1990) termed 'post-tourists', a group with distinctive socio-economic characteristics who are fundamental to the contemporary tourist industry. They belong to educated supervisory, managerial, clerical and professional middle-income groups and have a reflexive, self-conscious approach to their own leisure. Typically they reject the artificiality of mass tourism and bring with them an environmental awareness derived from an 'educated' interest in current affairs.

Their concern to experience 'real nature' and 'authentic' culture has resulted in a rapid expansion of tour operators developing specialist tourist destinations away from mass-tourist attractions (Urry, 1990:95). Promotion of the Forest of Dean with its emphasis on the experience of nature clearly aims to target them. In doing this, art and advertising for the Forest emphasises the 'reality' of the Forest and builds its tourist image on natural and human productive capacity. The Sculpture Trail leads people into the Forest and therefore follows what Wilson calls the current fashion in the design of ecological and zoological material, that of landscape immersion. Based on our understanding of plant and animal communities as well as human psychology the aim is to immerse the spectator in the habitat of the subject matter (Wilson, 1992:247).

However, the promotion of the Forest takes the current interest in environmentalism and 'real tourism' a stage further by making connections between the concepts of landscape immersion and productive symbiosis. The Forest of Dean Visitors' Centre, for example, suggests that they can help us 'discover Dean – the story of a Forest and its people'. The switch in reference from *the* Forest to *a* Forest is important because it indicates the insertion of 'Forest' as a universal signifier of symbiosis and bio-diversity into the specific history of Dean.

Using this language of 'sustainable tourism', the long-standing interpretation of the Forest of Dean as a land and a way of life set apart conflates the grounded modernist concern with locally rooted creativity and the post-tourist expectations of the exotic. Dean becomes analogous to a tropical rain forest, where a society lives in harmony with nature; a precious heritage for which tourism is both salvation and hazard. Tourism reflects the failure and vulnerability of this society while offering hope for the future. It is an ideal to be reclaimed, yet is further injured by the process of reclamation. It is a tourist experience at once exotic and mundane and, as such, falls within the mainstream of 'tourist gaze' encounters – proffering a glimpse of the new from the safety of the familiar. Yet, by making connections between the industrial decline of the Forest of Dean and wider ecological problems, promotion of tourism in the Forest is not just adding a synthetic or anachronistic free-floating symbolism to the 'real landscape'. Rather, it is the very grounding of this approach to landscape in 'the real world' which makes it worthy of critical attention.

The eclectic heritage landscapes of the 1980s have been roundly criticised by the political Left as promoting shallow and stereotyped representations of history and geography (Hewison, 1987). In fact as Urry (1990) pointed out, such heritage landscapes are understood as 'artificial' by the very people who enjoy them most. The 'post-tourist', he suggested, is well aware of the games which are being played. However, the landscape of eco-tourism is perhaps different. It adopts a language which is shared by both poles of the political spectrum. To the Right, it denotes the vitality of a competitive community and, to the Left, the harmony of cooperation.

The Sculpture Trail's many, often contradictory, objectives are reflected in the diversity of groups concerned with its creation. It is corporate advertising, the exemplification of local culture, a tourist attraction generating revenue, and a resource of uncommodifiable nature. The idea of 'immersion' pitches each individual into the landscape and takes the language and techniques of the ecological sciences to reconnect the individual physically and philosophically to the environment. This is not a problem-free landscape of ideologically simple, synthetic, hedonistic consumerism. Rather it is an ideologically complex landscape where the contested nature of the concepts used to justify its constitution are hidden by the very naturalism of the language used both to explain it and give it form. Moreover, by adopting this same language of naturalism, the promoters of the Forest become accomplices in the process of the mystification of place.

References

Bell, D. (1976) *The Cultural Contradictions of Capitalism*, London: Heinemann.

Bick, D. (1980) *The Old Industries of Dean*, Coleford, Gloucestershire: Douglas McLean.

Chambers, I. (1987) 'Maps for the metropolis: a possible guide to the present', *Cultural Studies*, 1, 1–22.

Christian, J. (1991) 'Paul Sandby and the military survey of Scotland' in N. Alfrey and S.D. Daniels, eds., *Mapping the Landscape*, Nottingham: Nottingham Castle Museum.

Clayre, A. (1977) *Nature and Industrialization*, Oxford: Oxford University Press.

Cosgrove, D. and Daniels, S.D., eds. (1988) *The Iconography of Landscape*, Cambridge: Cambridge University Press.

Daniels, S.D. (1992a) *Fields of Vision*, Cambridge: Polity Press.

Daniels, S.D. (1992b) 'Loutherbourg's chemical theatre: Coalbrookdale by night' in J. Barrell, ed., *Painting and the Politics of Culture: new essays on British Art, 1700–1850*, Oxford: Oxford University Press.

Forestry Commission (1984) *The Forestry Commission and Recreation*, Policy Paper 2, Edinburgh: Forestry Commission.

Forestry Commission (1989) *Forest of Dean Sculpture Walk: art in the Forest*, Coleford, Gloucestershire: Forestry Commission.

Gilg, A.W. (1978) *Countryside Planning: the first three decades 1945–76*, London: Methuen.

Godwin, F. (1986) *The Secret Forest of Dean*, Bristol: Redcliffe Press.

Hart, C. (1971) *The Industrial History of Dean*, Newton Abbot: David and Charles.

Harvey, D. (1989) *The Condition of Postmodernity*, Oxford: Blackwell.

Herrmann, L. (1986) *Paul and Thomas Sandby*, London: Batsford.

Hewison, R. (1987) *The Heritage Industry: Britain in a climate of decline*, London: Methuen.

Hudson, K. (1965) *The Industrial Past and the Industrial Present*, Bath: University of Bath.

Jameson, F. (1984) 'Postmodernism, or the cultural logic of late capitalism', *New Left Review*, 146, 53–92.

Jencks, C. (1984) *What is Post-Modernism?*, London: St. Martin's Press.

Katz, E. (1992) 'The big lie: human restoration of nature', *Research in Philosophy and Technology*, 12, 231–41.

Lee, M.S. (1990) *Rural Tourism Planning: lessons of the Forest of Dean Tourism Development Action Programme*, unpublished MA dissertation, University of Nottingham.

Lowenthal, D. (1985) *The Past is a Foreign Country*, Cambridge: Cambridge University Press.

Martin, R. (1990) *The Sculptured Forest*, Bristol: Redcliffe Press.

Ousby, I. (1990) *The Englishman's England: taste travel and the rise of tourism*, Cambridge: Cambridge University Press.

Rees, G. (1980) *Early Railway Prints*, Oxford: Phaidon.

Revill, G.E. (1989) 'Coal mining and "picturesque theory", the landscaping of Coleorton Hall, Leicestershire, 1800–1820', *East Midland Geographer*, 12(1–2), 14–25.

Revill, G.E. (forthcoming, 1994) 'Working the system: journeys through corporate culture in the railway age', *Society and Space*.

Robbins, K. (1983) *The Eclipse of A Great Power: modern Britain, 1870–1975*, London: Longman.

Rosenthal, M. (1982) *British Landscape Painting*, Oxford: Phaidon.

Sked, A. (1987) *Britain's Decline: problems and perspectives*, Oxford: Blackwell.

Thomas, J. (1992) 'Temporality, material culture and the self', in C. Philo, ed., *New Words, New Worlds: Reconceptualising Social and Cultural Geography*, Lampeter: Social and Cultural Geography Study Group, 119–24.

Urry, J. (1990) *The Tourist Gaze: leisure and travel in contemporary societies*, London: Sage.

Watkins, C. (1983) *Woodlands in Nottinghamshire since 1945: a study of changing distribution type and use*, unpublished PhD, University of Nottingham.

Wiener, M.J. (1981) *English Culture and the Decline of the Industrial Spirit, 1850–1980*, Cambridge: Cambridge University Press.

Wilson, A. (1992) *The Culture of Nature: North American landscape from Disney to the Exxon Valdez*, Oxford: Blackwell

Wright, R. (1990) *Visitors' Guide To The Royal Forest of Dean*, Ross on Wye: Bradley Hill Workshop.

14 Selling the countryside: representations of rural Britain

PYRS GRUFFUDD

Much of this book, quite properly, is concerned with the self-conscious place promotion that is conducted by public or quasi-public agencies. Yet the place marketeers who work for these agencies – preoccupied with inward investment, visitor figures and events programmes – are also part of a wider place representational process. It is important to recognise the reality that places are also promoted by other, less conscious means.

This chapter is concerned with the ways in which certain environments come, at certain times, to assume a particular importance that makes them worthy of promotion (*see also* Gruffudd, 1990). The countryside is one such environment and this chapter considers the nature and the role of the ways in which the rural was represented in early-20th-century Britain, with examples particularly drawn from rural Wales. In the course of this chapter, I argue that promotion can be achieved through a variety of means more subtle than the overtly propagandist text or image. A range of cultural products – travel books, landscape art, popular treatises on rural life, academic studies – contributed to the creation of a ruralist cultural discourse between the two World Wars, each stressing the integrity of rural life and landscapes. I further argue that the promotion of the rural is as much to do with the transmission of 'enduring values' as with narrow environmental concerns; values which remain heavily promoted in the tourist and industrial place marketing of the late-20th century.

The search for the picturesque

To locate the origins of these 'enduring values', it is necessary to go back more than two centuries (*see also* Chapter 13). It is widely argued that the awakening to landscape aesthetics in Britain was a feature of the Picturesque movement of the 18th century and the later work of the Romantics. While space does not permit detailed analysis of the lasting impact of these movements (see Zaring, 1977; Morgan, 1983; Howard, 1985), a brief analysis is helpful in understanding later developments.

The replacement of the classical landscape ideal of Claude and Poussin by the more vernacular Picturesque made the rugged terrain of, for instance, Wales and the Lake

District attractive to travellers from the mid-18th century. After receiving no mentions in the *Gentleman's Magazine* for most of the century, an article on Wales appeared in every issue in the 1780s and 1790s (Zaring, 1977). In 1798, one writer noted that an excursion on the River Wye had 'become an essential part of the education . . . of all who aspire to the reputation of elegance, taste, and fashion' (quoted in Wordsworth, 1987:96).

The emerging genre of the travel book created and mediated this fashionable search for the Picturesque. A travel book was a personal narration of an apparently seamless jaunt around a country or region. Through the descriptions of writers like Gilpin and Thomas Pennant, the charms of particular districts were added to the rigorously structured itinerary of the Picturesque tour. In the case of Wales, about 50 books recording tours were published between 1770 and 1800, including Pennant's *Tour of Wales* (published in three parts between 1778 and 1783).

Through these tours and landscape painting, the Picturesque and Romantic movements established a dominant way of imagining the countryside. They constructed Wales as a place with both aesthetic and social and moral virtues. Its landscapes were seen through the lenses of aesthetic theory and taste (or in the case of the Romantics, through the primacy of emotional responses), and its people were viewed as noble, sturdy peasants.

This was not, however, a wholly nostalgic representation of place. Some emphasis has recently been given to those picturesque and romantic writers and artists equally comfortable with modernity and urbanity (Wordsworth, 1987). The impacts of the industrialisation were seen by artists such as Turner in terms of the harnessing of nature's power, often for enterprises of patriotic resonance such as industry or transport (Daniels, 1993). The owners of industrial sites in the early 19th century were well aware of the touristic interest in their work; the owners of Coalbrookdale, for instance, arranged a spectacular promotional route around their ironworks (*see* Chapter 13). Picturesque landscape gardeners like Humphry Repton proved able to accommodate industrial buildings into their newly created rural vistas (Daniels, 1981). Others have suggested that picturesque tourists would generally shy away from the products of the industrial age, but made exceptions if there were stimulating contrasts to be exploited. One writer, confronted by a Scottish aqueduct, remarked that 'where objects of art enter into a direct rivalship, as it were, with the objects of Nature, and are of sufficient magnitude, and importance, to maintain the composition, the suspense in which the mind is held, is of the most pleasing kind' (quoted in Andrews, 1989:120).

Tradition and modernity

There is remarkable similarity between this 19th-century sense of an aesthetic dialogue between modern industrial and natural forms and that exhibited by a number of writers on landscape in the first half of this century – another period of burgeoning interest in the countryside. The archaeologist and leading conservationist Cyril Fox (1930) argued for developments characteristic of the time, nobly planned and worthily executed. Telford's bridge over the Menai Straits reminded him that 'the grandeur of Nature and of Man . . . act and react on each other', and he devoted particular attention to arterial roads and electricity pylons, a row of which, in perspective, were 'as noble as . . . the arches of an aqueduct on the Campagna'.

Fox wrote during a period which had witnessed an immense interest in the countryside, promoted by travel and guide books, and publications on rural virtues. This cult of the countryside was facilitated by the immense growth in personal mobility. Between 1920 and 1934, the number of privately-owned cars increased tenfold (Duchen, 1983) and the introduction of the motor bus was little short of a revolution.

Published tours again played a great part in disseminating notions of the countryside into the 20th century. In 1902, the Poet Laureate Alfred Austin (1902) set out 'to see Old England' and found it in abundance. He came across a countryside which had the abiding charm of ancientness and a population which pleased him, as it had 18th- and 19th-century travellers, with its servility and its moral sense. According to Martin Wiener (1981:45):

> Austin's trip was to be followed by an ever-increasing number of similar trips as the automobile made the countryside more accessible to town dwellers. Yet if the scale altered, the character of perception did not. By the turn of the century, writers like Austin had helped establish a mental framework for domestic tourists – the quest for 'Old England'.

A quest for Old Wales also emerged. In 1905 Edward Thomas found Wales to be a land of cultured, God-fearing peasants, with its wild hills imbued with mythology. Thomas (1983:31) first 'discovered' Wales, appropriately enough, through a picture which hung in his childhood home in outer London: 'the last October sunlight used to fall upon it when the silence set in. The picture meant Wales'. Its picturesque composition yielded to his imagination as did the land itself on his later travels. As well as artistic convention, literary convention shaped his promotion of Wales. He acknowledged his debt to other writers within the genre, most notably George Borrow. However he denied the effect of fashion on his representation of Wales, discerning a lack of 'authenticity' amongst the 'lovers of the Celt'. These were a cosmopolitan crowd of aesthetes whose 'aim and ideal is to go about the world in a state of self-satisfied dejection, interrupted, and perhaps sustained, by days when they consume strange mixed liquors to the tune of all the fine old Celtic songs which are fashionable' (Thomas, 1983:10). Thomas's quest was for authenticity, narrated through his travels within the landscapes of rural Wales and through a series of encounters with the wise and colourful peasantry.

Whatever the particular view taken, the works of travel writers are selectively constructed. Peter Bishop (1989), in stressing the importance of an imaginative approach to the reading of travel texts, has noted that they were written not as faithful records of place, although some purported to be, but rather as part of a process of imagining and re-imagining. Hence writers acknowledge their debt to their predecessors and comment on their self-conscious approach to their task. Edmund Vale (1914:258), for instance, mused on the inadequacy of certain media for the promotion of his notion of the rural. Walking into a post office:

> My first act was to purchase a thing that is really an abomination unto me, namely, a pictorial post-card. This miserable device for distorting people's impressions of rural England is only fit to be trafficked in by those who aver that they can see the

How a North to South Wales arterial road would cross the mountain barriers.
—Sketch by Roy Saunders.

SECOND ARTICLE

Retaining Rural Charm on Arterial Road Route

Figure 14.1 Scenery from behind the wheel (from the *Western Mail*, 23 September 1937).

country from a motor car. For the flat anaemic landscapes and dull buildings and hideous streets these things wear upon their faces, without life or light or perspective or atmosphere, are the exact replica of the impressions one records in one's mind of the country when travelling in a motor car.

The mode of transport was a crucial part of the author's narrative. Yet if the motor car was still an enemy for writers such as Vale, for many others, it was a revolutionary force in a modern perception of landscape (e.g. Priestley, 1935:2–3). A proposal for a road linking North and South Wales during the 1940s, for instance, was couched in terms of the views of Welsh heritage afforded the speeding motorist (Figure 14.1). Wright (1985) also claimed that Shell advertising helped redefine the countryside in terms of the motor car, given that the population had become disassociated from the land. Although the car was removed in the late 1930s due to preservationist tensions, in visual imagery the road became a principle of perspective, providing the continuity between foreground and viewed distance.

In search of Wales

There is a hint, in a number of travel accounts, of writers' self-conscious roles in constructing a new notion of place. In 1935, Edmund Vale could imagine no better thing happening to England 'than an awakening of a more perfect understanding with the people of Wales. Just now West Britain is an accumulator of imaginative forces standing at full charge, waiting to be put into circuit' (1935a:x). Vale (1935a:5) imagined himself in the role of conductor for:

> Wales has neither written herself up for the consumption of English readers, nor spent money on publicity, nor embroiled herself with the Government. She has neither tartans, nor crow-step gables, nor jaunting cars, nor bog-oak souvenirs to catch the eye when you cross the Border. Her most distinctive thing is a separate language, but that has the unfortunate effect of repelling the English stranger rather than attracting him.

The native Welsh had failed to promote themselves for the benefit of the English and travel writers therefore often lapsed into the role of communicator of all that was worthy in Wales and the Welsh. In this way, the itinerary became a crucial indicator of discernment, the reaching of remote villages and communion with their natives a ritual feature, if not a matter of honour.

The text also became the medium for imparting certain messages to the readership. In the case of Wales, these messages would often be a plea for cultural sensitivity or an ode to rural society and its presumed values. As Paul Fussell notes, 'it is . . . possible to consider the between-the-wars travel book as a subtle instrument of ethics, replacing such former vehicles as sermons and essays' (1980:204).

Matless (1988) claimed to discern the same attitude in the work of H.V. Morton, probably the most successful travel writer of the period. His *In Search of England*, published in 1927, had reached its thirty-second edition by 1944 and had been serialised in the *Daily Express*. Matless (1988) suggested that there were links between Morton's works and preservationist discourses, notably those relating to the modernist ordering of people, society and landscapes. Crucial in this process of ordering was the presentation of a 'collective' definition of the countryside and a collective manner in which it is to be appreciated. Morton was well aware of his task. In the introduction to *In Search of England*, he noted that: 'a writer on England to-day addresses himself to a wider and a more intelligent public than ever before. And the reason is, I think, that never before have so many people been searching for England' (1931:vii). He went on to enthuse over the 'remarkable system of motor coach services' and of the popularity of the motor car as catalysts for the new pilgrimage to the countryside. The danger of the mass pilgrimage, though, was the vulgarisation of the countryside:

> I have seen charabanc parties from the large manufacturing towns, providing a mournful text for an essay on Progress, playing cornets on village greens and behaving with a barbaric lack of manners which might have been outrageous had it not been unconscious, and therefore only pathetic.

Fussell's argument, then, seems to be supported by Morton's didactic rhetoric.

Morton's *In Search of Wales* was first published in 1932, reaching its tenth edition six years later. The didactic strain is evident here too. Most books about Wales, he argued, 'treat the country as if it is something to look at and not understand' (1932:vii). Morton's task, it is clear, was to dispense understanding. The book's frontispiece (Figure 14.2) mused on the fluctuating stereotypes of Wales, women in Welsh costume labelled 'a vanished generation'. Yet Morton's tour was a sympathetic, humorous and often sensitive interpretation of Wales and the Welsh. He was sensitive to cultural and political distinctiveness and sympathetic towards those who must bear the depredations of the vulgar tourist rather than the enlightened traveller: 'It is amusing to sit in a corner and watch some worthy man, whose life has been spent among crowds in Manchester or Birmingham doing his best to cultivate the native . . . . He talks to a man who can see corpse-lights as if he was talking to a mechanic in his factory' (Morton, 1932:135–6). Here Morton set up a sympathetic resonance between the enlightened traveller and the spiritual Welsh peasantry, a people who could see 'corpse lights' (i.e. souls departing dead bodies). Neither is Morton unduly worried about following in the well-worn footsteps of earlier or contemporary writers.

Perhaps his most radical reworking of the travel book genre was his descent into what he called 'Black Wales', the industrial and mining valleys of the South. Matless (1988) commented on the assertive modernity of some travellers' thoughts on industry. However, Morton largely avoided industrial areas in *In Search of England* but in the North West 'stood impressed and thrilled by the grim power of these ugly chimneys rising in groups, by the black huddle of factories, and the still, silent wheels at pit-mouth and the drifting haze of smoke' (1931:186). Morton's encounter with industry in Wales, however, is more sustained and evokes a profounder response. In Swansea he:

> explored a grim and terrible valley. A century ago, it was, like all South Wales, a pretty, peaceful spot. Then the Industrial Revolution changed it. The most hideous creation of man, the foundry, with its bleak chimney-stack, took possession of it. They now stand the length of it, frightful and ogreish. The smoke drifts before the wind. In works and factories Fire and Force are torturing the intractable, transforming it and sending it out into the world in a thousand shapes. That is the drama of Swansea. And to Fire and Force – those primitive begetters of metal – has been added Science. Behind the smith with his hammer is now a chemist in spectacles (Morton, 1932:223).

This assertion of the industrial sublime was repeated elsewhere, but most remarkable was Morton's representation of the proud, humane and wise communities of the

Figure 14.2 'A Vanished Generation'. The frontispiece to H. V. Morton's *In Search of Wales*.

mining valleys, graphically represented by the photographs of James Jarche. The Welsh miner emerged as a heroic but sensitive figure, the women of the valleys equally heroic within the domestic realm. Despite these virtues, the communities of South Wales were a national problem for 'life in a mining valley is dominated by the pit shaft. The pit sucks all the male energy into its black depths' (1932:264). Extracts from Morton's book dealing with the mining valleys were serialised in the *Daily Herald*, illustrating the political resonance of Morton's sympathetic perceptions of the area.

Countryside companions

Travel books such as Morton's were outwardly factual yet, as Bishop (1989) has argued, we must regard them as the imaginative, creative works of specific authors. The same is largely true of the vast body of guide books and volumes of topographical information designed to accompany the independent traveller. These differ from travel books in that they do not have a narrative structure. Nonetheless, they are equally resonant with a particular notion of the countryside and the correct manner of its appreciation. As in the case of the travel book, these guide books are didactic texts. The leading publisher was probably Batsford, whose texts were subtle odes to tradition and to the rural, published under such series titles as 'British Heritage' and the 'Face of Britain'. Many had colourful jackets designed by the artist Brian Cook (Batsford, 1987) and in their bold colours and modern, stylised representations of the countryside they represented an optimism and energy that characterised the recreation movement between the wars. They also represented a dialogue between the modern world and the traditions of the countryside.

By 1939, 18 titles had been published in the 'British Heritage' series, ranging from *The English Castle* – 'a review of the origin, evolution and vicissitudes of medieval fortresses, with accounts of military engines, famous sieges etc.' – to more conventional topographic texts like Eiluned and Peter Lewis's *The Land of Wales*. First published in 1937, the book warned the reader that 'the traveller who buys a ticket at Paddington or Euston should be warned that he is about to travel backwards as well as westwards, for Wales is a storehouse of the past' (Lewis and Lewis, 1949:1–2). Wales was now constructed for the general reader in terms of its topography, its history, folklore and sociology. More explicitly than in travel texts, places are interrogated according to a sustained intellectual interest. From the mists of Celtic mythology, to folk tales (complete with footnotes recording the hearing of fairy music while researching the book), to the industrial revolution, and the prospects for Welsh nationalism, the book typifies the educated interest in place promoted by Batsford and offers the reader a frame for correct, ordered appreciation. Photographs, however, offered a more conventional narrative – from composed landscapes to a remarkable photograph of thirteen women, each with a child in arms, anxiously facing pit winding gear and 'Waiting for News' (Figure 14.3). What emerges from this gaze is the spirit of Wales, the quest of the enlightened traveller. The landscape haunts that Welsh spirit, a spirit characterised by 'a keenness of comprehension, the understanding heart as well as the ready tongue, an interest in spiritual and intellectual matters that characterises even the casual occupant of a third class railway carriage, west of Offa's Dyke' (Lewis and Lewis, 1949:111).

The Lewis' claim echoes that of the geographer H.J. Fleure, who noted a wit's comment that 'as one travels from England to rural Wales the talk in a railway compartment changes from betting to chapels, or from horse racing to the eisteddfod' (1940:883). Edmund Vale's contribution to *The Beauty of Britain* (Vale, 1935b) also exhibits this spirituality amid what are often characterised as the sterile pages of the guide book. The whole of Wales, he argued 'is pervaded by an invisible essence which issues from invisible sources and which we may call Welsh atmosphere' (Vale, 1935b:161). The Welsh spirit shrank away from the tourist's touch; it was not easily represented in costume, food, architecture or even souvenirs. Wales was constructed by Vale as essentially mysterious, yielding only to the worthy traveller.

Figure 14.3 'Waiting for News at the Pithead', from Eiluned and Peter Lewis, *The Land of Wales*.

Recent work on the Neo-Romantic movement in art – memorably described as a fusion of King Arthur, William Blake and Picasso (Mellor, 1987) – has suggested that the tendency to idealise and mythologise the landscapes of the 'Celtic fringes' was apparent in a variety of media including painting, photography and film. We might also suggest that the travel book and guide book exhibit some of this characteristic dialogue between tradition and modernity. Yet while the 'Celtic fringes' of Britain were likely to be promoted in this way, so too was lowland England. *The Beauty of Britain* had much to relate about the character of the downs, fens and moors. In *The Heart of England*, Ivor Brown (1939, originally 1935) made a vigorous defence of the new age and an attack on over-romanticised aspects of the old yet suggested that the English character exhibited a continuity of understatement and phlegmatism: 'We crack jests where our Continental neighbours would be cracking skulls' (Brown, 1939:117).

This allusion to different political cultures on continental Europe was significant, for tension on the Continent and finally the outbreak of World War II provided a huge stimulus to the continued promotion of the countryside. Crucially, rural values were seen as being under attack and not just rural landscapes. The stylistic modernism of Brian Cook's guide book covers and the posters of railway companies was translated into propaganda posters such as the series depicting the traditional landscapes of Britain (or more accurately England) under the banner 'Your Britain – Fight for it Now!'

Artistic representations of Britain in general, in fact, demonstrated remarkable continuity into wartime. Eric Ravilious translated his humour and understatement from pictures of agricultural machinery to pictures of military aircraft; John Piper's search for pleasing decay amid the ancient ruins of Britain turned into elegiac views of bomb damage; and the fusion of tradition and modernity in Paul Nash's views of ancient earthworks easily accommodated the symbolism of the clash of civilisations (Gruffudd, 1991). The peculiarly Neo-Romantic sense of a dialogue between past and present is plain in the four-volume artistic survey *Recording Britain*, a record of the heritage threatened by war but also by schemes of 'modernisation' (Recording Britain, 1946 *et seq.*). It demonstrated a familiar topographical itinerary. Antiquarian, ecclesiastical and pastoral scenes are favoured although industrial Britain was vindicated aesthetically by the war effort. The spirituality of rural topography was also evident. John Piper's picture of the *Tithe Barn, Great Coxwell* – viewed from below, its powerful diagonals soaring into a brooding sky – directly recalls H.J. Massingham's (1937:57) account of it in 'The Face of Britain' series:

> When the world of to-day is too much with me I go off to see it again that it may fill me with a fragment of its valour and greatness, and that I may stand in the shadow of its ancient peace. It rises from the land with a dignity so gnomic and lofty that it is impossible to think of it except as a holy place and so as a bond between heaven and earth.

The new conditions of wartime provided an added stimulus to Batsford's endeavours. The 'Home Front Handbooks', published in 1940, were designed for those evacuees and billeted soldiers living in the country for the first time. Essentially pocket manuals, they advised on *How to See Nature, How to Look at Old Buildings* and even *How to Grow Food*. Harry Batsford himself advised readers on *How to See the Country*. He was motivated by wartime events which 'led or compelled thousands of English urban-dwellers to a first-hand acquaintance with the country for the first time in their lives' (Batsford, 1945, originally 1940:1). This was perhaps the most explicitly didactic of the Batsford books designed, as it was, for the uninitiated or untutored (to borrow from Cyril Joad's, 1945, *The Untutored Townsman's Invasion of the Country*) visitor to the countryside. Curiously, it recalled the charismatic figure of Colpeper, the feudal patriarch of Powell and Pressburger's film *A Canterbury Tale* (1944), who saw wartime as an opportunity to educate the barbarian townsfolk, in the guise of the soldiers billeted in his village, in the ways of the country.

Batsford began by arguing that while landscape can be appreciated without being understood, it was best appreciated given an understanding of form and structure. The tutored visitor, therefore, examined the countryside via its components of geology, topography, architecture, history, custom and so on. Country crafts and industries were reverentially treated and the mysteries of rural travel and accommodation unravelled. The mode of behaviour at the village inn, for instance, was a minefield for the innocent urbanite:

> In the taproom you are in more crowded quarters, and must be careful not to get in the line of fire of a game of darts, or unwittingly occupy the seat of a local patriarch . . . . Of course, some counties are friendlier to strangers than others, and if (though the chance is rare) you find that your presence in the taproom is creating an awkward pause, you should seize the first suitable opportunity to transfer yourself

Figure 14.4 'Il Penseroso: Old Cronies; Fisherman and Rug-Maker, Looe, Cornwall', from Harry Batsford's *How to see the Country.*

to the smoke room . . . . Don't be shocked if of a Saturday night you run into a spot of tipsiness (Batsford, 1945:72).

Despite these pitfalls of the organic community for the unwitting traveller, the pub remained the place to meet the locals, many of whom were depicted in the volume at work or at play, most notably a bewhiskered pair of characters captioned thus: 'Il Penseroso: Old Cronies; Fisherman and Rug-Maker, Looe, Cornwall' (Figure 14.4).

The way of the land

In *How to See the Country*, Batsford advised his readers to consult the flood of books on the countryside and country life which had appeared since the beginning of World War II. These books did not explicitly promote the countryside for recreation or even education but were, nevertheless, subtle reinforcements of the promotional theme. Anthologies like *Countryside Mood* (Harman, 1943) or *Countryside Character* (Harman, 1946) were comprised of prose, recollections and the odd photographic essay, often on agriculture (Figure 14.5). Many were openly propagandist. They served to define the national character during wartime, and to locate it firmly in the heart of the

Figure 14.5 *The Rural Idyll.* The frontispiece to R. Harman's *Countryside Mood.*

country. For Harman (1943), a revitalised agriculture owing to the wartime drive for production was the clearest indication of a rebirth of the 'national soul'.

Other chronicles of rural life, like C. Henry Warren's *England is a Village* (1940), likewise located the national character in the countryside. Warren's book was a richly textured document of life, its hardships and pleasures, in the imaginary village of Larkfield. The sub-text was a eulogy for the countryside as the foundation and front-line of Englishness. The calm of Larkfield has been shattered but 'it is from the ashes (if such must be) of the Larkfields of England that our phoenix strength shall rise. England's might is still in her fields and villages, and though the weight of mechanized armies rolls over them to crush them, in the end they will triumph. The best of England is a village' (1940:5).

Such themes also appealed to the political and nationalist Right. H.J. Massingham, author of the Batsford book *Cotswold Country* (1937) and a long list of other books on country life, was one such figure. A self-taught naturalist, he disliked formal education and the bureaucracy of government, and he also violently attacked the free-market system. According to Bramwell (1989:129), for Massingham 'individualism meant an atomized, exploitable work-force, and an exploitative attitude to all natural resources. By regaining the knowledge of our ordered, craft-oriented country roots, man would rescue himself from the trough of urban despair'.

This philosophical underpinning relates much of the didactic material on country life to academic and more explicitly political and pragmatic treatises. Massingham, for instance, was inspired by Rolf Gardiner's – 'organic farmer and Nordic racialist' (Bramwell, 1989:107) – work on rural revivalism. Gardiner established youth movements and, at Springhead in Wessex in the 1930s, a centre for the study of rural life and reconstruction. Its motivation was the realisation that 'we could not do without order, beauty, and rhythm, and that these things came of the soil and not of machine and machine-made surroundings' (Gardiner, 1943:51). The restoration of rural England was to be a spiritual and moral crusade, as well as a practical process. The revival of agriculture would be meaningless without the revival of the rural way of life. Therefore, alongside schemes of agricultural instruction, and especially organic techniques, were founded experiments in the revival of folk song and dance. As Gardiner (1943:127) put it:

> The rhythmic order of the cosmos is the pattern of earth-life and of those who husband and cultivate the soil; it is the shape of time expressed in the cycle of the year .... Modern, industrial and urbanized society has forgotten or suppressed all this and become uprooted from the earth and from the shapes of time. It is denying the Natural Order. With a return to these fundamentals there will, therefore, be a need to restore the calendar and its celebration.

According to Bramwell (1989:121; also Griffiths, 1980) the interlocking circles around people like Gardiner included 'British National Socialists, men with ugly hair cuts and razor-scarred faces, (and) researchers and experimenters like Sir George Stapledon, the grass breeding specialist at Aberystwyth'. Stapledon is interesting in his own right. A mystic, he had read Henri Bergson 'and was deeply imbued with the feeling that an evolving Spirit of Life was immanent in Nature' (Waller, 1962:74). This spirit, however, was being denied by modern, urban life. City life was, Stapledon argued, one-sided in its appeal to the mental, as opposed to the pre-mental, aspects of character. Harmony and understanding could only come through the contemplation of nature. In addition, Stapledon feared the physical degeneracy caused by city life and is, as such, linked to the eugenics movement (*see* e.g. Searle, 1976, 1979). The 'country stock' was, he argued, sounder than the urban; the countryside of Britain 'carries in its population the genes, unsullied and uncontaminated, that maintain and perpetuate our national vigour and national characteristics' (Stapledon, 1944, originally 1935:231). To alleviate this general waning of the influence of the rural on British life, Stapledon was a vocal campaigner for National Parks and for the inculcation of rural values through the schools and universities.

It is vital, however, to realise that this promotion of the rural was by no means confined to conservative or Right-wing elements in British society. Many radicals drew on co-operative experiments in Denmark, for instance, or on earlier socialist back-to-the-land movements in Britain (Hardy 1979; Gould, 1988). Among writers and academics there was also a radical notion of the countryside and its values.

At Aberystwyth, like Stapledon, was the geographer H.J. Fleure, an internationalist and a political radical. Through racial surveys, Fleure elevated the rural population to a position of sociological, but not physical, importance (Gruffudd, 1989). In his opinion, the Celtic fringe in general and rural Wales in particular was 'the ultimate refuge in the far west, wherein persist, among valleys that look towards the sunset, old thoughts and visions that else had been lost to the world' (Fleure, 1926:1, 1940). The spiritual qualities of the peasantry were of importance in combatting the materialism of unbridled *laissez-faire* and its destructive social effects. He argued (Fleure, 1921) that society's one hope of avoiding collapse was to have a stream of supply from the remote corners where the treasures of ancient thought survived, imparting those faculties and discernment and creativity that Fleure felt were the possession of rural society. Industrial civilisation, he suggested, was facing collapse. The cry was for a new vision of the future that could only come from those who retained their rural roots. He rejected the blind attachment to 'Progress' and its effects, as he saw it, on personality, enforcing specialisation and dependence by contrast with the rich variety of peasant life.

In this way, Wales was 'a fount whence may well up streams of inspiration refreshing to the jaded and overstrained business life of our perplexed modern England' (Fleure, 1922:xi). In one sense, this quotation of Fleure's brings us full circle, for it was written as part of his introduction to the volume on Wales in *The Blue Guides* series (Muirhead, 1922). Curiously, he adopts the narrative position of a Wales seen from a railway carriage:

> The visitor approaching Wales feels he is nearing his destination when the hills begin to crowd upon his path, when the views from the train window or the motor are of the fair valleys that run among the hills, and the conversation of the people who come into the railway carriage at the little wayside stations takes a new tone and begins to deal with matters unfamiliar to dwellers on the open plains or in the industrial districts of England . . . (1922:xi).

This is not, however, the superficial glimpse of an aesthetic Wales thrown briefly onto the train's window. Rather, Fleure's academic theorisation of Wales depends on the issue of accessibility and the contact between cultures. His essay for *The Blue Guides* is a narrative in historical geography, dotted with the tales of successive invasions, population shifts and more recent incursions. All such changes have left their mark on the land, interpreted by Fleure in this dynamic, theoretical sense and by topographers in a more statically poetic one.

Conclusion

As we have seen, however, Fleure's discourse is not lacking in poetry and this is particularly true when he mourns the submerging of rural Wales by a broader, British national life including, ironically, tourism. It was the increase in personal mobility afforded by public transport which helped transcend the geographical protectors of Welsh distinctness: 'Berwyn, the Cader Idris and Plynlymon ranges long provided a strong barrier which is likely to count for less and less in these days of powerful charabancs, listening-in and universal education' (1926:1–2). Elsewhere, Fleure (1917) wrote of the moral and civic imperative of freeing rural Wales from dependence on 'the city tourist'. It is, therefore, ironic yet appropriate that Fleure should so often adopt the traveller's view from the railway carriage in his analysis of the Welsh countryside and his promotion of its remaining values. It is equally ironic that a tourism in part based on the promotion of rural spiritual values should be implicated in the decline of those values.

The overall conclusion must also sustain this note of irony. The self-conscious place promotion of today continues to struggle with the same basic dilemmas that were apparent in Fleure's writings. Contemporary place promotion is heir to, and in large measure prisoner of, a long tradition of rural place representation. It is a tradition that has laden the countryside with its deeper meanings as an embodiment of the virtues of nature, beauty, mystery and fundamental truths of human experience and cultural value. These same meanings continue to pervade the promotion of rural Wales, and many other parts of the British countryside, as a tourist experience and a 'life-style' adjunct to business investment. Although we have been able to identify, in other chapters of this book, many instances in which places have been able to reinvent themselves, countryside promotion continues to rely on its stock of 'enduring values'.

References

Andrews, M. (1989) *The Search for the Picturesque: landscape aesthetics and tourism, 1760–1800*, Aldershot: Scolar Press.

Austin, A. (1902) *Haunts of Ancient Peace*, London: Macmillan.

Batsford, B.C. (1987) *The Britain of Brian Cook*, London: Batsford.

Batsford, H. (1945) *How to See the Country*, London: Batsford (Home Front Handbooks).

Bishop, P. (1989) *The Myth of Shangri-La: Tibet, travel writing and the Western creation of sacred landscape*, London: Athlone.

Bramwell, A. (1989) *Ecology in the Twentieth Century: a history*, New Haven, CN: Yale University Press.

Brown, I. (1939) *The Heart of England*, London: Batsford (The British Heritage Series)

Daniels, S. (1981) 'Landscaping for a manufacturer: Humphry Repton's commission for Benjamin Gott at Armley in 1809–10', *Journal of Historical Geography*, 7, 379–96.

Daniels, S. (1991) 'Envisioning England', *Journal of Historical Geography*, 17, 95–9.

Daniels, S. (1993) *Fields of Vision: landscape imagery and national identity in England and the United States*, Cambridge: Polity Press.

Duchen, M.B. (1983) 'Chronology: a decade by decade summary of artistic and social life in Britain, 1850–1950', in Arts Council, *Landscape in Britain, 1850–1950*, London: Arts Council, 45–54.

Fleure, H.J. (1917) 'Inshore fisheries and their development', *Welsh Housing and Development Yearbook 1917*, Cardiff: W.H.D.A., 60–65.

Fleure, H.J. (1921) 'Countries as personalities', *Nature*, 108(2722), 573–5.

Fleure, H.J. (1922) 'The Land of Wales' in F. Muirhead, ed., *Wales – The Blue Guides*, London: Macmillan, xi–xxvi.

Fleure, H.J. (1926) *Wales and Her People*, Wrexham: Hughes and Son.

Fleure, H.J. (1940) 'The Celtic West', *Journal of the Royal Society of Arts*, 4 October, 882–4.

Fox, C. (1930) *Memorandum on Policy*, CPRW 95, Council for the Preservation of Rural Wales Papers, National Library of Wales.

Fussell, P. (1980) *Abroad: British literary travelling between the wars*, Oxford: Oxford University Press.

Gardiner, R. (1943) *England Herself: ventures in rural restoration*, London: Faber and Faber.

Gould, P. (1988) *Early Green Politics: back to nature, back to the land and socialism in Britain 1880–1900*, Hassocks, Sussex: Harvester Press.

Griffiths, R. (1980) *Fellow Travellers of the Right: British enthusiasts for Nazi Germany 1933–9*, London: Constable.

Gruffudd, P. (1989) *Landscape and Nationhood: tradition and modernity in rural Wales 1900–50*, unpublished PhD Thesis, Loughborough University.

Gruffudd, P. (1990) 'Uncivil engineering: nature, nationalism and hydro-electrics', in D. Cosgrove and G. Petts, eds., *Water, Engineering and Landscape*, London: Belhaven, 159–73.

Gruffudd, P. (1991) 'Reach for the sky: the air and English cultural nationalism', *Landscape Research*, 16, 19–24.

Hardy, D. (1979) *Alternative Communities in Nineteenth Century England*, London: Longman.

Harman, R. (1943) *Countryside Mood*, London: Blandford Press.

Harman, R. (1946) *Countryside Character*, London: Blandford Press.

Howard, P. (1985) 'Painters' preferred places', *Journal of Historical Geography*, 11, 138–54.

Joad, C.E.M. (1945) *The Untutored Townsman's Invasion of the Country*, London: Faber.

Lewis, E. and P. (1949, originally 1937) *The Land of Wales*, London: Batsford (The British Heritage Series).

Massingham, H.J. (1937) *Cotswold Country*, London: Batsford (The Face of Britain Series).

Matless, D. (1988) 'Seeing England with Morton and Cornish: travel writing and a quest for order', in M. Heffernan and P. Gruffudd, eds., *A Land fit for Heroes: essays in the human geography of inter-war Britain*, Occasional Paper 14, Department of Geography, Loughborough University, 110–29.

Mellor, D., ed., (1987) *A Paradise Lost: the neo-Romantic imagination in Britain 1935–55*, London: Lund Humphries/Barbican Art Gallery.

Morgan, P. (1983) 'From a death to a view: the hunt for the Welsh past in the romantic period' in E.J. Hobsbawm and T. Ranger, eds., *The Invention of Tradition*, Cambridge: Cambridge University Press, 43–100.

Morton, H.V. (1931, originally 1927), *In Search of England*, London: Methuen.

Morton, H.V. (1932) *In Search of Wales*, London: Methuen.

Muirhead, F., ed. (1922) *Wales – The Blue Guides*, London: Macmillan.

Pennant, T. (1991, originally 1778) *A Tour in Wales*, Wrexham: Bridge Books.

Priestley, J.B. (1935) 'The beauty of Britain', in *The Beauty of Britain*, London: Batsford, 1–10.

Recording Britain (1946 et seq.), Oxford: Oxford University Press, 4 volumes.

Searle, G.R. (1976) *Eugenics and Politics in Britain 1900–1914*, Leyden: Noordhoff International.

Searle, G.R. (1979) 'Eugenics and politics in Britain in the 1930s', *Annals of Science*, 36, 159–69.

Stapledon, R.G. (1944, originally 1935) *The Land Now and Tomorrow*, London: Faber and Faber.

Thomas, E. (1983, originally 1905) *Wales*, Oxford: Oxford University Press.

Vale, E. (1914) 'A Welsh Walk', *Blackwood's Magazine*, February, 249–270.

Vale, E. (1935a) *The World of Wales*, London: Dent.

Vale, E. (1935b) 'Wales: the spirit and the face', in J.B. Priestley, ed., *The Beauty of Britain*, London: Batsford, 160–76.

Waller, D. (1962) *Prophet of the New Age*, London: Faber and Faber.

Warren, C.H. (1940) *England is a Village*, London: Eyre and Spottiswoode.

Wiener, M.J. (1981) *English Culture and the Decline of the Industrial Spirit, 1850–1980*, Cambridge: Cambridge University Press.

Wordsworth, J. (1987) *William Wordsworth and the Age of English Romanticism*, New Brunswick, NJ: Rutgers University Press.

Wright, P. (1985) *On Living in an Old Country*, London: Verso.

Zaring, J. (1977) 'The romantic face of Wales', *Annals of the Association of American Geographers*, 67, 397–418.

Index

advertising 4–7, 11, 22, 23, 44. 49, 54, 57,
    61, 62, 75–92, 116, 138–48, 154, 195,
    243, 251
  budgets 4, 62, 79
  campaigns 4, 121, 138–48
  copy 6, 23
  creative strategies 4, 22, 29–34, 138–48
  media strategies 13, 79–80
  revenue 195
aesthetics 248
airports 32
American Indians 218, 222, 231
Archigram 190
architects 140, 145, 171, 182, 189
archives 21, 90, 200
attitudinal marketing 42
authenticity 86, 111, 242, 249
authority, appeals to 31
art 14, 21, 153 79, 182
art history 12, 21, 34, 181

Batsford 254–9
billboards 80, 191, 230
boosterism 12–14, 23, 32, 53–4, 62, 67,
    118–19, 196, 203, 226
bonusing 58–61, 67
brochures 6, 11, 65, 97, 115, 149, 167, 218,
    221, 227
brutalism 170
builders 75
building societies 12, 75–92

Canary Wharf 13, 133, 136, 143–6, 171–2
cars 220, 223–31, 251
cartography 32, 235
centrality 31, 122
Chambers of Commerce 62, 119
cinema 4, 80
coalfields 1, 233, 237
cognitive-behaviouralism 12, 20, 22–7, 34
collages 22

colonisation 2, 23
commodification
  of art 21, 117
  of place 9, 11, 99, 111, 181
community art 158–63
competition analysis 47
conference centres 116, 127, 196, 199
conservation 205, 235
consumer durables 79
consumerism 191
content analysis 6, 12, 14, 20–1, 34,
    200–11
cooperatives 8, 260
council housing 78
cultural capitals 2, 34
cultural studies 12, 14, 20, 22, 27, 34
culture 12, 14, 19, 27–34, 233–63
  elite 27
  'enterprise' 32–3, 190
  popular 27, 34

Dean, Forest of 14, 233–45
deindustrialisation 1, 70, 233, 239
de-skilling 70
Desert, Great American 213–14
development agencies 1, 61, 64–5
Direct Link 199–200, 207–10
direct selling 6
Disneyland 4, 9, 157, 234
display boards 80
disposable incomes 78
Docklands, London 11, 13, 23, 71, 109,
    133–51
dude ranches 222–3

ecology 14, 233–45
editorials 14, 196, 200–11
empiricism 19
engineering 66, 235
Enterprise Zones 135
environmental education 157

environmental quality 40, 122
estate agencies 75, 81, 86
ethics 251
ethnicity 22, 29, 126, 149
eugenics 260
exhibitions 2, 186–8
experiences 4, 158, 191
Explore 197–8, 200–4

fact sheets 97–8
fairs 2, 4, 186
fascism 186, 259
festivals 14
film 4, 49, 223, 235
forestry 238, 240
functional regions 195–212

garden cities 62
Garden Festivals 173–5, 181, 188–90
gardening 87
gender 29, 149
globalisation 2, 14, 62, 196
gold rush 215
Grands Projets 163–7
guide books 23, 188, 224–5, 248–9, 253–61

Harvey, Fred 220, 222
hegemony 28, 182, 187
heritage 2, 22, 106–8, 154, 157, 163, 167,
    169, 233, 239–41
hermeneutics 28
high-technology 2, 99, 100, 102, 133
historicism 241
home ownership 12, 75–92
homelessness 149
Hotel Roanoke 198–9, 204–7
household formation 78
housing,
    building 78
    for rent 77–9
    shortages 78
hyper-reality 2, 190

iconography 14, 21, 154, 157, 184
identity 93–114, 154
ideology 8–9, 20, 28–9, 41, 116, 147–50,
    181, 243
image communication 7, 12, 19–37
image marketing 42
imagery 1, 2, 7, 15, 19–37, 75–90, 93–114,
    115, 147–50, 182, 191
immigration 2, 116

industrial archaeology 234–6, 238
industrial tourism 102–3, 157, 167, 235,
    248
industrialisation 14, 20, 54, 57, 96
infrastructure 137, 235
inner cities 65, 117, 133–51
interpretation
    countryside 15, 234, 247–61
    urban 155
inward investment 1, 8, 12, 71, 109
ironworks 234–5, 237

journalism 197–212

labour
    discontent 125, 136
    relations 117, 125
landlords 78
landscape 14–15, 188, 213–61
landscape immersion 242
language 27–8, 243
leisure 2, 22, 104, 191, 254–9
leverage 8–9
lifestyle 34, 58, 77, 104, 122, 125, 130, 203,
    261
logograms 22, 97–9

make-overs 13, 115
malls 4, 116, 127
marketing 2, 9–11, 12, 15, 39–52, 93, 121,
    157, 230
Marxism 27–8
mass communication research 19
megastructures 165
memorials 154, 166
migration 2, 6, 31, 110, 216
modernism 80, 90, 96, 236, 242, 252, 255,
    259
monumentality 163–7, 170–2, 186, 237
Mormonism 217
mortgages 78–80, 117
motorways 32, 199
muckraking 197
municipal bonds 57
murals 158–61
museums 141, 165, 238–9, 240
music 50, 190–1
mysticism 259
mythology 182, 184, 228–30, 235, 249,
    254, 255

National Parks 14, 213–31, 260

naturalism 243
nature 4, 248
Neo-Romantic movement 255–6
New South, USA 54–8, 69
new towns 23, 32, 236
news filtering 195–212
newspapers 6, 14, 20–1, 23, 195–212
NIMBY 51, 199
nostalgia 205

Olympic Games 2, 58, 65, 167, 189, 190
overspill 20

pageants 181
paintings 81, 183–4, 235
photography 6, 221, 234, 239
pictorial representations 12, 20, 21–2,
    79–86
Picturesque movement 81, 188, 234–5, 237,
    247–8
planning 7–8, 40, 135–51
plot-sizes 80
pollution 27, 189
post-colonial theory 28
posters 9–11, 21–2, 75–92
post-industrialism 1, 62, 129, 189, 190, 233
post-modernism 1, 22, 28, 105, 116, 191
post-structuralism 28
post-tourism 242
potency analysis 47–9
preservation 251
processions 183
propaganda 181–93, 257
property value 8, 135, 140–1, 146, 165, 226
protectionism 67, 68
public policy 7–9, 12–13, 15, 53–74,
    133–51
publicity 2, 57, 62, 236
puns 30

racism 69
railways 4, 9, 11, 62, 65, 75, 117, 133, 135,
    146, 163, 197–8, 215, 219, 222, 235
Reaganomics 34
recession 1, 67
regeneration 12, 13, 23, 66, 133–51, 154,
    191, 196, 201
regional definition 195–212
regional incentives 1, 8, 57, 59
re-imaging 115, 191
resorts 2, 4, 39, 62, 65
revolutionary art 183
rhetoric 20, 29–34, 55, 59, 75–7, 150, 252

rock music 190–1
Romantic movement 234–5, 247–8
royal courts 182
ruins 256

sculpture 14, 161–2, 167, 176, 228, 233–45
security 4, 88
selling propositions 6,
semiotics 27
sense of place 95, 203
slogans 6, 22, 30, 49, 86, 97–8, 100–2
smart highways 207
social marketing 42
sociolinguistics 20
spectacle 181, 184, 188–90
statues 153–4, 182
stereotypes 2, 23, 29, 252
structural change 53, 93
structuralism 27–8
suburbia 4, 12, 39, 64, 65, 75–92, 158, 166,
    189, 196
sunbelt, USA 117
sunlight 81, 88–9
surveying 235
symbols 77, 86–9, 97–9, 116, 158, 182–3,
    185, 237, 239

tax exemptions 57
telecommunications 105, 117
television 11, 49, 138, 182, 187, 188, 235
tenure change 77–9
testimonials 31
Thatcherism 13, 32, 41, 65
theatre 173, 185–6, 191
thresholds 86–7
tourism 1–2, 14, 64, 106–8, 120, 154, 158,
    187, 196, 198, 200, 215–16, 218–31,
    234, 241, 261
tournaments 182
town directories 95
town guides 96, 98
town trails 155
Toyota 1, 31
transience 14, 110, 181–93
travel books, see guide books
triumphal arches 165–6, 182–3, 184

unemployment 1, 93, 103, 233
universities 196, 200, 204–7
urban design 13–14, 153–79, 182
urban hierarchies 2, 43, 65, 195
urban history 53–92

vernacular, the   78, 80, 86, 181, 191
video recordings   227, 230
villas   84
violence   23, 27
visitors' centres   234, 243

waterfronts   27, 104, 133–51, 167

West, American   20, 54, 228–30
wildlife conservation   198

yuppies   71

zoos   198